D1636250

New *Saint Joseph*

SUNDAY MISSAL
PRAYERBOOK AND HYMNAL

CANADIAN MISSAL
For 2018 - 2019
Year C

How easy it is to use this Missal

- Refer to the Calendar inside the front cover for the page of the Sunday Mass (the "Proper").

- This arrow (↓) means continue to read. This arrow (→) indicates a reference back to the Order of Mass ("Ordinary") or to another part of the "Proper."

- Boldface type always indicates the people's parts that are to be recited aloud.

"Take this, all of you, and eat of it, for this is my Body, which will be given up for you."

CANADIAN EDITION

New . . . St. Joseph

SUNDAY MISSAL

PRAYERBOOK AND HYMNAL

For 2018 - 2019

THE COMPLETE MASSES FOR
SUNDAYS, ASH WEDNESDAY, and the
SACRED PASCHAL TRIDUUM

With the People's Parts Printed in Boldface Type
and Arranged for Parish Participation

The liturgical texts are approved by
the Canadian Conference of Catholic Bishops.

**IN ACCORD WITH THE THIRD TYPICAL EDITION
OF THE ROMAN MISSAL**

With the
"NEW REVISED STANDARD VERSION" Text

Dedicated to St. Joseph
Patron of the Universal Church

CATHOLIC BOOK PUBLISHING CORP.
New Jersey

The *St. Joseph Sunday Missal for 2018-2019* is approved
for use in Canada by the National Liturgy Office, Canadian
Conference of Catholic Bishops.

Acknowledgements:

The St. Joseph Missals have been diligently prepared with the invaluable
assistance of a special Board of Editors, including specialists in Liturgy and
Sacred Scripture, Catechetics, and Sacred Music and Art.

Excerpts from the English translation and chants of *The Roman Missal*
© 2010, International Commission on English in the Liturgy Corporation (ICEL);
the English translation of the Psalm Responses, Alleluia Verses and Titles of the
Readings from *Lectionary for Mass* © 1969, 1981, 1997, ICEL; excerpts from the
English translation of *Rite of Christian Initiation of Adults* © 1985, ICEL. All
rights reserved.

The lectionary texts contained herein are from the *Lectionary, Sundays
and Solemnities* of the Canadian Conference of Catholic Bishops, copyright
© Concacan Inc., 1992, 2009. All rights reserved. Used by permission of the
Canadian Conference of Catholic Bishops.

This revised edition of the *Lectionary, Sundays and Solemnities* follows the
Ordo Lectionum Missae, editio typica altera, Typis Polyglottis Vaticanus, 1981.

The Scripture quotations contained herein (including the texts of the readings, the Psalms, the Psalm refrains and the Gospel verses) are based on the
New Revised Standard Version of the Bible, copyright © 1989 National Council
of the Churches of Christ in the USA. Adapted and used by permission. All
rights reserved.

Adaptations for liturgical use have been made to selected Scripture texts.
These adaptations have been made to bring the readings into conformity
with the *Ordo Lectionum Missae, editio typica altera*, the *Lectionarium* and
Liturgiam Authenticam, as well as to facilitate proclamation. These adaptations
were prepared by and are the sole responsibility of the Canadian Conference
of Catholic Bishops. Adaptations copyright © 2009 National Council of the
Churches of Christ in the USA. Used by permission. All rights reserved.

Psalm settings – Texts: New Revised Standard Version of the Bible
© 1989, National Council of Churches of Christ in the USA (NCCC). Adapted by
the Canadian Conference of Catholic Bishops, Adaptations © 2009, NCCC. All
rights reserved. Used with permission. – Music: © Concacan Inc., 2011-2015. All
rights reserved. Used with permission.

English translation of the Sequence for Easter, copyright © Peter J.
Scagnelli. All rights reserved. English translation of the Sequence for Pentecost,
Edward Caswell (+1878); adaptations, copyright © Peter J. Scagnelli. All rights
reserved.

Texts on pages 647-660 in the "Treasury of Prayers"—copyright ©
Concacan Inc., 1983. Used by permission.

All other texts and illustrations © Copyright by Catholic Book Publishing
Corp., N.J.

(T-2119)

ISBN 978-1-947070-24-0

© 2018 by *Catholic Book Publishing Corp.*, N.J.
www.catholicbookpublishing.com
Printed in the U.S.A.

PREFACE

IN the words of the Second Vatican Council in the *Constitution on the Sacred Liturgy*, the Mass "is an action of Christ the priest and of his body which is the Church; it is a sacred action surpassing all others; no other action of the Church can equal its efficacy by the same title and to the same degree" (art. 7). Hence the Mass is a sacred sign, something visible which brings the invisible reality of Christ to us in the worship of the Father.

The Mass was first instituted as a meal at the Last Supper and became a living memorial of Christ's sacrifice on the Cross:

"At the Last Supper, on the night when he was betrayed, our Saviour instituted the Eucharistic sacrifice of his body and blood. He did this in order to perpetuate the sacrifice of the Cross throughout the centuries until he should come again, and so to entrust to his beloved spouse, the Church, a memorial of his death and resurrection: a sacrament of love, a sign of unity, a bond of charity, a paschal banquet in which Christ is eaten, the mind is filled with grace, and a pledge of future glory is given to us.

"The Church, therefore, earnestly desires that Christ's faithful, when present at this mystery of faith, should not be there as strangers or silent spectators; on the contrary, through a good understanding of the rites and prayers they should take part in the sacred action conscious of what they are doing, with devotion and full collaboration. They should be instructed by God's word and be nourished at the table of the Lord's body; they should give thanks to God; by offering the immaculate Victim, not only through the hands of the priest, but also with him, they should learn also to offer themselves; through Christ the Mediator, they should be drawn day by day into ever more perfect union with God and with each other, so that . . . God may be all in all" (art. 47-48).

A simple method of identifying the various parts of the Mass has been designed using different typefaces:

(1) **boldface type**—clearly identifies all people's parts

(2) lightface type—indicates the Priest's, Deacon's, or reader's parts.

In order to enable the faithful to prepare for each Mass at home and so participate more actively at Mass, the editors have added short, helpful explanations of the scripture readings, geared to the spiritual needs of daily life. A large selection of hymns for congregational singing has been included, as well as a treasury of personal prayers.

We trust that all these special features will help Catholics who use this new St. Joseph Missal to be led—in keeping with the desire of the Church—"to that full, conscious, and active participation in liturgical celebrations which is demanded by the very nature of the liturgy. Such participation by the Christian people as a chosen race, a royal priesthood, a holy nation, a redeemed people (1 Pt. 2.9; cf. 2.4-5), is their right and duty by reason of their baptism" (art. 14).

PLAN OF THE MASS

THE INTRODUCTORY RITES
1. Entrance Chant
2. Greeting
3. Rite for the Blessing and Sprinkling of Water
4. Penitential Act
5. Kyrie
6. Gloria
7. Collect **(Proper)**

THE LITURGY OF THE WORD
8. First Reading **(Proper)**
9. Responsorial Psalm **(Proper)**
10. Second Reading **(Proper)**
11. Gospel Acclamation **(Proper)**
12. Gospel Dialogue
13. Gospel Reading **(Proper)**
14. Homily
15. Profession of Faith **(Creed)**
16. Universal Prayer

THE LITURGY OF THE EUCHARIST
17. Presentation and Preparation of the Gifts
18. Invitation to Prayer
19. Prayer over the Offerings **(Proper)**
20. Eucharistic Prayer
21. Preface Dialogue
22. Preface
23. Preface Acclamation
    Eucharistic Prayer
    1, 2, 3, 4
    Reconciliation 1, 2
    Various Needs 1, 2, 3, 4

The Communion Rite
24. The Lord's Prayer
25. Sign of Peace
26. Lamb of God
27. Invitation to Communion
28. Communion
29. Prayer after Communion **(Proper)**

THE CONCLUDING RITES
30. Solemn Blessing
31. Final Blessing
32. Dismissal

THE ORDER OF MASS

Options are indicated by A, B, C, D in the margin.

THE INTRODUCTORY RITES

Acts of prayer and penitence prepare us to meet Christ as he comes in Word and Sacrament. We gather as a worshipping community to celebrate our unity with him and with one another in faith.

1 ENTRANCE CHANT   `STAND`

If it is not sung, it is recited by all or some of the people.

Joined together as Christ's people, we open the celebration by raising our voices in praise of God who is present among us. This song should deepen our unity as it introduces the Mass we celebrate today.

→ `Turn to Today's Mass`

2 GREETING (3 forms)

When the Priest comes to the altar, he makes the customary reverence with the ministers and kisses the altar. Then, with the ministers, he goes to his chair. After the Entrance Chant, all make the Sign of the Cross:

Priest: In the name of the Father, and of the Son, and of the Holy Spirit.

PEOPLE: Amen.

10

MASS CALENDAR FOR 2018-2019

Using this Book in Prayer

*You can use this book to help your prayer,
alone or with your family and friends:*

- Read the Gospel or other readings for last Sunday, and pray about them.

- Read the Gospel or other readings for next Sunday, and begin to pray about them.

- Think about God's Word: what is the Holy Spirit telling you?

- Pray the Responsorial Psalm from any of the Masses in the book.

- Reflect on the Collect from last Sunday's Mass, and pray it slowly.

- Use some of the prayers in the treasury.

- Say the Lord's Prayer slowly (page 72).

The Priest welcomes us in the name of the Lord. We show our union with God, our neighbour, and the Priest by a united response to his greeting.

A

Priest: The grace of our Lord Jesus Christ,
and the love of God,
and the communion of the Holy Spirit
be with you all.

PEOPLE: And with your spirit.

B ——————— OR ———————

Priest: Grace to you and peace from God our Father
and the Lord Jesus Christ.

PEOPLE: And with your spirit.

C ——————— OR ———————

Priest: The Lord be with you.

PEOPLE: And with your spirit.

[Bishop: Peace be with you.

PEOPLE: And with your spirit.]

3 RITE FOR the BLESSING and SPRINKLING of WATER

From time to time on Sundays, especially in Easter Time, instead of the customary Penitential Act, the Blessing and Sprinkling of Water may take place (see pp. 78-81) as a reminder of Baptism.

4 PENITENTIAL ACT (3 forms)

(Omitted when the Rite for the Blessing and Sprinkling of Water [see pp. 78-81] has taken place or some part of the liturgy of the hours has preceded.)

Before we hear God's word, we acknowledge our sins humbly, ask for mercy, and accept his pardon.

Invitation to repent:

After the introduction to the day's Mass, the Priest invites the people to recall their sins and to repent of them in silence:

Priest: Brethren (brothers and sisters), let us acknowledge our sins,
and so prepare ourselves to celebrate the sacred mysteries.

Then, after a brief silence, one of the following forms is used.

Priest and **PEOPLE**:

> I confess to almighty God
> and to you, my brothers and sisters,
> that I have greatly sinned,
> in my thoughts and in my words,
> in what I have done and in what I have failed to do,

They strike their breast:

> through my fault, through my fault,
> through my most grievous fault;

Then they continue:

> therefore I ask blessed Mary ever-Virgin,
> all the Angels and Saints,
> and you, my brothers and sisters,
> to pray for me to the Lord our God.

B ————————— OR —————————

Priest: Have mercy on us, O Lord.

PEOPLE: For we have sinned against you.

Priest: Show us, O Lord, your mercy.

PEOPLE: And grant us your salvation.

C ————————— OR —————————

Priest, or a Deacon or another minister:

> You were sent to heal the contrite of heart:
> Lord, have mercy.

PEOPLE: Lord, have mercy.

Priest or other minister:

> You came to call sinners:
> Christ, have mercy.

PEOPLE: Christ, have mercy.

Priest or other minister:

> You are seated at the right hand of the Father to intercede for us:
>
> Lord, have mercy.

PEOPLE: Lord, have mercy.

———————

Absolution:

At the end of any of the forms of the Penitential Act:

Priest: May almighty God have mercy on us,
forgive us our sins,
and bring us to everlasting life.

PEOPLE: Amen.

5 KYRIE

Unless included in the Penitential Act, the Kyrie is sung or said by all, with alternating parts for the choir or cantor and for the people:

℣. Lord, have mercy.

℞. **Lord, have mercy.**

℣. Christ, have mercy.

℞. **Christ, have mercy.**

℣. Lord, have mercy.

℞. **Lord, have mercy.**

6 GLORIA

As the Church assembled in the Spirit we praise and pray to the Father and the Lamb.

When the Gloria is sung or said, the Priest or the cantors or everyone together may begin it:

Glory to God in the highest,
and on earth peace to people of good will.

We praise you,
we bless you,
we adore you,
we glorify you,
we give you thanks for your great glory,
Lord God, heavenly King,
O God, almighty Father.

Lord Jesus Christ, Only Begotten Son,
Lord God, Lamb of God, Son of the Father,
you take away the sins of the world,
    have mercy on us;

you take away the sins of the world,
    receive our prayer;
you are seated at the right hand of the Father,
    have mercy on us.

For you alone are the Holy One,
you alone are the Lord,
you alone are the Most High,
Jesus Christ,
with the Holy Spirit,
in the glory of God the Father.
Amen.

7 COLLECT

The Priest invites us to pray silently for a moment and then,
in our name, expresses the theme of the day's celebration
and petitions God the Father through the mediation of Christ
in the Holy Spirit.

Priest: Let us pray.

→ **Turn to Today's Mass**

*Priest and people pray silently for a while. Then the
Priest says the Collect prayer, at the end of which the
people acclaim:*

PEOPLE: **Amen.**

Liturgy of the WORD

The proclamation of God's Word is always centred on Christ, present through his Word. Old Testament writings prepare for him; New Testament books speak of him directly. All of scripture calls us to believe once more and to follow. After the reading we reflect on God's words and respond to them.

As in Today's Mass **SIT**

8 FIRST READING

At the end of the reading: Reader: The word of the Lord.

PEOPLE: **Thanks be to God.**

9 RESPONSORIAL PSALM

The people repeat the response sung by the cantor the first time and then after each verse.

10 SECOND READING

At the end of the reading: Reader: The word of the Lord.

PEOPLE: **Thanks be to God.**

11 GOSPEL ACCLAMATION **STAND**

Jesus will speak to us in the Gospel. We rise now out of respect and prepare for his message with the Alleluia.

The people repeat the Alleluia after the cantor's Alleluia and then after the verse. During Lent one of the following invocations is used as a response instead of the Alleluia:

(a) **Glory and praise to you, Lord Jesus Christ!**
(b) **Glory to you, Lord Jesus Christ, Wisdom of God the Father!**
(c) **Glory to you, Word of God, Lord Jesus Christ!**
(d) **Glory to you, Lord Jesus Christ, Son of the living God!**

(e)   Praise and honour to you, Lord Jesus Christ!
(f)   Praise to you, Lord Jesus Christ, King of endless glory!
(g)   Marvellous and great are your works, O Lord!
(h)   Salvation, glory, and power to the Lord Jesus Christ!

12 GOSPEL DIALOGUE

Before proclaiming the Gospel, the Deacon asks the Priest: Your blessing, Father. *The Priest says:*

May the Lord be in your heart and on your lips,
that you may proclaim his Gospel worthily and well,
in the name of the Father, and of the Son, ✚ and of
the Holy Spirit. *The Deacon answers:* Amen.

If there is no Deacon, the Priest says inaudibly:

Cleanse my heart and my lips, almighty God,
that I may worthily proclaim your holy Gospel.

13 GOSPEL READING

Deacon (or Priest):
            The Lord be with you.
PEOPLE: And with your spirit.

Deacon (or Priest):

✚ A reading from the holy Gospel according to N.

PEOPLE: Glory to you, O Lord.

At the end:

Deacon (or Priest):
            The Gospel of the Lord.

PEOPLE: Praise to you, Lord Jesus Christ.

Then the Deacon (or Priest) kisses the book, saying inaudibly: Through the words of the Gospel may our sins be wiped away.

14 HOMILY   SIT

God's word is spoken again in the Homily. The Holy Spirit speaking through the lips of the preacher explains and applies today's biblical readings to the needs of this particular congregation. He calls us to respond to Christ through the life we lead.

15 PROFESSION OF FAITH (CREED) STAND

As a people we express our acceptance of God's message in the Scriptures and Homily. We summarize our faith by proclaiming a creed handed down from the early Church.

All say the Profession of Faith on Sundays.

THE NICENE CREED

I believe in one God,
the Father almighty,
maker of heaven and earth,
of all things visible and invisible.

I believe in one Lord Jesus Christ,
the Only Begotten Son of God,
born of the Father before all ages.
God from God, Light from Light,
true God from true God,
begotten, not made, consubstantial with the Father;
through him all things were made.
For us men and for our salvation
he came down from heaven,
and by the Holy Spirit was incarnate of the Virgin ⎫ *bow*
    Mary,
and became man.

For our sake he was crucified under Pontius Pilate,
he suffered death and was buried,
and rose again on the third day
in accordance with the Scriptures.
He ascended into heaven
and is seated at the right hand of the Father.
He will come again in glory
to judge the living and the dead
and his kingdom will have no end.

I believe in the Holy Spirit, the Lord, the giver of life,
who proceeds from the Father and the Son,
who with the Father and the Son is adored and
    glorified,
who has spoken through the prophets.

I believe in one, holy, catholic and apostolic Church.
I confess one Baptism for the forgiveness of sins
and I look forward to the resurrection of the dead
and the life of the world to come. Amen.

OR ———— APOSTLES' CREED ————

*Especially during Lent and Easter Time, the Apostles'
Creed may be said after the Homily.*

I believe in God,
the Father almighty,
Creator of heaven and earth,
and in Jesus Christ, his only Son, our Lord,
who was conceived by the Holy Spirit,⎫
born of the Virgin Mary,⎭ *bow*
suffered under Pontius Pilate,
was crucified, died and was buried;
he descended into hell;
on the third day he rose again from the dead;
he ascended into heaven,
and is seated at the right hand of God the Father
    almighty;
from there he will come to judge the living and the dead.

I believe in the Holy Spirit,
the holy catholic Church,
the communion of saints,
the forgiveness of sins,
the resurrection of the body,
and life everlasting. Amen.

16 UNIVERSAL PRAYER (Prayer of the Faithful)

As a priestly people we unite with one another to pray for today's
needs in the Church and the world.

*After the Priest gives the introduction the Deacon or other
minister sings or says the invocations.*

PEOPLE: Lord, hear our prayer.
(or other response, according to local custom)
At the end the Priest says the concluding prayer:
PEOPLE: Amen.

THE LITURGY OF THE EUCHARIST

17 PRESENTATION AND PREPARATION `SIT` OF THE GIFTS

While the people's gifts are brought forward to the Priest and are placed on the altar, the Offertory Chant is sung.

Before placing the bread on the altar, the Priest says inaudibly:

Blessed are you, Lord God of all creation,
for through your goodness we have received
the bread we offer you:
fruit of the earth and work of human hands,
it will become for us the bread of life.

If there is no singing, the Priest may say this prayer aloud, and the people may respond:

PEOPLE: Blessed be God for ever.

When he pours wine and a little water into the chalice, the Deacon (or the Priest) says inaudibly:

By the mystery of this water and wine
may we come to share in the divinity of Christ
who humbled himself to share in our humanity.

Before placing the chalice on the altar, he says:

Blessed are you, Lord God of all creation,
for through your goodness we have received
the wine we offer you:
fruit of the vine and work of human hands,
it will become our spiritual drink.

If there is no singing, the Priest may say this prayer aloud, and the people may respond:

PEOPLE: **Blessed be God for ever.**

The Priest says inaudibly:

With humble spirit and contrite heart
may we be accepted by you, O Lord,
and may our sacrifice in your sight this day
be pleasing to you, Lord God.

Then he washes his hands, saying:

Wash me, O Lord, from my iniquity
and cleanse me from my sin.

18 INVITATION TO PRAYER

Priest: Pray, brethren (brothers and sisters),
          that my sacrifice and yours
          may be acceptable to God,
          the almighty Father.

`STAND`

PEOPLE:

**May the Lord accept the sacrifice at your hands
for the praise and glory of his name,
for our good
and the good of all his holy Church.**

19 PRAYER OVER THE OFFERINGS

*The Priest, speaking in our name, asks the Father to
bless and accept these gifts.*

→ `Turn to Today's Mass`

At the end, **PEOPLE:** **Amen.**

20 EUCHARISTIC PRAYER

We begin the eucharistic service of praise and thanksgiving, the centre of the entire celebration, the central prayer of worship. We lift our hearts to God, and offer praise and thanks as the Priest addresses this prayer to the Father through Jesus Christ. Together we join Christ in his sacrifice, celebrating his memorial in the holy meal and acknowledging with him the wonderful works of God in our lives.

21 PREFACE DIALOGUE

Priest: The Lord be with you.
PEOPLE: And with your spirit.
Priest: Lift up your hearts.
PEOPLE: We lift them up to the Lord.
Priest: Let us give thanks to the Lord our God.
PEOPLE: It is right and just.

22 PREFACE

As indicated in the individual Masses of this Missal, the Priest may say one of the following Prefaces (listed in numerical order).

23   PREFACE ACCLAMATION

Priest and **PEOPLE:**
Holy, Holy, Holy Lord, God of hosts.
Heaven and earth are full of your glory.
Hosanna in the highest.
Blessed is he who comes in the name of the Lord.
Hosanna in the highest.   `KNEEL`

Then the Priest continues with one of the following Eucharistic Prayers.

EUCHARISTIC PRAYER .... **Choice of ten**

1	To you, therefore, most merciful Father	p. 24
2	You are indeed Holy, O Lord, the fount	p. 31
3	You are indeed Holy, O Lord, and all	p. 34
4	We give you praise, Father most holy	p. 39
R1	You are indeed Holy, O Lord, and from	p. 44
R2	You, therefore, almighty Father	p. 49
V1	You are indeed Holy and to be glorified	p. 53
V2	You are indeed Holy and to be glorified	p. 58
V3	You are indeed Holy and to be glorified	p. 63
V4	You are indeed Holy and to be glorified	p. 68

EUCHARISTIC PRAYER No. 1

The Roman Canon

(This Eucharistic Prayer is especially suitable for Sundays and Masses with proper Communicantes *and* Hanc igitur.*)*

[The words within parentheses may be omitted.]

To you, therefore, most merciful Father,
we make humble prayer and petition
through Jesus Christ, your Son, our Lord:
that you accept
and bless ✠ these gifts, these offerings,
these holy and unblemished sacrifices,
which we offer you firstly
for your holy catholic Church.
Be pleased to grant her peace,
to guard, unite and govern her
throughout the whole world,
together with your servant N. our Pope,
and N. our Bishop,
and all those who, holding to the truth,
hand on the catholic and apostolic faith.

Remember, Lord, your servants N. and N.
and all gathered here,
whose faith and devotion are known to you.
For them, we offer you this sacrifice of praise
or they offer it for themselves
and all who are dear to them:
for the redemption of their souls,
in hope of health and well-being,
and paying their homage to you,
the eternal God, living and true.

In communion with those whose memory we **1**
  venerate,
especially the glorious ever-Virgin Mary,
Mother of our God and Lord, Jesus Christ,
† and blessed Joseph, her Spouse,
your blessed Apostles and Martyrs
Peter and Paul, Andrew,
(James, John,
Thomas, James, Philip,
Bartholomew, Matthew,
Simon and Jude;
Linus, Cletus, Clement, Sixtus,
Cornelius, Cyprian,
Lawrence, Chrysogonus,
John and Paul,
Cosmas and Damian)
and all your Saints;
we ask that through their merits and prayers,
in all things we may be defended
by your protecting help.
(Through Christ our Lord. Amen.)

Therefore, Lord, we pray:*
graciously accept this oblation of our service,
that of your whole family;
order our days in your peace,
and command that we be delivered from eternal
  damnation
and counted among the flock of those you have
  chosen.
(Through Christ our Lord. Amen.)

Be pleased, O God, we pray,
to bless, acknowledge,
and approve this offering in every respect;

† * *See p. 95 for proper* Communicantes *and* Hanc igitur.

1 make it spiritual and acceptable,
so that it may become for us
the Body and Blood of your most beloved Son,
our Lord Jesus Christ.

On the day before he was to suffer,
he took bread in his holy and venerable hands,
and with eyes raised to heaven
to you, O God, his almighty Father,
giving you thanks, he said the blessing,
broke the bread
and gave it to his disciples, saying:

Take this, all of you, and eat of it,
for this is my Body,
which will be given up for you.

In a similar way when supper was ended,
he took this precious chalice
in his holy and venerable hands,
and once more giving you thanks, he said the
    blessing
and gave the chalice to his disciples, saying:

Take this, all of you, and drink from it, ·
for this is the chalice of my Blood,
the Blood of the new and eternal covenant,
which will be poured out for you and for many
for the forgiveness of sins.
Do this in memory of me.

Priest: The mystery of faith. *(Memorial Acclamation)*

PEOPLE:

A We proclaim your Death, O Lord,
    and profess your Resurrection
    until you come again.

B **When we eat this Bread and drink this Cup,
we proclaim your Death, O Lord,
until you come again.**

C **Save us, Saviour of the world,
for by your Cross and Resurrection
you have set us free.**

Therefore, O Lord,
as we celebrate the memorial of the blessed Passion,
the Resurrection from the dead,
and the glorious Ascension into heaven
of Christ, your Son, our Lord,
we your servants and your holy people,
offer to your glorious majesty
from the gifts that you have given us,
this pure victim,
this holy victim,
this spotless victim,
the holy Bread of eternal life
and the Chalice of everlasting salvation.

Be pleased to look upon these offerings
with a serene and kindly countenance,
and to accept them,
as once you were pleased to accept
the gifts of your servant Abel the just,
the sacrifice of Abraham, our father in faith,
and the offering of your high priest Melchizedek,
a holy sacrifice, a spotless victim.

In humble prayer we ask you, almighty God:
command that these gifts be borne
by the hands of your holy Angel
to your altar on high
in the sight of your divine majesty,

1 so that all of us, who through this participation at
    the altar
receive the most holy Body and Blood of your Son,
may be filled with every grace and heavenly
    blessing.
(Through Christ our Lord. Amen)

Remember also, Lord, your servants, *N.* and *N.*,
who have gone before us with the sign of faith
and rest in the sleep of peace.
Grant them, O Lord, we pray,
and all who sleep in Christ,
a place of refreshment, light and peace.
(Through Christ our Lord. Amen)

To us, also your servants, who, though sinners,
hope in your abundant mercies,
graciously grant some share
and fellowship with your holy Apostles and
    Martyrs:
with John the Baptist, Stephen,
Matthias, Barnabas,
(Ignatius, Alexander,
Marcellinus, Peter,
Felicity, Perpetua,
Agatha, Lucy,
Agnes, Cecilia, Anastasia)
and all your Saints;
admit us, we beseech you,
into their company,
not weighing our merits,
but granting us your pardon,
through Christ our Lord.

1

Through whom
you continue to make all these good things,
   O Lord;
you sanctify them, fill them with life,
bless them, and bestow them upon us.

(Concluding Doxology)

Through him, and with him, and in him,
O God, almighty Father,
in the unity of the Holy Spirit,
all glory and honour is yours,
for ever and ever.

The people acclaim: **Amen.**

Continue with the Mass, as on p. 72.

(This Eucharistic Prayer is particularly suitable on Weekdays or for special circumstances.)

STAND

℣. The Lord be with you.

℟. **And with your spirit.**

℣. Lift up your hearts.

℟. **We lift them up to the Lord.**

℣. Let us give thanks to the Lord our God.

℟. **It is right and just.**

It is truly right and just, our duty and our
    salvation,
always and everywhere to give you thanks, Father
    most holy,
through your beloved Son, Jesus Christ,
your Word through whom you made all things,
whom you sent as our Saviour and Redeemer,
incarnate by the Holy Spirit and born of the
    Virgin.

Fulfilling your will
    and gaining for you a holy people,
he stretched out his hands
    as he endured his Passion,
so as to break the bonds of death
    and manifest the resurrection.

And so, with the Angels and all the Saints
we declare your glory,
as with one voice we acclaim:

2

Holy, Holy, Holy Lord God of hosts.
Heaven and earth are full of your glory.
Hosanna in the highest.
Blessed is he who comes in the name of the Lord.
Hosanna in the highest.

KNEEL

You are indeed Holy, O Lord,
the fount of all holiness.

Make holy, therefore, these gifts, we pray,
by sending down your Spirit upon them like the
    dewfall,
so that they may become for us
the Body and ✠ Blood of our Lord Jesus Christ.

At the time he was betrayed
and entered willingly into his Passion,
he took bread and, giving thanks, broke it,
and gave it to his disciples, saying:

Take this, all of you, and eat of it,
for this is my Body,
which will be given up for you.

In a similar way, when supper was ended,
he took the chalice
and, once more giving thanks,
he gave it to his disciples, saying:

Take this, all of you, and drink from it,
for this is the chalice of my Blood,
the Blood of the new and eternal covenant,
which will be poured out for you and for many
for the forgiveness of sins.
Do this in memory of me.

2 Priest: The mystery of faith. *(Memorial Acclamation)*
PEOPLE:

A   We proclaim your Death, O Lord,
and profess your Resurrection
until you come again.

B   When we eat this Bread and drink this Cup,
we proclaim your Death, O Lord,
until you come again.

C   Save us, Saviour of the world,
for by your Cross and Resurrection
you have set us free.

Therefore, as we celebrate
the memorial of his Death and Resurrection,
we offer you, Lord,
the Bread of life and the Chalice of salvation,
giving thanks that you have held us worthy
to be in your presence and minister to you.

Humbly we pray
that, partaking of the Body and Blood of Christ,
we may be gathered into one by the Holy Spirit.

Remember, Lord, your Church,
spread throughout the world,
and bring her to the fullness of charity,
together with N. our Pope and N. our Bishop
and all the clergy.

In Masses for the Dead the following may be added:

Remember your servant N. ,
whom you have called (today)
from this world to yourself.

Grant that he (she) who was united with your Son in a
    death like his,
may also be one with him in his Resurrection.

2

Remember also our brothers and sisters
who have fallen asleep in the hope of the
    resurrection,
and all who have died in your mercy:
welcome them into the light of your face.
Have mercy on us all, we pray,
that with the Blessed Virgin Mary, Mother of God,
with blessed Joseph, her Spouse,
with the blessed Apostles,
and all the Saints who have pleased you
    throughout the ages,
we may merit to be co-heirs to eternal life,
and may praise and glorify you
through your Son, Jesus Christ.

(Concluding Doxology)

Through him, and with him, and in him,
O God, almighty Father,
in the unity of the Holy Spirit,
all glory and honour is yours,
for ever and ever.

The people acclaim: **Amen.**

Continue with the Mass, as on p. 72.

(This Eucharistic Prayer may be used with any Preface and preferably on Sundays and feast days.)

KNEEL

You are indeed Holy, O Lord,
and all you have created
rightly gives you praise,
for through your Son our Lord Jesus Christ,
by the power and working of the Holy Spirit,
you give life to all things and make them holy,
and you never cease to gather a people to yourself,
so that from the rising of the sun to its setting
a pure sacrifice may be offered to your name.

Therefore, O Lord, we humbly implore you:
by the same Spirit graciously make holy
these gifts we have brought to you for
    consecration,
that they may become the Body and ✠ Blood
of your Son our Lord Jesus Christ,
at whose command we celebrate these mysteries.

For on the night he was betrayed
he himself took bread,
and, giving you thanks, he said the blessing,
broke the bread and gave it to his disciples,
    saying:

*Take this, all of you, and eat of it,
for this is my Body,
which will be given up for you.*

In a similar way, when supper was ended,
he took the chalice,

3

and, giving you thanks, he said the blessing,
and gave the chalice to his disciples, saying:

Take this, all of you, and drink from it,
for this is the chalice of my Blood,
the Blood of the new and eternal covenant,
which will be poured out for you and for many
for the forgiveness of sins.

Do this in memory of me.

Priest: The mystery of faith. *(Memorial Acclamation)*

PEOPLE:

A **We proclaim your Death, O Lord,**
and profess your Resurrection
until you come again.

B **When we eat this Bread and drink this Cup,**
we proclaim your Death, O Lord,
until you come again.

C **Save us, Saviour of the world,**
for by your Cross and Resurrection
you have set us free.

Therefore, O Lord, as we celebrate the memorial
of the saving Passion of your Son,
his wondrous Resurrection
and Ascension into heaven,
and as we look forward to his second coming,
we offer you in thanksgiving
this holy and living sacrifice.

Look, we pray, upon the oblation of your Church
and, recognizing the sacrificial Victim by whose
   death
you willed to reconcile us to yourself,

3 grant that we, who are nourished
by the Body and Blood of your Son
and filled with his Holy Spirit,
may become one body, one spirit in Christ.

May he make us
an eternal offering to you,
so that we may obtain an inheritance with your
    elect,
especially with the most Blessed Virgin Mary,
    Mother of God,
with blessed Joseph, her Spouse,
with your blessed Apostles and glorious Martyrs
(with Saint N. : the Saint of the day or Patron Saint)
and with all the Saints,
on whose constant intercession in your presence
we rely for unfailing help.

May this Sacrifice of our reconciliation,
we pray, O Lord,
advance the peace and salvation of all the world.
Be pleased to confirm in faith and charity
your pilgrim Church on earth,
with your servant N. our Pope and N. our Bishop,
the Order of Bishops, all the clergy,
and the entire people you have gained for your own.

Listen graciously to the prayers of this family,
whom you have summoned before you:
in your compassion, O merciful Father,
gather to yourself all your children
scattered throughout the world.

† To our departed brothers and sisters
and to all who were pleasing to you
at their passing from this life,
give kind admittance to your Kingdom.

3

There we hope to enjoy for ever the fullness of
   your glory
through Christ our Lord,
through whom you bestow on the world all that
   is good. †

(Concluding Doxology)

Through him, and with him, and in him,
O God, almighty Father,
in the unity of the Holy Spirit,
all glory and honour is yours,
for ever and ever.

The people acclaim: **Amen.**

Continue with the Mass, as on p. 72.

---

* *In Masses for the Dead the following may be said:*

† Remember your servant *N.*
whom you have called (today)
from this world to yourself.
Grant that he (she) who was united with your Son in a
   death like his,
may also be one with him in his Resurrection,
when from the earth
he will raise up in the flesh those who have died,
and transform our lowly body
after the pattern of his own glorious body.
To our departed brothers and sisters, too,
and to all who were pleasing to you
at their passing from this life,
give kind admittance to your Kingdom.
There we hope to enjoy for ever the fullness of your glory,
when you will wipe away every tear from our eyes.
For seeing you, our God, as you are,
we shall be like you for all the ages
and praise you without end,
through Christ our Lord,
through whom you bestow on the world all that is good. †

℣. The Lord be with you.   **STAND**
℟. **And with your spirit.**

℣. Lift up your hearts.
℟. **We lift them up to the Lord.**

℣. Let us give thanks to the Lord our God.
℟. **It is right and just.**

It is truly right to give you thanks,
truly just to give you glory, Father most holy,
for you are the one God living and true,
existing before all ages and abiding for all eternity,
dwelling in unapproachable light;
yet you, who alone are good, the source of life,
have made all that is,
so that you might fill your creatures with blessings
and bring joy to many of them by the glory of your
    light.

And so, in your presence are countless hosts of
    Angels,
who serve you day and night
and, gazing upon the glory of your face,
glorify you without ceasing.

With them we, too, confess your name in exultation,
giving voice to every creature under heaven,
as we acclaim:

Holy, Holy, Holy Lord God of hosts.
Heaven and earth are full of your glory.
Hosanna in the highest.

**Blessed is he who comes in the name of the Lord.
Hosanna in the highest.**

4

KNEEL

We give you praise, Father most holy,
for you are great
and you have fashioned all your works
in wisdom and in love.
You formed man in your own image
and entrusted the whole world to his care,
so that in serving you alone, the Creator,
he might have dominion over all creatures.
And when through disobedience he had lost your
    friendship,
you did not abandon him to the domain of death.
For you came in mercy to the aid of all,
so that those who seek might find you.
Time and again you offered them covenants
and through the prophets
taught them to look forward to salvation.

And you so loved the world, Father most holy,
that in the fullness of time
you sent your Only Begotten Son to be our Saviour.
Made incarnate by the Holy Spirit
and born of the Virgin Mary,
he shared our human nature
in all things but sin.
To the poor he proclaimed the good news of
    salvation,
to prisoners, freedom,
and to the sorrowful of heart, joy.
To accomplish your plan,
he gave himself up to death,
and, rising from the dead,
he destroyed death and restored life.

4 And that we might live no longer for ourselves
but for him who died and rose again for us,
he sent the Holy Spirit from you, Father,
as the first fruits for those who believe,
so that, bringing to perfection his work in the world,
he might sanctify creation to the full.

Therefore, O Lord, we pray:
may this same Holy Spirit
graciously sanctify these offerings,
that they may become
the Body and ✚ Blood of our Lord Jesus Christ
for the celebration of this great mystery,
which he himself left us
as an eternal covenant.

For when the hour had come
for him to be glorified by you, Father most holy,
having loved his own who were in the world,
he loved them to the end:
and while they were at supper,
he took bread, blessed and broke it,
and gave it to his disciples, saying:

Take this, all of you, and eat of it,
for this is my Body,
which will be given up for you.

In a similar way,
taking the chalice filled with the fruit of the vine,
he gave thanks,
and gave the chalice to his disciples, saying:

Take this, all of you, and drink from it,
for this is the chalice of my Blood,
the Blood of the new and eternal covenant,

*which will be poured out for you and for many
for the forgiveness of sins.*
Do this in memory of me.

Priest: The mystery of faith. *(Memorial Acclamation)*

PEOPLE:

A We proclaim your Death, O Lord,
and profess your Resurrection
until you come again.

B When we eat this Bread and drink this Cup,
we proclaim your Death, O Lord,
until you come again.

C Save us, Saviour of the world,
for by your Cross and Resurrection
you have set us free.

Therefore, O Lord,
as we now celebrate the memorial of our
redemption,
we remember Christ's Death
and his descent to the realm of the dead,
we proclaim his Resurrection
and his Ascension to your right hand,
and, as we await his coming in glory,
we offer you his Body and Blood,
the sacrifice acceptable to you
which brings salvation to the whole world.

Look, O Lord, upon the Sacrifice
which you yourself have provided for your Church,
and grant in your loving kindness
to all who partake of this one Bread and one
Chalice
that, gathered into one body by the Holy Spirit,

4 they may truly become a living sacrifice in Christ
to the praise of your glory.

Therefore, Lord, remember now
all for whom we offer this sacrifice:
especially your servant N. our Pope,
N. our Bishop, and the whole Order of Bishops,
all the clergy,
those who take part in this offering,
those gathered here before you,
your entire people,
and all who seek you with a sincere heart.

Remember also
those who have died in the peace of your Christ
and all the dead,
whose faith you alone have known.

To all of us, your children,
grant, O merciful Father,
that we may enter into a heavenly inheritance
with the Blessed Virgin Mary, Mother of God,
with blessed Joseph, her Spouse,
and with your Apostles and Saints in your
   Kingdom.
There, with the whole of creation,
freed from the corruption of sin and death,
may we glorify you through Christ our Lord,
through whom you bestow on the world all that
   is good.

(Concluding Doxology)

Through him, and with him, and in him,
O God, almighty Father,
in the unity of the Holy Spirit,
all glory and honour is yours,
for ever and ever.

The people acclaim: **Amen.**

Continue with the Mass, as on p. 72.

EUCHARISTIC PRAYER FOR RECONCILIATION I

STAND

℣. The Lord be with you.

℟. **And with your spirit.**

℣. Lift up your hearts.

℟. **We lift them up to the Lord.**

℣. Let us give thanks to the Lord our God.

℟. **It is right and just.**

It is truly right and just
that we should always give you thanks,
Lord, holy Father, almighty and eternal God.

For you do not cease to spur us on
to possess a more abundant life
and, being rich in mercy,
you constantly offer pardon
and call on sinners
to trust in your forgiveness alone.

Never did you turn away from us,
and, though time and again we have broken your
    covenant,
you have bound the human family to yourself
through Jesus your Son, our Redeemer,
with a new bond of love so tight
that it can never be undone.

Even now you set before your people
a time of grace and reconciliation,
and, as they turn back to you in spirit,
you grant them hope in Christ Jesus
and a desire to be of service to all,

43

R 1

while they entrust themselves
more fully to the Holy Spirit.

And so, filled with wonder,
we extol the power of your love,
and, proclaiming our joy
at the salvation that comes from you,
we join in the heavenly hymn of countless hosts,
as without end we acclaim:

Holy, Holy, Holy Lord God of hosts.
Heaven and earth are full of your glory.
Hosanna in the highest.
Blessed is he who comes in the name of the Lord.
Hosanna in the highest.

KNEEL

You are indeed Holy, O Lord,
and from the world's beginning
are ceaselessly at work,
so that the human race may become holy,
just as you yourself are holy.

Look, we pray, upon your people's offerings
and pour out on them the power of your Spirit,
that they may become the Body and ✚ Blood
of your beloved Son, Jesus Christ,
in whom we, too, are your sons and daughters.

Indeed, though we once were lost
and could not approach you,
you loved us with the greatest love:
for your Son, who alone is just,
handed himself over to death,

and did not disdain to be nailed for our sake
to the wood of the Cross.

But before his arms were outstretched between
 heaven and earth,
to become the lasting sign of your covenant,
he desired to celebrate the Passover with his
 disciples.

As he ate with them,
he took bread
and, giving you thanks, he said the blessing,
broke the bread and gave it to them, saying:

Take this, all of you, and eat of it,
for this is my Body,
which will be given up for you.

In a similar way, when supper was ended,
knowing that he was about to reconcile all things
 in himself
through his Blood to be shed on the Cross,
he took the chalice, filled with the fruit of the
 vine,
and once more giving you thanks,
handed the chalice to his disciples, saying:

Take this, all of you, and drink from it,
for this is the chalice of my Blood,
the Blood of the new and eternal covenant,
which will be poured out for you and for many
for the forgiveness of sins.
Do this in memory of me.

R1 Priest: The mystery of faith. *(Memorial Acclamation)*

PEOPLE:

A We proclaim your Death, O Lord,
and profess your Resurrection
until you come again.

B When we eat this Bread and drink this Cup,
we proclaim your Death, O Lord,
until you come again.

C Save us, Saviour of the world,
for by your Cross and Resurrection
you have set us free.

Therefore, as we celebrate
the memorial of your Son Jesus Christ,
who is our Passover and our surest peace,
we celebrate his Death and Resurrection from the
   dead,
and looking forward to his blessed Coming,
we offer you, who are our faithful and merciful
   God,
this sacrificial Victim
who reconciles to you the human race.

Look kindly, most compassionate Father,
on those you unite to yourself
by the Sacrifice of your Son,
and grant that, by the power of the Holy Spirit,
as they partake of this one Bread and one
   Chalice,
they may be gathered into one Body in Christ,
who heals every division.

Be pleased to keep us always
in communion of mind and heart,
together with N. our Pope and N. our Bishop.
Help us to work together
for the coming of your Kingdom,
until the hour when we stand before you,
Saints among the Saints in the halls of heaven,
with the Blessed Virgin Mary, Mother of God,
the blessed Apostles and all the Saints,
and with our deceased brothers and sisters,
whom we humbly commend to your mercy.

Then, freed at last from the wound of corruption
and made fully into a new creation,
we shall sing to you with gladness
the thanksgiving of Christ,
who lives for all eternity.

(Concluding Doxology)

Through him, and with him, and in him,
O God, almighty Father,
in the unity of the Holy Spirit,
all glory and honour is yours,
for ever and ever.

The people acclaim: **Amen.**

Continue with the Mass, as on p. 72.

EUCHARISTIC PRAYER FOR
RECONCILIATION II

STAND

℣. The Lord be with you.
℟. **And with your spirit.**

℣. Lift up your hearts.
℟. **We lift them up to the Lord.**

℣. Let us give thanks to the Lord our God.
℟. **It is right and just.**

It is truly right and just
that we should give you thanks and praise,
O God, almighty Father,
for all you do in this world,
through our Lord Jesus Christ.

For though the human race
is divided by dissension and discord,
yet we know that by testing us
you change our hearts
to prepare them for reconciliation.

Even more, by your Spirit you move human hearts
that enemies may speak to each other again,
adversaries join hands,
and peoples seek to meet together.

By the working of your power
it comes about, O Lord,
that hatred is overcome by love,
revenge gives way to forgiveness,
and discord is changed to mutual respect.

Therefore, as we give you ceaseless thanks
with the choirs of heaven,

R 2

we cry out to your majesty on earth,
and without end we acclaim:

Holy, Holy, Holy Lord God of hosts.
Heaven and earth are full of your glory.
Hosanna in the highest.
Blessed is he who comes in the name of the Lord.
Hosanna in the highest.

`KNEEL`

You, therefore, almighty Father,
we bless through Jesus Christ your Son,
who comes in your name.
He himself is the Word that brings salvation,
the hand you extend to sinners,
the way by which your peace is offered to us.
When we ourselves had turned away from you
on account of our sins,
you brought us back to be reconciled, O Lord,
so that, converted at last to you,
we might love one another
through your Son,
whom for our sake you handed over to death.

And now, celebrating the reconciliation
Christ has brought us,
we entreat you:
sanctify these gifts by the outpouring of your
    Spirit,
that they may become the Body and ✚ Blood of
    your Son,
whose command we fulfill
when we celebrate these mysteries.

For when about to give his life to set us free,
as he reclined at supper,

R 2 he himself took bread into his hands,
and, giving you thanks, he said the blessing,
broke the bread and gave it to his disciples, saying:

Take this, all of you, and eat of it,
for this is my Body,
which will be given up for you.

In a similar way, on that same evening,
he took the chalice of blessing in his hands,
confessing your mercy,
and gave the chalice to his disciples, saying:

Take this, all of you, and drink from it,
for this is the chalice of my Blood,
the Blood of the new and eternal covenant,
which will be poured out for you and for many
for the forgiveness of sins.

Do this in memory of me.

Priest: The mystery of faith. *(Memorial Acclamation)*

PEOPLE:

A We proclaim your Death, O Lord,
and profess your Resurrection
until you come again.

B When we eat this Bread and drink this Cup,
we proclaim your Death, O Lord,
until you come again.

C Save us, Saviour of the world,
for by your Cross and Resurrection
you have set us free.

Celebrating, therefore, the memorial
of the Death and Resurrection of your Son,
who left us this pledge of his love,
we offer you what you have bestowed on us,
the Sacrifice of perfect reconciliation.

Holy Father, we humbly beseech you
to accept us also, together with your Son,
and in this saving banquet
graciously to endow us with his very Spirit,
who takes away everything
that estranges us from one another.

May he make your Church a sign of unity
and an instrument of your peace among all people
and may he keep us in communion
with N. our Pope and N. our Bishop
and all the Bishops
and your entire people.

Just as you have gathered us now at the table of
   your Son,
so also bring us together,
with the glorious Virgin Mary, Mother of God,
with your blessed Apostles and all the Saints,
with our brothers and sisters
and those of every race and tongue
who have died in your friendship.
Bring us to share with them the unending banquet
   of unity
in a new heaven and a new earth,
where the fullness of your peace will shine forth
in Christ Jesus our Lord.

(Concluding Doxology)

Through him, and with him, and in him,
O God, almighty Father,
in the unity of the Holy Spirit,
all glory and honour is yours,
for ever and ever.

The people acclaim: **Amen.**

Continue with the Mass, as on p. 72.

STAND

℣. The Lord be with you.

℟. **And with your spirit.**

℣. Lift up your hearts.

℟. **We lift them up to the Lord.**

℣. Let us give thanks to the Lord our God.

℟. **It is right and just.**

It is truly right to give you thanks
and raise to you a hymn of glory and praise,
O Lord, Father of infinite goodness.

For by the word of your Son's Gospel
you have brought together one Church
from every people, tongue, and nation,
and, having filled her with life by the power of
     your Spirit,
you never cease through her
to gather the whole human race into one.

Manifesting the covenant of your love,
she dispenses without ceasing
the blessed hope of your Kingdom
and shines bright as the sign of your faithfulness,
which in Christ Jesus our Lord
you promised would last for eternity.

And so, with all the Powers of heaven,
we worship you constantly on earth,
while, with all the Church,
as one voice we acclaim:

V
1

Holy, Holy, Holy Lord God of hosts.
Heaven and earth are full of your glory.
Hosanna in the highest.
Blessed is he who comes in the name of the Lord.
Hosanna in the highest.

`KNEEL`

You are indeed Holy and to be glorified, O God,
who love the human race
and who always walk with us on the journey of life.
Blessed indeed is your Son,
present in our midst
when we are gathered by his love,
and when, as once for the disciples, so now for us,
he opens the Scriptures and breaks the bread.

Therefore, Father most merciful,
we ask that you send forth your Holy Spirit
to sanctify these gifts of bread and wine,
that they may become for us
the Body and ✠ Blood
of our Lord Jesus Christ.

On the day before he was to suffer,
on the night of the Last Supper,
he took bread and said the blessing,
broke the bread and gave it to his disciples, saying:

Take this, all of you, and eat of it,
for this is my Body,
which will be given up for you.

In a similar way, when supper was ended,
he took the chalice, gave you thanks
and gave the chalice to his disciples, saying:

V 1

Take this, all of you, and drink from it,
for this is the chalice of my Blood,
the Blood of the new and eternal covenant,
which will be poured out for you and for many
for the forgiveness of sins.

Do this in memory of me.

Priest: The mystery of faith. *(Memorial Acclamation)*

PEOPLE:

A We proclaim your Death, O Lord,
and profess your Resurrection
until you come again.

B When we eat this Bread and drink this Cup,
we proclaim your Death, O Lord,
until you come again.

C Save us, Saviour of the world,
for by your Cross and Resurrection
you have set us free.

Therefore, holy Father,
as we celebrate the memorial of Christ your Son,
    our Saviour,
whom you led through his Passion and Death on
    the Cross
to the glory of the Resurrection,
and whom you have seated at your right hand,
we proclaim the work of your love until he comes
    again
and we offer you the Bread of life
and the Chalice of blessing.

Look with favour on the oblation of your Church,
in which we show forth

V 1

the paschal Sacrifice of Christ that has been handed
    on to us,
and grant that, by the power of the Spirit of your
    love,
we may be counted now and until the day of
    eternity
among the members of your Son,
in whose Body and Blood we have communion.

Lord, renew your Church (which is in N.)
by the light of the Gospel.
Strengthen the bond of unity
between the faithful and the pastors of your
    people,
together with N. our Pope, N. our Bishop,
and the whole Order of Bishops,
that in a world torn by strife
your people may shine forth
as a prophetic sign of unity and concord.

Remember our brothers and sisters (N. and N.),
who have fallen asleep in the peace of your Christ,
and all the dead, whose faith you alone have
    known.
Admit them to rejoice in the light of your face,
and in the resurrection give them the fullness of
    life.

Grant also to us,
when our earthly pilgrimage is done,
that we may come to an eternal dwelling place
and live with you for ever;
there, in communion with the Blessed Virgin Mary,
    Mother of God,
with the Apostles and Martyrs,

V 1 (with Saint N.: the Saint of the day or Patron)
and with all the Saints,
we shall praise and exalt you
through Jesus Christ, your Son.

(Concluding Doxology)

Through him, and with him, and in him,
O God, almighty Father,
in the unity of the Holy Spirit,
all glory and honour is yours,
for ever and ever.

The people acclaim: **Amen.**

Continue with the Mass, as on p. 72.

EUCHARISTIC PRAYER FOR USE IN MASSES FOR VARIOUS NEEDS II

V 2

STAND

℣. The Lord be with you.

℟. **And with your spirit.**

℣. Lift up your hearts.

℟. **We lift them up to the Lord.**

℣. Let us give thanks to the Lord our God.

℟. **It is right and just.**

It is truly right and just, our duty and our salvation,
always and everywhere to give you thanks,
Lord, holy Father,
creator of the world and source of all life.

For you never forsake the works of your wisdom,
but by your providence are even now at work in our midst.
With mighty hand and outstretched arm
you led your people Israel through the desert.
Now, as your Church makes her pilgrim journey in the world,
you always accompany her
by the power of the Holy Spirit
and lead her along the paths of time
to the eternal joy of your Kingdom,
through Christ our Lord.

And so, with the Angels and Saints,
we, too, sing the hymn of your glory,
as without end we acclaim:

V 2 Holy, Holy, Holy Lord God of hosts.
Heaven and earth are full of your glory.
Hosanna in the highest.
Blessed is he who comes in the name of the Lord.
Hosanna in the highest.

KNEEL

You are indeed Holy and to be glorified, O God,
who love the human race
and who always walk with us on the journey of life.
Blessed indeed is your Son,
present in our midst
when we are gathered by his love,
and when, as once for the disciples, so now for us,
he opens the Scriptures and breaks the bread.

Therefore, Father most merciful,
we ask that you send forth your Holy Spirit
to sanctify these gifts of bread and wine,
that they may become for us
the Body and ✤ Blood
of our Lord Jesus Christ.

On the day before he was to suffer,
on the night of the Last Supper,
he took bread and said the blessing,
broke the bread and gave it to his disciples, saying:

Take this, all of you, and eat of it,
for this is my Body,
which will be given up for you.

In a similar way, when supper was ended,
he took the chalice, gave you thanks
and gave the chalice to his disciples, saying:

V2

Take this, all of you, and drink from it,
for this is the chalice of my Blood,
the Blood of the new and eternal covenant,
which will be poured out for you and for many
for the forgiveness of sins.

Do this in memory of me.

Priest: The mystery of faith. *(Memorial Acclamation)*

PEOPLE:

A We proclaim your Death, O Lord,
   and profess your Resurrection
   until you come again.

B When we eat this Bread and drink this Cup,
   we proclaim your Death, O Lord,
   until you come again.

C Save us, Saviour of the world,
   for by your Cross and Resurrection
   you have set us free.

Therefore, holy Father,
as we celebrate the memorial of Christ your Son,
   our Saviour,
whom you led through his Passion and Death on
   the Cross
to the glory of the Resurrection,
and whom you have seated at your right hand,
we proclaim the work of your love until he comes
   again
and we offer you the Bread of life
and the Chalice of blessing.

Look with favour on the oblation of your Church,
in which we show forth

V 2

the paschal Sacrifice of Christ that has been handed
    on to us,
and grant that, by the power of the Spirit of your
    love,
we may be counted now and until the day of
    eternity
among the members of your Son,
in whose Body and Blood we have communion.

And so, having called us to your table, Lord,
confirm us in unity,
so that, together with N. our Pope and N. our
    Bishop,
with all Bishops, Priests and Deacons,
and your entire people,
as we walk your ways with faith and hope,
we may strive to bring joy and trust into the world.

Remember our brothers and sisters (N. and N.),
who have fallen asleep in the peace of your Christ,
and all the dead, whose faith you alone have
    known.
Admit them to rejoice in the light of your face,
and in the resurrection give them the fullness of
    life.

Grant also to us,
when our earthly pilgrimage is done,
that we may come to an eternal dwelling place
and live with you for ever;
there, in communion with the Blessed Virgin Mary,
    Mother of God,
with the Apostles and Martyrs,
(with Saint N.: the Saint of the day or Patron)

and with all the Saints,
we shall praise and exalt you
through Jesus Christ, your Son.

(Concluding Doxology)

Through him, and with him, and in him,
O God, almighty Father,
in the unity of the Holy Spirit,
all glory and honour is yours,
for ever and ever.

The people acclaim: **Amen.**

Continue with the Mass, as on p. 72.

STAND

℣. The Lord be with you.
℟. **And with your spirit.**

℣. Lift up your hearts.
℟. **We lift them up to the Lord.**

℣. Let us give thanks to the Lord our God.
℟. **It is right and just.**

It is truly right and just, our duty and our salvation,
always and everywhere to give you thanks,
holy Father, Lord of heaven and earth,
through Christ our Lord.

For by your Word you created the world
and you govern all things in harmony.
You gave us the same Word made flesh as Mediator,
and he has spoken your words to us
and called us to follow him.
He is the way that leads us to you,
the truth that sets us free,
the life that fills us with gladness.

Through your Son
you gather men and women,
whom you made for the glory of your name,
into one family,
redeemed by the Blood of his Cross
and signed with the seal of the Spirit.

Therefore, now and for ages unending,
with all the Angels,

V 3

we proclaim your glory,
as in joyful celebration we acclaim:

Holy, Holy, Holy Lord God of hosts.
Heaven and earth are full of your glory.
Hosanna in the highest.
Blessed is he who comes in the name of the Lord.
Hosanna in the highest.

KNEEL

You are indeed Holy and to be glorified, O God,
who love the human race
and who always walk with us on the journey of life.
Blessed indeed is your Son,
present in our midst
when we are gathered by his love,
and when, as once for the disciples, so now for us,
he opens the Scriptures and breaks the bread.

Therefore, Father most merciful,
we ask that you send forth your Holy Spirit
to sanctify these gifts of bread and wine,
that they may become for us
the Body and ✠ Blood
of our Lord Jesus Christ.

On the day before he was to suffer,
on the night of the Last Supper,
he took bread and said the blessing,
broke the bread and gave it to his disciples, saying:

Take this, all of you, and eat of it,
for this is my Body,
which will be given up for you.

V 3 In a similar way, when supper was ended,
he took the chalice, gave you thanks
and gave the chalice to his disciples, saying:

Take this, all of you, and drink from it,
for this is the chalice of my Blood,
the Blood of the new and eternal covenant,
which will be poured out for you and for many
for the forgiveness of sins.

Do this in memory of me.

Priest: The mystery of faith. *(Memorial Acclamation)*

PEOPLE:

A **We proclaim your Death, O Lord,**
and profess your Resurrection
until you come again.

B **When we eat this Bread and drink this Cup,**
we proclaim your Death, O Lord,
until you come again.

C **Save us, Saviour of the world,**
for by your Cross and Resurrection
you have set us free.

Therefore, holy Father,
as we celebrate the memorial of Christ your Son,
     our Saviour,
whom you led through his Passion and Death on
     the Cross
to the glory of the Resurrection,
and whom you have seated at your right hand,
we proclaim the work of your love until he comes
     again
and we offer you the Bread of life
and the Chalice of blessing.

V 3

Look with favour on the oblation of your Church,
in which we show forth
the paschal Sacrifice of Christ that has been handed
    on to us,
and grant that, by the power of the Spirit of your
    love,
we may be counted now and until the day of
    eternity
among the members of your Son,
in whose Body and Blood we have communion.

By our partaking of this mystery, almighty Father,
give us life through your Spirit,
grant that we may be conformed to the image of
    your Son,
and confirm us in the bond of communion,
together with N. our Pope and N. our Bishop,
with all other Bishops,
with Priests and Deacons,
and with your entire people.

Grant that all the faithful of the Church,
looking into the signs of the times by the light of
    faith,
may constantly devote themselves
to the service of the Gospel.

Keep us attentive to the needs of all
that, sharing their grief and pain,
their joy and hope,
we may faithfully bring them the good news of
    salvation
and go forward with them
along the way of your Kingdom.

V 3 Remember our brothers and sisters (*N.* and *N.*),
who have fallen asleep in the peace of your Christ,
and all the dead, whose faith you alone have known.
Admit them to rejoice in the light of your face,
and in the resurrection give them the fullness of
  life.

Grant also to us,
when our earthly pilgrimage is done,
that we may come to an eternal dwelling place
and live with you for ever;
there, in communion with the Blessed Virgin Mary,
  Mother of God,
with the Apostles and Martyrs,
(with Saint *N.*: the Saint of the day or Patron)
and with all the Saints,
we shall praise and exalt you
through Jesus Christ, your Son.

(Concluding Doxology)

Through him, and with him, and in him,
O God, almighty Father,
in the unity of the Holy Spirit,
all glory and honour is yours,
for ever and ever.

The people acclaim: **Amen.**

Continue with the Mass, as on p. 72.

EUCHARISTIC PRAYER FOR USE IN MASSES FOR VARIOUS NEEDS IV

V 4

STAND

℣. The Lord be with you.
℟. **And with your spirit.**

℣. Lift up your hearts.
℟. **We lift them up to the Lord.**

℣. Let us give thanks to the Lord our God.
℟. **It is right and just.**

It is truly right and just, our duty and our salvation,
always and everywhere to give you thanks,
Father of mercies and faithful God.

For you have given us Jesus Christ, your Son,
as our Lord and Redeemer.

He always showed compassion
for children and for the poor,
for the sick and for sinners,
and he became a neighbour
to the oppressed and the afflicted.

By word and deed he announced to the world
that you are our Father
and that you care for all your sons and daughters.

And so, with all the Angels and Saints,
we exalt and bless your name
and sing the hymn of your glory,
as without end we acclaim:

V 4

Holy, Holy, Holy Lord God of hosts.
Heaven and earth are full of your glory.
Hosanna in the highest.
Blessed is he who comes in the name of the Lord.
Hosanna in the highest.

KNEEL

You are indeed Holy and to be glorified, O God,
who love the human race
and who always walk with us on the journey of life.
Blessed indeed is your Son,
present in our midst
when we are gathered by his love
and when, as once for the disciples, so now for us,
he opens the Scriptures and breaks the bread.

Therefore, Father most merciful,
we ask that you send forth your Holy Spirit
to sanctify these gifts of bread and wine,
that they may become for us
the Body and ✚ Blood
of our Lord Jesus Christ.

On the day before he was to suffer,
on the night of the Last Supper,
he took bread and said the blessing,
broke the bread and gave it to his disciples, saying:

Take this, all of you, and eat of it,
for this is my Body,
which will be given up for you.

In a similar way, when supper was ended,
he took the chalice, gave you thanks
and gave the chalice to his disciples, saying:

V 4

Take this, all of you, and drink from it,
for this is the chalice of my Blood,
the Blood of the new and eternal covenant,
which will be poured out for you and for many
for the forgiveness of sins.

Do this in memory of me.

Priest: The mystery of faith. *(Memorial Acclamation)*

PEOPLE:

A We proclaim your Death, O Lord,
and profess your Resurrection
until you come again.

B When we eat this Bread and drink this Cup,
we proclaim your Death, O Lord,
until you come again.

C Save us, Saviour of the world,
for by your Cross and Resurrection
you have set us free.

Therefore, holy Father,
as we celebrate the memorial of Christ your Son,
    our Saviour,
whom you led through his Passion and Death on
    the Cross
to the glory of the Resurrection,
and whom you have seated at your right hand,
we proclaim the work of your love until he comes
    again
and we offer you the Bread of life
and the Chalice of blessing.

Look with favour on the oblation of your Church,
in which we show forth

**V
4** the paschal Sacrifice of Christ that has been handed
on to us,
and grant that, by the power of the Spirit of your
love,
we may be counted now and until the day of
eternity
among the members of your Son,
in whose Body and Blood we have communion.

Bring your Church, O Lord,
to perfect faith and charity,
together with N. our Pope and N. our Bishop,
with all Bishops, Priests and Deacons,
and the entire people you have made your own.

Open our eyes
to the needs of our brothers and sisters;
inspire in us words and actions
to comfort those who labour and are burdened.
Make us serve them truly,
after the example of Christ and at his command.
And may your Church stand as a living witness
to truth and freedom,
to peace and justice,
that all people may be raised up to a new hope.

Remember our brothers and sisters (N. and N.),
who have fallen asleep in the peace of your Christ,
and all the dead, whose faith you alone have
known.
Admit them to rejoice in the light of your face,
and in the resurrection give them the fullness of
life.

Grant also to us,
when our earthly pilgrimage is done,
that we may come to an eternal dwelling place
and live with you for ever;
there, in communion with the Blessed Virgin Mary,
    Mother of God,
with the Apostles and Martyrs,
(with Saint *N.*: the Saint of the day or Patron)
and with all the Saints,
we shall praise and exalt you
through Jesus Christ, your Son.

(Concluding Doxology)

Through him, and with him, and in him,
O God, almighty Father,
in the unity of the Holy Spirit,
all glory and honour is yours,
for ever and ever.

The people acclaim: **Amen.**

Continue with the Mass, as on p. 72.

THE COMMUNION RITE

To prepare for the paschal meal, to welcome the Lord, we pray for forgiveness and exchange a sign of peace. Before eating Christ's Body and drinking his Blood, we must be one with him and with all our brothers and sisters in the Church.

24 THE LORD'S PRAYER

STAND

Priest: At the Saviour's command
and formed by divine teaching,
we dare to say:

Priest and **PEOPLE:**

**Our Father, who art in heaven,
hallowed be thy name;
thy kingdom come;
thy will be done
on earth as it is in heaven.
Give us this day our daily bread,
and forgive us our trespasses,
as we forgive those who trespass against us;
and lead us not into temptation,
but deliver us from evil.**

Priest: Deliver us, Lord, we pray, from every evil,
graciously grant us peace in our days,
that, by the help of your mercy,
we may be always free from sin
and safe from all distress,
as we await the blessed hope
and the coming of our Saviour, Jesus
Christ.

PEOPLE: **For the kingdom,**
               the power and the glory are yours
               now and for ever.

25 SIGN OF PEACE

The Church is a community of Christians joined by the Spirit in love. It needs to express, deepen, and restore its peaceful unity before eating the one Body of the Lord and drinking from the one cup of salvation. We do this by a sign of peace.

The Priest says the prayer for peace:

Lord Jesus Christ,
who said to your Apostles:
Peace I leave you, my peace I give you,
look not on our sins,
but on the faith of your Church,
and graciously grant her peace and unity
in accordance with your will.
Who live and reign for ever and ever.

PEOPLE: **Amen.**

Priest: The peace of the Lord be with you always.

PEOPLE: **And with your spirit.**

Deacon (or Priest):
   Let us offer each other the sign of peace.

The people exchange a sign of peace, communion and charity, according to local customs.

26 LAMB OF GOD

Christians are gathered for the "breaking of the bread," another name for the Mass. In Communion, though many we are made one body in the one bread, which is Christ.

The Priest breaks the host over the paten and places a small piece in the chalice, saying quietly:

May this mingling of the Body and Blood
of our Lord Jesus Christ
bring eternal life to us who receive it.

Meanwhile the following is sung or said:

PEOPLE:

> **Lamb of God, you take away the sins of the world,**
>> **have mercy on us.**
> **Lamb of God, you take away the sins of the world,**
>> **have mercy on us.**
> **Lamb of God, you take away the sins of the world,**
>> **grant us peace.**

The invocation may even be repeated several times if the breaking of the bread is prolonged. Only the final time, however, is grant us peace *said.*

We pray in silence and then voice words of humility and hope as our final preparation before meeting Christ in the Eucharist.

Before Communion, the Priest says quietly one of the following prayers:

Lord Jesus Christ, Son of the living God,
who, by the will of the Father
and the work of the Holy Spirit,
through your Death gave life to the world,
free me by this, your most holy Body and Blood,
from all my sins and from every evil;
keep me always faithful to your commandments,
and never let me be parted from you.

———————— **OR** ————————

May the receiving of your Body and Blood,
Lord Jesus Christ,
not bring me to judgment and condemnation,
but through your loving mercy
be for me protection in mind and body
and a healing remedy.

27 INVITATION TO COMMUNION

The Priest genuflects, takes the host and, holding it slightly raised above the paten or above the chalice, while facing the people, says aloud:

Priest: Behold the Lamb of God,
          behold him who takes away the sins of the
            world.
          Blessed are those called to the supper of
            the Lamb.

Priest and **PEOPLE** (once only):

**Lord, I am not worthy
that you should enter under my roof,
but only say the word
and my soul shall be healed.**

Before reverently consuming the Body of Christ, the Priest says quietly:

May the Body of Christ
keep me safe for eternal life.

Then, before reverently consuming the Blood of Christ, he takes the chalice and says quietly:

May the Blood of Christ
keep me safe for eternal life.

28 COMMUNION

He then gives Communion to the people.

Priest: **The Body of Christ.** Communicant: **Amen.**
Priest: **The Blood of Christ.** Communicant: **Amen.**

The Communion Psalm or other appropriate chant is sung while Communion is given to the faithful. If there is no singing, the Communion Antiphon is said.

> ➜ **Turn to Today's Mass**

The vessels are purified by the Priest or Deacon or acolyte. Meanwhile he says quietly:

What has passed our lips as food, O Lord,
may we possess in purity of heart,
that what has been given to us in time
may be our healing for eternity.

After Communion there may be a period of sacred silence, or a canticle of praise or a hymn may be sung.

29 PRAYER AFTER COMMUNION   STAND

The Priest prays in our name that we may live the life of faith since we have been strengthened by Christ himself. Our *Amen* makes his prayer our own.

Priest: **Let us pray.**

Priest and people may pray silently for a while unless silence has just been observed. Then the Priest says the Prayer after Communion.

> ➜ **Turn to Today's Mass**

At the end, **PEOPLE: Amen.**

THE CONCLUDING RITES

We have heard God's Word and eaten the Body of Christ. Now it is time for us to leave, to do good works, to praise and bless the Lord in our daily lives.

30 SOLEMN BLESSING STAND

After any brief announcements, the Blessing and Dismissal follow:

Priest: The Lord be with you.

PEOPLE: And with your spirit.

31 FINAL BLESSING

Priest: May almighty God bless you,
the Father, and the Son, ✠ and the Holy Spirit.

PEOPLE: Amen.

On certain days or occasions, this formula of blessing is preceded, in accordance with the rubrics, by another more solemn formula of blessing (pp. 97-105) or by a prayer over the people (pp. 105-110).

32 DISMISSAL

Deacon (or Priest):

A Go forth, the Mass is ended.

B Go and announce the Gospel of the Lord.

C Go in peace, glorifying the Lord by your life.

D Go in peace.

PEOPLE: Thanks be to God.

If any liturgical service follows immediately, the rites of dismissal are omitted.

RITE FOR THE BLESSING AND SPRINKLING OF WATER

If this rite is celebrated during Mass, it takes the place of the usual Penitential Act at the beginning of Mass.

After the greeting, the Priest stands at his chair and faces the people. With a vessel containing the water to be blessed before him, he calls upon the people to pray in these or similar words:

Dear brethren (brothers and sisters),
let us humbly beseech the Lord our God
to bless this water he has created,
which will be sprinkled on us
as a memorial of our Baptism.
May he help us by his grace
to remain faithful to the Spirit we have received.

And after a brief pause for silence, he continues with hands joined:

Almighty ever-living God,
who willed that through water,
the fountain of life and the source of purification,
even souls should be cleansed
and receive the gift of eternal life;
be pleased, we pray, to ✠ bless this water,
by which we seek protection on this your day, O Lord.
Renew the living spring of your grace within us
and grant that by this water we may be defended
from all ills of spirit and body,
and so approach you with hearts made clean
and worthily receive your salvation.
Through Christ our Lord. ℟. **Amen.**

Or:

Almighty Lord and God,
who are the source and origin of all life,

whether of body or soul,
we ask you to ✠ bless this water,
which we use in confidence
to implore forgiveness for our sins
and to obtain the protection of your grace
against all illness and every snare of the enemy.
Grant, O Lord, in your mercy,
that living waters may always spring up for our
    salvation,
and so may we approach you with a pure heart
and avoid all danger to body and soul.
Through Christ our Lord. ℞. **Amen.**

Or (during Easter Time):

Lord our God,
in your mercy be present to your people's prayers,
and, for us who recall the wondrous work of our
    creation
and the still greater work of our redemption,
graciously ✠ bless this water.
For you created water to make the fields fruitful
and to refresh and cleanse our bodies.
You also made water the instrument of your mercy:
for through water you freed your people from slavery
and quenched their thirst in the desert;
through water the Prophets proclaimed the new
    covenant
you were to enter upon with the human race;
and last of all,
through water, which Christ made holy in the Jordan,
you have renewed our corrupted nature
in the bath of regeneration.
Therefore, may this water be for us
a memorial of the Baptism we have received,
and grant that we may share
in the gladness of our brothers and sisters
who at Easter have received their Baptism.
Through Christ our Lord. ℞. **Amen.**

Where the circumstances of the place or the custom of the people suggest that the mixing of salt be preserved in the blessing of water, the Priest may bless salt, saying:

We humbly ask you, almighty God:
be pleased in your faithful love to bless ✠ this salt
you have created,
for it was you who commanded the prophet Elisha
to cast salt into water,
that impure water might be purified.
Grant, O Lord, we pray,
that, wherever this mixture of salt and water is sprinkled,
every attack of the enemy may be repulsed
and your Holy Spirit may be present
to keep us safe at all times.
Through Christ our Lord. ℟. **Amen.**

Then he pours the salt into the water, without saying anything.

Afterward, taking the aspergillum, the Priest sprinkles himself and the ministers, then the clergy and people, moving through the church, if appropriate.

Meanwhile, one of the following chants, or another appropriate chant is sung.

Outside Easter Time

ANTIPHON 1 Ps. 51(50).9

Sprinkle me with hyssop, O Lord, and I shall be cleansed; wash me and I shall be whiter than snow.

ANTIPHON 2 Ez. 36.25-26

I will pour clean water upon you, and you will be made clean of all your impurities, and I shall give you a new spirit, says the Lord.

HYMN Cf. 1 Pt. 1.3-5

Blessed be the God and Father of our Lord Jesus Christ, who in his great mercy has given us new birth into a living hope through the Resurrection of Jesus Christ from

the dead, into an inheritance that will not perish, preserved for us in heaven for the salvation to be revealed in the last time!

During Easter Time

ANTIPHON 1 Cf. Ez. 47.1-2, 9

I saw water flowing from the Temple, from its right-hand side, alleluia: and all to whom this water came were saved and shall say: Alleluia, alleluia.

ANTIPHON 2 Cf. Zeph. 3.8; Ez. 36.25

On the day of my resurrection, says the Lord, alleluia, I will gather the nations and assemble the kingdoms and I will pour clean water upon you, alleluia.

ANTIPHON 3 Cf. Dn. 3.77, 79

You springs and all that moves in the waters, sing a hymn to God, alleluia.

ANTIPHON 4 1 Pt. 2.9

O chosen race, royal priesthood, holy nation, proclaim the mighty works of him who called you out of darkness into his wonderful light, alleluia.

ANTIPHON 5

From your side, O Christ, bursts forth a spring of water, by which the squalor of the world is washed away and life is made new again, alleluia.

When he returns to his chair and the singing is over, the Priest stands facing the people and, with hands joined, says:

May almighty God cleanse us of our sins,
and through the celebration of this Eucharist
make us worthy to share at the table of his Kingdom.
℞. **Amen**.

Then, when it is prescribed, the hymn Gloria in excelsis (Glory to God in the highest) *is sung or said.*

PREFACES

PREFACE I OF ADVENT (1)

The two comings of Christ

(From the First Sunday of Advent to December 16)

It is truly right and just, our duty and our salvation,
always and everywhere to give you thanks,
Lord, holy Father, almighty and eternal God,
through Christ our Lord.

For he assumed at his first coming
the lowliness of human flesh,
and so fulfilled the design you formed long ago,
and opened for us the way to eternal salvation,
that, when he comes again in glory and majesty
and all is at last made manifest,
we who watch for that day
may inherit the great promise
in which now we dare to hope.

And so, with Angels and Archangels,
with Thrones and Dominions,
and with all the hosts and Powers of heaven,
we sing the hymn of your glory,
as without end we acclaim: → No. 23, p. 23

PREFACE II OF ADVENT (2)

The twofold expectation of Christ

(From December 17 to December 24)

It is truly right and just, our duty and our salvation,
always and everywhere to give you thanks,
Lord, holy Father, almighty and eternal God,
through Christ our Lord.

For all the oracles of the prophets foretold him,
the Virgin Mother longed for him
with love beyond all telling,

John the Baptist sang of his coming
and proclaimed his presence when he came.

It is by his gift that already we rejoice
at the mystery of his Nativity,
so that he may find us watchful in prayer
and exultant in his praise.

And so, with Angels and Archangels,
with Thrones and Dominions,
and with all the hosts and Powers of heaven,
we sing the hymn of your glory,
as without end we acclaim: → No. 23, p. 23

PREFACE I OF THE NATIVITY OF THE LORD (3)
Christ the Light

(For the Nativity of the Lord, its Octave Day and within the Octave)

It is truly right and just, our duty and our salvation,
always and everywhere to give you thanks,
Lord, holy Father, almighty and eternal God.

For in the mystery of the Word made flesh
a new light of your glory has shone upon the eyes of our
    mind,
so that, as we recognize in him God made visible,
we may be caught up through him in love of things invisible.

And so, with Angels and Archangels,
with Thrones and Dominions,
and with all the hosts and Powers of heaven,
we sing the hymn of your glory,
as without end we acclaim: → No. 23, p. 23

PREFACE II OF THE NATIVITY OF THE LORD (4)
The restoration of all things in the Incarnation

(For the Nativity of the Lord, its Octave Day and within the Octave)

It is truly right and just, our duty and our salvation,
always and everywhere to give you thanks,
Lord, holy Father, almighty and eternal God,
through Christ our Lord.

For on the feast of this awe-filled mystery,
though invisible in his own divine nature,

he has appeared visibly in ours;
and begotten before all ages,
he has begun to exist in time;
so that, raising up in himself all that was cast down,
he might restore unity to all creation
and call straying humanity back to the heavenly Kingdom.

And so, with all the Angels, we praise you,
as in joyful celebration we acclaim: → No. 23, p. 23

PREFACE III OF THE NATIVITY OF THE LORD (5)

The exchange in the Incarnation of the Word

(For the Nativity of the Lord, its Octave Day and within the Octave)

It is truly right and just, our duty and our salvation,
always and everywhere to give you thanks,
Lord, holy Father, almighty and eternal God,
through Christ our Lord.

For through him the holy exchange that restores our life
has shone forth today in splendour:
when our frailty is assumed by your Word
not only does human mortality receive unending honour
but by this wondrous union we, too, are made eternal.

And so, in company with the choirs of Angels,
we praise you, and with joy we proclaim: → No. 23, p. 23

PREFACE I OF LENT (8)

The spiritual meaning of Lent

It is truly right and just, our duty and our salvation,
always and everywhere to give you thanks,
Lord, holy Father, almighty and eternal God,
through Christ our Lord.

For by your gracious gift each year
your faithful await the sacred paschal feasts
with the joy of minds made pure,
so that, more eagerly intent on prayer
and on the works of charity,
and participating in the mysteries
by which they have been reborn,

they may be led to the fullness of grace
that you bestow on your sons and daughters.

And so, with Angels and Archangels,
with Thrones and Dominions,
and with all the hosts and Powers of heaven,
we sing the hymn of your glory,
as without end we acclaim: ➙ No. 23, p. 23

PREFACE II OF LENT (9)

Spiritual penance

It is truly right and just, our duty and our salvation,
always and everywhere to give you thanks,
Lord, holy Father, almighty and eternal God.

For you have given your children a sacred time
for the renewing and purifying of their hearts,
that, freed from disordered affections,
they may so deal with the things of this passing world
as to hold rather to the things that eternally endure.

And so, with all the Angels and Saints,
we praise you, as without end we acclaim: ➙ No. 23, p. 23

PREFACE I OF EASTER I (21)

The Paschal Mystery

(Easter Vigil, Easter Sunday and during the Octave and Easter Time)

(At the Easter Vigil, is said "on this night"; on Easter Sunday and throughout the Octave
of Easter, is said "on this day"; on other days of Easter Time, is said "in this time.")

It is truly right and just, our duty and our salvation,
at all times to acclaim you, O Lord,
but (on this night / on this day / in this time) above all
to laud you yet more gloriously,
when Christ our Passover has been sacrificed.

For he is the true Lamb
who has taken away the sins of the world;
by dying he has destroyed our death,
and by rising, restored our life.

Therefore, overcome with paschal joy,
every land, every people exults in your praise
and even the heavenly Powers, with the angelic hosts,
sing together the unending hymn of your glory,
as they acclaim: ➙ No. 23, p. 23

PREFACE II OF EASTER (22)
New life in Christ

It is truly right and just, our duty and our salvation,
at all times to acclaim you, O Lord,
but in this time above all to laud you yet more gloriously,
when Christ our Passover has been sacrificed.

Through him the children of light rise to eternal life
and the halls of the heavenly Kingdom
are thrown open to the faithful;
for his Death is our ransom from death,
and in his rising the life of all has risen.

Therefore, overcome with paschal joy,
every land, every people exults in your praise
and even the heavenly Powers, with the angelic hosts,
sing together the unending hymn of your glory,
as they acclaim: ➔ No. 23, p. 23

PREFACE III OF EASTER (23)
Christ living and always interceding for us

It is truly right and just, our duty and our salvation,
at all times to acclaim you, O Lord,
but in this time above all to laud you yet more gloriously,
when Christ our Passover has been sacrificed.

He never ceases to offer himself for us
but defends us and ever pleads our cause before you:
he is the sacrificial Victim who dies no more,
the Lamb, once slain, who lives for ever.

Therefore, overcome with paschal joy,
every land, every people exults in your praise
and even the heavenly Powers, with the angelic hosts,
sing together the unending hymn of your glory,
as they acclaim: ➔ No. 23, p. 23

PREFACE IV OF EASTER (24)
*The restoration of the universe through the
Paschal Mystery*

It is truly right and just, our duty and our salvation,
at all times to acclaim you, O Lord,

but in this time above all to laud you yet more gloriously,
when Christ our Passover has been sacrificed.

For, with the old order destroyed,
a universe cast down is renewed,
and integrity of life is restored to us in Christ.

Therefore, overcome with paschal joy,
every land, every people exults in your praise
and even the heavenly Powers, with the angelic hosts,
sing together the unending hymn of your glory,
as they acclaim: → No. 23, p. 23

PREFACE V OF EASTER (25)

Christ, Priest and Victim

It is truly right and just, our duty and our salvation,
at all times to acclaim you, O Lord,
but in this time above all to laud you yet more gloriously,
when Christ our Passover has been sacrificed.

By the oblation of his Body,
he brought the sacrifices of old to fulfillment
in the reality of the Cross
and, by commending himself to you for our salvation,
showed himself the Priest, the Altar, and the Lamb of
    sacrifice.

Therefore, overcome with paschal joy,
every land, every people exults in your praise
and even the heavenly Powers, with the angelic hosts,
sing together the unending hymn of your glory,
as they acclaim: → No. 23, p. 23

PREFACE I OF THE ASCENSION OF THE LORD (26)

The mystery of the Ascension
(Ascension to the Saturday before Pentecost inclusive)

It is truly right and just, our duty and our salvation,
always and everywhere to give you thanks,
Lord, holy Father, almighty and eternal God.

For the Lord Jesus, the King of glory,
conqueror of sin and death,

ascended (today) to the highest heavens,
as the Angels gazed in wonder.

Mediator between God and man,
judge of the world and Lord of hosts,
he ascended, not to distance himself from our lowly state
but that we, his members, might be confident of following
where he, our Head and Founder, has gone before.

Therefore, overcome with paschal joy,
every land, every people exults in your praise
and even the heavenly Powers, with the angelic hosts,
sing together the unending hymn of your glory,
as they acclaim: ➙ No. 23, p. 23

PREFACE II OF THE ASCENSION OF THE LORD (27)

The mystery of the Ascension
(Ascension to the Saturday before Pentecost inclusive)

It is truly right and just, our duty and our salvation,
always and everywhere to give you thanks,
Lord, holy Father, almighty and eternal God,
through Christ our Lord.

For after his Resurrection
he plainly appeared to all his disciples
and was taken up to heaven in their sight,
that he might make us sharers in his divinity.

Therefore, overcome with paschal joy,
every land, every people exults in your praise
and even the heavenly Powers, with the angelic hosts,
sing together the unending hymn of your glory,
as they acclaim: ➙ No. 23, p. 23

PREFACE I OF THE SUNDAYS IN ORDINARY TIME (29)

The Paschal Mystery and the People of God

It is truly right and just, our duty and our salvation,
always and everywhere to give you thanks,
Lord, holy Father, almighty and eternal God,
through Christ our Lord.

For through his Paschal Mystery,
he accomplished the marvellous deed,

by which he has freed us from the yoke of sin and death,
summoning us to the glory of being now called
a chosen race, a royal priesthood,
a holy nation, a people for your own possession,
to proclaim everywhere your mighty works,
for you have called us out of darkness
into your own wonderful light.

And so, with Angels and Archangels,
with Thrones and Dominions,
and with all the hosts and Powers of heaven,
we sing the hymn of your glory,
as without end we acclaim: → No. 23, p. 23

PREFACE II OF THE SUNDAYS IN ORDINARY TIME (30)

The mystery of salvation

It is truly right and just, our duty and our salvation,
always and everywhere to give you thanks,
Lord, holy Father, almighty and eternal God,
through Christ our Lord.

For out of compassion for the waywardness that is ours,
he humbled himself and was born of the Virgin;
by the passion of the Cross he freed us from unending death,
and by rising from the dead he gave us life eternal.

And so, with Angels and Archangels,
with Thrones and Dominions,
and with all the hosts and Powers of heaven,
we sing the hymn of your glory,
as without end we acclaim: → No. 23, p. 23

PREFACE III OF THE SUNDAYS IN ORDINARY TIME (31)

The salvation of man by a man

It is truly right and just, our duty and our salvation,
always and everywhere to give you thanks,
Lord, holy Father, almighty and eternal God.

For we know it belongs to your boundless glory,
that you came to the aid of mortal beings with your divinity
and even fashioned for us a remedy out of mortality itself,
that the cause of our downfall

might become the means of our salvation,
through Christ our Lord.

Through him the host of Angels adores your majesty
and rejoices in your presence for ever.
May our voices, we pray, join with theirs
in one chorus of exultant praise, as we acclaim:

➙ No. 23, p. 23

PREFACE IV OF THE SUNDAYS IN ORDINARY TIME (32)
The history of salvation

It is truly right and just, our duty and our salvation,
always and everywhere to give you thanks,
Lord, holy Father, almighty and eternal God,
through Christ our Lord.

For by his birth he brought renewal
to humanity's fallen state,
and by his suffering, cancelled out our sins;
by his rising from the dead
he has opened the way to eternal life,
and by ascending to you, O Father,
he has unlocked the gates of heaven.

And so, with the company of Angels and Saints,
we sing the hymn of your praise,
as without end we acclaim:

➙ No. 23, p. 23

PREFACE V OF THE SUNDAYS IN ORDINARY TIME (33)
Creation

It is truly right and just, our duty and our salvation,
always and everywhere to give you thanks,
Lord, holy Father, almighty and eternal God.

For you laid the foundations of the world
and have arranged the changing of times and seasons;
you formed man in your own image
and set humanity over the whole world in all its wonder,
to rule in your name over all you have made
and for ever praise you in your mighty works,
through Christ our Lord.

And so, with all the Angels, we praise you,
as in joyful celebration we acclaim: → No. 23, p. 23

PREFACE VI OF THE SUNDAYS IN ORDINARY TIME (34)

The pledge of the eternal Passover

It is truly right and just, our duty and our salvation,
always and everywhere to give you thanks,
Lord, holy Father, almighty and eternal God.

For in you we live and move and have our being,
and while in this body
we not only experience the daily effects of your care,
but even now possess the pledge of life eternal.

For, having received the first fruits of the Spirit,
through whom you raised up Jesus from the dead,
we hope for an everlasting share in the Paschal Mystery.

And so, with all the Angels, we praise you,
as in joyful celebration we acclaim: → No. 23, p. 23

PREFACE VII OF THE SUNDAYS IN ORDINARY TIME (35)

Salvation through the obedience of Christ

It is truly right and just, our duty and our salvation,
always and everywhere to give you thanks,
Lord, holy Father, almighty and eternal God.

For you so loved the world
that in your mercy you sent us the Redeemer,
to live like us in all things but sin,
so that you might love in us what you loved in your Son,
by whose obedience we have been restored to those gifts
    of yours
that, by sinning, we had lost in disobedience.

And so, Lord, with all the Angels and Saints,
we, too, give you thanks, as in exultation we acclaim:
→ No. 23, p. 23

PREFACE VIII OF THE SUNDAYS IN ORDINARY TIME (36)

The Church united by the unity of the Trinity

It is truly right and just, our duty and our salvation,
always and everywhere to give you thanks,
Lord, holy Father, almighty and eternal God.

For, when your children were scattered afar by sin,
through the Blood of your Son and the power of the Spirit,
you gathered them again to yourself,
that a people, formed as one by the unity of the Trinity,
made the body of Christ and the temple of the Holy Spirit,
might, to the praise of your manifold wisdom,
be manifest as the Church.

And so, in company with the choirs of Angels,
we praise you, and with joy we proclaim: → No. 23, p. 23

PREFACE I OF THE MOST HOLY EUCHARIST (47)
The Sacrifice and the Sacrament of Christ

It is truly right and just, our duty and our salvation,
always and everywhere to give you thanks,
Lord, holy Father, almighty and eternal God,
through Christ our Lord.

For he is the true and eternal Priest,
who instituted the pattern of an everlasting sacrifice
and was the first to offer himself as the saving Victim,
commanding us to make this offering as his memorial.
As we eat his flesh that was sacrificed for us,
we are made strong,
and, as we drink his Blood that was poured out for us,
we are washed clean.

And so, with Angels and Archangels,
with Thrones and Dominions,
and with all the hosts and Powers of heaven,
we sing the hymn of your glory,
as without end we acclaim: → No. 23, p. 23

PREFACE II OF THE MOST HOLY EUCHARIST (48)
The fruits of the Most Holy Eucharist

It is truly right and just, our duty and our salvation,
always and everywhere to give you thanks,
Lord, holy Father, almighty and eternal God,
through Christ our Lord.

For at the Last Supper with his Apostles,
establishing for the ages to come the saving memorial of
    the Cross,
he offered himself to you as the unblemished Lamb,
the acceptable gift of perfect praise.

Nourishing your faithful by this sacred mystery,
you make them holy, so that the human race,
bounded by one world,
may be enlightened by one faith
and united by one bond of charity.

And so, we approach the table of this wondrous Sacrament,
so that, bathed in the sweetness of your grace,
we may pass over to the heavenly realities here
    foreshadowed.

Therefore, all creatures of heaven and earth
sing a new song in adoration,
and we, with all the host of Angels,
cry out, and without end we acclaim: → No. 23, p. 23

PREFACE I FOR THE DEAD (77)
The hope of resurrection in Christ

It is truly right and just, our duty and our salvation,
always and everywhere to give you thanks,
Lord, holy Father, almighty and eternal God,
through Christ our Lord.

In him the hope of blessed resurrection has dawned,
that those saddened by the certainty of dying
might be consoled by the promise of immortality to come.
Indeed for your faithful, Lord,
life is changed not ended,
and, when this earthly dwelling turns to dust,
an eternal dwelling is made ready for them in heaven.

And so, with Angels and Archangels,
with Thrones and Dominions,
and with all the hosts and Powers of heaven,
we sing the hymn of your glory,
as without end we acclaim: → No. 23, p. 23

PREFACE II FOR THE DEAD (78)
Christ died so that we might live

It is truly right and just, our duty and our salvation,
always and everywhere to give you thanks,
Lord, holy Father, almighty and eternal God,
through Christ our Lord.

For as one alone he accepted death,
so that we might all escape from dying;
as one man he chose to die,
so that in your sight we all might live for ever.

And so, in company with the choirs of Angels,
we praise you, and with joy we proclaim: ➙ No. 23, p. 23

PREFACE III FOR THE DEAD (79)
Christ, the salvation and the life

It is truly right and just, our duty and our salvation,
always and everywhere to give you thanks,
Lord, holy Father, almighty and eternal God,
through Christ our Lord.

For he is the salvation of the world,
the life of the human race,
the resurrection of the dead.

Through him the host of Angels adores your majesty
and rejoices in your presence for ever.
May our voices, we pray, join with theirs
in one chorus of exultant praise, as we acclaim:
➙ No. 23, p. 23

PREFACE IV FOR THE DEAD (80)
From earthly life to heavenly glory

It is truly right and just, our duty and our salvation,
always and everywhere to give you thanks,
Lord, holy Father, almighty and eternal God.

For it is at your summons that we come to birth,
by your will that we are governed,
and at your command that we return,
on account of sin,
to that earth from which we came.

And when you give the sign,
we who have been redeemed by the Death of your Son
shall be raised up to the glory of his Resurrection.

And so, with the company of Angels and Saints,
we sing the hymn of your praise,
as without end we acclaim: ➜ No. 23, p. 23

PREFACE V FOR THE DEAD (81)
Our resurrection through the victory of Christ

It is truly right and just, our duty and our salvation,
always and everywhere to give you thanks,
Lord, holy Father, almighty and eternal God.

For even though by our own fault we perish,
yet by your compassion and your grace,
when seized by death according to our sins,
we are redeemed through Christ's great victory,
and with him called back into life.

And so, with the Powers of heaven,
we worship you constantly on earth,
and before your majesty
without end we acclaim: ➜ No. 23, p. 23

PROPER COMMUNICANTES
AND HANC IGITUR

FOR EUCHARISTIC PRAYER I (THE ROMAN CANON)

Communicantes for the Nativity of the Lord
and throughout the Octave

Celebrating the most sacred night (day)
on which blessed Mary the immaculate Virgin
brought forth the Saviour for this world,
and in communion with those whose memory we venerate,
especially the glorious ever-Virgin Mary,
Mother of our God and Lord, Jesus Christ,† etc., p. 25.

Communicantes for the Epiphany of the Lord

Celebrating the most sacred day
on which your Only Begotten Son,
eternal with you in your glory,
appeared in a human body, truly sharing our flesh,

and in communion with those whose memory we venerate,
especially the glorious ever-Virgin Mary,
Mother of our God and Lord, Jesus Christ,† etc., p. 25.

Communicantes for Easter

Celebrating the most sacred night (day)
of the Resurrection of our Lord Jesus Christ in the flesh,
and in communion with those whose memory we venerate,
especially the glorious ever-Virgin Mary,
Mother of our God and Lord, Jesus Christ,† etc., p. 25.

Hanc Igitur for the Easter Vigil
until the Second Sunday of Easter

Therefore, Lord, we pray:
graciously accept this oblation of our service,
that of your whole family,
which we make to you
also for those to whom you have been pleased to give
the new birth of water and the Holy Spirit,
granting them forgiveness of all their sins;
order our days in your peace,
and command that we be delivered from eternal damnation
and counted among the flock of those you have chosen.
(Through Christ our Lord. Amen.)   ➔ *Canon*, p. 25.

Communicantes for the Ascension of the Lord

Celebrating the most sacred day
on which your Only Begotten Son, our Lord,
placed at the right hand of your glory
our weak human nature,
which he had united to himself,
and in communion with those whose memory we venerate,
especially the glorious ever-Virgin Mary,
Mother of our God and Lord, Jesus Christ,† etc., p. 25.

Communicantes for Pentecost Sunday

Celebrating the most sacred day of Pentecost,
on which the Holy Spirit
appeared to the Apostles in tongues of fire,
and in communion with those whose memory we venerate,
especially the glorious ever-Virgin Mary,
Mother of our God and Lord, Jesus Christ,† etc., p. 25.

BLESSINGS AT THE END OF MASS AND PRAYERS OVER THE PEOPLE

SOLEMN BLESSINGS

The following blessings may be used, at the discretion of the Priest, at the end of the celebration of Mass, or of a Liturgy of the Word, or of the Office, or of the Sacraments.

The Deacon or, in his absence, the Priest himself, says the invitation: Bow down for the blessing. *Then the Priest, with hands extended over the people, says the blessing, with all responding:* **Amen**.

I. For Celebrations in the Different Liturgical Times

1. ADVENT

May the almighty and merciful God,
by whose grace you have placed your faith
in the First Coming of his Only Begotten Son
and yearn for his coming again,
sanctify you by the radiance of Christ's Advent
and enrich you with his blessing. ℟. **Amen.**

As you run the race of this present life,
may he make you firm in faith,
joyful in hope and active in charity. ℟. **Amen.**

So that, rejoicing now with devotion.
at the Redeemer's coming in the flesh,
you may be endowed with the rich reward of eternal life
when he comes again in majesty. ℟. **Amen.**

And may the blessing of almighty God,
the Father, and the Son, ✠ and the Holy Spirit,
come down on you and remain with you for ever. ℟. **Amen.**

2. THE NATIVITY OF THE LORD

May the God of infinite goodness,
who by the Incarnation of his Son has driven darkness
    from the world

and by that glorious Birth has illumined this most holy
    night (day),
drive far from you the darkness of vice
and illumine your hearts with the light of virtue. ℟. **Amen.**

May God, who willed that the great joy
of his Son's saving Birth
be announced to shepherds by the Angel,
fill your minds with the gladness he gives
and make you heralds of his Gospel. ℟. **Amen.**

And may God, who by the Incarnation
brought together the earthly and heavenly realm,
fill you with the gift of his peace and favour
and make you sharers with the Church in heaven. ℟. **Amen.**

And may the blessing of almighty God,
the Father, and the Son, ✠ and the Holy Spirit,
come down on you and remain with you for ever. ℟. **Amen.**

3. THE BEGINNING OF THE YEAR

May God, the source and origin of all blessing,
grant you grace,
pour out his blessing in abundance,
and keep you safe from harm throughout the year.
    ℟. **Amen.**

May he give you integrity in the faith,
endurance in hope,
and perseverance in charity
with holy patience to the end. ℟. **Amen.**

May he order your days and your deeds in his peace,
grant your prayers in this and in every place,
and lead you happily to eternal life. ℟. **Amen.**

And may the blessing of almighty God,
the Father, and the Son, ✠ and the Holy Spirit,
come down on you and remain with you for ever. ℟. **Amen.**

4. THE EPIPHANY OF THE LORD

May God, who has called you
out of darkness into his wonderful light,
pour out in kindness his blessing upon you
and make your hearts firm
in faith, hope and charity. ℟. **Amen.**

And since in all confidence you follow Christ,
who today appeared in the world
as a light shining in darkness,
may God make you, too,
a light for your brothers and sisters. ℟. **Amen.**

And so when your pilgrimage is ended,
may you come to him
whom the Magi sought as they followed the star
and whom they found with great joy, the Light from Light,
who is Christ the Lord. ℟. **Amen.**

And may the blessing of almighty God,
the Father, and the Son, ✠ and the Holy Spirit,
come down on you and remain with you for ever. ℟. **Amen.**

5. THE PASSION OF THE LORD

May God, the Father of mercies,
who has given you an example of love
in the Passion of his Only Begotten Son,
grant that, by serving God and your neighbour,
you may lay hold of the wondrous gift of his blessing.
℟. **Amen.**

So that you may receive the reward of everlasting life from
him,
through whose earthly Death
you believe that you escape eternal death. ℟. **Amen.**

And by following the example of his self-abasement,
may you possess a share in his Resurrection. ℟. **Amen.**

And may the blessing of almighty God,
the Father, and the Son, ✠ and the Holy Spirit,
come down on you and remain with you for ever. ℟. **Amen.**

6. EASTER TIME

May God, who by the Resurrection of his Only Begotten
Son
was pleased to confer on you
the gift of redemption and of adoption,
give you gladness by his blessing. ℟. **Amen.**

May he, by whose redeeming work
you have received the gift of everlasting freedom,
make you heirs to an eternal inheritance. ℟. **Amen.**

And may you, who have already risen with Christ
in Baptism through faith,
by living in a right manner on this earth,
be united with him in the homeland of heaven. ℟. **Amen.**

And may the blessing of almighty God,
the Father, and the Son, ✠ and the Holy Spirit,
come down on you and remain with you for ever. ℟. **Amen.**

7. THE ASCENSION OF THE LORD

May almighty God bless you,
for on this very day his Only Begotten Son
pierced the heights of heaven
and unlocked for you the way
to ascend to where he is. ℟. **Amen.**

May he grant that,
as Christ after his Resurrection
was seen plainly by his disciples,
so when he comes as Judge
he may show himself merciful to you for all eternity.
℟. **Amen.**

And may you, who believe he is seated
with the Father in his majesty,
know with joy the fulfillment of his promise
to stay with you until the end of time. ℟. **Amen.**

And may the blessing of almighty God,
the Father, and the Son, ✠ and the Holy Spirit,
come down on you and remain with you for ever. ℟. **Amen.**

8. THE HOLY SPIRIT

May God, the Father of lights,
who was pleased to enlighten the disciples' minds
by the outpouring of the Spirit, the Paraclete,
grant you gladness by his blessing
and make you always abound with the gifts of the same
    Spirit. ℟. **Amen.**

May the wondrous flame that appeared above the disciples,
powerfully cleanse your hearts from every evil
and pervade them with its purifying light. ℟. **Amen.**

And may God, who has been pleased to unite many
  tongues
in the profession of one faith,
give you perseverance in that same faith
and, by believing, may you journey from hope to clear
  vision. ℟. **Amen.**

And may the blessing of almighty God,
the Father, and the Son, ✠ and the Holy Spirit,
come down on you and remain with you for ever. ℟. **Amen.**

9. ORDINARY TIME I

May the Lord bless you and keep you. ℟. **Amen.**

May he let his face shine upon you
and show you his mercy. ℟. **Amen.**

May he turn his countenance towards you
and give you his peace. ℟. **Amen.**

And may the blessing of almighty God,
the Father, and the Son, ✠ and the Holy Spirit,
come down on you and remain with you for ever. ℟. **Amen.**

10. ORDINARY TIME II

May the peace of God,
which surpasses all understanding,
keep your hearts and minds
in the knowledge and love of God,
and of his Son, our Lord Jesus Christ. ℟. **Amen.**

And may the blessing of almighty God,
the Father, and the Son, ✠ and the Holy Spirit,
come down on you and remain with you for ever. ℟. **Amen.**

11. ORDINARY TIME III

May almighty God bless you in his kindness
and pour out saving wisdom upon you. ℟. **Amen.**

May he nourish you always with the teachings of the faith
and make you persevere in holy deeds. ℟. **Amen.**

May he turn your steps towards himself
and show you the path of charity and peace. ℟. **Amen.**

And may the blessing of almighty God,
the Father, and the Son, ✠ and the Holy Spirit,
come down on you and remain with you for ever. ℟. **Amen.**

12. ORDINARY TIME IV

May the God of all consolation order your days in his peace
and grant you the gifts of his blessing. ℟. **Amen.**

May he free you always from every distress
and confirm your hearts in his love. ℟. **Amen.**

So that on this life's journey
you may be effective in good works,
rich in the gifts of hope, faith and charity,
and may come happily to eternal life. ℟. **Amen.**

And may the blessing of almighty God,
the Father, and the Son, ✠ and the Holy Spirit,
come down on you and remain with you for ever. ℟. **Amen.**

13. ORDINARY TIME V

May almighty God always keep every adversity far from
you
and in his kindness pour out upon you the gifts of his
blessing. ℟. **Amen.**

May God keep your hearts attentive to his words,
that they may be filled with everlasting gladness. ℟. **Amen.**

And so, may you always understand what is good and right,
and be found ever hastening along
in the path of God's commands,
made co-heirs with the citizens of heaven. ℟. **Amen.**

And may the blessing of almighty God,
the Father, and the Son, ✠ and the Holy Spirit,
come down on you and remain with you for ever. ℟. **Amen.**

14. ORDINARY TIME VI

May God bless you with every heavenly blessing,
make you always holy and pure in his sight,
pour out in abundance upon you the riches of his glory,
and teach you with the words of truth;
may he instruct you in the Gospel of salvation,
and ever endow you with fraternal charity.
Through Christ our Lord. ℟. **Amen.**

And may the blessing of almighty God,
the Father, and the Son, ✠ and the Holy Spirit,
come down on you and remain with you for ever. ℟. **Amen.**

II. For Celebrations of the Saints

15. THE BLESSED VIRGIN MARY

May God, who through the childbearing of the Blessed
    Virgin Mary
willed in his great kindness to redeem the human race,
be pleased to enrich you with his blessing. ℟. **Amen.**

May you know always and everywhere the protection
    of her,
through whom you have been found worthy to receive the
    author of life. ℟. **Amen.**

May you, who have devoutly gathered on this day,
carry away with you the gifts of spiritual joys and heavenly
    rewards. ℟. **Amen.**

And may the blessing of almighty God,
the Father, and the Son, ✠ and the Holy Spirit,
come down on you and remain with you for ever. ℟. **Amen.**

16. SAINTS PETER AND PAUL, APOSTLES

May almighty God bless you,
for he has made you steadfast in Saint Peter's saving
    confession
and through it has set you on the solid rock of the Church's
    faith. ℟. **Amen.**

And having instructed you
by the tireless preaching of Saint Paul,
may God teach you constantly by his example
to win brothers and sisters for Christ. ℟. **Amen.**

So that by the keys of Saint Peter and the words of Saint
    Paul,
and by the support of their intercession,
God may bring us happily to that homeland
that Peter attained on a cross
and Paul by the blade of a sword. ℟. **Amen.**

And may the blessing of almighty God,
the Father, and the Son, ✤ and the Holy Spirit,
come down on you and remain with you for ever. ℟. **Amen.**

17. THE APOSTLES

May God, who has granted you
to stand firm on apostolic foundations,
graciously bless you through the glorious merits
of the holy Apostles *N.* and *N.* (the holy Apostle *N.*).
　℟. **Amen.**

And may he, who endowed you
with the teaching and example of the Apostles,
make you, under their protection,
witnesses to the truth before all. ℟. **Amen.**

So that through the intercession of the Apostles,
you may inherit the eternal homeland,
for by their teaching you possess firmness of faith. ℟. **Amen.**

And may the blessing of almighty God,
the Father, and the Son, ✤ and the Holy Spirit,
come down on you and remain with you for ever. ℟. **Amen.**

18. ALL SAINTS

May God, the glory and joy of the Saints,
who has caused you to be strengthened
by means of their outstanding prayers,
bless you with unending blessings. ℟. **Amen.**

Freed through their intercession from present ills
and formed by the example of their holy way of life,
may you be ever devoted
to serving God and your neighbour. ℟. **Amen.**

So that, together with all,
you may possess the joys of the homeland,
where Holy Church rejoices
that her children are admitted in perpetual peace
to the company of the citizens of heaven. ℟. **Amen.**

And may the blessing of almighty God,
the Father, and the Son, ✤ and the Holy Spirit,
come down on you and remain with you for ever. ℟. **Amen.**

III. Other Blessings

19. FOR THE DEDICATION OF A CHURCH

May God, the Lord of heaven and earth,
who has gathered you today for the dedication of this
    church,
make you abound in heavenly blessings. ℟. **Amen.**

And may he, who has willed that all his scattered children
should be gathered together in his Son,
grant that you may become his temple
and the dwelling place of the Holy Spirit. ℟. **Amen.**

And so, when you are thoroughly cleansed,
may God dwell within you
and grant you to possess with all the Saints
the inheritance of eternal happiness. ℟. **Amen.**

And may the blessing of almighty God,
the Father, ✚ and the Son, ✚ and the Holy ✚ Spirit,
come down on you and remain with you for ever. ℟. **Amen.**

20. IN CELEBRATIONS FOR THE DEAD

May the God of all consolation bless you,
for in his unfathomable goodness he created the human
    race,
and in the Resurrection of his Only Begotten Son
he has given believers the hope of rising again. ℟. **Amen.**

To us who are alive, may God grant pardon for our sins,
and to all the dead, a place of light and peace. ℟. **Amen.**

So may we all live happily for ever with Christ,
whom we believe truly rose from the dead. ℟. **Amen.**

And may the blessing of almighty God,
the Father, and the Son, ✚ and the Holy Spirit,
come down on you and remain with you for ever. ℟. **Amen.**

PRAYERS OVER THE PEOPLE

*The following prayers may be used, at the discretion
of the Priest, at the end of the celebration of Mass,
or of a Liturgy of the Word, or of the Office, or of the
Sacraments.*

The Deacon or, in his absence, the Priest himself, says the invitation: Bow down for the blessing. *Then the Priest, with hands outstretched over the people, says the prayer, with all responding:* **Amen**.

After the prayer, the Priest always adds: And may the blessing of almighty God, the Father, and the Son, ✠ and the Holy Spirit, come down on you and remain with you for ever. ℟. **Amen.**

1. Be gracious to your people, O Lord,
   and do not withhold consolation on earth
   from those you call to strive for heaven.
   Through Christ our Lord.

2. Grant, O Lord, we pray,
   that the Christian people
   may understand the truths they profess
   and love the heavenly liturgy
   in which they participate.
   Through Christ our Lord.

3. May your people receive your holy blessing,
   O Lord, we pray,
   and, by that gift,
   spurn all that would harm them
   and obtain what they desire.
   Through Christ our Lord.

4. Turn your people to you with all their heart,
   O Lord, we pray,
   for you protect even those who go astray,
   but when they serve you with undivided heart,
   you sustain them with still greater care.
   Through Christ our Lord.

5. Graciously enlighten your family, O Lord, we pray,
   that by holding fast to what is pleasing to you,
   they may be worthy to accomplish all that is good.
   Through Christ our Lord.

6. Bestow pardon and peace, O Lord, we pray,
   upon your faithful,
   that they may be cleansed from every offence

and serve you with untroubled hearts.
Through Christ our Lord.

7. May your heavenly favour, O Lord, we pray,
increase in number the people subject to you
and make them always obedient to your commands.
Through Christ our Lord.

8. Be propitious to your people, O God,
that, freed from every evil,
they may serve you with all their heart
and ever stand firm under your protection.
Through Christ our Lord.

9. May your family always rejoice together, O God,
over the mysteries of redemption they have celebrated,
and grant its members the perseverance
to attain the effects that flow from them.
Through Christ our Lord.

10. Lord God, from the abundance of your mercies
provide for your servants and ensure their safety,
so that, strengthened by your blessings,
they may at all times abound in thanksgiving
and bless you with unending exultation.
Through Christ our Lord.

11. Keep your family, we pray, O Lord,
in your constant care,
so that, under your protection,
they may be free from all troubles
and by good works show dedication to your name.
Through Christ our Lord.

12. Purify your faithful, both in body and in mind,
O Lord, we pray,
so that, feeling the compunction you inspire,
they may be able to avoid harmful pleasures
and ever feed upon your delights.
Through Christ our Lord.

13. May the effects of your sacred blessing, O Lord,
make themselves felt among your faithful,

to prepare with spiritual sustenance the minds of all,
that they may be strengthened by the power of your
   love
to carry out works of charity.
Through Christ our Lord.

14. The hearts of your faithful submitted to your name,
entreat your help, O Lord,
and since without you they can do nothing that is just,
grant by your abundant mercy
that they may both know what is right
and receive all that they need for their good.
Through Christ our Lord.

15. Hasten to the aid of your faithful people
who call upon you, O Lord, we pray,
and graciously give strength in their human weakness,
so that, being dedicated to you in complete sincerity,
they may find gladness in your remedies
both now and in the life to come.
Through Christ our Lord.

16. Look with favour on your family, O Lord,
and bestow your endless mercy on those who seek it:
and just as without your mercy
they can do nothing truly worthy of you,
so through it,
may they merit to obey your saving commands.
Through Christ our Lord.

17. Bestow increase of heavenly grace
on your faithful, O Lord;
may they praise you with their lips,
with their souls, with their lives;
and since it is by your gift that we exist,
may our whole lives be yours.
Through Christ our Lord.

18. Direct your people, O Lord, we pray,
with heavenly instruction,
that by avoiding every evil
and pursuing all that is good,
they may earn not your anger

but your unending mercy.
Through Christ our Lord.

19. Be near to those who call on you, O Lord,
and graciously grant your protection
to all who place their hope in your mercy,
that they may remain faithful in holiness of life
and, having enough for their needs in this world,
they may be made full heirs of your promise for eternity.
Through Christ our Lord.

20. Bestow the grace of your kindness
upon your supplicant people, O Lord,
that, formed by you, their Creator,
and restored by you, their sustainer,
through your constant action they may be saved.
Through Christ our Lord.

21. May your faithful people, O Lord, we pray,
always respond to the promptings of your love
and, moved by wholesome compunction,
may they do gladly what you command,
so as to receive the things you promise.
Through Christ our Lord.

22. May the weakness of your devoted people
stir your compassion, O Lord, we pray,
and let their faithful pleading win your mercy,
that what they do not presume upon by their merits
they may receive by your generous pardon.
Through Christ our Lord.

23. In defence of your children, O Lord, we pray,
stretch forth the right hand of your majesty,
so that, obeying your fatherly will,
they may have the unfailing protection
of your fatherly care.
Through Christ our Lord.

24. Look, O Lord, on the prayers of your family,
and grant them the assistance they humbly implore,
so that, strengthened by the help they need,
they may persevere in confessing your name.
Through Christ our Lord.

25. Keep your family safe, O Lord, we pray,
    and grant them the abundance of your mercies,
    that they may find growth
    through the teachings and the gifts of heaven.
    Through Christ our Lord.

26. May your faithful people rejoice, we pray, O Lord,
    to be upheld by your right hand,
    and, progressing in the Christian life,
    may they delight in good things
    both now and in the time to come.
    Through Christ our Lord.

ON FEASTS OF SAINTS

27. May the Christian people exult, O Lord,
    at the glorification of the illustrious members of your
        Son's Body,
    and may they gain a share in the eternal lot
    of the Saints on whose feast day
    they reaffirm their devotion to you,
    rejoicing with them for ever in your glory.
    Through Christ our Lord.

28. Turn the hearts of your people
    always to you, O Lord, we pray,
    and, as you give them the help of such great patrons as
        these,
    grant also the unfailing help of your protection.
    Through Christ our Lord.

"Be alert at all times, praying . . . to escape
all these things . . . and to stand before the Son of Man."

YEAR C
DECEMBER 2, 2018

1st SUNDAY OF ADVENT

ENTRANCE ANTIPHON Cf. Ps. 24.1-3

**To you, I lift up my soul, O my God. In you, I have
trusted; let me not be put to shame. Nor let my
enemies exult over me; and let none who hope in
you be put to shame.** → No. 2, p. 10 (Omit Gloria)

COLLECT

Grant your faithful, we pray, almighty God,
the resolve to run forth to meet your Christ
with righteous deeds at his coming,
so that, gathered at his right hand,
they may be worthy to possess the heavenly
    Kingdom.
Through our Lord Jesus Christ, your Son,

who lives and reigns with you in the unity of the
   Holy Spirit,
one God, for ever and ever. ℟. **Amen.** ↓

FIRST READING Jer. 33.14-16

**Jeremiah reveals the promise of the Lord made to the
house of Israel. A Branch from David shall do what is
right and just. Judah and Jerusalem shall be saved.**

A reading from the book of the Prophet Jeremiah.

THE days are surely coming, says the Lord,
when I will fulfill the promise I made to the
house of Israel and the house of Judah.

   In those days and at that time I will cause a
righteous Branch to spring up for David; and he
shall execute justice and righteousness in the
land.

   In those days Judah will be saved and Jerusalem will live in safety. And this is the name by
which it will be called: "The Lord is our righteousness."—The word of the Lord. ℟. **Thanks be
to God.** ↓

RESPONSORIAL PSALM Ps. 25

Michel Guimont

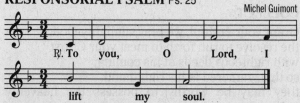

℟. To you, O Lord, I lift my soul.

Make me to know your ways, O Lord,
teach me your paths.
Lead me in your truth and teach me,
for you are the God of my salvation.—℟. ↓

Good and upright is the Lord;
therefore he instructs sinners in the way.
He leads the humble in what is right,
and teaches the humble his way.—℟. ↓

All the paths of the Lord are steadfast love and
   faithfulness,
for those who keep his covenant and his decrees.
The friendship of the Lord is for those who fear
   him,
and he makes his covenant known to them.—℟. ↓

SECOND READING 1 Thess. 3.12—4.2

> Paul prays that the Lord will increase love among the
> Thessalonians. In turn they must live a life pleasing to
> God so that they may progress in the way of perfection.

A reading from the first Letter of Saint Paul
            to the Thessalonians.

BROTHERS and sisters: May the Lord make
you increase and abound in love for one another and for all, just as we abound in love for
you. And may he so strengthen your hearts in
holiness that you may be blameless before our
God and Father at the coming of our Lord Jesus
with all his saints.

Finally, brothers and sisters, we ask and urge
you in the Lord Jesus that, as you learned from
us how you ought to live and to please God, as,
in fact, you are doing, you should do so more
and more. For you know what instructions we
gave you through the Lord Jesus.—The word of
the Lord. ℟. **Thanks be to God.** ↓

GOSPEL ACCLAMATION Ps. 85.7

℣. Alleluia. ℟. **Alleluia.**
℣. Show us your steadfast love, O Lord,
and grant us your salvation.
℟. **Alleluia.** ↓

GOSPEL Lk. 21.25-28, 34-36

Jesus tells his disciples that there will be signs before his
second coming. The sun, moon, stars, anguish among
people, fright—these will warn of his coming. They
should watch and pray to be able to stand with confidence before the Son of Man.

℣. The Lord be with you. ℟. **And with your spirit.**
✠ A reading from the holy Gospel according to
Luke. ℟. **Glory to you, O Lord.**

JESUS spoke to his disciples: "There will be
signs in the sun, the moon, and the stars and
on the earth distress among nations confused by
the roaring of the sea and the waves. People will
faint from fear and foreboding of what is coming upon the world, for the powers of the heavens will be shaken.

Then they will see 'the Son of Man coming in
a cloud' with power and great glory. Now when
these things begin to take place, stand up and
raise your heads, because your redemption is
drawing near.

Be on guard so that your hearts are not
weighed down with dissipation and drunken-
ness and the worries of this life, and that day
catch you unexpectedly, like a trap. For it will
come upon all who live on the face of the whole
earth. Be alert at all times, praying that you may

have the strength to escape all these things that
will take place, and to stand before the Son of
Man."—The Gospel of the Lord. ℟. **Praise to you,
Lord Jesus Christ.**   ➜ No. 15, p. 18

PRAYER OVER THE OFFERINGS

Accept, we pray, O Lord, these offerings we make,
gathered from among your gifts to us,
and may what you grant us to celebrate devoutly
    here below
gain for us the prize of eternal redemption.
Through Christ our Lord.
℟. **Amen.**   ➜ No. 21, p. 22 (Pref. 1)

COMMUNION ANTIPHON Ps. 84.13

**The Lord will bestow his bounty, and our earth
shall yield its increase.** ↓

PRAYER AFTER COMMUNION

May these mysteries, O Lord,
in which we have participated,
profit us, we pray,
for even now, as we walk amid passing things,
you teach us by them
to love the things of heaven
and hold fast to what endures.
Through Christ our Lord.
℟. **Amen.**   ➜ No. 30, p. 77

Optional Solemn Blessings, p. 97, and Prayers over the People, p. 105

"He went into all the region around the Jordan,
proclaiming a baptism of repentance."

DECEMBER 9

2nd SUNDAY OF ADVENT

ENTRANCE ANTIPHON Cf. Isa. 30.19, 30 [Saving Lord]

O people of Sion, behold, the Lord will come to save the nations, and the Lord will make the glory of his voice heard in the joy of your heart.

➜ No. 2, p. 10 (Omit Gloria)

COLLECT

Almighty and merciful God,
may no earthly undertaking hinder those
who set out in haste to meet your Son,
but may our learning of heavenly wisdom
gain us admittance to his company.
Who lives and reigns with you in the unity of the
 Holy Spirit,
one God, for ever and ever.
℟. **Amen.** ↓

FIRST READING Bar. 5.1-9

Baruch tells Jerusalem of God's favour. God will gather
the people together that Israel may grow secure in the
glory of God. God leads Israel in joy, mercy, and righteousness.

A reading from the book of the Prophet Baruch.

TAKE off the garment of your sorrow and affliction, O Jerusalem,

and put on forever the beauty of the glory from
God.

Put on the robe of the righteousness that comes
from God;

put on your head the diadem of the glory of the
Everlasting;

for God will show your splendour everywhere
under heaven.

For God will give you evermore the name,

"Righteous Peace, Godly Glory."

Arise, O Jerusalem, stand upon the height;

look toward the east,

and see your children gathered from west and east

at the word of the Holy One,

rejoicing that God has remembered them.

For they went out from you on foot,

led away by their enemies;

but God will bring them back to you,

carried in glory, as on a royal throne.

For God has ordered that every high mountain

and the everlasting hills be made low

and the valleys filled up, to make level ground,

so that Israel may walk safely in the glory of
God.

The woods and every fragrant tree
have shaded Israel at God's command.
For God will lead Israel with joy,
in the light of his glory,
with the mercy and righteousness that come from
    him.

The word of the Lord. ℟. **Thanks be to God.** ↓

RESPONSORIAL PSALM Ps. 126

Leo Marchildon

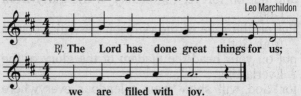

℟. The Lord has done great things for us;
we are filled with joy.

When the Lord restored the fortunes of Zion,
we were like those who dream.
Then our mouth was filled with laughter,
and our tongue with shouts of joy.—℟.

Then it was said among the nations,
"The Lord has done great things for them."
The Lord has done great things for us,
and we rejoiced.—℟.

Restore our fortunes, O Lord,
like the watercourses in the desert of the Negev.
May those who sow in tears
reap with shouts of joy.—℟.

Those who go out weeping,
bearing the seed for sowing,
shall come home with shouts of joy,
carrying their sheaves.—℟. ↓

SECOND READING Phil. 1.3-6, 8-11

Paul rejoices in the progress of faith among the Philippians. He is sure that God who began this good work will help it grow. Paul prays that their love may continue to grow so that they may be rich in harvest.

A reading from the Letter of Saint Paul
to the Philippians.

BROTHERS and sisters, I thank my God every time I remember you, constantly praying with joy in every one of my prayers for all of you, because of your sharing in the Gospel from the first day until now.

I am confident of this, that the one who began a good work among you will bring it to completion by the day of Jesus Christ.

For God is my witness, how I long for all of you with the compassion of Christ Jesus. And this is my prayer, that your love may overflow more and more with knowledge and full insight to help you determine what is best, so that in the day of Christ you may be pure and blameless, having produced the harvest of righteousness that comes through Jesus Christ for the glory and praise of God.—The word of the Lord. ℟. **Thanks be to God.** ↓

GOSPEL ACCLAMATION Lk. 3.4, 6

℣. Alleluia. ℟. **Alleluia.**
℣. Prepare the way of the Lord, make straight his paths:
all flesh shall see the salvation of God.
℟. **Alleluia.** ↓

GOSPEL Lk. 3.1-6

> Luke outlines some historical facts at the time of John the Baptist's preaching. It is the fulfillment of the prophecy of Isaiah. John prepares the way for the Lord.

℣. The Lord be with you. ℟. **And with your spirit.**
✤ A reading from the holy Gospel according to Luke. ℟. **Glory to you, O Lord.**

IN the fifteenth year of the reign of Emperor Tiberius, when Pontius Pilate was governor of Judea, and Herod was ruler of Galilee, and his brother Philip ruler of the region of Ituraea and Trachonitis, and Lysanias ruler of Abilene, during the high priesthood of Annas and Caiaphas, the word of God came to John son of Zechariah in the wilderness.

He went into all the region around the Jordan, proclaiming a baptism of repentance for the forgiveness of sins, as it is written in the book of the words of the Prophet Isaiah,

"The voice of one crying out in the wilderness:
'Prepare the way of the Lord,
    make his paths straight.
Every valley shall be filled,
    and every mountain and hill shall be made
        low,
and the crooked shall be made straight,
    and the rough ways made smooth;
and all flesh shall see the salvation of God.'"

The Gospel of the Lord. ℟. **Praise to you, Lord Jesus Christ.**   ➔ No. 15, p. 18

PRAYER OVER THE OFFERINGS

Be pleased, O Lord, with our humble prayers and
    offerings,
and, since we have no merits to plead our cause,
come, we pray, to our rescue
with the protection of your mercy.
Through Christ our Lord.
℟. **Amen.**   ➥ No. 21, p. 22 (Pref. 1)

COMMUNION ANTIPHON Bar. 5.5; 4.36

**Jerusalem, arise and stand upon the heights, and
behold the joy which comes to you from God.** ↓

PRAYER AFTER COMMUNION

Replenished by the food of spiritual nourishment,
we humbly beseech you, O Lord,
that, through our partaking in this mystery,
you may teach us to judge wisely the things of
    earth
and hold firm to the things of heaven.
Through Christ our Lord.
℟. **Amen.**   ➥ No. 30, p. 77

Optional Solemn Blessings, p. 97, and Prayers over the People, p. 105

"John proclaimed the good news to the people."

DECEMBER 16

3rd SUNDAY OF ADVENT

ENTRANCE ANTIPHON Phil. 4.4, 5
Rejoice in the Lord always; again I say, rejoice. Indeed, the Lord is near.

➔ No. 2, p. 10 (Omit Gloria)

COLLECT
O God, who see how your people
faithfully await the feast of the Lord's Nativity,
enable us, we pray,
to attain the joys of so great a salvation
and to celebrate them always
with solemn worship and glad rejoicing.
Through our Lord Jesus Christ, your Son,
who lives and reigns with you in the unity of the
    Holy Spirit,
one God, for ever and ever. ℟. **Amen.** ↓

FIRST READING Zeph. 3.14-18a

Zephaniah writes that Israel should shout for joy. Her king, the Lord, is in her midst. The Lord is a mighty saviour. Israel should not be discouraged.

A reading from the book of the
Prophet Zephaniah.

SING aloud, O daughter Zion; shout, O Israel!
Rejoice and exult with all your heart,
O daughter of Jerusalem!
The Lord has taken away the judgments against
    you,
he has turned away your enemies.
The king of Israel, the Lord, is in your midst;
you shall fear disaster no more.

On that day it shall be said to Jerusalem:
Do not fear, O Zion;
do not let your hands grow weak.
The Lord, your God, is in your midst,
a warrior who gives victory;
he will rejoice over you with gladness,
he will renew you in his love.
The Lord, your God, will exult over you with
    loud singing
as on a day of festival.

The word of the Lord. ℟. **Thanks be to God.** ↓

RESPONSORIAL PSALM Isa. 12

Frank Lynch

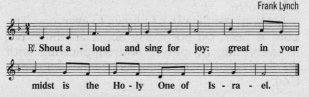

℟. Shout a - loud and sing for joy: great in your
midst is the Ho - ly One of Is - ra - el.

Surely God is my salvation;
I will trust, and will not be afraid,
for the Lord God is my strength and my might;
he has become my salvation.
With joy you will draw water
from the wells of salvation.

℟. **Shout aloud and sing for joy: great in your
midst is the Holy One of Israel.**

Give thanks to the Lord,
call on his name;
make known his deeds among the nations;
proclaim that his name is exalted.—℟.

Sing praises to the Lord,
for he has done gloriously;
let this be known in all the earth.
Shout aloud and sing for joy, O royal Zion,
for great in your midst
is the Holy One of Israel.—℟. ↓

SECOND READING Phil. 4.4-7

**Christians should rejoice in the Lord. We should take our
prayers and petitions to God, who watches over us as
beloved children.**

A reading from the Letter of Saint Paul
to the Philippians.

REJOICE in the Lord always; again I will say,
Rejoice.
Let your gentleness be known to everyone. The
Lord is near. Do not worry about anything, but
in everything by prayer and supplication with
thanksgiving let your requests be made known to
God.

And the peace of God, which surpasses all understanding, will guard your hearts and your minds in Christ Jesus.—The word of the Lord. ℟. **Thanks be to God.** ↓

GOSPEL ACCLAMATION Lk. 4.18 (Isa. 61.1)

℣. Alleluia. ℟. **Alleluia.**

℣. The Spirit of the Lord is upon me;
he has sent me to bring good news to the poor.
℟. **Alleluia.** ↓

GOSPEL Lk. 3.10-18

> John preached a law of sharing. He baptized and admonished all to be just and loving and to pray. John tells the people about the majesty of the Messiah.

℣. The Lord be with you. ℟. **And with your spirit.**
✛ A reading from the holy Gospel according to Luke. ℟. **Glory to you, O Lord.**

THE crowds, who were gathering to be baptized by John, asked him, "What should we do?" In reply John said to them, "Whoever has two coats must share with anyone who has none; and whoever has food must do likewise."

Even tax collectors came to be baptized, and they asked him, "Teacher, what should we do?" He said to them, "Collect no more than the amount prescribed for you." Soldiers also asked him, "And we, what should we do?" He said to them, "Do not extort money from anyone by threats or false accusation, and be satisfied with your wages."

As the people were filled with expectation, and all were questioning in their hearts concerning John, whether he might be the Messiah, John answered all of them by saying, "I baptize you with water; but one who is more powerful than I is coming; I am not worthy to untie the thong of his sandals. He will baptize you with the Holy Spirit and fire. His winnowing fork is in his hand, to clear his threshing floor and to gather the wheat into his granary; but the chaff he will burn with unquenchable fire."

So, with many other exhortations, John proclaimed the good news to the people.—The Gospel of the Lord. ℟. **Praise to you, Lord Jesus Christ.**   ➔ No. 15, p. 18

PRAYER OVER THE OFFERINGS

May the sacrifice of our worship, Lord, we pray, be offered to you unceasingly,
to complete what was begun in sacred mystery
and powerfully accomplish for us your saving work.
Through Christ our Lord.
℟. **Amen.**   ➔ No. 21, p. 22 (Pref. 1 or 2)

COMMUNION ANTIPHON Cf. Isa. 35.4

Say to the faint of heart: Be strong and do not fear. Behold, our God will come, and he will save us. ↓

PRAYER AFTER COMMUNION

We implore your mercy, Lord,
that this divine sustenance may cleanse us of our faults
and prepare us for the coming feasts.
Through Christ our Lord.
℟. **Amen.**   ➔ No. 30, p. 77

Optional Solemn Blessings, p. 97, and Prayers over the People, p. 105

"Blessed are you among women, and blessed
is the fruit of your womb."

DECEMBER 23

4th SUNDAY OF ADVENT

ENTRANCE ANTIPHON Cf. Isa. 45.8

**Drop down dew from above, you heavens, and let
the clouds rain down the Just One; let the earth
be opened and bring forth a Saviour.**

➜ No. 2, p. 10 (Omit Gloria)

COLLECT

Pour forth, we beseech you, O Lord,
your grace into our hearts,
that we, to whom the Incarnation of Christ your
　Son
was made known by the message of an Angel,
may by his Passion and Cross
be brought to the glory of his Resurrection.
Who lives and reigns with you in the unity of the
　Holy Spirit,
one God, for ever and ever. ℟. **Amen.** ↓

FIRST READING Mic. 5.2-5a

> Micah speaks of the glory of Bethlehem, a little town of Judah. From Bethlehem will come forth the promised one who will stand firm and strong in the Lord.

A reading from the book of the Prophet Micah.

THE Lord says to his people:
    "You, O Bethlehem of Ephrathah,
who are one of the little clans of Judea,
from you shall come forth for me
one who is to rule in Israel,
whose origin is from of old, from ancient days."

Therefore he shall give them up until the time
when she who is in labour has brought forth;
then the rest of his kindred
shall return to the children of Israel.
And he shall stand and feed his flock
in the strength of the Lord,
in the majesty of the name of the Lord his God.

And they shall live secure,
for now he shall be great to the ends of the
    earth;
and he shall be peace.

The word of the Lord. ℞. **Thanks be to God.** ↓

RESPONSORIAL PSALM Ps. 80

Normand L. Blanchard

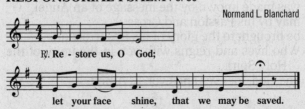

℞. Re - store us, O God; let your face shine, that we may be saved.

Give ear, O Shepherd of Israel,
you who are enthroned upon the cherubim,
    shine forth.
Stir up your might,
and come to save us.—R̥.

Turn again, O God of hosts;
look down from heaven, and see;
have regard for this vine,
the stock that your right hand has planted.—R̥.

But let your hand be upon the man at your right,
the son of man you have made strong for your-
    self.
Then we will never turn back from you;
give us life, and we will call on your name.—R̥. ↓

SECOND READING Heb. 10.5-10

Jesus said that sacrifices, sin offerings, and burnt offerings did not delight the Lord. But he has come to do the
will of God—to establish a second covenant.

A reading from the Letter to the Hebrews.

BROTHERS and sisters: When Christ came
into the world, he said,
"Sacrifices and offerings you have not desired,
    but a body you have prepared for me;
in burnt offerings and sin offerings
    you have taken no pleasure.
Then I said,
    as it is written of me in the scroll of the
        book,
    'See, God, I have come to do your will, O
        God.'"

When Christ said, "You have neither desired nor taken pleasure in sacrifices and offerings and burnt offerings and sin offerings" (these are offered according to the Law), then he added, "See, I have come to do your will." He abolishes the first in order to establish the second.

And it is by God's will that we have been sanctified through the offering of the body of Jesus Christ once for all.—The word of the Lord. ℟. **Thanks be to God.** ↓

GOSPEL ACCLAMATION Lk. 1.38

℣. Alleluia. ℟. **Alleluia.**
℣. Here am I, the servant of the Lord:
let it be done to me according to your word.
℟. **Alleluia.** ↓

GOSPEL Lk. 1.39-45

> Mary went to visit Elizabeth who was also blessed by the Holy Spirit. Elizabeth greeted Mary: "Blessed are you among women, and blessed is the fruit of your womb."

℣. The Lord be with you. ℟. **And with your spirit.**
✚ A reading from the holy Gospel according to Luke. ℟. **Glory to you, O Lord.**

MARY set out and went with haste to a Judean town in the hill country, where she entered the house of Zechariah and greeted Elizabeth.

When Elizabeth heard Mary's greeting, the child leaped in her womb. And Elizabeth was filled with the Holy Spirit and exclaimed with a loud cry, "Blessed are you among women, and blessed is the fruit of your womb. And why has this happened to me, that the mother of my Lord comes to me? For as soon as I heard the sound of your greeting, the child in my womb leaped for joy. And blessed is she who believed that there would be a fulfillment of what was spoken to her by the Lord."—The Gospel of the Lord. ℟. **Praise to you, Lord Jesus Christ.**   → No. 15, p. 18

PRAYER OVER THE OFFERINGS

May the Holy Spirit, O Lord,
sanctify these gifts laid upon your altar,
just as he filled with his power the womb of the
    Blessed Virgin Mary.
Through Christ our Lord.
℟. **Amen.**   → No. 21, p. 22 (Pref. 2)

COMMUNION ANTIPHON Isa. 7.14

Behold, a Virgin shall conceive and bear a son; and his name will be called Emmanuel. ↓

PRAYER AFTER COMMUNION

Having received this pledge of eternal redemption,
we pray, almighty God,
that, as the feast day of our salvation draws ever
    nearer,
so we may press forward all the more eagerly
to the worthy celebration of the mystery of your
    Son's Nativity.
Who lives and reigns for ever and ever.
℟. **Amen.**   → No. 30, p. 77

Optional Solemn Blessings, p. 97, and Prayers over the People, p. 105

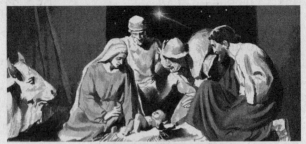

The Word is made flesh.

DECEMBER 25
THE NATIVITY OF THE LORD
[CHRISTMAS]

Solemnity

AT THE MASS DURING THE NIGHT

ENTRANCE ANTIPHON Ps. 2.7

The Lord said to me: You are my Son. It is I who have begotten you this day. → No. 2, p. 10

OR

Let us all rejoice in the Lord, for our Saviour has been born in the world. Today true peace has come down to us from heaven. → No. 2, p. 10

COLLECT

O God, who have made this most sacred night
radiant with the splendour of the true light,
grant, we pray, that we, who have known the
   mysteries of his light on earth,
may also delight in his gladness in heaven.
Who lives and reigns with you in the unity of the
   Holy Spirit,
one God, for ever and ever. ℟. **Amen.** ↓

FIRST READING Isa. 9.2-4, 6-7

The Messiah is a promise of peace for the world. His reign shall be vast and filled with justice. The power of God is revealed through the weakness of humans.

A reading from the book of the Prophet Isaiah.

THE people who walked in darkness have
    seen a great light;
those who lived in a land of deep darkness—
on them light has shone.
You have multiplied the nation,
you have increased its joy;
they rejoice before you
as with joy at the harvest,
as people exult when dividing plunder.

For the yoke of their burden,
and the bar across their shoulders,
the rod of their oppressor,
you have broken as on the day of Midian.

For a child has been born for us,
a son given to us;
authority rests upon his shoulders;
and he is named
Wonderful Counsellor, Mighty God,
Everlasting Father, Prince of Peace.
His authority shall grow continually,
and there shall be endless peace
for the throne of David and his kingdom.
He will establish and uphold it
with justice and with righteousness
from this time onward and forevermore.
The zeal of the Lord of hosts will do this.

The word of the Lord. ℟. **Thanks be to God.** ↓

RESPONSORIAL PSALM Ps. 96

Leo Marchildon

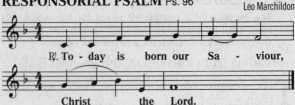

R). To-day is born our Sa-viour, Christ____ the Lord.

O sing to the Lord a new song;
sing to the Lord, all the earth.
Sing to the Lord, bless his name;
tell of his salvation from day to day. —R).

Declare his glory among the nations,
his marvellous works among all the peoples.
For great is the Lord, and greatly to be praised;
he is to be revered above all gods.—R).

Let the heavens be glad, and let the earth rejoice;
let the sea roar, and all that fills it;
let the field exult, and everything in it.
Then shall all the trees of the forest sing for joy.
    —R).

Rejoice before the Lord; for he is coming,
for he is coming to judge the earth.
He will judge the world with righteousness,
and the peoples with his truth.—R). ↓

SECOND READING Tit. 2.11-14

God offers salvation to all people. His way asks us to reject worldly desires—to live temperately and justly. He
even asked the only Son to sacrifice himself to redeem us.

A reading from the Letter of Saint Paul to Titus.

BELOVED: The grace of God has appeared,
bringing salvation to all, training us to re-

nounce impiety and worldly passions, and in the present age to live lives that are self-controlled, upright, and godly, while we wait for the blessed hope and the manifestation of the glory of our great God and Saviour, Jesus Christ.

He it is who gave himself for us that he might redeem us from all iniquity and purify for himself a people of his own who are zealous for good deeds.—The word of the Lord. ℟. **Thanks be to God.** ↓

GOSPEL ACCLAMATION Lk. 2.10-11

℣. Alleluia. ℟. **Alleluia.**
℣. Good news and great joy to all the world:
today is born our Saviour, Christ the Lord.
℟. **Alleluia.** ↓

GOSPEL Lk. 2.1-16

Caesar Augustus desired a world census. Joseph and Mary go to Bethlehem where Jesus, the Lord of the universe, is born in a stable. Glory to God and peace on earth!

℣. The Lord be with you. ℟. **And with your spirit.**
✠ A reading from the holy Gospel according to Luke. ℟. **Glory to you, O Lord.**

IN those days a decree went out from Caesar Augustus that all the world should be registered. This was the first registration and was taken while Quirinius was governor of Syria. All went to their own towns to be registered. Joseph also went from the town of Nazareth in Galilee to Judea, to the city of David called Bethlehem, because he was descended from the house and family of David. He went to be registered with Mary, to whom he was engaged and who was expecting a child.

While they were there, the time came for her to deliver her child. And she gave birth to her first-born son and wrapped him in swaddling clothes, and laid him in a manger, because there was no place for them in the inn.

In that region there were shepherds living in the fields, keeping watch over their flock by night. Then an Angel of the Lord stood before them, and the glory of the Lord shone around them, and they were terrified. But the Angel said to them, "Do not be afraid; for see—I am bringing you good news of great joy for all the people: to you is born this day in the city of David a Saviour, who is the Christ, the Lord. This will be a sign for you: you will find a child wrapped in swaddling clothes and lying in a manger."

And suddenly there was with the Angel a multitude of the heavenly host, praising God and saying,

"Glory to God in the highest heaven,
       and on earth peace among those whom he
       favours!"

When the Angels had left them and gone into heaven, the shepherds said to one another, "Let us go now to Bethlehem and see this thing that has taken place, which the Lord has made known to us." So they went with haste and found Mary and Joseph, and the child lying in the manger.—The Gospel of the Lord. ℟. **Praise to you, Lord Jesus Christ.**   ➙ No. 15, p. 18

The Creed is said. All kneel at the words and by the Holy Spirit was incarnate.

PRAYER OVER THE OFFERINGS

May the oblation of this day's feast
be pleasing to you, O Lord, we pray,
that through this most holy exchange
we may be found in the likeness of Christ,
in whom our nature is united to you.
Who lives and reigns for ever and ever.
℟. **Amen.**   → No. 21, p. 22 (Pref. 3-5)

When the Roman Canon is used, the proper form of the
Communicantes (In communion with those) *is said.*

COMMUNION ANTIPHON Jn. 1.14

**The Word became flesh, and we have seen his
glory.** ↓

PRAYER AFTER COMMUNION

Grant us, we pray, O Lord our God,
that we, who are gladdened by participation
in the feast of our Redeemer's Nativity,
may through an honourable way of life become
    worthy of union with him.
Who lives and reigns for ever and ever.
℟. **Amen.**   → No. 30, p. 77

Optional Solemn Blessings, p. 97, and Prayers over the People, p. 105

AT THE MASS AT DAWN

ENTRANCE ANTIPHON Cf. Isa. 9.1, 5; Lk. 1.33

**Today a light will shine upon us, for the Lord is
born for us; and he will be called Wondrous God,
Prince of peace, Father of future ages: and his
reign will be without end.**   → No. 2, p. 10

COLLECT

Grant, we pray, almighty God,
that, as we are bathed in the new radiance of your
    incarnate Word,
the light of faith, which illumines our minds,
may also shine through in our deeds.
Through our Lord Jesus Christ, your Son,
who lives and reigns with you in the unity of the
    Holy Spirit,
one God, for ever and ever. ℟. **Amen.** ↓

FIRST READING Isa. 62.11-12

> Isaiah foretells the birth of the Saviour who will come to
> Zion. These people will be called holy, and they shall be
> redeemed.

A reading from the book of the Prophet Isaiah.

THE Lord has proclaimed to the end of the
    earth:
"Say to daughter Zion,
See, your salvation comes;
his reward is with him,
and his recompense before him.

They shall be called 'The Holy People,'
'The Redeemed of the Lord';
and you shall be called 'Sought Out,'
'A City Not Forsaken.'"

The word of the Lord. ℟. **Thanks be to God.** ↓

RESPONSORIAL PSALM Ps. 97

James Howells

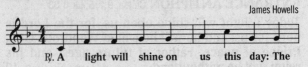

℟. A   light will   shine on   us   this   day: The

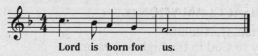

Lord   is   born for   us.

The Lord is king! Let the earth rejoice;
let the many coastlands be glad!
Clouds and thick darkness are all around him;
righteousness and justice are the foundation of
    his throne.—℟.

The mountains melt like wax before the Lord,
before the Lord of all the earth.
The heavens proclaim his righteousness;
and all the peoples behold his glory. —℟.

Light dawns for the righteous,
and joy for the upright in heart.
Rejoice in the Lord, O you righteous,
and give thanks to his holy name!—℟. ↓

SECOND READING Tit. 3.4-7

Christians are saved not because of their own merits but because of the mercy of God. We are saved through baptism and renewal in the Holy Spirit.

A reading from the Letter of Saint Paul to Titus.

WHEN the goodness and loving kindness of God our Saviour appeared, he saved us, not because of any works of righteousness that we had done, but according to his mercy, through the water of rebirth and renewal by the Holy Spirit. This Spirit he poured out on us richly through Jesus Christ our Saviour, so that, having been justified by his grace, we might become heirs according to the hope of eternal life.—The word of the Lord. ℟. **Thanks be to God.** ↓

GOSPEL ACCLAMATION Lk. 2.14

℣. Alleluia. ℟. **Alleluia.**
℣. Glory to God in the highest heaven;
peace on earth to people of good will.
℟. **Alleluia.** ↓

GOSPEL Lk. 2.15-20

The shepherds, the poor of the people of God, come to pay homage to Jesus. Mary ponders and prays over the great event of God becoming one of us.

℣. The Lord be with you. ℟. **And with your spirit.**
✛ A reading from the holy Gospel according to Luke. ℟. **Glory to you, O Lord.**

WHEN the Angels had left them and gone into heaven, the shepherds said to one another, "Let us go now to Bethlehem and see this thing that has taken place, which the Lord has made known to us."

So they went with haste and found Mary and Joseph, and the child lying in the manger. When they saw this, they made known what had been told them about this child; and all who heard it were amazed at what the shepherds told them.

But Mary treasured all these words and pondered them in her heart. The shepherds returned, glorifying and praising God for all they had heard and seen, as it had been told them.— The Gospel of the Lord. ℟. **Praise to you, Lord Jesus Christ.**   ➜ No. 15, p. 18

The Creed is said. All kneel at the words and by the Holy Spirit was incarnate.

PRAYER OVER THE OFFERINGS

May our offerings be worthy, we pray, O Lord,
of the mysteries of the Nativity this day,
that, just as Christ was born a man and also
   shone forth as God,
so these earthly gifts may confer on us what is
   divine.
Through Christ our Lord.
R̸. **Amen.**   → No. 21, p. 22 (Pref. 3-5)

When the Roman Canon is used, the proper form of the
Communicantes *(In communion with those) is said.*

COMMUNION ANTIPHON Cf. Zech. 9.9

Rejoice, O Daughter Sion; lift up praise, Daughter Jerusalem: Behold, your King will come, the Holy One and Saviour of the world. ↓

PRAYER AFTER COMMUNION

Grant us, Lord, as we honour with joyful devotion
the Nativity of your Son,
that we may come to know with fullness of faith
the hidden depths of this mystery
and to love them ever more and more.
Through Christ our Lord.
R̸. **Amen.**   → No. 30, p. 77

Optional Solemn Blessings, p. 97, and Prayers over the People, p. 105

AT THE MASS DURING THE DAY

ENTRANCE ANTIPHON Cf. Isa. 9.5

A child is born for us, and a son is given to us; his sceptre of power rests upon his shoulder, and his name will be called Messenger of great counsel.
                                   → No. 2, p. 10

COLLECT

O God, who wonderfully created the dignity of
    human nature
and still more wonderfully restored it,
grant, we pray,
that we may share in the divinity of Christ,
who humbled himself to share in our humanity.
Who lives and reigns with you in the unity of the
    Holy Spirit,
one God, for ever and ever. ℟. **Amen.** ↓

FIRST READING Isa. 52.7-10

God shows salvation to all people. God brings peace and
good news. God comforts and redeems the faithful.

A reading from the book of the Prophet Isaiah.

HOW beautiful upon the mountains
    are the feet of the messenger who announces
    peace,
who brings good news,
who announces salvation,
who says to Zion, "Your God reigns."

Listen! Your watchmen lift up their voices,
together they sing for joy;
for in plain sight they see
the return of the Lord to Zion.

Break forth together into singing,
you ruins of Jerusalem;
for the Lord has comforted his people,
he has redeemed Jerusalem.
The Lord has bared his holy arm
before the eyes of all the nations;
and all the ends of the earth shall see the salva-
    tion of our God.

The word of the Lord. ℟. **Thanks be to God.** ↓

RESPONSORIAL PSALM Ps. 98

Normand L. Blanchard

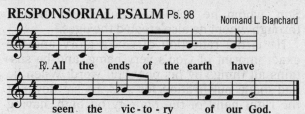

℟. All the ends of the earth have seen the vic-to-ry of our God.

O sing to the Lord a new song,
for he has done marvellous things.
His right hand and his holy arm
have brought him victory.—℟.

The Lord has made known his victory;
he has revealed his vindication in the sight of
    the nations.
He has remembered his steadfast love
and faithfulness to the house of Israel.—℟.

All the ends of the earth have seen
the victory of our God.
Make a joyful noise to the Lord, all the earth;
break forth into joyous song and sing praises.—℟.

Sing praises to the Lord with the lyre,
with the lyre and the sound of melody.
With trumpets and the sound of the horn
make a joyful noise before the King, the Lord.—℟. ↓

SECOND READING Heb. 1.1-6

God now speaks through Jesus, the Son, who reflects God's glory. The Son cleanses us from sin. Heaven and earth should worship him.

A reading from the Letter to the Hebrews.

LONG ago God spoke to our ancestors in many and various ways by the Prophets, but in these last days he has spoken to us by the

Son, whom he appointed heir of all things, through whom he also created the ages.

He is the reflection of God's glory and the exact imprint of God's very being, and he sustains all things by his powerful word. When he had made purification for sins, he sat down at the right hand of the Majesty on high, having become as much superior to Angels as the name he has inherited is more excellent than theirs.

For to which of the Angels did God ever say,
    "You are my Son;
        today I have begotten you"?
Or again,
    "I will be his Father,
        and he will be my Son"?
And again, when he brings the firstborn into the world, he says,
    "Let all God's Angels worship him."

The word of the Lord. ℟. **Thanks be to God.** ↓

GOSPEL ACCLAMATION

℣. Alleluia. ℟. **Alleluia.**
℣. A holy day has dawned upon us.
Come you nations and adore the Lord.
Today a great light has come down upon the earth.
℟. **Alleluia.** ↓

GOSPEL Jn. 1.1-18 or 1.1-5, 9-14

John's opening words parallel the Book of Genesis. Jesus is the Word made flesh, the light of the world, who always was and will ever be.

[If the "Shorter Form" is used, the indented text in brackets is omitted.]

℣. The Lord be with you. ℟. **And with your spirit.**
✚ A reading from the holy Gospel according to
John. ℟. **Glory to you, O Lord.**

IN the beginning was the Word, and the Word
was with God, and the Word was God. He was
in the beginning with God. All things came into
being through him, and without him not one
thing came into being. What has come into
being in him was life, and the life was the light
of the human race. The light shines in the darkness, and the darkness did not overcome it.

[There was a man sent from God, whose
name was John. He came as a witness to
testify to the light, so that all might believe
through him. He himself was not the light,
but he came to testify to the light.]

The true light, which enlightens everyone, was
coming into the world. He was in the world, and
the world came into being through him; yet the
world did not know him. He came to what was his
own, and his own people did not accept him. But
to all who received him, who believed in his name,
he gave power to become children of God, who
were born, not of blood or of the will of the flesh
or of the will of man, but of God. And the Word
became flesh and lived among us, and we have
seen his glory, the glory as of a father's only-
begotten son, full of grace and truth.

[John testified to him and cried out, "This
was he of whom I said, 'He who comes after
me ranks ahead of me because he was before me.'"]

From his fullness we have all received,
grace upon grace. The law indeed was

given through Moses; grace and truth came
through Jesus Christ. No one has ever seen
God. It is God the only-begotten Son, who
is close to the Father's heart, who has made
him known.]

The Gospel of the Lord. R̠. **Praise to you, Lord
Jesus Christ.** ➔ No. 15, p. 18

The Creed is said. All kneel at the words and by the
Holy Spirit was incarnate.

PRAYER OVER THE OFFERINGS

Make acceptable, O Lord, our oblation on this
   solemn day,
when you manifested the reconciliation
that makes us wholly pleasing in your sight
and inaugurated for us the fullness of divine
   worship.
Through Christ our Lord.
R̠. **Amen.** ➔ No. 21, p. 22 (Pref. 3-5)

When the Roman Canon is used, the proper form of the
Communicantes (In communion with those) *is said.*

COMMUNION ANTIPHON Cf. Ps. 97.3

**All the ends of the earth have seen the salvation
of our God.** ↓

PRAYER AFTER COMMUNION

Grant, O merciful God,
that, just as the Saviour of the world, born this
   day,
is the author of divine generation for us,
so he may be the giver even of immortality.
Who lives and reigns for ever and ever.
R̠. **Amen.** ➔ No. 30, p. 77

Optional Solemn Blessings, p. 97, and Prayers over the People, p. 105

"Jesus went down with them and came to Nazareth, and was obedient to them."

DECEMBER 30

THE HOLY FAMILY OF JESUS, MARY AND JOSEPH

Feast

ENTRANCE ANTIPHON Lk. 2.16

The shepherds went in haste, and found Mary and Joseph and the Infant lying in a manger.

➥ No. 2, p. 10

COLLECT

O God, who were pleased to give us
the shining example of the Holy Family,
graciously grant that we may imitate them
in practising the virtues of family life and in the
    bonds of charity,
and so, in the joy of your house,
delight one day in eternal rewards.
Through our Lord Jesus Christ, your Son,

who lives and reigns with you in the unity of the
  Holy Spirit,
one God, for ever and ever. ℟. **Amen.** ↓

FIRST READING 1 Sam. 1.20-22, 24-28

This reading teaches us that motherhood and life are a
gift of God. The presence of children in a family signals
the continuation of life and manifests the newness of
God's love, which gives origin to ever new creatures.

A reading from the first book of Samuel.

IN due time Hannah conceived and bore a son.
  She named him Samuel, for she said, "I have
asked him of the Lord." Elkanah and all his household went up to offer to the Lord the yearly sacrifice, and to pay his vow. But Hannah did not go
up, for she said to her husband, "As soon as the
child is weaned, I will bring him, that he may appear in the presence of the Lord, and remain there
forever; I will offer him as a nazirite for all time."

When she had weaned him, she took him up
with her, along with a three-year-old bull, a measure of flour, and a skin of wine. She brought him
to the house of the Lord at Shiloh; and the child
was young. Then they slaughtered the bull, and
they brought the child to Eli. And she said, "Oh,
my lord! As you live, my lord, I am the woman
who was standing here in your presence, praying
to the Lord.

For this child I prayed; and the Lord has granted
me the petition that I made to him. Therefore I have
lent him to the Lord; as long as he lives, he is given
to the Lord." She left him there for the Lord.—The
word of the Lord. ℟. **Thanks be to God.** ↓

RESPONSORIAL PSALM Ps. 84

Geoffrey Angeles

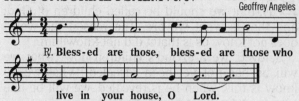

℟. Bless-ed are those, bless-ed are those who live in your house, O Lord.

How lovely is your dwelling place,
O Lord of hosts!
My soul longs, indeed it faints for the courts of
    the Lord;
my heart and my flesh sing for joy to the living
    God.—℟.

Blessed are those who live in your house,
ever singing your praise.
Blessed are those whose strength is in you,
in whose heart are the highways to Zion.—℟.

O Lord God of hosts, hear my prayer;
give ear, O God of Jacob!
Behold our shield, O God;
look on the face of your anointed.—℟.

For a day in your courts is better
than a thousand elsewhere.
I would rather be a doorkeeper in the house of
    my God
than live in the tents of wickedness.—℟. ↓

SECOND READING 1 Jn. 3.1-2, 21-24

Every family must be a mirror of the divine love because
the root of every love is God. Therefore, members of a
family should deal lovingly with one another.

A reading from the first Letter of Saint John.

Beloved: See what love the Father has given us, that we should be called children of God; and that is what we are. The reason the world does not know us is that it did not know him.

Beloved, we are God's children now; what we will be has not yet been revealed. What we do know is this: when he is revealed, we will be like him, for we will see him as he is.

Beloved, if our hearts do not condemn us, we have boldness before God; and we receive from him whatever we ask, because we obey his commandments and do what pleases him.

And this is his commandment, that we should believe in the name of his Son Jesus Christ and love one another, just as he has commanded us. Whoever obeys his commandments abides in him, and he abides in them. And by this we know that he abides in us, by the Spirit that he has given us.—The word of the Lord. ℟. **Thanks be to God.** ↓

GOSPEL ACCLAMATION See Acts 16.14b

℣. Alleluia. ℟. **Alleluia.**
℣. Open our hearts, O Lord,
to listen to the words of your Son.
℟. **Alleluia.** ↓

GOSPEL Lk. 2.41-52

Jesus and his parents go to Jerusalem for the Passover. Upon returning, Jesus is separated from them. Mary and Joseph find him in the temple teaching. When Mary asks why, Jesus replies that he must be doing his Father's work. Jesus returns with Mary and Joseph to Nazareth.

℣. The Lord be with you. ℟. **And with your spirit.**
✠ A reading from the holy Gospel according to
Luke. ℟. **Glory to you, O Lord.**

EVERY year the parents of Jesus went to
Jerusalem for the festival of the Passover.
And when he was twelve years old, they went
up as usual for the festival.

When the festival was ended and they started
to return, the boy Jesus stayed behind in Jerusalem, but his parents did not know it. Assuming
that he was in the group of travellers, they went
a day's journey. Then they started to look for
him among their relatives and friends. When
they did not find him, they returned to Jerusalem to search for him.

After three days they found him in the temple, sitting among the teachers, listening to
them and asking them questions. And all who
heard him were amazed at his understanding
and his answers. When his parents saw him
they were astonished; and his mother said to
him, "Child, why have you treated us like this?
Look, your father and I have been searching for
you in great anxiety." He said to them, "Why
were you searching for me? Did you not know
that I must be in my Father's house?" But they
did not understand what he said to them.

Then he went down with them and came to
Nazareth, and was obedient to them. His mother
treasured all these things in her heart. And
Jesus increased in wisdom and in years, and in
favour with God and human beings.—The

Gospel of the Lord. ℟. **Praise to you, Lord Jesus Christ.**   ➜ No. 15, p. 18

PRAYER OVER THE OFFERINGS

We offer you, Lord, the sacrifice of conciliation, humbly asking that,
through the intercession of the Virgin Mother of
    God and Saint Joseph,
you may establish our families firmly in your
    grace and your peace.
Through Christ our Lord.
℟. **Amen.**   ➜ No. 21, p. 22 (Pref. 3-5)

When the Roman Canon is used, the proper form of the
Communicantes *(In communion with those) is said.*

COMMUNION ANTIPHON Bar. 3.38

Our God has appeared on the earth, and lived among us. ↓

PRAYER AFTER COMMUNION

Bring those you refresh with this heavenly
    Sacrament,
most merciful Father,
to imitate constantly the example of the Holy
    Family,
so that, after the trials of this world,
we may share their company for ever.
Through Christ our Lord.
℟. **Amen.**   ➜ No. 30, p. 77

Optional Solemn Blessings, p. 97, and Prayers over the People, p. 105

"He was called Jesus. . . ."

JANUARY 1, 2019

The Octave Day of the Nativity of the Lord [Christmas]
SOLEMNITY OF MARY, THE HOLY MOTHER OF GOD

ENTRANCE ANTIPHON

Hail, Holy Mother, who gave birth to the King who rules heaven and earth for ever. ➔ No. 2, p. 10

OR Cf. Isa. 9.1, 5; Lk. 1.33

Today a light will shine upon us, for the Lord is born for us; and he will be called Wondrous God, Prince of peace, Father of future ages: and his reign will be without end. ➔ No. 2, p. 10

COLLECT

O God, who through the fruitful virginity of
    Blessed Mary
bestowed on the human race

the grace of eternal salvation,
grant, we pray,
that we may experience the intercession of her,
through whom we were found worthy
to receive the author of life,
our Lord Jesus Christ, your Son.
Who lives and reigns with you in the unity of the
    Holy Spirit,
one God, for ever and ever. ℟. **Amen.** ↓

FIRST READING Num. 6.22-27

**Aaron and the Israelites are to pray that God will answer
their prayers with blessings.**

    A reading from the book of Numbers.

THE Lord spoke to Moses:
    Speak to Aaron and his sons, saying,
Thus you shall bless the children of Israel:
You shall say to them,

The Lord bless you and keep you;
the Lord make his face to shine upon you,
and be gracious to you;
the Lord lift up his countenance upon you,
and give you peace.
So they shall put my name on the children of
    Israel,
and I will bless them.

The word of the Lord. ℟. **Thanks be to God.** ↓

RESPONSORIAL PSALM Ps. 67

Paul K. McKay

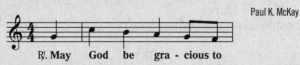

℟. May   God   be   gra - cious to

us　　　and bless＿＿＿　　us.

May God be gracious to us and bless us
and make his face to shine upon us,
that your way may be known upon earth,
your saving power among all nations.—℟.

Let the nations be glad and sing for joy,
for you judge the peoples with equity
and guide the nations upon earth.
Let the peoples praise you, O God;
let all the peoples praise you.—℟.

The earth has yielded its increase;
God, our God, has blessed us.
May God continue to bless us;
let all the ends of the earth revere him.—℟. ↓

SECOND READING Gal. 4.4-7

**God sent Jesus, his Son, born of Mary, to deliver all peo-
ple from the bondage of sin and slavery of the law. By
God's choice we are heirs of heaven.**

A reading from the Letter of Saint Paul
to the Galatians.

B ROTHERS and sisters: When the fullness of
time had come, God sent his Son, born of a
woman, born under the law, in order to redeem
those who were under the law, so that we might
receive adoption to sonship.

And because you are sons and daughters,
God has sent the Spirit of his Son into our
hearts, crying, "Abba! Father!" So you are no
longer slave but son, and if son then also heir,
through God.—The word of the Lord. ℟. **Thanks
be to God.** ↓

GOSPEL ACCLAMATION Heb. 1.1-2

℣. Alleluia. ℟. **Alleluia.**

℣. Long ago God spoke to our ancestors by the Prophets;

in these last days he has spoken to us by the Son.
℟. **Alleluia.** ↓

GOSPEL Lk. 2.16-21

When the shepherds came to Bethlehem, they began to understand the message of the angels. Mary prayed about this great event. Jesus received his name according to the Jewish ritual of circumcision.

℣. The Lord be with you. ℟. **And with your spirit.**
✚ A reading from the holy Gospel according to Luke. ℟. **Glory to you, O Lord.**

THE shepherds went with haste to Bethlehem and found Mary and Joseph, and the child lying in the manger. When they saw this, they made known what had been told them about this child; and all who heard it were amazed at what the shepherds told them. But Mary treasured all these words and pondered them in her heart.

The shepherds returned, glorifying and praising God for all they had heard and seen, as it had been told them.

After eight days had passed, it was time to circumcise the child; and he was called Jesus, the name given by the Angel before he was conceived in the womb.—The Gospel of the Lord.
℟. **Praise to you, Lord Jesus Christ.** → No. 15, p. 18

PRAYER OVER THE OFFERINGS

O God, who in your kindness begin all good
   things
and bring them to fulfillment,
grant to us, who find joy in the Solemnity of the
   holy Mother of God,
that, just as we glory in the beginnings of your
   grace,
so one day we may rejoice in its completion.
Through Christ our Lord.
℟. **Amen.** ↓

PREFACE (56)

℣. The Lord be with you. ℟. **And with your spirit.**
℣. Lift up your hearts. ℟. **We lift them up to the
Lord.** ℣. Let us give thanks to the Lord our God.
℟. **It is right and just.**

It is truly right and just, our duty and our
   salvation,
always and everywhere to give you thanks,
Lord, holy Father, almighty and eternal God,
and to praise, bless, and glorify your name
on the Solemnity of the Motherhood
of the Blessed ever-Virgin Mary.

For by the overshadowing of the Holy Spirit
she conceived your Only Begotten Son,
and without losing the glory of virginity,
brought forth into the world the eternal Light,
Jesus Christ our Lord.

Through him the Angels praise your majesty,
Dominions adore and Powers tremble before you.

Heaven and the Virtues of heaven and the blessed
  Seraphim
worship together with exultation.
May our voices, we pray, join with theirs
in humble praise, as we acclaim: ➜ No. 23, p. 23

When the Roman Canon is used, the proper form of the
Communicantes (In communion with those) *is said.*

COMMUNION ANTIPHON Heb. 13.8

**Jesus Christ is the same yesterday, today, and for
ever.** ↓

PRAYER AFTER COMMUNION

We have received this heavenly Sacrament with
  joy, O Lord:
grant, we pray,
that it may lead us to eternal life,
for we rejoice to proclaim the blessed ever-Virgin
  Mary
Mother of your Son and Mother of the Church.
Through Christ our Lord.
℟. **Amen.**   ➜ No. 30, p. 77

Optional Solemn Blessings, p. 97, and Prayers over the People, p. 105

"They knelt down and paid him homage."

JANUARY 6

THE EPIPHANY OF THE LORD

Solemnity

AT THE VIGIL MASS (January 5)

ENTRANCE ANTIPHON Cf. Bar. 5.5

Arise, Jerusalem, and look to the East and see your children gathered from the rising to the setting of the sun. ➜ No. 2, p. 10

COLLECT

May the splendour of your majesty, O Lord, we pray,

shed its light upon our hearts,

that we may pass through the shadows of this world

and reach the brightness of our eternal home.

Through our Lord Jesus Christ, your Son,

who lives and reigns with you in the unity of the Holy Spirit,

one God, for ever and ever. ℟. **Amen.** ↓

The readings for this Mass can be found beginning on p. 162.

PRAYER OVER THE OFFERINGS

Accept we pray, O Lord, our offerings,
in honour of the appearing of your Only Begotten
    Son
and the first fruits of the nations,
that to you praise may be rendered
and eternal salvation be ours.
Through Christ our Lord.
℟. **Amen.** ↓

PREFACE (6)

℣. The Lord be with you. ℟. **And with your spirit.**
℣. Lift up your hearts. ℟. **We lift them up to the
Lord.** ℣. Let us give thanks to the Lord our God.
℟. **It is right and just.**

It is truly right and just, our duty and our
    salvation,
always and everywhere to give you thanks,
Lord, holy Father, almighty and eternal God.

For today you have revealed the mystery
of our salvation in Christ
as a light for the nations,
and, when he appeared in our mortal nature,
you made us new by the glory of his immortal
    nature.

And so, with Angels and Archangels,
with Thrones and Dominions,
and with all the hosts and Powers of heaven,
we sing the hymn of your glory,
as without end we acclaim: ➔ No. 23, p. 23

COMMUNION ANTIPHON Cf. Rev. 21.23

The brightness of God illumined the holy city Jerusalem, and the nations will walk by its light. ↓

PRAYER AFTER COMMUNION

Renewed by sacred nourishment,
we implore your mercy, O Lord,
that the star of your justice
may shine always bright in our minds
and that our true treasure may ever consist in our
   confession of you.
Through Christ our Lord.
℞. Amen.   ➜ No. 30, p. 77

Optional Solemn Blessings, p. 97, and Prayers over the People, p. 105

AT THE MASS DURING THE DAY

ENTRANCE ANTIPHON Cf. Mal. 3.1; 1 Chr. 29.12

Behold, the Lord, the Mighty One, has come; and kingship is in his grasp, and power and dominion.   ➜ No. 2, p. 10

COLLECT

O God, who on this day
revealed your Only Begotten Son to the nations
by the guidance of a star,
grant in your mercy
that we, who know you already by faith,
may be brought to behold the beauty of your
   sublime glory.

Through our Lord Jesus Christ, your Son,
who lives and reigns with you in the unity of the
    Holy Spirit,
one God, for ever and ever. ℟. **Amen.** ↓

FIRST READING Isa. 60.1-6

Jerusalem is favoured by the Lord. Kings and peoples will
come there, and the riches of the earth will be placed at
its gates.

A reading from the book of the Prophet Isaiah.

ARISE, shine, for your light has come,
    and the glory of the Lord has risen upon you!
For darkness shall cover the earth,
and thick darkness the peoples;
but the Lord will arise upon you,
and his glory will appear over you.

Nations shall come to your light,
and kings to the brightness of your dawn.
Lift up your eyes and look around;
they all gather together, they come to you;
your sons shall come from far away,
and your daughters shall be carried on their
    nurses' arms.

Then you shall see and be radiant;
your heart shall thrill and rejoice,
because the abundance of the sea shall be
    brought to you,
the wealth of the nations shall come to you.
A multitude of camels shall cover you,
the young camels of Midian and Ephah;
all those from Sheba shall come.
They shall bring gold and frankincense,
and shall proclaim the praise of the Lord.

The word of the Lord. ℟. **Thanks be to God.** ↓

RESPONSORIAL PSALM Ps. 72

David Szanto

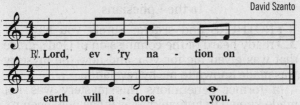

℟. Lord, ev-'ry na - tion on earth will a - dore you.

Give the king your justice, O God,
and your righteousness to a king's son.
May he judge your people with righteousness,
and your poor with justice.—℟.

In his days may righteousness flourish
and peace abound, until the moon is no more.
May he have dominion from sea to sea,
and from the River to the ends of the earth.—℟.

May the kings of Tarshish and of the isles render
    him tribute,
may the kings of Sheba and Seba bring gifts.
May all kings fall down before him,
all nations give him service.—℟.

For he delivers the needy one who calls,
the poor and the one who has no helper.
He has pity on the weak and the needy,
and saves the lives of the needy.—℟. ↓

SECOND READING Eph. 3.2-3a, 5-6

**Paul admits that God has revealed the divine plan of sal-
vation to him. Not only the Jews, but also the whole
world will share in the good news.**

A reading from the Letter of Saint Paul
to the Ephesians.

BROTHERS and sisters: Surely you have already heard of the commission of God's grace that was given me for you, and how the mystery was made known to me by revelation.

In former generations this mystery was not made known to humankind as it has now been revealed to his holy Apostles and Prophets by the Spirit: that is, the Gentiles have become fellow heirs, members of the same body, and sharers in the promise in Christ Jesus through the Gospel.—The word of the Lord. ℟. **Thanks be to God.** ↓

GOSPEL ACCLAMATION See Mt. 2.2

℣. Alleluia. ℟. **Alleluia.**
℣. We observed his star at its rising,
and have come to pay homage to the Lord.
℟. **Alleluia.** ↓

GOSPEL Mt. 2.1-12

The wise men from the East followed the star to Bethlehem, from which a ruler was to come.

℣. The Lord be with you. ℟. **And with your spirit.**
✠ A reading from the holy Gospel according to Matthew. ℟. **Glory to you, O Lord.**

IN the time of King Herod, after Jesus was born in Bethlehem of Judea, wise men from the East came to Jerusalem, asking, "Where is the child who has been born king of the Jews? For we observed his star at its rising, and have come to pay him homage."

When King Herod heard this, he was frightened, and all Jerusalem with him; and calling together all the chief priests and scribes of the people, he inquired of them where the Messiah was to be born. They told him, "In Bethlehem of Judea; for so it has been written by the Prophet:

'And you, Bethlehem, in the land of Judah,
　　are by no means least among the rulers of
　　　Judah;
for from you shall come a ruler
　　who is to shepherd my people Israel.'"

Then Herod secretly called for the wise men and learned from them the exact time when the star had appeared. Then he sent them to Bethlehem, saying, "Go and search diligently for the child; and when you have found him, bring me word so that I may also go and pay him homage."

When they had heard the king, they set out; and there, ahead of them, went the star that they had seen at its rising, until it stopped over the place where the child was. When they saw that the star had stopped, they were overwhelmed with joy.

On entering the house, they saw the child with Mary his mother; and they knelt down and paid him homage. Then, opening their treasure chests, they offered him gifts of gold, frankincense, and myrrh.

And having been warned in a dream not to return to Herod, they left for their own country by another road.—The Gospel of the Lord.
℟. **Praise to you, Lord Jesus Christ.** → No. 15, p. 18

PRAYER OVER THE OFFERINGS

Look with favour, Lord, we pray,
on these gifts of your Church,
in which are offered now not gold or
    frankincense or myrrh,
but he who by them is proclaimed,
sacrificed and received, Jesus Christ.
Who lives and reigns for ever and ever. ℟. **Amen.**

➜ Pref. 6, p. 160

When the Roman Canon is used, the proper form of the
Communicantes *(In communion with those) is said.*

COMMUNION ANTIPHON Cf. Mt. 2.2

**We have seen his star in the East, and have come
with gifts to adore the Lord. ↓**

PRAYER AFTER COMMUNION

Go before us with heavenly light, O Lord,
always and everywhere,
that we may perceive with clear sight
and revere with true affection
the mystery in which you have willed us to
    participate.
Through Christ our Lord.
℟. **Amen.**

➜ No. 30, p. 77

Optional Solemn Blessings, p. 97, and Prayers over the People, p. 105

"You are my Son, the Beloved; with you I am well pleased."

JANUARY 13
THE BAPTISM OF THE LORD
Feast

ENTRANCE ANTIPHON Cf. Mt. 3.16-17

After the Lord was baptized, the heavens were opened, and the Spirit descended upon him like a dove, and the voice of the Father thundered: This is my beloved Son, with whom I am well pleased. ➜ No. 2, p. 10

COLLECT

Almighty ever-living God,
who, when Christ had been baptized in the River Jordan
and as the Holy Spirit descended upon him,
solemnly declared him your beloved Son,
grant that your children by adoption,
reborn of water and the Holy Spirit,
may always be well pleasing to you.
Through our Lord Jesus Christ, your Son,
who lives and reigns with you in the unity of the Holy Spirit,

one God, for ever and ever.
℟. **Amen.** ↓

OR

O God, whose Only Begotten Son
has appeared in our very flesh,
grant, we pray, that we may be inwardly
 transformed
through him whom we recognize as outwardly
 like ourselves.
Who lives and reigns with you in the unity of the
 Holy Spirit,
one God, for ever and ever. ℟. **Amen.** ↓

FIRST READING Isa. 40.1-5, 9-11

> Isaiah's central message is an announcement of salvation
> for the people of God. He reveals God as a Shepherd-
> King, attracting and ever caring for his people.

A reading from the book of the Prophet Isaiah.

COMFORT, O comfort my people,
 says your God.
Speak tenderly to Jerusalem,
and cry to her
that she has served her term,
that her penalty is paid,
that she has received from the Lord's hand
double for all her sins.

A voice cries out:
"In the wilderness prepare the way of the Lord,
make straight in the desert a highway for our God.
Every valley shall be lifted up,
and every mountain and hill be made low;
the uneven ground shall become level,
and the rough places a plain.

Then the glory of the Lord shall be revealed,
and all people shall see it together,
for the mouth of the Lord has spoken."

Get you up to a high mountain,
O Zion, herald of good tidings;
lift up your voice with strength,
O Jerusalem, herald of good tidings,
lift it up, do not fear;
say to the cities of Judah,
"Here is your God!"

See, the Lord God comes with might,
and his arm rules for him;
his reward is with him,
and his recompense before him.

He will feed his flock like a shepherd;
he will gather the lambs in his arms,
and carry them in his bosom,
and gently lead the mother sheep.

The word of the Lord. ℟. **Thanks be to God.** ↓

RESPONSORIAL PSALM Ps. 104

Leo Marchildon

℟. O   bless the   Lord,   my   soul!

O Lord my God, you are very great.
You are clothed with honour and majesty,
wrapped in light as with a garment.
You stretch out the heavens like a tent.—℟.

You set the beams of your dwelling place on the
    waters,
you make the clouds your chariot,

you ride on the wings of the wind,
you make the winds your messengers,
fire and flame your ministers.
℟. **O bless the Lord, my soul!**

O Lord, how manifold are your works!
In wisdom you have made them all;
the earth is full of your creatures.
Yonder is the sea, great and wide,
creeping things innumerable are there,
living things both small and great.—℟.

Living things all look to you
to give them their food in due season;
when you give to them, they gather it up;
when you open your hand, they are filled with
    good things.—℟.

When you take away their breath,
they die and return to their dust.
When you send forth your spirit, they are
    created;
and you renew the face of the earth.—℟. ↓

SECOND READING Tit. 2.11-14; 3.4-7

Paul proclaims that the "grace of God has appeared" in
Christ. This has set us on the road to salvation by giving
us the gifts of God, especially Baptism, and by calling us
to lead lives dedicated to Christ.

A reading from the Letter of Saint Paul to Titus.

BELOVED: The grace of God has appeared,
bringing salvation to all, training us to renounce impiety and worldly passions, and in the

present age to live lives that are self-controlled, upright, and godly, while we wait for the blessed hope and the manifestation of the glory of our great God and Saviour, Jesus Christ.

He it is who gave himself for us that he might redeem us from all iniquity and purify for himself a people of his own who are zealous for good deeds.

For when the goodness and loving kindness of God our Saviour appeared, he saved us, not because of any works of righteousness that we had done, but according to his mercy, through the water of rebirth and renewal by the Holy Spirit. This Spirit he poured out on us richly through Jesus Christ our Saviour, so that, having been justified by his grace, we might become heirs according to the hope of eternal life.—The word of the Lord. ℟. **Thanks be to God.** ↓

GOSPEL ACCLAMATION See Lk. 3.16

℣. Alleluia. ℟. **Alleluia.**
℣. John said: One more powerful than I is coming;
he will baptize you with the Holy Spirit and fire.
℟. **Alleluia.** ↓

GOSPEL Lk. 3.15-16, 21-22

The Spirit of God is seen coming upon Christ. And God the Father bears witness to his Son on whom his favour rests.

℣. The Lord be with you. ℟. **And with your spirit.**
✛ A reading from the holy Gospel according to Luke. ℟. **Glory to you, O Lord.**

AS the people were filled with expectation, and all were questioning in their hearts concerning John, whether he might be the Messiah, John answered all of them by saying, "I baptize you with water; but one who is more powerful than I is coming; I am not worthy to untie the thong of his sandals. He will baptize you with the Holy Spirit and fire."

Now when all the people were baptized, and when Jesus also had been baptized and was praying, the heaven was opened, and the Holy Spirit descended upon him in bodily form like a dove. And a voice came from heaven, "You are my Son, the Beloved; with you I am well pleased."—The Gospel of the Lord. ℟. **Praise to you, Lord, Jesus Christ.**   → No. 15, p. 18

PRAYER OVER THE OFFERINGS

Accept, O Lord, the offerings
we have brought to honour the revealing of your
   beloved Son,
so that the oblation of your faithful
may be transformed into the sacrifice of him
who willed in his compassion
to wash away the sins of the world.
Who lives and reigns for ever and ever. ℟. **Amen.** ↓

PREFACE (7)

℣. The Lord be with you. ℟. **And with your spirit.**
℣. Lift up your hearts. ℟. **We lift them up to the Lord.** ℣. Let us give thanks to the Lord our God.
℟. **It is right and just.**

It is truly right and just, our duty and our
   salvation,

always and everywhere to give you thanks,
Lord, holy Father, almighty and eternal God.

For in the waters of the Jordan
you revealed with signs and wonders a new
    Baptism,
so that through the voice that came down from
    heaven
we might come to believe in your Word dwelling
    among us,
and by the Spirit's descending in the likeness of
    a dove
we might know that Christ your Servant
has been anointed with the oil of gladness
and sent to bring the good news to the poor.

And so, with the Powers of heaven,
we worship you constantly on earth,
and before your majesty
without end we acclaim: ➝ No. 23, p. 23

COMMUNION ANTIPHON Jn. 1.32, 34

**Behold the One of whom John said: I have seen
and testified that this is the Son of God.** ↓

PRAYER AFTER COMMUNION

Nourished with these sacred gifts,
we humbly entreat your mercy, O Lord,
that, faithfully listening to your Only Begotten
    Son,
we may be your children in name and in truth.
Through Christ our Lord.
℟. **Amen.**   ➝ No. 30, p. 77

Optional Solemn Blessings, p. 97, and Prayers over the People, p. 105

"Jesus said to the servants, 'Fill the jars with water.'"

JANUARY 20

2nd SUNDAY IN ORDINARY TIME

ENTRANCE ANTIPHON Ps. 65.4

All the earth shall bow down before you, O God, and shall sing to you, shall sing to your name, O Most High! → No. 2, p. 10

COLLECT

Almighty ever-living God,
who govern all things,
both in heaven and on earth,
mercifully hear the pleading of your people
and bestow your peace on our times.
Through our Lord Jesus Christ, your Son,
who lives and reigns with you in the unity of the
    Holy Spirit,
one God, for ever and ever. ℞. **Amen.** ↓

FIRST READING Isa. 62.1-5

"Zion," "Jerusalem," is the people of God, and God describes deep love and concern for us in terms of the joy of a bridegroom.

174

A reading from the book of the Prophet Isaiah.

FOR Zion's sake I will not keep silent,
and for Jerusalem's sake I will not rest,
until her vindication shines out like the dawn,
and her salvation like a burning torch.

The nations shall see your vindication,
and all the kings your glory;
and you shall be called by a new name
that the mouth of the Lord will give.
You shall be a crown of beauty in the hand of the
  Lord,
and a royal diadem in the hand of your God.

You shall no more be termed Forsaken,
and your land shall no more be termed Desolate;
but you shall be called My Delight Is in Her,
and your land Married;
for the Lord delights in you,
and your land shall be married.

For as a young man marries a young woman,
so shall your builder marry you,
and as the bridegroom rejoices over the bride,
so shall your God rejoice over you.

The word of the Lord. ℟. **Thanks be to God.** ↓

RESPONSORIAL PSALM Ps. 96

Paul McKay

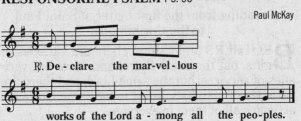

℟. De - clare   the mar - vel - lous
works of the Lord a - mong all   the peo - ples.

O sing to the Lord a new song;
sing to the Lord, all the earth.
Sing to the Lord, bless his name;
tell of his salvation from day to day.

℟. **Declare the marvellous works of the Lord**
   among all the peoples.

Declare his glory among the nations,
his marvellous works among all the peoples.
For great is the Lord, and greatly to be praised;
he is to be revered above all gods.—℟.

Ascribe to the Lord, O families of the peoples,
ascribe to the Lord glory and strength.
Ascribe to the Lord the glory due his name;
bring an offering, and come into his courts.—℟.

Worship the Lord in holy splendour;
tremble before him, all the earth.
Say among the nations, "The Lord is king!
He will judge the peoples with equity."—℟. ↓

SECOND READING 1 Cor. 12.4-11

The gifts of God come from the same Spirit. The gifts are
diverse but the Spirit is one; and the gifts are given to
unite not separate us.

A reading from the first Letter of Saint Paul
              to the Corinthians.

BROTHERS and sisters: There are varieties of
gifts, but the same Spirit; and there are varieties of services, but the same Lord; and there are
varieties of activities, but it is the same God who
activates all of them in everyone.

To each is given the manifestation of the Spirit for the common good. To one is given through the Spirit the utterance of wisdom, and to another the utterance of knowledge according to the same Spirit, to another faith by the same Spirit, to another gifts of healing by the one Spirit, to another the working of miracles, to another prophecy, to another the discernment of spirits, to another various kinds of tongues, to another the interpretation of tongues.

All these are activated by one and the same Spirit, who allots to each one individually just as the Spirit chooses.—The word of the Lord. ℟. **Thanks be to God.** ↓

GOSPEL ACCLAMATION 2 Thess. 2.14

℣. Alleluia. ℟. **Alleluia.**
℣. God has called us through the good news, that we may obtain the glory of our Lord Jesus Christ.
℟. **Alleluia.** ↓

In the place of the Gospel Acclamation given for each Sunday in Ordinary Time, another may be selected.

GOSPEL Jn. 2.1-12

Mary intercedes with her Son for the newlyweds, and Jesus changes water into wine. He thus reveals his glory and indicates that the kingdom of God is at hand.

℣. The Lord be with you. ℟. **And with your spirit.**
✝ A reading from the holy Gospel according to John. ℟. **Glory to you, O Lord.**

O N the third day there was a wedding in Cana of Galilee, and the mother of Jesus was there. Jesus and his disciples had also been invited to the wedding.

When the wine gave out, the mother of Jesus said to him, "They have no wine." And Jesus said to her, "Woman, what concern is that to you and to me? My hour has not yet come." His mother said to the servants, "Do whatever he tells you."

Now standing there were six stone water jars for the Jewish rites of purification, each holding about a hundred litres. Jesus said to the servants, "Fill the jars with water." And they filled them up to the brim. He said to them, "Now draw some out, and take it to the chief steward." So they took it.

When the steward tasted the water that had become wine, and did not know where it came from (though the servants who had drawn the water knew), the steward called the bridegroom and said to him, "Everyone serves the good wine first, and then the inferior wine after the guests have become drunk. But you have kept the good wine until now."

Jesus did this, the first of his signs, in Cana of Galilee, and revealed his glory; and his disciples believed in him. After this he went down to Capernaum with his mother, his brothers, and his disciples; and they remained there a few days.— The Gospel of the Lord. ℟. **Praise to you, Lord Jesus Christ.**   → No. 15, p. 18

PRAYER OVER THE OFFERINGS

Grant us, O Lord, we pray,
that we may participate worthily in these mysteries,

for whenever the memorial of this sacrifice is
  celebrated
the work of our redemption is accomplished.
Through Christ our Lord.
℟. **Amen.**   → No. 21, p. 22 (Pref. 29-36)

COMMUNION ANTIPHON Cf. Ps. 22.5

**You have prepared a table before me, and how
precious is the chalice that quenches my thirst.** ↓

OR 1 Jn. 4.16

**We have come to know and to believe in the love
that God has for us.** ↓

PRAYER AFTER COMMUNION

Pour on us, O Lord, the Spirit of your love,
and in your kindness
make those you have nourished
by this one heavenly Bread
one in mind and heart.
Through Christ our Lord.
℟. **Amen.**   → No. 30, p. 77

Optional Solemn Blessings, p. 97, and Prayers over the People, p. 105

"The eyes of all in the synagogue were fixed on him."

JANUARY 27

3rd SUNDAY IN ORDINARY TIME

ENTRANCE ANTIPHON Cf. Ps. 95.1, 6

O sing a new song to the Lord; sing to the Lord, all the earth. In his presence are majesty and splendour, strength and honour in his holy place.

→ No. 2, p. 10

COLLECT

Almighty ever-living God,
direct our actions according to your good
   pleasure,
that in the name of your beloved Son
we may abound in good works.
Through our Lord Jesus Christ, your Son,
who lives and reigns with you in the unity of the
   Holy Spirit,
one God, for ever and ever. ℟. **Amen.** ↓

FIRST READING Neh. 8.2-4a, 5-6, 8-10

The people of God return to their homeland, rebuild the temple, and now listen to the proclamation of the law of God.

A reading from the book of Nehemiah.

THE priest Ezra brought the Law before the assembly, both men and women and all who could hear with understanding. This was on the first day of the seventh month. He read from it facing the square before the Water Gate from early morning until midday, in the presence of the men and the women and those who could understand; and the ears of all the people were attentive to the book of the Law. The scribe Ezra stood on a wooden platform that had been made for the purpose.

And Ezra opened the book in the sight of all the people, for he was standing above all the people; and when he opened it, all the people stood up. Then Ezra blessed the Lord, the great God, and all the people answered, "Amen, Amen," lifting up their hands. Then they bowed their heads and worshipped the Lord with their faces to the ground.

So the Levites read from the book, from the Law of God, with interpretation. They gave the sense, so that the people understood the reading. And Nehemiah, who was the governor, and Ezra the priest and scribe, and the Levites who taught the people said to all the people, "This day is holy to the Lord your God; do not mourn or weep." For all the people wept when they heard the words of the Law.

Then Ezra said to them, "Go your way, eat the fat and drink sweet wine and send portions of them to those for whom nothing is prepared, for this day is holy to our Lord; and do not be grieved, for the joy of the Lord is your strength."—The word of the Lord. ℟. **Thanks be to God.** ↓

RESPONSORIAL PSALM Ps. 19   Scott Knarr

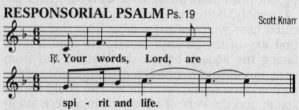

℟. Your words, Lord, are spi - rit and life.

The law of the Lord is perfect,
reviving the soul;
the decrees of the Lord are sure,
making wise the simple.—℟.

The precepts of the Lord are right,
rejoicing the heart;
the commandment of the Lord is clear,
enlightening the eyes.—℟.

The fear of the Lord is pure,
enduring forever;
the ordinances of the Lord are true
and righteous altogether.—℟.

Let the words of my mouth
and the meditation of my heart
be acceptable to you,
O Lord, my rock and my redeemer.—℟. ↓

SECOND READING 1 Cor. 12.12-30 or 12.12-14, 27

By baptism we begin to become Christians, Christ takes possession of us, and we must grow with him.

[If the "Shorter Form" is used, the indented text in brackets is omitted.]

A reading from the first Letter of Saint Paul
to the Corinthians.

BROTHERS and sisters: Just as the body is one and has many members, and all the members of the body, though many, are one body, so it is with Christ. For in the one Spirit we were all baptized into one body—Jews or Greeks, slaves or free—and we were all made to drink of one Spirit.

Indeed, the body does not consist of one member but of many.

[If the foot would say, "Because I am not a hand, I do not belong to the body," that would not make it any less a part of the body.

And if the ear would say, "Because I am not an eye, I do not belong to the body," that would not make it any less a part of the body. If the whole body were an eye, where would the hearing be? If the whole body were hearing, where would the sense of smell be?

But as it is, God arranged the members in the body, each one of them, as he chose. If all were a single member, where would the body be? As it is, there are many members, yet one body. The eye cannot say to the hand, "I have no need of you," nor again the head to the feet, "I have no need of you." On the contrary, the members of the body that seem to be weaker are indispensable, and those members of the body that we think less honourable we clothe with greater honour, and our less respectable members are treated with greater respect; whereas our more respectable members do not need this. But God has so arranged the body, giving the greater honour to the inferior member, that there may be no dissension within the body, but the members may have the same care for one another. If one member suffers, all suffer together with it; if one member is honoured, all rejoice together with it.]

Now you are the body of Christ and individually members of it.

[And God has appointed in the Church first Apostles, second Prophets, third Teachers; then deeds of power, then gifts of healing, forms of assistance, forms of leadership, various kinds of tongues.

Are all Apostles? Are all Prophets? Are all Teachers? Do all work miracles? Do all possess gifts of healing? Do all speak in tongues? Do all interpret?]

The word of the Lord. ℟. **Thanks be to God.** ↓

GOSPEL ACCLAMATION Lk. 4.18-19

℣. Alleluia. ℟. **Alleluia.**
℣. The Lord sent me to bring good news to the poor,
to proclaim release to the captives.
℟. **Alleluia.** ↓

GOSPEL Lk. 1.1-4; 4.14-21

Jesus proclaims the "good news" to the poor, and announces the fulfilment of the prophetic vision of Isaiah.

℣. The Lord be with you. ℟. **And with your spirit.**
✤ A reading from the holy Gospel according to Luke. ℟. **Glory to you, O Lord.**

SINCE many have undertaken to set down an orderly account of the events that have been fulfilled among us, just as they were handed on to us by those who from the beginning were eyewitnesses and servants of the word, I too decided, after investigating everything carefully from the very first, to write an orderly account for you, most excellent Theophilus, so that you may know the truth concerning the things about which you have been instructed.

Jesus, filled with the power of the Spirit, returned to Galilee, and a report about him spread through all the surrounding country. He began to teach in their synagogues and was praised by everyone.

When he came to Nazareth, where he had been brought up, he went to the synagogue on the Sabbath day, as was his custom.

He stood up to read, and the scroll of the Prophet Isaiah was given to him. He unrolled the scroll and found the place where it was written:

"The Spirit of the Lord is upon me,
　　because he has anointed me to bring good
　　news to the poor.
　　He has sent me to proclaim release to the
　　captives

and recovery of sight to the blind,
  to let the oppressed go free,
to proclaim the year of the Lord's favour."

And he rolled up the scroll, gave it back to the attendant, and sat down. The eyes of all in the synagogue were fixed on him.

Then he began to say to them, "Today this Scripture has been fulfilled in your hearing."— The Gospel of the Lord. ℟. **Praise to you, Lord Jesus Christ.**   → No. 15, p. 18

PRAYER OVER THE OFFERINGS

Accept our offerings, O Lord, we pray,
and in sanctifying them
grant that they may profit us for salvation.
Through Christ our Lord.
℟. **Amen.**   → No. 21, p. 22 (Pref. 29-36)

COMMUNION ANTIPHON Cf. Ps. 33.6

Look toward the Lord and be radiant; let your faces not be abashed. ↓

OR Jn. 8.12

I am the light of the world, says the Lord; whoever follows me will not walk in darkness, but will have the light of life. ↓

PRAYER AFTER COMMUNION

Grant, we pray, almighty God,
that, receiving the grace
by which you bring us to new life,
we may always glory in your gift.

Through Christ our Lord.
℟. **Amen.**   ➙ No. 30, p. 77

Optional Solemn Blessings, p. 97, and Prayers over the People, p. 105

"Jesus passed through the midst of them. . . ."

FEBRUARY 3

4th SUNDAY IN ORDINARY TIME

ENTRANCE ANTIPHON Ps. 105.47

Save us, O Lord our God! And gather us from the nations, to give thanks to your holy name, and make it our glory to praise you.   ➙ No. 2, p. 10

COLLECT

Grant us, Lord our God,
that we may honour you with all our mind,
and love everyone in truth of heart.
Through our Lord Jesus Christ, your Son,
who lives and reigns with you in the unity of the
    Holy Spirit,
one God, for ever and ever. ℟. **Amen.** ↓

FIRST READING Jer. 1.4-5, 17-19

Jeremiah is called by the Father to be his spokesman. He will be rejected but receives the promise of God that he will support him against his adversaries.

A reading from the book of the Prophet Jeremiah.

THE word of the Lord came to me saying, "Before I formed you in the womb I knew you, and before you were born I consecrated you; I appointed you a Prophet to the nations.

Therefore, gird up your loins; stand up and tell the people everything that I command you. Do not break down before them, or I will break you before them. And I for my part have made you today a fortified city, an iron pillar, and a bronze wall, against the whole land—against the kings of Judah, its princes, its priests, and the people of the land.

They will fight against you; but they shall not prevail against you, for I am with you, says the Lord, to deliver you."—The word of the Lord. ℟. **Thanks be to God.** ↓

RESPONSORIAL PSALM Ps. 71

Kathrine Bellamy

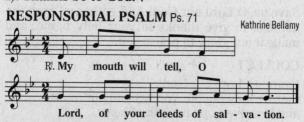

℟. **My mouth will tell, O Lord, of your deeds of sal - va - tion.**

In you, O Lord, I take refuge;
let me never be put to shame.
In your righteousness, deliver me and rescue me;
incline your ear to me and save me.—℟.

Be to me a rock of refuge,
a strong fortress, to save me,
for you are my rock and my fortress.
Rescue me, O my God, from the hand of the
    wicked.—R̲/.

For you, O Lord, are my hope,
my trust, O Lord, from my youth.
Upon you I have leaned from my birth;
from my mother's womb you have been my
    strength.—R̲/.

My mouth will tell of your righteous acts,
of your deeds of salvation all day long.
O God, from my youth you have taught me,
and I still proclaim your wondrous deeds.—R̲/. ↓

SECOND READING 1 Cor. 12.31—13.13 or 13.4-13

**Love, the virtue of charity, surpasses all. It rises above
everything. All gifts will pass away, but the supernatural
virtue of love will never fail.**

*[If the "Shorter Form" is used, the indented text in brackets
is omitted.]*

A reading from the first Letter of Saint Paul
to the Corinthians.

[B ROTHERS and sisters, strive for the
greater gifts. And I will show you a still
more excellent way.

If I speak in the tongues of human beings
and of Angels, but do not have love, I am a
noisy gong or a clanging cymbal. If I have
prophetic powers, and understand all mysteries and all knowledge, and if I have all
faith, so as to remove mountains, but do not

have love, I am nothing. If I give away all my possessions, and if I hand over my body so that I may boast, but do not have love, I gain nothing.]

Love is patient; love is kind; love is not envious or boastful or arrogant or rude. It does not insist on its own way; it is not irritable or resentful; it does not rejoice in wrongdoing, but rejoices in the truth. It bears all things, believes all things, hopes all things, endures all things. Love never ends.

But as for prophecies, they will come to an end; as for tongues, they will cease; as for knowledge, it will come to an end.

For we know only in part, and we prophesy only in part; but when the complete comes, the partial will come to an end. When I was a child, I spoke like a child, I thought like a child, I reasoned like a child; when I became a man, I put an end to childish ways.

For now we see in a mirror, dimly, but then we will see face to face. Now I know only in part; then I will know fully, even as I have been fully known.

Now faith, hope, and love abide, these three; and the greatest of these is love.—The word of the Lord. ℟. **Thanks be to God.** ↓

GOSPEL ACCLAMATION Lk. 4.18-19

℣. Alleluia. ℟. **Alleluia.**

℣. The Lord sent me to bring good news to the poor,

to proclaim release to the captives.

℟. **Alleluia.** ↓

GOSPEL Lk. 4.21-30

Jesus is rejected by his own neighbours. They resented his strong reminder of the past rejections of the prophets. In baptism and the sacraments we are united to Jesus. Like him we must bear our crosses.

℣. The Lord be with you. ℟. **And with your spirit.**
✠ A reading from the holy Gospel according to Luke. ℟. **Glory to you, O Lord.**

JESUS, filled with the power of the Spirit, came to Nazareth, where he had been brought up. He went to the synagogue on the Sabbath day, as was his custom, and read from the Prophet Isaiah. The eyes of all were fixed on him. Then he began to say to them,

"Today this Scripture has been fulfilled in your hearing." All spoke well of him and were amazed at the gracious words that came from his mouth. They said, "Is not this Joseph's son?"

Jesus said to them, "Doubtless you will quote to me this proverb, 'Doctor, cure yourself!' And you will say, 'Do here also in your hometown the things that we have heard you did at Capernaum.'"

And he said, "Truly I tell you, no Prophet is accepted in his hometown. But the truth is, there were many widows in Israel in the time of Elijah, when the heaven was shut up three years and six months, and there was a severe famine over all the land; yet Elijah was sent to none of them except to a widow at Zarephath in Sidon. There were also many lepers in Israel in the time of the Prophet Elisha, and none of them was cleansed except Naaman the Syrian."

When they heard this, all in the synagogue were filled with rage. They got up, drove Jesus out of the town, and led him to the brow of the hill on which their town was built, so that they might hurl him off the cliff. But Jesus passed through the midst of them and went on his way.—The Gospel of the Lord. ℟. **Praise to you, Lord Jesus Christ.**   → No. 15, p. 18

PRAYER OVER THE OFFERINGS

O Lord, we bring to your altar
these offerings of our service:
be pleased to receive them, we pray,
and transform them
into the Sacrament of our redemption.
Through Christ our Lord.
℟. **Amen.**   → No. 21, p. 22 (Pref. 29-36)

COMMUNION ANTIPHON Cf. Ps. 30.17-18

Let your face shine on your servant. Save me in your merciful love. O Lord, let me never be put to shame, for I call on you. ↓

OR Mt 5.3-4

Blessed are the poor in spirit, for theirs is the Kingdom of Heaven. Blessed are the meek, for they shall possess the land. ↓

PRAYER AFTER COMMUNION

Nourished by these redeeming gifts,
we pray, O Lord,
that through this help to eternal salvation
true faith may ever increase.

Through Christ our Lord.
℟. **Amen.**

➔ No. 30, p. 77

Optional Solemn Blessings, p. 97, and Prayers over the People, p. 105

"They caught so many fish that their nets
were beginning to break."

FEBRUARY 10

5th SUNDAY IN ORDINARY TIME

ENTRANCE ANTIPHON Ps. 94.6-7

**O come, let us worship God and bow low before
the God who made us, for he is the Lord our God.**

➔ No. 2, p. 10

COLLECT

Keep your family safe, O Lord, with unfailing care,
that, relying solely on the hope of heavenly grace,
they may be defended always by your protection.
Through our Lord Jesus Christ, your Son,
who lives and reigns with you in the unity of the
   Holy Spirit,
one God, for ever and ever. ℟. **Amen.** ↓

FIRST READING Isa. 6.1-2a, 3-8

> The prophet, aware of his own unworthiness, is fearful.
> Purged of sin, he accepts the call of the Father.

A reading from the book of the Prophet Isaiah.

IN the year that King Uzziah died, I saw the Lord sitting on a throne, high and lofty; and the hem of his robe filled the temple. Seraphs were in attendance above him; each had six wings. And one called to another and said:

"Holy, holy, holy is the Lord of hosts;
the whole earth is full of his glory."

The pivots on the thresholds shook at the voices of those who called, and the house filled with smoke.

And I said: "Woe is me! I am lost, for I am a man of unclean lips, and I live among a people of unclean lips; yet my eyes have seen the King, the Lord of hosts!"

Then one of the seraphs flew to me, holding a live coal that had been taken from the altar with a pair of tongs. The seraph touched my mouth with it and said: "Now that this has touched your lips, your guilt has departed and your sin is blotted out."

Then I heard the voice of the Lord saying, "Whom shall I send, and who will go for us?" And I said, "Here am I; send me!"—The word of the Lord. ℟. **Thanks be to God.** ↓

RESPONSORIAL PSALM Ps. 138

Frank Lynch

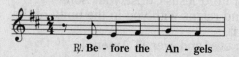

℟. Be - fore the   An - gels

I sing your praise, O Lord.

I give you thanks, O Lord, with my whole heart;
before the Angels I sing your praise;
I bow down toward your holy temple,
and give thanks to your name
for your steadfast love and your faithfulness.—R℣.

For you have exalted your name
and your word above everything.
On the day I called, you answered me,
you increased my strength of soul.—R℣.

All the kings of the earth shall praise you, O Lord,
for they have heard the words of your mouth.
They shall sing of the ways of the Lord,
for great is the glory of the Lord.—R℣.

You stretch out your hand, and your right hand
   delivers me.
The Lord will fulfill his purpose for me;
your steadfast love, O Lord, endures forever.
Do not forsake the work of your hands.—R℣. ↓

SECOND READING 1 Cor. 15.1-11 or 15.3-8, 11

> **Through God's favour, the apostles turned from persecution to preaching the "good news" like Isaiah. Christ has died, Christ is risen, Christ will come again.**

[If the "Shorter Form" is used, the indented text in brackets is omitted.]

A reading from the first Letter of Saint Paul
to the Corinthians.

[I WOULD remind you,] brothers and sisters, [of the good news that I proclaimed to you, which you in turn received, in which also you stand. This is the good news through which also you are being saved, if you hold firmly to the message that I proclaimed to you—unless you have come to believe in vain.]

[For] I handed on to you as of first importance what I in turn had received: that Christ died for our sins in accordance with the Scriptures, and that he was buried, and that he was raised on the third day in accordance with the Scriptures, and that he appeared to Cephas, then to the twelve.

Then he appeared to more than five hundred of the brothers and sisters at one time, most of whom are still alive, though some have died.

Then he appeared to James, then to all the Apostles. Last of all, as to one untimely born, he appeared also to me.

[For I am the least of the Apostles, unfit to be called an Apostle, because I persecuted the Church of God. But by the grace of God I am what I am, and his grace toward me has not been in vain. On the contrary, I worked harder than any of the Apostles—though it was not I, but the grace of God that is with me.]

Whether then it was I or they, so we proclaim and so you have come to believe.—The word of the Lord. ℟. **Thanks be to God.** ↓

GOSPEL ACCLAMATION Mt. 4.19

℣. Alleluia. ℟. **Alleluia.**
℣. Come follow me, says the Lord,
and I will make you fishers of people.
℟. **Alleluia.** ↓

GOSPEL Lk. 5.1-11

Peter confesses: "I am a sinful man," and is reassured by Christ. Then together with James and John he leaves everything to become his follower.

℣. The Lord be with you. ℟. **And with your spirit.**
✛ A reading from the holy Gospel according to Luke. ℟. **Glory to you, O Lord.**

WHILE Jesus was standing beside the lake of Gennesaret, and the crowd was pressing in on him to hear the word of God, he saw two boats there at the shore of the lake; the fishermen had gone out of them and were washing their nets.

Jesus got into one of the boats, the one belonging to Simon, and asked him to put out a little way from the shore. Then he sat down and taught the crowds from the boat. When he had finished speaking, he said to Simon, "Put out into the deep water and let down your nets for a catch." Simon answered, "Master, we have worked all night long but have caught nothing. Yet if you say so, I will let down the nets." When they had done this, they caught so many fish that their nets were beginning to break. So they signalled their partners in the other boat to come and help them. And they came and filled both boats, so that they began to sink.

But when Simon Peter saw it, he fell down at Jesus' knees, saying, "Go away from me, Lord, for I am a sinful man!"

For Simon Peter and all who were with him were amazed at the catch of fish that they had taken; and so also were James and John, sons of Zebedee, who were partners with Simon. Then Jesus said to Simon, "Do not be afraid; from now on you will be catching people."

When they had brought their boats to shore, they left everything and followed Jesus.—The Gospel of the Lord. ℟. **Praise to you, Lord Jesus Christ.**   ➜ No. 15, p. 18

PRAYER OVER THE OFFERINGS

O Lord our God,
who once established these created things
to sustain us in our frailty,
grant, we pray,
that they may become for us now
the Sacrament of eternal life.
Through Christ our Lord.
℟. **Amen.**   ➜ No. 21, p. 22 (Pref. 29-36)

COMMUNION ANTIPHON Cf. Ps. 106.8-9

Let them thank the Lord for his mercy, his wonders for the children of men, for he satisfies the thirsty soul, and the hungry he fills with good things. ↓

OR Mt. 5.5-6

Blessed are those who mourn, for they shall be consoled. Blessed are those who hunger and thirst for righteousness, for they shall have their fill. ↓

PRAYER AFTER COMMUNION

O God, who have willed that we be partakers
in the one Bread and the one Chalice,
grant us, we pray, so to live
that, made one in Christ,
we may joyfully bear fruit
for the salvation of the world.
Through Christ our Lord.
℟. **Amen.**   ➜ No. 30, p. 77

Optional Solemn Blessings, p. 97, and Prayers over the People, p. 105

"Blessed are you who are poor, for yours
is the kingdom of God."

FEBRUARY 17

6th SUNDAY IN ORDINARY TIME

ENTRANCE ANTIPHON Cf. Ps. 30.3-4

**Be my protector, O God, a mighty stronghold to
save me. For you are my rock, my stronghold!
Lead me, guide me, for the sake of your name.**

→ No. 2, p. 10

COLLECT

O God, who teach us that you abide
in hearts that are just and true,
grant that we may be so fashioned by your grace
as to become a dwelling pleasing to you.
Through our Lord Jesus Christ, your Son,
who lives and reigns with you in the unity of the
  Holy Spirit,
one God, for ever and ever. ℞. **Amen.** ↓

FIRST READING Jer. 17.5-8

> To put all one's trust in human strength leads to frustra-
> tion. Let us trust in the Lord and find fulfillment.

A reading from the book of the Prophet Jeremiah.

THUS says the Lord:
"Cursed is the one who trusts in mere mortals
and makes mere flesh their strength,
whose heart turns away from the Lord.
That person shall be like a shrub in the desert,
and shall not see when relief comes,
but shall live in the parched places of the
    wilderness,
in an uninhabited salt land.

Blessed is the one who trusts in the Lord,
whose trust is the Lord.
That person shall be like a tree planted by water,
sending out its roots by the stream.
It shall not fear when heat comes,
and its leaves shall stay green;
in the year of drought it is not anxious,
and it does not cease to bear fruit."

The word of the Lord. ℟. **Thanks be to God.** ↓

RESPONSORIAL PSALM Ps. 1

Michel Guimont

℟. Bless - ed the one who trusts in the Lord.

Blessed is the man who does not follow the ad-
    vice of the wicked,
or take the path that sinners tread, or sit in the
    seat of scoffers;
but whose delight is in the law of the Lord,
and on his law meditates day and night.—℟.

He is like a tree planted by streams of water,
which yields its fruit in its season,
and its leaves do not wither.
And everything he does, prospers.—℟.

The wicked are not so,
but are like chaff that the wind drives away,
for the Lord watches over the way of the right-
    eous,
but the way of the wicked will perish.—℟. ↓

SECOND READING 1 Cor. 15.12, 16-20

If our hopes in Christ are limited to this life only, we are the most pitiable of human beings.

A reading from the first Letter of Saint Paul
            to the Corinthians.

IF Christ is proclaimed as raised from the dead,
how can some of you say there is no resurrection of the dead?

For if the dead are not raised, then Christ has
not been raised. If Christ has not been raised,
your faith is futile and you are still in your sins.
Then those also who have died in Christ have per-
ished.

If for this life only we have hoped in Christ, we
are of all people most to be pitied. But in fact
Christ has been raised from the dead, the first
fruits of those who have fallen asleep.—The word
of the Lord. ℟. **Thanks be to God.** ↓

GOSPEL ACCLAMATION Lk. 6.23

℣. Alleluia. ℟. **Alleluia.**
℣. Rejoice and leap for joy;

for surely your reward is great in heaven.
℟. **Alleluia.** ↓

GOSPEL Lk. 6.17, 20-26

Happiness and blessing are the rewards of those who accept the Gospel and the Saviour. Sorrow and woe await
those who take wealth and pleasure as their goal in life.

℣. The Lord be with you. ℟. **And with your spirit.**
✠ A reading from the holy Gospel according to
Luke. ℟. **Glory to you, O Lord.**

JESUS came down with the twelve and stood on
a level place, with a great crowd of his disciples
and a great multitude of people from all Judea,
Jerusalem, and the coast of Tyre and Sidon.
Then Jesus looked up at his disciples and said:
"Blessed are you who are poor,
for yours is the kingdom of God.
Blessed are you who are hungry now,
for you will be filled.
Blessed are you who weep now,
for you will laugh.
Blessed are you when people hate you,
and when they exclude you, revile you, and
defame you
on account of the Son of Man.

Rejoice in that day and leap for joy,
for surely your reward is great in heaven;
for that is what their ancestors did to the
Prophets.

But woe to you who are rich,
for you have received your consolation.
Woe to you who are full now,
for you will be hungry.

Woe to you who are laughing now,
    for you will mourn and weep.
Woe to you when all speak well of you,
    for that is what their ancestors did to the
      false Prophets."

The Gospel of the Lord. ℟. **Praise to you, Lord Jesus Christ.**
        ➨ No. 15, p. 18

PRAYER OVER THE OFFERINGS

May this oblation, O Lord, we pray,
cleanse and renew us
and may it become for those who do your will
the source of eternal reward.
Through Christ our Lord.
℟. **Amen.**
        ➨ No. 21, p. 22 (Pref. 29-36)

COMMUNION ANTIPHON Cf. Ps. 77.29-30

They ate and had their fill, and what they craved the Lord gave them; they were not disappointed in what they craved. ↓

OR Jn. 3.16

God so loved the world that he gave his Only Begotten Son, so that all who believe in him may not perish, but may have eternal life. ↓

PRAYER AFTER COMMUNION

Having fed upon these heavenly delights,
we pray, O Lord,
that we may always long
for that food by which we truly live.
Through Christ our Lord.
℟. **Amen.**
        ➨ No. 30, p. 77

Optional Solemn Blessings, p. 97, and Prayers over the People, p. 105

"Do not condemn, and you will not be condemned."

FEBRUARY 24

7th SUNDAY IN ORDINARY TIME

ENTRANCE ANTIPHON Ps. 12.5-6

O Lord, I trust in your merciful love. My heart will rejoice in your salvation. I will sing to the Lord who has been bountiful with me.   ➜ No. 2, p. 10

COLLECT

Grant, we pray, almighty God,
that, always pondering spiritual things,
we may carry out in both word and deed
that which is pleasing to you.
Through our Lord Jesus Christ, your Son,
who lives and reigns with you in the unity of the
   Holy Spirit,
one God, for ever and ever. ℟. **Amen.** ↓

FIRST READING 1 Sam. 26.2, 7-9, 12-13, 22-25

King Saul has condemned David and is trying to capture
him. David has the opportunity to kill Saul, but refuses to
harm the king because Saul is anointed by the Lord.

A reading from the first book of Samuel.

SAUL rose and went down to the Wilderness of Ziph, with three thousand chosen men of Israel, to seek David in the Wilderness of Ziph. David and Abishai went into Saul's army by night; there Saul lay sleeping within the encampment, with his spear stuck in the ground at his head; and Abner and the army lay around him. Abishai said to David, "God has given your enemy into your hand today; now therefore let me pin him to the ground with one stroke of the spear; I will not strike him twice." But David said to Abishai, "Do not destroy him; for who can raise his hand against the Lord's anointed, and be guiltless?"

So David took the spear that was at Saul's head and the water jar, and they went away. No one saw it, or knew it, nor did anyone awake; for they were all asleep, because a deep sleep from the Lord had fallen upon them.

Then David went over to the other side, and stood on top of a hill far away, with a great distance between them. David called aloud to Saul, "Here is the spear, O king! Let one of the young men come over and get it. The Lord rewards everyone for his righteousness and his faithfulness; for the Lord gave you into my hand today, but I would not raise my hand against the Lord's anointed. As your life was precious today in my sight, so may my life be precious in the sight of the Lord, and may he rescue me from all tribulation."

Then Saul said to David, "Blessed be you, my son David! You will do many things and will succeed in them."

So David went his way, and Saul returned to his place.—The word of the Lord. ℟. **Thanks be to God.** ↓

RESPONSORIAL PSALM Ps. 103

Normand L. Blanchard

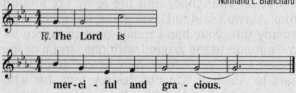

℟. The Lord is mer-ci-ful and gra-cious.

Bless the Lord, O my soul,
and all that is within me, bless his holy name.
Bless the Lord, O my soul,
and do not forget all his benefits.—℟.

It is the Lord who forgives all your iniquity,
who heals all your diseases,
who redeems your life from the Pit,
who crowns you with steadfast love and
    mercy.—℟.

The Lord is merciful and gracious,
slow to anger and abounding in steadfast love.
He does not deal with us according to our sins,
nor repay us according to our iniquities.—℟.

As far as the east is from the west,
so far he removes our transgressions from us.
As a father has compassion for his children,
so the Lord has compassion for those who fear
    him.—℟. ↓

SECOND READING 1 Cor. 15.45-49

> Grace builds on nature. In Christ we are formed in the spiritual order.

A reading from the first Letter of Saint Paul
to the Corinthians.

BROTHERS and sisters: "The first man, Adam, became a living being"; the last Adam became a life-giving spirit. But it is not the spiritual that is first, but the physical, and then the spiritual.

The first was from the earth, made of dust; the second man is from heaven. As was the one of dust, so are those who are of the dust; and as is the one of heaven, so are those who are of heaven.

Just as we have borne the image of the one of dust, we will also bear the image of the one of heaven.—The word of the Lord. ℟. **Thanks be to God.** ↓

GOSPEL ACCLAMATION Jn. 13.34

℣. Alleluia. ℟. **Alleluia.**
℣. I give you a new commandment:
love one another just as I have loved you.
℟. **Alleluia.** ↓

GOSPEL Lk. 6.27-38

> The supernatural virtues go beyond the natural virtues, which even sinners practise.

℣. The Lord be with you. ℟. **And with your spirit.**
✛ A reading from the holy Gospel according to Luke. ℟. **Glory to you, O Lord.**

JESUS said to his disciples: "I say to you that listen: Love your enemies, do good to those who hate you, bless those who curse you, pray for those who abuse you. If anyone strikes you on the cheek, offer the other also; and from anyone who takes away your coat do not withhold even your shirt. Give to everyone who begs from you; and if anyone takes away your goods, do not ask for them again. Do to others as you would have them do to you.

If you love those who love you, what credit is that to you? For even sinners love those who love them. If you do good to those who do good to you, what credit is that to you? For even sinners do the same. If you lend to those from whom you hope to receive, what credit is that to you? Even sinners lend to sinners, to receive as much again. But love your enemies, do good, and lend, expecting nothing in return. Your reward will be great, and you will be children of the Most High; for he is kind to the ungrateful and the wicked. Be merciful, just as your Father is merciful.

Do not judge, and you will not be judged; do not condemn, and you will not be condemned. Forgive, and you will be forgiven; give, and it will be given to you. A good measure, pressed down, shaken together, running over, will be put into your lap; for the measure you give will be the measure you get back."—The Gospel of the Lord. ℟. **Praise to you, Lord Jesus Christ.**

➔ No. 15, p. 18

PRAYER OVER THE OFFERINGS

As we celebrate your mysteries, O Lord,
with the observance that is your due,
we humbly ask you,
that what we offer to the honour of your
   majesty
may profit us for salvation.
Through Christ our Lord.
℞. Amen.   → No. 21, p. 22 (Pref. 29-36)

COMMUNION ANTIPHON Ps. 9.2-3

**I will recount all your wonders, I will rejoice in
you and be glad, and sing psalms to your name,
O Most High. ↓**

OR Jn. 11.27

**Lord, I have come to believe that you are the
Christ, the Son of the living God, who is coming
into this world. ↓**

PRAYER AFTER COMMUNION

Grant, we pray, almighty God,
that we may experience the effects of the salvation
which is pledged to us by these mysteries.
Through Christ our Lord.
℞. Amen.   → No. 30, p. 77

Optional Solemn Blessings, p. 97, and Prayers over the People, p. 105

"Each tree is known by its own fruit."

MARCH 3

8th SUNDAY IN ORDINARY TIME

ENTRANCE ANTIPHON Cf. Ps. 17.19-20

The Lord became my protector. He brought me out to a place of freedom; he saved me because he delighted in me. → No. 2, p. 10

COLLECT

Grant us, O Lord, we pray,
that the course of our world
may be directed by your peaceful rule
and that your Church may rejoice,
untroubled in her devotion.
Through our Lord Jesus Christ, your Son,
who lives and reigns with you in the unity of the
  Holy Spirit,
one God, for ever and ever. ℟. **Amen.** ↓

FIRST READING Sir. 27.4-7

> The Sage indicates that our speech reveals what we are. He anticipates the Gospel maxim: "Out of the abundance of the heart . . . the mouth speaks" (Mt. 12.34).

210

A reading from the book of Sirach.

WHEN a sieve is shaken, the refuse appears;
so do one's faults when one speaks.
The kiln tests the potter's vessels;
so the test of a person is in tribulation.

Its fruit discloses the cultivation of a tree;
so a person's speech discloses the cultivation of
the mind.
Do not praise people before they speak,
for this is the way people are tested.
The word of the Lord. ℟. **Thanks be to God.** ↓

RESPONSORIAL PSALM Ps. 92

David Paines

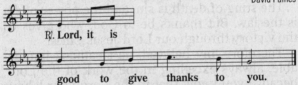

℟. Lord, it is good to give thanks to you.

It is good to give thanks to the Lord,
to sing praises to your name, O Most High;
to declare your steadfast love in the morning,
and your faithfulness by night.—℟.

The righteous flourish like the palm tree,
and grow like a cedar in Lebanon.
They are planted in the house of the Lord;
they flourish in the courts of our God.—℟.

In old age they still produce fruit;
they are always green and full of sap,
showing that the Lord is upright;
he is my rock, and there is no unrighteousness
in him.—℟. ↓

SECOND READING 1 Cor. 15.54-58

The Risen Christ is the source of our new life that will produce in us all its fruits at the time of our resurrection. We must never stop working toward that goal.

A reading from the first Letter of Saint Paul
to the Corinthians.

BROTHERS and sisters: When this perishable body puts on imperishability, and this mortal body puts on immortality, then the saying that is written will be fulfilled:

"Death has been swallowed up in victory."
"Where, O death, is your victory?
Where, O death, is your sting?"

The sting of death is sin, and the power of sin is the law. But thanks be to God, who gives us the victory through our Lord Jesus Christ.

Therefore, my beloved, be steadfast, immovable, always excelling in the work of the Lord, because you know that in the Lord your labour is not in vain.—The word of the Lord. ℟. **Thanks be to God.** ↓

GOSPEL ACCLAMATION Phil. 2.15-16

℣. Alleluia. ℟. **Alleluia.**
℣. Shine like stars in the world,
holding fast to the word of life.
℟. **Alleluia.** ↓

GOSPEL Lk. 6.39-45

We must receive the Word of God with complete openness. Only then can we draw from our hearts words that will lead others to Christ.

℣. The Lord be with you. ℟. **And with your spirit.**
✚ A reading from the holy Gospel according to
Luke. ℟. **Glory to you, O Lord.**

JESUS told his disciples a parable: "Can a
blind person guide a blind person? Will not
both fall into a pit? A disciple is not above the
teacher, but everyone who is fully qualified will
be like their teacher.

Why do you see the speck in your neighbour's
eye, but do not notice the log in your own eye?
Or how can you say to your neighbour, 'Friend,
let me take out the speck in your eye,' when you
yourself do not see the log in your own eye? You
hypocrite, first take the log out of your own eye,
and then you will see clearly to take the speck
out of your neighbour's eye.

No good tree bears bad fruit, nor again does a
bad tree bear good fruit; for each tree is known
by its own fruit. Figs are not gathered from
thorns, nor are grapes picked from a bramble
bush.

Out of the good treasure of the heart, the
good person produces good, and out of evil treasure, the evil person produces evil; for it is out
of the abundance of the heart that the mouth
speaks."—The Gospel of the Lord. ℟. **Praise to
you, Lord Jesus Christ.**   → No. 15, p. 18

PRAYER OVER THE OFFERINGS

O God, who provide gifts to be offered to your
    name
and count our oblations as signs

of our desire to serve you with devotion,
we ask of your mercy
that what you grant as the source of merit
may also help us to attain merit's reward.
Through Christ our Lord.
℟. **Amen.**   → No. 21, p. 22 (Pref. 29-36)

COMMUNION ANTIPHON Cf. Ps. 12.6

**I will sing to the Lord who has been bountiful
with me, sing psalms to the name of the Lord
Most High.** ↓

OR Mt. 28.20

**Behold, I am with you always, even to the end
of the age, says the Lord.** ↓

PRAYER AFTER COMMUNION

Nourished by your saving gifts,
we beseech your mercy, Lord,
that by this same Sacrament
with which you feed us in the present age,
you may make us partakers of life eternal.
Through Christ our Lord.
℟. **Amen.**   → No. 30, p. 77

Optional Solemn Blessings, p. 97, and Prayers over the People, p. 105

"Whenever you fast, do not look dismal,
like the hypocrites."

MARCH 6

ASH WEDNESDAY

ENTRANCE ANTIPHON Wis. 11.24, 25, 27

You are merciful to all, O Lord, and despise nothing that you have made. You overlook people's sins, to bring them to repentance, and you spare them, for you are the Lord our God. → No. 2, p. 10 (Omit Penitential Act)

COLLECT

Grant, O Lord, that we may begin with holy fasting
this campaign of Christian service,
so that, as we take up battle against spiritual evils,
we may be armed with weapons of self-restraint.
Through our Lord Jesus Christ, your Son,
who lives and reigns with you in the unity of the Holy
    Spirit,
one God, for ever and ever.
℟. **Amen.** ↓

FIRST READING Jl. 2.12-18

The prophet points to the fact that "works" of penance, if not related to that inner conversion to God in love, are worthless.

A reading from the book of the Prophet Joel.

EVEN now, says the Lord,
   return to me with all your heart,
with fasting, with weeping, and with mourning;
rend your hearts and not your clothing.
Return to the Lord, your God,
for he is gracious and merciful,
slow to anger, and abounding in steadfast love,
and relents from punishing.
Who knows whether the Lord will not turn and relent,
and leave a blessing behind him:
a grain offering and a drink offering
to be presented to the Lord, your God?

Blow the trumpet in Zion;
sanctify a fast;
call a solemn assembly;
gather the people.
Sanctify the congregation;
assemble the aged;
gather the children, even infants at the breast.
Let the bridegroom leave his room,
and the bride her canopy.

Between the vestibule and the altar
let the priests, the ministers of the Lord, weep.
Let them say, "Spare your people, O Lord,
and do not make your heritage a mockery,
a byword among the nations.
Why should it be said among the peoples,
'Where is their God?'"

Then the Lord became jealous for his land,
and had pity on his people.

The word of the Lord. ℟. **Thanks be to God.** ↓

RESPONSORIAL PSALM Ps. 51

Michel Guimont

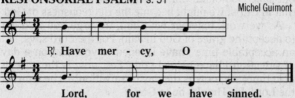

℟. Have mer - cy, O Lord, for we have sinned.

Have mercy on me, O God,
according to your steadfast love;
according to your abundant mercy
blot out my transgressions
Wash me thoroughly from my iniquity,
and cleanse me from my sin.—℟.

For I know my transgressions,
and my sin is ever before me.
Against you, you alone, have I sinned,
and done what is evil in your sight.—℟.

Create in me a clean heart, O God,
and put a new and right spirit within me.
Do not cast me away from your presence,
and do not take your holy spirit from me.—℟.

Restore to me the joy of your salvation,
and sustain in me a willing spirit.
O Lord, open my lips,
and my mouth will declare your praise.—℟. ↓

SECOND READING 2 Cor. 5.20—6.2

**Paul insists on conversion now! Forgiveness is available.
Ask for it now! "Now is the acceptable time!"**

A reading from the second Letter of Saint Paul
to the Corinthians.

Brothers and sisters: We are ambassadors for
Christ, since God is making his appeal through us; we
entreat you on behalf of Christ, be reconciled to God. For

our sake God made Christ to be sin who knew no sin, so
that in Christ we might become the righteousness of God.

As we work together with him, we urge you also not
to accept the grace of God in vain. For the Lord says, "At
an acceptable time I have listened to you, and on a day
of salvation I have helped you." See, now is the acceptable time; see, now is the day of salvation!—The word of
the Lord. ℟. **Thanks be to God.** ↓

GOSPEL ACCLAMATION Ps. 95.7-8

℣. Praise to you, Lord Jesus Christ, King of endless
    glory! *
℟. **Praise to you, Lord Jesus Christ, King of endless
    glory!**
℣. Today, do not harden your hearts,
but listen to the voice of the Lord.
℟. **Praise to you, Lord Jesus Christ, King of endless
    glory!** ↓

GOSPEL Mt. 6.1-6, 16-18

> External works of penance have no value in themselves. You
> must relate them to the real penance, your conversion to God.

℣. The Lord be with you. ℟. **And with your spirit.**
✛ A reading from the holy Gospel according to Matthew.
℟. **Glory to you, O Lord.**

JESUS said to his disciples: "Beware of practising your
piety before people in order to be seen by them; for
then you have no reward from your Father in heaven.

So whenever you give alms, do not sound a trumpet
before you, as the hypocrites do in the synagogues and in
the streets, so that they may be praised by others. Truly I
tell you, they have received their reward. But when you
give alms, do not let your left hand know what your right
hand is doing, so that your alms may be done in secret;
and your Father who sees in secret will reward you.

---

* See p. 16 for other Gospel Acclamations.

And whenever you pray, do not be like the hypocrites; for they love to stand and pray in the synagogues and on the street corners, so that they may be seen by others. Truly I tell you, they have received their reward. But whenever you pray, go into your room and shut the door and pray to your Father who is in secret; and your Father who sees in secret will reward you.

And whenever you fast, do not look dismal, like the hypocrites, for they disfigure their faces so as to show others that they are fasting. Truly I tell you, they have received their reward. But when you fast, put oil on your head and wash your face, so that your fasting may be seen not by others but by your Father who is in secret; and your Father who sees in secret will reward you."—The Gospel of the Lord. ℟. **Praise to you, Lord Jesus Christ.** ↓

BLESSING AND DISTRIBUTION OF ASHES

After the Homily, the Priest, standing with his hands joined, says:

Dear brethren (brothers and sisters), let us humbly ask God our Father
that he be pleased to bless with the abundance of his grace
these ashes, which we will put on our heads in penitence. ↓

After a brief prayer in silence, and, with hands extended, he continues:

O God, who are moved by acts of humility
and respond with forgiveness to works of penance,
lend your merciful ear to our prayers
and in your kindness pour out the grace of your ✠ blessing
on your servants who are marked with these ashes,
that, as they follow the Lenten observances,
they may be worthy to come with minds made pure
to celebrate the Paschal Mystery of your Son.
Through Christ our Lord. ℟. **Amen.** ↓

OR:

O God, who desire not the death of sinners,
but their conversion,
mercifully hear our prayers
and in your kindness be pleased to bless ✠ these ashes,
which we intend to receive upon our heads,
that we, who acknowledge we are but ashes
and shall return to dust,
may, through a steadfast observance of Lent,
gain pardon for sins and newness of life
after the likeness of your Risen Son.
Who lives and reigns for ever and ever. ℟. **Amen.** ↓

He sprinkles the ashes with holy water, without saying anything.

Then the Priest places ashes on the head of all those present who come to him, and says to each one:

Repent, and believe in the Gospel.

OR:

Remember that you are dust, and to dust you shall return.

Meanwhile, the following are sung.

ANTIPHON 1

Let us change our garments to sackcloth and ashes, let us fast and weep before the Lord, that our God, rich in mercy, might forgive us our sins.

ANTIPHON 2 Cf. Jl. 2.17; Est. 4.17

Let the priests, the ministers of the Lord, stand between the porch and the altar and weep and cry out: Spare, O Lord, spare your people; do not close the mouths of those who sing your praise, O Lord.

ANTIPHON 3 Ps. 51.3

Blot out my transgressions, O Lord.

This may be repeated after each verse of Psalm 51 (Have mercy on me, O God).

RESPONSORY Cf. Bar. 3.2; Ps. 79.9

℟. **Let us correct our faults which we have committed in ignorance, let us not be taken unawares by the day of our death, looking in vain for leisure to repent. Hear us, O Lord, and show us your mercy, for we have sinned against you.**

℣. **Help us, O God our Savior; for the sake of your name, O Lord, set us free. Hear us, O Lord . . .**

Another appropriate chant may also be sung.

After the distribution of ashes, the Priest washes his hands and proceeds to the Universal Prayer, and continues the Mass in the usual way.

The Creed is not said.

PRAYER OVER THE OFFERINGS

As we solemnly offer
the annual sacrifice for the beginning of Lent,
we entreat you, O Lord,
that, through works of penance and charity,
we may turn away from harmful pleasures
and, cleansed from our sins, may become worthy
to celebrate devoutly the Passion of your Son.
Who lives and reigns for ever and ever. ℟. **Amen.** ↓

PREFACE (10)

℣. The Lord be with you. ℟. **And with your spirit.** ℣. Lift up your hearts. ℟. **We lift them up to the Lord.** ℣. Let us give thanks to the Lord our God. ℟. **It is right and just.**

It is truly right and just, our duty and our salvation,
always and everywhere to give you thanks,
Lord, holy Father, almighty and eternal God.

For you will that our self-denial should give you thanks,
humble our sinful pride,
contribute to the feeding of the poor,
and so help us imitate you in your kindness.

And so we glorify you with countless Angels,
as with one voice of praise we acclaim: → No. 23, p. 23
OR:

PREFACE (11)

℣. The Lord be with you. ℟. **And with your spirit.** ℣. Lift up your hearts. ℟. **We lift them up to the Lord.** ℣. Let us give thanks to the Lord our God. ℟. **It is right and just.**

It is truly right and just, our duty and our salvation,
always and everywhere to give you thanks,
Lord, holy Father, almighty and eternal God.

For through bodily fasting you restrain our faults,
raise up our minds,
and bestow both virtue and its rewards,
through Christ our Lord.

Through him the Angels praise your majesty,
Dominions adore and Powers tremble before you.
Heaven and the Virtues of heaven and the blessed Seraphim
worship together with exultation.
May our voices, we pray, join with theirs
in humble praise, as we acclaim: → No. 23, p. 23

COMMUNION ANTIPHON Cf. Ps. 1.2-3

**He who ponders the law of the Lord day and night will
yield fruit in due season.** ↓

PRAYER AFTER COMMUNION

May the Sacrament we have received sustain us, O Lord,
that our Lenten fast may be pleasing to you
and be for us a healing remedy.
Through Christ our Lord. ℟. **Amen.** ↓

PRAYER OVER THE PEOPLE

*For the dismissal, the Priest stands facing the people and, ex-
tending his hands over them, says this prayer:*

Pour out a spirit of compunction, O God,
on those who bow before your majesty,
and by your mercy may they merit the rewards you
    promise
to those who do penance.
Through Christ our Lord. ℟. **Amen.**   → No. 32, p. 77

"Jesus answered . . . , 'Do not put the Lord
your God to the test.'"

MARCH 10

1st SUNDAY OF LENT

ENTRANCE ANTIPHON Cf. Ps. 90.15-16

**When he calls on me, I will answer him; I will de-
liver him and give him glory, I will grant him
length of days.** ➔ No. 2, p. 10 (Omit Gloria)

COLLECT

Grant, almighty God,
through the yearly observances of holy Lent,
that we may grow in understanding
of the riches hidden in Christ
and by worthy conduct pursue their effects.
Through our Lord Jesus Christ, your Son,
who lives and reigns with you in the unity of the
    Holy Spirit,
one God, for ever and ever.
R̰. **Amen.** ↓

223

FIRST READING Deut. 26.4-10

The fruits of our labour are from God. Before we use and enjoy them we should first acknowledge God's bounty with dedication and thanks.

A reading from the book of Deuteronomy.

MOSES spoke to the people, saying: "When the priest takes the basket from your hand and sets it down before the altar of the Lord your God, you shall make this response before the Lord your God:

'A wandering Aramean was my father; he went down into Egypt and lived there as an alien, few in number, and there he became a great nation, mighty and populous. When the Egyptians treated us harshly and afflicted us, by imposing hard labour on us, we cried to the Lord, the God of our fathers; the Lord heard our voice and saw our affliction, our toil, and our oppression.

The Lord brought us out of Egypt with a mighty hand and an outstretched arm, with a terrifying display of power, and with signs and wonders; and he brought us into this place and gave us this land, a land flowing with milk and honey. So now I bring the first of the fruit of the ground that you, O Lord, have given me.

And Moses continued, "You shall set it down before the Lord your God and bow down before the Lord your God."—The word of the Lord. ℟. **Thanks be to God.** ↓

RESPONSORIAL PSALM Ps. 91

David Szanto

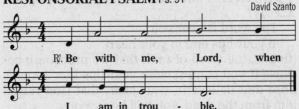

℟. Be with me, Lord, when I am in trou - ble.

You who live in the shelter of the Most High,
who abide in the shadow of the Almighty,
will say to the Lord, "My refuge and my fortress;
my God, in whom I trust."—℟.

No evil shall befall you,
no scourge come near your tent.
For he will command his Angels concerning you
to guard you in all your ways.—℟.

On their hands they will bear you up,
so that you will not dash your foot against a stone.
You will tread on the lion and the adder,
the young lion and the serpent you will trample
    under foot.—℟.

The one who loves me, I will deliver;
I will protect the one who knows my name.
When he calls to me, I will answer him;
I will be with him in trouble, I will rescue him
    and honour him.—℟. ↓

SECOND READING Rom. 10.8-13

**Holiness (justification) is rooted in faith. Believe in your
heart that Jesus is raised from the dead.**

A reading from the Letter of Saint Paul
to the Romans.

B ROTHERS and sisters, what does Scripture say?

"The word is near you,
　on your lips and in your heart"
(that is, the word of faith that we proclaim); because if you confess with your lips that Jesus is Lord and believe in your heart that God raised him from the dead, you will be saved.

For one believes with the heart and so is justified, and one confesses with the mouth and so is saved.

The Scripture says, "No one who believes in him will be put to shame." For there is no distinction between Jew and Greek; the same Lord is Lord of all and is generous to all who call on him. For, "Everyone who calls on the name of the Lord shall be saved."—The word of the Lord. ℟. **Thanks be to God.** ↓

GOSPEL ACCLAMATION Mt. 4.4

℣. Praise and honour to you, Lord Jesus Christ!*
℟. **Praise and honour to you, Lord Jesus Christ!**
℣. Man does not live by bread alone,
but by every word that comes from the mouth of
　God.

℟. **Praise and honour to you, Lord Jesus Christ!** ↓

GOSPEL Lk. 4.1-13

Jesus is fully human and overcomes the temptation of Satan. As Messiah he will not resort to expediency.

℣. The Lord be with you. ℟. **And with your spirit.**

* See p. 16 for other Gospel Acclamations.

✠ A reading from the holy Gospel according to Luke. ℟. **Glory to you, O Lord.**

JESUS, full of the Holy Spirit, returned from the Jordan and was led by the Spirit in the wilderness, where for forty days he was tempted by the devil. He ate nothing at all during those days, and when they were over, he was famished.

The devil said to him, "If you are the Son of God, command this stone to become a loaf of bread." Jesus answered him, "It is written, 'Man does not live by bread alone.'"

Then the devil led him up and showed him in an instant all the kingdoms of the world. And the devil said to him, "To you I will give their glory and all this authority; for it has been given over to me, and I give it to anyone I please. If you, then, will worship me, it will all be yours." Jesus answered him, "It is written,

'Worship the Lord your God,
    and serve only him.'"
Then the devil took him to Jerusalem, and placed him on the pinnacle of the temple, saying to him, "If you are the Son of God, throw yourself down from here, for it is written,

'He will command his Angels concerning you,
        to protect you,'
and
'On their hands they will bear you up,
    so that you will not dash your foot against a
        stone.'"
Jesus answered him, "It is said, 'Do not put the Lord your God to the test.'"

When the devil had finished every test, he departed from him until an opportune time.—The Gospel of the Lord. ℞. **Praise to you, Lord Jesus Christ.**   → No. 15, p. 18

PRAYER OVER THE OFFERINGS

Give us the right dispositions, O Lord, we pray,
to make these offerings,
for with them we celebrate the beginning
of this venerable and sacred time.
Through Christ our Lord. ℞. **Amen.** ↓

PREFACE (12)

℣. The Lord be with you. ℞. **And with your spirit.**
℣. Lift up your hearts. ℞. **We lift them up to the Lord.** ℣. Let us give thanks to the Lord our God.
℞. **It is right and just.**

It is truly right and just, our duty and our salvation,
always and everywhere to give you thanks,
Lord, holy Father, almighty and eternal God,
through Christ our Lord.

By abstaining forty long days from earthly food,
he consecrated through his fast
the pattern of our Lenten observance
and, by overturning all the snares of the ancient
    serpent,
taught us to cast out the leaven of malice,
so that, celebrating worthily the Paschal Mystery,
we might pass over at last to the eternal paschal
    feast.

And so, with the company of Angels and Saints,
we sing the hymn of your praise,
as without end we acclaim: → No. 23, p. 23

COMMUNION ANTIPHON Mt. 4.4

**One does not live by bread alone, but by every
word that comes forth from the mouth of God.** ↓

OR Cf. Ps. 90.4

**The Lord will conceal you with his pinions, and
under his wings you will trust.** ↓

PRAYER AFTER COMMUNION

Renewed now with heavenly bread,
by which faith is nourished, hope increased,
and charity strengthened,
we pray, O Lord,
that we may learn to hunger for Christ,
the true and living Bread,
and strive to live by every word
which proceeds from your mouth.
Through Christ our Lord.
℟. **Amen.** ↓

*The Deacon or, in his absence, the Priest himself, says
the invitation:* Bow down for the blessing.

PRAYER OVER THE PEOPLE

May bountiful blessing, O Lord, we pray,
come down upon your people,
that hope may grow in tribulation,
virtue be strengthened in temptation,
and eternal redemption be assured.
Through Christ our Lord.
℟. **Amen.**   → No. 32, p. 77

"They saw . . . Moses and Elijah, talking to Jesus.
They appeared in glory."

MARCH 17

2nd SUNDAY OF LENT

ENTRANCE ANTIPHON Cf. Ps. 26.8-9

Of you my heart has spoken: Seek his face. It is your face, O Lord, that I seek; hide not your face from me. → No. 2, p. 10 (Omit Gloria)

OR Cf. Ps. 24.6, 2, 22

Remember your compassion, O Lord, and your merciful love, for they are from of old. Let not our enemies exult over us. Redeem us, O God of Israel, from all our distress.

→ No. 2, p. 10 (Omit Gloria)

COLLECT

O God, who have commanded us
to listen to your beloved Son,
be pleased, we pray,
to nourish us inwardly by your word,

that, with spiritual sight made pure,
we may rejoice to behold your glory.
Through our Lord Jesus Christ, your Son,
who lives and reigns with you in the unity of the
    Holy Spirit,
one God, for ever and ever. ℟. **Amen.** ↓

FIRST READING Gen. 15.5-12, 17-18

> By faith Abram finds favour with the Lord. The Lord
> makes a covenant, that is, establishes a special relation-
> ship, with Abram and his descendants.

A reading from the book of Genesis.

THE Lord said to Abram: "Look toward
heaven and count the stars, if you are able to
count them." Then he said to him, "So shall your
descendants be." And he believed the Lord; and
the Lord reckoned it to him as righteousness.

Then the Lord said to Abram, "I am the Lord
who brought you from Ur of the Chaldeans, to
give you this land to possess."

But Abram said, "O Lord God, how am I to
know that I shall possess it?"

The Lord said to him, "Bring me a heifer three
years old, a female goat three years old, a ram
three years old, a turtledove, and a young pi-
geon." Abram brought the Lord all these and cut
them in two, laying each half over against the
other; but he did not cut the birds in two. And
when birds of prey came down on the carcasses,
Abram drove them away.

As the sun was going down, a deep sleep fell
upon Abram, and a deep and terrifying darkness
descended upon him. When the sun had gone

down and it was dark, a smoking fire pot and a flaming torch passed between these pieces.

On that day the Lord made a covenant with Abram, saying, "To your descendants I give this land, from the river of Egypt to the great river, the river Euphrates."—The word of the Lord. ℟. **Thanks be to God.** ↓

RESPONSORIAL PSALM Ps. 27

Leo Marchildon

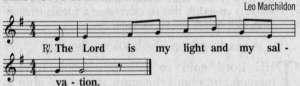

℟. The Lord is my light and my sal-va-tion.

The Lord is my light and my salvation;
whom shall I fear?
The Lord is the stronghold of my life;
of whom shall I be afraid?—℟.

Hear, O Lord, when I cry aloud,
be gracious to me and answer me!
"Come," my heart says, "seek his face!"
Your face, Lord, do I seek.—℟.

Do not hide your face from me.
Do not turn your servant away in anger,
you who have been my help.
Do not cast me off, do not forsake me, O God of
my salvation!—℟.

I believe that I shall see the goodness of the Lord
in the land of the living.
Wait for the Lord; be strong,
and let your heart take courage; wait for the
Lord!—℟. ↓

SECOND READING Phil. 3.17—4.1 or 3.20—4.1

Paul exhorts us to turn away from worldly pleasure and pride, to reject sin. He reminds us that we are not of this world.

[If the "Shorter Form" is used, the indented text in brackets is omitted.]

A reading from the Letter of Saint Paul
to the Philippians.

[B ROTHERS and sisters, join in imitating me, and observe those who live according to the example you have in us. For many live as enemies of the Cross of Christ; I have often told you of them, and now I tell you even with tears. Their end is destruction; their god is the belly; and their glory is in their shame; their minds are set on earthly things.]

But our citizenship is in heaven, and it is from there that we are expecting a Saviour, the Lord Jesus Christ. He will transform the body of our humiliation that it may be conformed to the body of his glory, by the power that also enables him to make all things subject to himself.

Therefore, my brothers and sisters, whom I love and long for, my joy and crown, stand firm, my beloved, in the Lord in this way.—The word of the Lord. ℟. **Thanks be to God.** ↓

GOSPEL ACCLAMATION Lk. 9.35

℣. Praise and honour to you, Lord Jesus Christ!*
℟. **Praise and honour to you, Lord Jesus Christ!**

---

* *See p. 16 for other Gospel Acclamations.*

℣. From the bright cloud the Father's voice is heard:

This is my Son, the Beloved; listen to him.

℟. **Praise and honour to you, Lord Jesus Christ!**

GOSPEL Lk. 9.28b-36

> The glory of Christ is revealed, and God manifests the special mission of Christ.

℣. The Lord be with you. ℟. **And with your spirit.**
✠ A reading from the holy Gospel according to Luke. ℟. **Glory to you, O Lord.**

JESUS took with him Peter and John and James, and went up on the mountain to pray. And while he was praying, the appearance of his face changed, and his clothes became dazzling white.

Suddenly they saw two men, Moses and Elijah, talking to Jesus. They appeared in glory and were speaking of his exodus, which he was about to accomplish at Jerusalem.

Now Peter and his companions were weighed down with sleep; but since they had stayed awake, they saw his glory and the two men who stood with him.

Just as they were leaving him, Peter said to Jesus, "Master, it is good for us to be here; let us make three dwellings, one for you, one for Moses, and one for Elijah," but Peter did not know what he said.

While he was saying this, a cloud came and overshadowed them; and they were terrified as they entered the cloud. Then from the cloud came a voice that said, "This is my Son, my Chosen; listen to him!" When the voice had spoken, Jesus was found alone. And the disciples kept silent and in those days told no one any of the things they had seen.—The Gospel of the Lord. ℟. **Praise to you, Lord Jesus Christ.**   → No. 15, p. 18

PRAYER OVER THE OFFERINGS

May this sacrifice, O Lord, we pray,
cleanse us of our faults
and sanctify your faithful in body and mind
for the celebration of the paschal festivities.
Through Christ our Lord. ℟. **Amen.** ↓

PREFACE (13)

℣. The Lord be with you. ℟. **And with your spirit.**
℣. Lift up your hearts. ℟. **We lift them up to the Lord.** ℣. Let us give thanks to the Lord our God.
℟. **It is right and just.**

It is truly right and just, our duty and our salvation,
always and everywhere to give you thanks,
Lord, holy Father, almighty and eternal God,
through Christ our Lord.

For after he had told the disciples of his coming Death,
on the holy mountain he manifested to them his glory,
to show, even by the testimony of the law and the prophets,
that the Passion leads to the glory of the Resurrection.

And so, with the Powers of heaven,
we worship you constantly on earth,
and before your majesty
without end we acclaim: → No. 23, p. 23

COMMUNION ANTIPHON Mt. 17.5

This is my beloved Son, with whom I am well pleased; listen to him. ↓

PRAYER AFTER COMMUNION

As we receive these glorious mysteries,
we make thanksgiving to you, O Lord,
for allowing us while still on earth
to be partakers even now of the things of heaven.
Through Christ our Lord.
℟. **Amen.** ↓

*The Deacon or, in his absence, the Priest himself, says
the invitation:* Bow down for the blessing.

PRAYER OVER THE PEOPLE

Bless your faithful, we pray, O Lord,
with a blessing that endures for ever,
and keep them faithful
to the Gospel of your Only Begotten Son,
so that they may always desire and at last attain
that glory whose beauty he showed in his own
  Body,
to the amazement of his Apostles.
Through Christ our Lord.
℟. **Amen.**   ➜ No. 32, p. 77

"Let it alone for one more year."

MARCH 24

3rd SUNDAY OF LENT

On this Sunday is celebrated the First Scrutiny in preparation for the Baptism of the catechumens who are to be admitted to the Sacraments of Christian Initiation at the Easter Vigil. The Ritual Mass for the First Scrutiny is found on p. 243.

ENTRANCE ANTIPHON Cf. Ps. 24.15-16

My eyes are always on the Lord, for he rescues my feet from the snare. Turn to me and have mercy on me, for I am alone and poor.

➡ No. 2, p. 10 (Omit Gloria)

OR Ez. 36.23-26

When I prove my holiness among you, I will gather you from all the foreign lands; and I will pour clean water upon you and cleanse you from all your impurities, and I will give you a new spirit, says the Lord. ➡ No. 2, p. 10 (Omit Gloria)

COLLECT

O God, author of every mercy and of all goodness,
who in fasting, prayer and almsgiving
have shown us a remedy for sin,
look graciously on this confession of our
  lowliness,
that we, who are bowed down by our conscience,
may always be lifted up by your mercy.
Through our Lord Jesus Christ, your Son,
who lives and reigns with you in the unity of the
  Holy Spirit,
one God, for ever and ever. ℟. **Amen.** ↓

FIRST READING Ex. 3.1-8a, 13-15

The Lord calls Moses to lead the chosen people, and reveals God's name to Moses.

A reading from the book of Exodus.

MOSES was keeping the flock of his father-in-law Jethro, the priest of Midian; he led his flock beyond the wilderness, and came to Horeb, the mountain of God. There the Angel of the Lord appeared to him in a flame of fire out of a bush; Moses looked, and the bush was blazing, yet it was not consumed.

Then Moses said, "I must turn aside and look at this great sight, and see why the bush is not burned up."

When the Lord saw that Moses had turned aside to see, God called to him out of the bush, "Moses, Moses!" And Moses said, "Here I am." Then God said, "Come no closer! Remove the sandals from your feet, for the place on which you are standing is holy ground."

God said further, "I am the God of your fathers, the God of Abraham, the God of Isaac, and the God of Jacob." And Moses hid his face, for he was afraid to look at God.

Then the Lord said, "I have observed the misery of my people who are in Egypt; I have heard their cry on account of their taskmasters. Indeed, I know their sufferings, and I have come down to deliver them from the Egyptians, and to bring them up out of that land to a good and broad land, a land flowing with milk and honey." But Moses said to God, "If I come to the children of Israel and say to them, 'The God of your fathers has sent me to you,' and they ask me, 'What is his name?' what shall I say to them?"

God said to Moses, "I AM WHO I AM." He said further, "Thus you shall say to the children of Israel, 'I AM has sent me to you.'"

God also said to Moses, "Thus you shall say to the children of Israel, 'The Lord, the God of your fathers, the God of Abraham, the God of Isaac, and the God of Jacob, has sent me to you.' This is my name forever, and this my memorial for all generations."—The word of the Lord. ℟. **Thanks be to God.** ↓

RESPONSORIAL PSALM Ps. 103

David Szanto

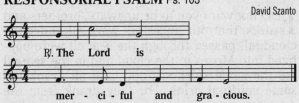

℟. The Lord is mer - ci - ful and gra - cious.

Bless the Lord, O my soul,
and all that is within me, bless his holy name.
Bless the Lord, O my soul,
and do not forget all his benefits.
℟. **The Lord is merciful and gracious.**

It is the Lord who forgives all your iniquity,
who heals all your diseases,
who redeems your life from the Pit,
who crowns you with steadfast love and
   mercy.—℟.

The Lord works vindication
and justice for all who are oppressed.
He made known his ways to Moses,
his acts to the people of Israel.—℟.

The Lord is merciful and gracious,
slow to anger and abounding in steadfast love.
For as the heavens are high above the earth,
so great is his steadfast love toward those who
   fear him.—℟. ↓

SECOND READING 1 Cor. 10.1-6, 10-12

> We must remain steadfast in our faith. We cannot be-
> come overconfident even though we are the recipients of
> God's favour and grace.

A reading from the first Letter of Saint Paul
to the Corinthians.

I DO not want you to be unaware, brothers and
sisters, that our ancestors were all under the
cloud; all passed through the sea; all were baptized into Moses in the cloud and in the sea; all
ate the same spiritual food, and all drank the
same spiritual drink. For they drank from the

spiritual rock that followed them, and the rock was Christ.

Nevertheless, God was not pleased with most of them, and they were struck down in the wilderness.

Now these things occurred as examples for us, so that we might not desire evil as they did. And do not complain as some of them did, and were destroyed by the destroyer.

These things happened to them to serve as an example, and they were written down to instruct us, on whom the ends of the ages have come. So if you think you are standing, watch out that you do not fall.—The word of the Lord. ℟. **Thanks be to God.** ↓

GOSPEL ACCLAMATION Mt. 4.17

℣. Praise and honour to you, Lord Jesus Christ!*
℟. **Praise and honour to you, Lord Jesus Christ!**
℣. Repent, says the Lord;
the kingdom of heaven is at hand.
℟. **Praise and honour to you, Lord Jesus Christ!** ↓

GOSPEL Lk. 13.1-9

Jesus tells us to repent. Time will run out, and no one can ever count on another year. Now is the time!

℣. The Lord be with you. ℟. **And with your spirit.**
✛ A reading from the holy Gospel according to Luke. ℟. **Glory to you, O Lord.**

JESUS was teaching the crowds; some of those present told Jesus about the Galileans whose blood Pilate had mingled with their sacrifices.

---

* See p. 16 for other Gospel Acclamations.

Jesus asked them, "Do you think that because these Galileans suffered in this way they were worse sinners than all other Galileans? No, I tell you; but unless you repent, you will all perish as they did. Or those eighteen who were killed when the tower of Siloam fell on them—do you think that they were worse offenders than all the others living in Jerusalem? No, I tell you; but unless you repent, you will all perish just as they did."

Then Jesus told this parable: "A man had a fig tree planted in his vineyard; and he came looking for fruit on it and found none. So he said to the gardener, 'See here! For three years I have come looking for fruit on this fig tree, and still I find none. Cut it down! Why should it be wasting the soil?'

The gardener replied, 'Sir, let it alone for one more year, until I dig around it and put manure on it. If it bears fruit next year, well and good; but if not, you can cut it down.'" —The Gospel of the Lord. ℟. **Praise to you, Lord Jesus Christ.**

→ No. 15, p. 18

PRAYER OVER THE OFFERINGS

Be pleased, O Lord, with these sacrificial offerings, and grant that we who beseech pardon for our
    own sins,
may take care to forgive our neighbour.
Through Christ our Lord.
℟. **Amen.**   → No. 21, p. 22 (Pref. 8-9)

COMMUNION ANTIPHON Cf. Ps. 83.4-5
The sparrow finds a home, and the swallow a nest for her young: by your altars, O Lord of hosts, my

King and my God. Blessed are they who dwell in
your house, for ever singing your praise. ↓

PRAYER AFTER COMMUNION

As we receive the pledge
of things yet hidden in heaven
and are nourished while still on earth
with the Bread that comes from on high,
we humbly entreat you, O Lord,
that what is being brought about in us in mystery
may come to true completion.
Through Christ our Lord. ℟. **Amen.** ↓

The Deacon or, in his absence, the Priest himself, says the
invitation: Bow down for the blessing.

PRAYER OVER THE PEOPLE

Direct, O Lord, we pray, the hearts of your faithful,
and in your kindness grant your servants this grace:
that, abiding in the love of you and their neighbour,
they may fulfill the whole of your commands.
Through Christ our Lord.
℟. **Amen.**   → No. 32, p. 77

———————————

MARCH 24

MASS FOR THE FIRST SCRUTINY

This Mass is celebrated when the First Scrutiny takes
place during the Rite of Christian Initiation of Adults,
usually on the Third Sunday of Lent.

ENTRANCE ANTIPHON Ez. 36.23-26

When I prove my holiness among you, I will gather you
from all the foreign lands and I will pour clean water

upon you and cleanse you from all your impurities, and
I will give you a new spirit, says the Lord.

→ No. 2 p. 10 (Omit Gloria)

OR Cf. Isa. 55.1

Come to the waters, you who are thirsty, says the Lord;
you who have no money, come and drink joyfully.

→ No. 2 p. 10 (Omit Gloria)

COLLECT

Grant, we pray, O Lord,
that these chosen ones may come worthily and wisely
to the confession of your praise,
so that in accordance with that first dignity
which they lost by original sin
they may be fashioned anew through your glory.
Through our Lord Jesus Christ, your Son,
who lives and reigns with you in the unity of the Holy
  Spirit,
one God, for ever and ever. ℟. **Amen.** ↓

FIRST READING Ex. 17.3-7

The Israelites murmured against God in their thirst. God
directs Moses to strike a rock with his staff, and water is-
sues forth.

A reading from the book of Exodus.

IN the wilderness the people thirsted for water; and
the people complained against Moses and said, "Why
did you bring us out of Egypt, to kill us and our children and livestock with thirst?" So Moses cried out to
the Lord, "What shall I do with this people? They are
almost ready to stone me."

The Lord said to Moses, "Go on ahead of the people,
and take some of the elders of Israel with you; take in
your hand the staff with which you struck the Nile, and
go. I will be standing there in front of you on the rock
at Horeb. Strike the rock, and water will come out of it,
so that the people may drink."

Moses did so, in the sight of the elders of Israel. He called the place Massah and Meribah, because the children of Israel quarrelled and tested the Lord, saying, "Is the Lord among us or not?"—The word of the Lord. ℟. **Thanks be to God.** ↓

RESPONSORIAL PSALM Ps. 95

Michael Gauthier

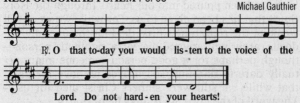

℟. O that to-day you would lis-ten to the voice of the

Lord. Do not hard-en your hearts!

O come, let us sing to the Lord;
let us make a joyful noise to the rock of our salvation!
Let us come into his presence with thanksgiving;
let us make a joyful noise to him with songs of
    praise!—℟.

O come, let us worship and bow down,
let us kneel before the Lord, our Maker!
For he is our God, and we are the people of his pasture,
and the sheep of his hand. —℟.

O that today you would listen to his voice!
Do not harden your hearts, as at Meribah,
as on the day at Massah in the wilderness,
when your ancestors tested me,
and put me to the proof,
though they had seen my work.—℟. ↓

SECOND READING Rom. 5.1-2, 5-8

Through Jesus we have received the grace of faith. The love of God has been poured upon us. Jesus laid down his life for us while we were still sinners.

A reading from the Letter of Saint Paul to the Romans.

Brothers and sisters: Since we are justified by faith, we have peace with God through our Lord Jesus Christ, through whom we have obtained access to this grace in which we stand; and we boast in our hope of sharing the glory of God.

And hope does not disappoint us, because God's love has been poured into our hearts through the Holy Spirit that has been given to us. For while we were still weak, at the right time Christ died for the ungodly. Indeed, rarely will anyone die for a righteous person— though perhaps for a good person someone might actually dare to die. But God proves his love for us in that while we still were sinners Christ died for us.— The word of the Lord. ℟. **Thanks be to God.** ↓

GOSPEL ACCLAMATION Jn. 4.42, 15

℣. Glory to you, Word of God, Lord Jesus Christ!*
℟. **Glory to you, Word of God, Lord Jesus Christ!**
℣. Lord, you are truly the Saviour of the world;
give me living water, that I may never be thirsty.
℟. **Glory to you, Word of God, Lord Jesus Christ!** ↓

GOSPEL Jn. 4.5-42 or 4.5-15, 19-26, 39a, 40-42

Jesus speaks to the Samaritan woman at the well. He searches her soul, and she recognizes him as a prophet. Jesus speaks of the water of eternal life.

[If the "Shorter Form" is used, the indented text in brackets is omitted.]

℣. The Lord be with you. ℟. **And with your spirit.**
✛ A reading from the holy Gospel according to John.
℟. **Glory to you, O Lord.**

Jesus came to a Samaritan city called Sychar, near the plot of ground that Jacob had given to his son Joseph. Jacob's well was there, and Jesus, tired out by his journey, was sitting by the well. It was about noon.

---

* See p. 16 for other Gospel Acclamations.

A Samaritan woman came to draw water, and Jesus said to her, "Give me a drink." (His disciples had gone to the city to buy food.)

The Samaritan woman said to him, "How is it that you, a Jew, ask a drink of me, a woman of Samaria?" (Jews do not share things in common with Samaritans.) Jesus answered her, "If you knew the gift of God, and who it is that is saying to you, 'Give me a drink,' you would have asked him, and he would have given you living water."

The woman said to him, "Sir, you have no bucket, and the well is deep. Where do you get that living water? Are you greater than our father Jacob, who gave us the well, and with his children and his flocks drank from it?" Jesus said to her, "Everyone who drinks of this water will be thirsty again, but the one who drinks of the water that I will give will never be thirsty. The water that I will give him will become in him a spring of water gushing up to eternal life." The woman said to him, "Sir, give me this water, so that I may never be thirsty or have to keep coming here to draw water."

[Jesus said to her, "Go, call your husband, and come back." The woman answered him, "I have no husband." Jesus said to her, "You are right in saying, 'I have no husband'; for you have had five husbands, and the one you have now is not your husband. What you have said is true!"]

[The woman said to him, "Sir,] I see that you are a Prophet. Our ancestors worshipped on this mountain, but you say that the place where people must worship is in Jerusalem."

Jesus said to her, "Woman, believe me, the hour is coming when you will worship the Father neither on this mountain nor in Jerusalem. You worship what you do not know; we worship what we know, for salvation is from the Jews. But the hour is coming, and is now here, when the true worshippers will worship the Father in spirit and truth, for the Father seeks such as these to worship him.

God is spirit, and those who worship him must worship in spirit and truth."

The woman said to him, "I know that the Messiah is coming" (who is called the Christ). "When he comes, he will proclaim all things to us." Jesus said to her, "I am he, the one who is speaking to you."

[Just then his disciples came. They were astonished that he was speaking with a woman, but no one said, "What do you want?" or, "Why are you speaking with her?" Then the woman left her water jar and went back to the city. She said to the people, "Come and see a man who told me everything I have ever done! He cannot be the Messiah, can he?" They left the city and were on their way to him. Meanwhile the disciples were urging him, "Rabbi, eat something." But he said to them, "I have food to eat that you do not know about." So the disciples said to one another, "Surely no one has brought him something to eat?"

Jesus said to them, "My food is to do the will of him who sent me and to complete his work. Do you not say, 'Four months more, then comes the harvest'? But I tell you, look around you, and see how the fields are ripe for harvesting. The reaper is already receiving wages and is gathering fruit for eternal life, so that sower and reaper may rejoice together. For here the saying holds true, 'One sows and another reaps.' I sent you to reap that for which you did not labour. Others have laboured, and you have entered into their labour."]

Many Samaritans from that city believed in Jesus [because of the woman's testimony, "He told me everything I have ever done."]

So when the Samaritans came to him, they asked him to stay with them; and he stayed there two days. And many more believed because of his word. They said to the woman, "It is no longer because of what you said that we believe, for we have heard for ourselves, and we

know that this is truly the Saviour of the world."—The
Gospel of the Lord. ℟. **Praise to you, Lord Jesus Christ.**

→ No. 15, p. 18

PRAYER OVER THE OFFERINGS

May your merciful grace prepare your servants, O Lord,
for the worthy celebration of these mysteries
and lead them to it by a devout way of life.
Through Christ our Lord. ℟. **Amen.** ↓

PREFACE (14)

℣. The Lord be with you. ℟. **And with your spirit.**
℣. Lift up your hearts. ℟. **We lift them up to the Lord.**
℣. Let us give thanks to the Lord our God. ℟. **It is right
and just.**

It is truly right and just, our duty and our salvation,
always and everywhere to give you thanks,
Lord, holy Father, almighty and eternal God,
through Christ our Lord.

For when he asked the Samaritan woman for water to
  drink,
he had already created the gift of faith within her
and so ardently did he thirst for her faith,
that he kindled in her the fire of divine love.

And so we, too, give you thanks
and with the Angels
praise your mighty deeds, as we acclaim: → No. 23, p. 23

When the Roman Canon is used, in the section Memento,
Domine (Remember, Lord, your servants) *there is a com-
memoration of the godparents, and the proper form of the*
Hanc igitur (Therefore, Lord, we pray), *is said.*

Remember, Lord, your servants
who are to present your chosen ones
for the holy grace of your Baptism,

(Here the names of the godparents are read out.)

and all gathered here,
whose faith and devotion are known to you ... (p. 24).

Therefore, Lord, we pray:
graciously accept this oblation
which we make to you for your servants,
whom you have been pleased
to enroll, choose and call for eternal life
and for the blessed gift of your grace.
(Through Christ our Lord. Amen.)

The rest follows the Roman Canon, pp. 25-29.

When Eucharistic Prayer II is used, after the words and all
the clergy, *the following is added:*

Remember also, Lord, your servants
who are to present these chosen ones
at the font of rebirth.

When Eucharistic Prayer III is used, after the words and the
entire people you have gained for your own, *the following is
added:*

Assist your servants with your grace,
O Lord, we pray,
that they may lead these chosen ones by word and
    example
to new life in Christ, our Lord.

COMMUNION ANTIPHON Jn. 4.14

**For anyone who drinks it, says the Lord, the water I
shall give will become in him a spring welling up to eternal life.** ↓

PRAYER AFTER COMMUNION

Give help, O Lord, we pray,
by the grace of your redemption
and be pleased to protect and prepare
those you are to initiate
through the Sacraments of eternal life.
Through Christ our Lord.
℟. **Amen.**   ➔ No. 30, p. 77

Optional Solemn Blessings, p. 97, and Prayers over the People, p. 105

"Father, I have sinned against heaven and before you."

MARCH 31

4th SUNDAY OF LENT

On this Sunday is celebrated the Second Scrutiny in preparation for the Baptism of the catechumens who are to be admitted to the Sacraments of Christian Initiation at the Easter Vigil. The Ritual Mass for the Second Scrutiny is found on p. 257.

ENTRANCE ANTIPHON Cf. Isa. 66.10-11

Rejoice, Jerusalem, and all who love her. Be joyful, all who were in mourning; exult and be satisfied at her consoling breast.

➜ No. 2, p. 10 (Omit Gloria)

COLLECT

O God, who through your Word
reconcile the human race to yourself in a
    wonderful way,
grant, we pray,
that with prompt devotion and eager faith
the Christian people may hasten

251

toward the solemn celebrations to come.
Through our Lord Jesus Christ, your Son,
who lives and reigns with you in the unity of the
   Holy Spirit,
one God, for ever and ever. ℟. **Amen.** ↓

FIRST READING Jos. 5.9a, 10-12

> The people of God celebrate the Passover in the promised
> land. As a sign that they are "home," the manna from
> heaven is no longer provided.

A reading from the book of Joshua.

THE Lord said to Joshua, "Today I have rolled
away from you the disgrace of Egypt."
   While the children of Israel were camped in Gilgal they kept the Passover in the evening on the fourteenth day of the month in the plains of Jericho.
   On the day after the Passover, on that very day, they ate the produce of the land, unleavened cakes and parched grain. The manna ceased on the day they ate the produce of the land, and the children of Israel no longer had manna; they ate the crops of the land of Canaan that year.—The word of the Lord. ℟. **Thanks be to God.** ↓

RESPONSORIAL PSALM Ps. 34

Michel Guimont

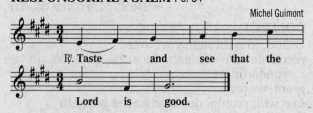

℟. Taste_____ and see that the Lord is good.

I will bless the Lord at all times;
his praise shall continually be in my mouth.

My soul makes its boast in the Lord;
let the humble hear and be glad.—℟.

O magnify the Lord with me,
and let us exalt his name together.
I sought the Lord, and he answered me,
and delivered me from all my fears.—℟.

Look to him, and be radiant;
so your faces shall never be ashamed.
The poor one called, and the Lord heard,
and saved that person from every trouble.—℟. ↓

SECOND READING 2 Cor. 5.17-21

Christ, the ambassador, reconciles all to God. Our transgressions find forgiveness in him so that we might become the very holiness of God.

A reading from the second Letter of Saint Paul
to the Corinthians.

BROTHERS and sisters: If anyone is in Christ, there is a new creation: everything old has passed away; see, everything has become new! All this is from God, who reconciled us to himself through Christ, and has given us the ministry of reconciliation; that is, in Christ, God was reconciling the world to himself, not counting their trespasses against them, and entrusting the message of reconciliation to us.

So we are ambassadors for Christ, since God is making his appeal through us; we entreat you on behalf of Christ, be reconciled to God. For our sake God made Christ to be sin who knew no sin, so that in Christ we might become the

righteousness of God.—The word of the Lord.
℟. **Thanks be to God.** ↓

GOSPEL ACCLAMATION Lk. 15.18

℣. Praise and honour to you, Lord Jesus Christ!*
℟. **Praise and honour to you, Lord Jesus Christ!**
℣. I will get up and go to my father and say to him:
Father, I have sinned against heaven and before
you.
℟. **Praise and honour to you, Lord Jesus Christ!** ↓

GOSPEL Lk. 15.1-3, 11-32

**Our loving Father is always ready to forgive those who
are truly repentant.**

℣. The Lord be with you. ℟. **And with your spirit.**
✝ A reading from the holy Gospel according to
Luke. ℟. **Glory to you, O Lord.**

A LL the tax collectors and sinners were coming
near to listen to Jesus. And the Pharisees and
the scribes were grumbling and saying, "This fellow welcomes sinners and eats with them."

So he told them a parable: "There was a man
who had two sons. The younger of them said to
his father, 'Father, give me the share of the property that will belong to me.' So the father divided
his property between them.

A few days later the younger son gathered all he
had and travelled to a distant country, and there he
squandered his property in dissolute living.

When he had spent everything, a severe famine
took place throughout that country, and he began

* See p. 16 for other Gospel Acclamations.

to be in need. So he went and hired himself out to one of the citizens of that country, who sent him to his fields to feed the pigs. The young man would gladly have filled himself with the pods that the pigs were eating; and no one gave him anything.

But when he came to himself he said, 'How many of my father's hired hands have bread enough and to spare, but here I am dying of hunger! I will get up and go to my father, and I will say to him, "Father, I have sinned against heaven and before you; I am no longer worthy to be called your son; treat me like one of your hired hands."'

So he set off and went to his father. But while he was still far off, his father saw him and was filled with compassion; he ran and put his arms around him and kissed him.

Then the son said to him, 'Father, I have sinned against heaven and before you; I am no longer worthy to be called your son.' But the father said to his slaves, 'Quickly, bring out a robe—the best one—and put it on him; put a ring on his finger and sandals on his feet. And get the fatted calf and kill it, and let us eat and celebrate; for this son of mine was dead and is alive again; he was lost and is found!' And they began to celebrate.

Now his elder son was in the field; and when he came and approached the house, he heard music and dancing. He called one of the slaves and asked what was going on. The slave replied, 'Your brother has come, and your father has killed the fatted calf, because he has got him back safe and sound.'

Then the elder son became angry and refused to go in. His father came out and began to plead with him. But he answered his father, 'Listen! For all these years I have been working like a slave for you, and I have never disobeyed your command; yet you have never given me even a young goat so that I might celebrate with my friends. But when this son of yours came back, who has devoured your property with prostitutes, you killed the fatted calf for him!'

Then the father said to him, 'Son, you are always with me, and all that is mine is yours. But we had to celebrate and rejoice, because this brother of yours was dead and has come to life; he was lost and has been found.'" —The Gospel of the Lord. ℟. **Praise to you, Lord Jesus Christ.**

→ No. 15, p. 18

PRAYER OVER THE OFFERINGS

We place before you with joy these offerings,
which bring eternal remedy, O Lord,
praying that we may both faithfully revere them
and present them to you, as is fitting,
for the salvation of all the world.
Through Christ our Lord.
℟. **Amen.**   → No. 21, p. 22 (Pref. 8-9)

COMMUNION ANTIPHON Lk 15.32

You must rejoice, my son, for your brother was dead and has come to life; he was lost and is found. ↓

PRAYER AFTER COMMUNION

O God, who enlighten everyone who comes into this world,

illuminate our hearts, we pray,
with the splendour of your grace,
that we may always ponder
what is worthy and pleasing to your majesty
and love you in all sincerity.
Through Christ our Lord. ℟. **Amen.** ↓

*The Deacon or, in his absence, the Priest himself, says
the invitation:* Bow down for the blessing.

PRAYER OVER THE PEOPLE

Look upon those who call to you, O Lord,
and sustain the weak;
give life by your unfailing light
to those who walk in the shadow of death,
and bring those rescued by your mercy from every
    evil
to reach the highest good.
Through Christ our Lord.
℟. **Amen.**   → No. 32, p. 77

_____

MARCH 31

MASS FOR THE SECOND SCRUTINY

*This Mass is celebrated when the Second Scrutiny takes place
during the Rite of Christian Initiation of Adults, usually on
the Fourth Sunday of Lent.*

ENTRANCE ANTIPHON Cf. Ps. 24.15-16
**My eyes are always on the Lord, for he rescues my feet
from the snare. Turn to me and have mercy on me, for
I am alone and poor.**   → No. 2, p. 10 (Omit Gloria)

COLLECT
Almighty ever-living God,
give to your Church an increase in spiritual joy,
so that those once born of earth

may be reborn as citizens of heaven.
Through our Lord Jesus Christ, your Son,
who lives and reigns with you in the unity of the Holy
    Spirit,
one God, for ever and ever. ℟. **Amen.** ↓

FIRST READING 1 Sam. 16.1b, 6-7, 10-13

**God directs Samuel to anoint David king. God looks into
the heart of each person.**

A reading from the first book of Samuel.

THE Lord said to Samuel, "Fill your horn with oil and
    set out; I will send you to Jesse of Bethlehem, for I
have provided for myself a king among his sons."

When the sons of Jesse came, Samuel looked on Eliab
and thought, "Surely the Lord's anointed is now before
the Lord." But the Lord said to Samuel, "Do not look on
his appearance or on the height of his stature, because I
have rejected him; for the Lord does not see as the
human sees; the human looks on the outward appearance, but the Lord looks on the heart."

Jesse made seven of his sons pass before Samuel, and
Samuel said to Jesse, "The Lord has not chosen any of
these." Samuel said to Jesse, "Are all your sons here?"
And he said, "There remains yet the youngest, but he is
keeping the sheep." And Samuel said to Jesse, "Send and
bring him; for we will not sit down until he comes here."
Jesse sent and brought David in. Now he was ruddy, and
had beautiful eyes, and was handsome. The Lord said,
"Rise and anoint him; for this is the one."

Then Samuel took the horn of oil, and anointed him in
the presence of his brothers; and the spirit of the Lord
came mightily upon David from that day forward.—The
word of the Lord. ℟. **Thanks be to God.** ↓

RESPONSORIAL PSALM Ps. 23

Michel Guimont

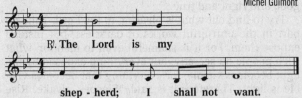

R̸. The Lord is my shep-herd; I shall not want.

The Lord is my shepherd, I shall not want.
He makes me lie down in green pastures;
he leads me beside still waters;
he restores my soul.—R̸.

He leads me in right paths for his name's sake.
Even though I walk through the darkest valley, I fear
no evil;
for you are with me;
your rod and your staff—they comfort me.—R̸.

You prepare a table before me
in the presence of my enemies;
you anoint my head with oil;
my cup overflows—R̸.

Surely goodness and mercy shall follow me
all the days of my life,
and I shall dwell in the house of the Lord
my whole life long.—R̸. ↓

SECOND READING Eph. 5.8-14

We are to walk in the light which shows goodness, justice, and truth. Evil deeds are condemned. Christ gives this light whereby we live.

A reading from the Letter of Saint Paul
to the Ephesians.

BROTHERS and sisters: Once you were darkness,
but now in the Lord you are light. Live as children

of light—for the fruit of the light is found in all that is good and right and true.

Try to find out what is pleasing to the Lord. Take no part in the unfruitful works of darkness, but instead expose them. For it is shameful even to mention what such people do secretly; but everything exposed by the light becomes visible, for everything that becomes visible is light. Therefore it is said, "Sleeper, awake! Rise from the dead, and Christ will shine on you."—The word of the Lord. ℟. **Thanks be to God.** ↓

GOSPEL ACCLAMATION Jn. 8.12

℣. Praise and honour to you, Lord Jesus Christ!*
℟. **Praise and honour to you, Lord Jesus Christ!**
℣. I am the light of the world, says the Lord;
whoever follows me will have the light of life.
℟. **Praise and honour to you, Lord Jesus Christ!** ↓

GOSPEL Jn. 9.1-41 or 9.1, 6-9, 13-17, 34-38

Jesus is the light. He cures a man born blind by bringing him to see. Jesus identifies himself as the Son of Man.

[If the "Shorter Form" is used, the indented text in brackets is omitted.]

℣. The Lord be with you. ℟. **And with your spirit.**
✠ A reading from the holy Gospel according to John.
℟. **Glory to you, O Lord.**

AS Jesus walked along, he saw a man blind from birth.

[His disciples asked him, "Rabbi, who sinned, this man or his parents, that he was born blind?"

Jesus answered, "Neither this man nor his parents sinned; he was born blind so that God's works might be revealed in him. We must work the works of him who sent me while it is day; night is coming when no one can work. As long

---

* *See p. 16 for other Gospel Acclamations.*

as I am in the world, I am the light of the world."
When he had said this,]
he spat on the ground and made mud with the saliva
and spread the mud on the man's eyes, saying to him,
"Go, wash in the pool of Siloam" (which means Sent).

Then the man who was blind went and washed, and
came back able to see. The neighbours and those who
had seen him before as a beggar began to ask, "Is this
not the man who used to sit and beg?" Some were saying, "It is he." Others were saying, "No, but it is someone like him." He kept saying, "I am the man."

[But they kept asking him, "Then how were your
eyes opened?" He answered, "The man called
Jesus made mud, spread it on my eyes, and said
to me, 'Go to Siloam and wash.' Then I went and
washed and received my sight." They said to him,
"Where is he?" He said, "I do not know."]

They brought to the Pharisees the man who had formerly been blind. Now it was a Sabbath day when Jesus
made the mud and opened his eyes. Then the Pharisees
also began to ask him how he had received his sight. He
said to them, "He put mud on my eyes. Then I washed,
and now I see." Some of the Pharisees said, "This man is
not from God, for he does not observe the Sabbath." But
others said, "How can a man who is a sinner perform
such signs?" And they were divided. So they said again to
the blind man, "What do you say about him? It was your
eyes he opened." He said, "He is a Prophet."

[They did not believe that he had been blind and
had received his sight until they called the parents of the man who had received his sight and
asked them, "Is this your son, who you say was
born blind? How then does he now see?" His parents answered, "We know that this is our son, and
that he was born blind; but we do not know how
it is that now he sees, nor do we know who
opened his eyes. Ask him; he is of age. He will
speak for himself." His parents said this because

they were afraid of the Jewish authorities, who had already agreed that anyone who confessed Jesus to be the Messiah would be put out of the synagogue. Therefore his parents said, "He is of age; ask him."

So for the second time they called the man who had been blind, and they said to him, "Give glory to God! We know that this man is a sinner." He answered, "I do not know whether he is a sinner. One thing I do know, that though I was blind, now I see." They said to him, "What did he do to you? How did he open your eyes?" He answered them, "I have told you already, and you would not listen. Why do you want to hear it again? Do you also want to become his disciples?" Then they reviled him, saying, "You are his disciple, but we are disciples of Moses. We know that God has spoken to Moses, but as for this man, we do not know where he comes from."

The man answered, "Here is an astonishing thing! You do not know where he comes from, and yet he opened my eyes. We know that God does not listen to sinners, but he does listen to one who worships him and obeys his will. Never since the world began has it been heard that anyone opened the eyes of a person born blind. If this man were not from God, he could do nothing."]

They answered him, "You were born entirely in sins, and are you trying to teach us?" And they drove him out.

Jesus heard that they had driven him out, and when he found him, he said, "Do you believe in the Son of Man?" He answered, "And who is he, sir? Tell me, so that I may believe in him." Jesus said to him, "You have seen him, and the one speaking with you is he." He said, "Lord, I believe." And he worshipped him.

[Jesus said, "I came into this world for judgment so that those who do not see may see, and those who do see may become blind." Some of the Pharisees near him heard this and said to him, "Surely we are not blind, are we?" Jesus said to

them, "If you were blind, you would have no sin.
But now that you say, 'We see,' your sin remains.]
The Gospel of the Lord. ℟. **Praise to you, Lord Jesus
Christ.**   ➔ No. 15, p. 18

PRAYER OVER THE OFFERINGS

We place before you with joy these offerings,
which bring eternal remedy, O Lord,
praying that we may both faithfully revere them
and present them to you, as is fitting,
for those who seek salvation.
Through Christ our Lord. ℟. **Amen.** ↓

PREFACE (15)

℣. The Lord be with you. ℟. **And with your spirit.**
℣. Lift up your hearts. ℟. **We lift them up to the Lord.**
℣. Let us give thanks to the Lord our God. ℟. **It is right
and just.**

It is truly right and just, our duty and our salvation,
always and everywhere to give you thanks,
Lord, holy Father, almighty and eternal God,
through Christ our Lord.

By the mystery of the Incarnation,
he has led the human race that walked in darkness
into the radiance of the faith
and has brought those born in slavery to ancient sin
through the waters of regeneration
to make them your adopted children.

Therefore, all creatures of heaven and earth
sing a new song in adoration,
and we, with all the host of Angels,
cry out, and without end acclaim: ➔ No. 23, p. 23

*The commemoration of the godparents in the Eucharistic
Prayers takes place as above (pp. 249, 250) and, if the Roman
Canon is used, the proper form of the* Hanc igitur *(Therefore,
Lord, we pray) is said, as in the First Scrutiny (p. 250).*

The rest follows the Roman Canon, pp. 25-29.

COMMUNION ANTIPHON Cf. Jn. 9.11, 38

The Lord anointed my eyes; I went, I washed, I saw and I believed in God. ↓

PRAYER AFTER COMMUNION

Sustain your family always in your kindness,
O Lord, we pray,
correct them, set them in order,
graciously protect them under your rule,
and in your unfailing goodness
direct them along the way of salvation.
Through Christ our Lord.
℟. **Amen.**

➜ No. 30, p. 77

Optional Solemn Blessings, p. 97, and Prayers over the People, p. 105

"Go your way, and from now on do not sin again."

APRIL 7

5th SUNDAY OF LENT

On this Sunday is celebrated the Third Scrutiny in preparation for the Baptism of the catechumens who are to be admitted to the Sacraments of Christian Initiation at the Easter Vigil. The Ritual Mass for the Third Scrutiny is found on p. 270.

ENTRANCE ANTIPHON Cf. Ps. 42.1-2

Give me justice, O God, and plead my cause against a nation that is faithless. From the deceitful and cunning rescue me, for you, O God, are my strength.   → No. 2, p. 10 (Omit Gloria)

COLLECT

By your help, we beseech you, Lord our God,
may we walk eagerly in that same charity
with which, out of love for the world,
your Son handed himself over to death.
Through our Lord Jesus Christ, your Son,
who lives and reigns with you in the unity of the
    Holy Spirit,
one God, for ever and ever. ℟. **Amen.** ↓

FIRST READING Isa. 43.16-21

A call to look with hope to the future. God is not dead.
Look around you and see God's wonderful works.

A reading from the book of the Prophet Isaiah.

T HUS says the Lord,
who makes a way in the sea,
a path in the mighty waters,
who brings out chariot and horse, army and
    warrior;
they lie down, they cannot rise,
they are extinguished, quenched like a wick:
"Do not remember the former things,
or consider the things of old.

I am about to do a new thing;
now it springs forth, do you not perceive it?
I will make a way in the wilderness
and rivers in the desert.

The wild animals will honour me,
the jackals and the ostriches;

for I give water in the wilderness, rivers in the desert,
to give drink to my chosen people,
the people whom I formed for myself
so that they might declare my praise."

The word of the Lord. ℟. **Thanks be to God.** ↓

RESPONSORIAL PSALM Ps. 126

Gloria Gassi

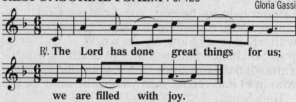

℟. The Lord has done great things for us; we are filled with joy.

When the Lord restored the fortunes of Zion,
we were like those who dream.
Then our mouth was filled with laughter,
and our tongue with shouts of joy.—℟.

Then it was said among the nations,
"The Lord has done great things for them."
The Lord has done great things for us,
and we rejoiced.—℟.

Restore our fortunes, O Lord,
like the watercourses in the desert of the Negev.
May those who sow in tears
reap with shouts of joy.—℟.

Those who go out weeping,
bearing the seed for sowing,
shall come home with shouts of joy,
carrying their sheaves.—℟. ↓

SECOND READING Phil. 3.8-14

Faith in Christ is our salvation, but we cannot relax. We must continue, while in this life, to strive for the good things of life in Christ—heaven.

A reading from the Letter of Saint Paul
to the Philippians.

Brothers and sisters: I regard everything
as loss because of the surpassing value of
knowing Christ Jesus my Lord. For his sake I
have suffered the loss of all things, and I regard
them as rubbish, in order that I may gain Christ
and be found in him, not having a righteousness
of my own that comes from the law, but one that
comes through faith in Christ, the righteousness
from God based on faith.

I want to know Christ and the power of his resurrection and the sharing of his sufferings by becoming like him in his death, if somehow I may
attain the resurrection from the dead.

Not that I have already obtained this or have already reached the goal; but I press on to make it
my own, because Christ Jesus has made me his
own.

Brothers and sisters, I do not consider that I
have made it my own; but this one thing I do: for-
getting what lies behind and straining forward to
what lies ahead, I press on toward the goal for the
prize of the heavenly call of God in Christ Jesus.—
The word of the Lord. ℟. **Thanks be to God.** ↓

GOSPEL ACCLAMATION Joel 2.12-13

℣. Praise and honour to you, Lord Jesus Christ!*
℟. **Praise and honour to you, Lord Jesus Christ!**
℣. Return to me with all your heart, says the
Lord,

---

* See p. 16 for other Gospel Acclamations.

for I am gracious and merciful.

℟. **Praise and honour to you, Lord Jesus Christ!** ↓

GOSPEL Jn. 8.1-11

> By his example and works the Lord teaches us that God extends mercy to sinners to free them from slavery to sin.

℣. The Lord be with you. ℟. **And with your spirit.**
✝ A reading from the holy Gospel according to John. ℟. **Glory to you, O Lord.**

JESUS went to the Mount of Olives. Early in the morning he came again to the temple. All the people came to him and he sat down and began to teach them.

The scribes and the Pharisees brought a woman who had been caught in adultery; and making her stand before the people, they said to Jesus, "Teacher, this woman was caught in the very act of committing adultery. In the law, Moses commanded us to stone such women. Now what do you say?" They said this to test Jesus, so that they might have some charge to bring against him.

Jesus bent down and wrote with his finger on the ground. When the scribes and Pharisees kept on questioning him, Jesus straightened up and said to them, "Let anyone among you who is without sin be the first to throw a stone at her." And once again Jesus bent down and wrote on the ground.

When the scribes and Pharisees heard what Jesus had said, they went away, one by one, beginning with the elders; and Jesus was left alone with the woman standing before him.

Jesus straightened up and said to her, "Woman, where are they? Has no one condemned you?"

She said, "No one, sir." And Jesus said, "Neither do I condemn you. Go your way, and from now on do not sin again."—The Gospel of the Lord.
℟. **Praise to you, Lord Jesus Christ.** → No. 15, p. 18

PRAYER OVER THE OFFERINGS

Hear us, almighty God,
and, having instilled in your servants
the teachings of the Christian faith,
graciously purify them
by the working of this sacrifice.
Through Christ our Lord.
℟. **Amen.**   → No. 21, p. 22 (Pref. 8-9)

COMMUNION ANTIPHON Jn. 8.10-11

Has no one condemned you, woman? No one, Lord. Neither shall I condemn you. From now on, sin no more. ↓

PRAYER AFTER COMMUNION

We pray, almighty God,
that we may always be counted among the
    members of Christ,
in whose Body and Blood we have communion.
Who lives and reigns for ever and ever. ℟. **Amen.** ↓

The Deacon or, in his absence, the Priest himself, says the invitation: Bow down for the blessing.

PRAYER OVER THE PEOPLE

Bless, O Lord, your people,
who long for the gift of your mercy,
and grant that what, at your prompting, they
    desire
they may receive by your generous gift.
Through Christ our Lord.
℟. **Amen.**   → No. 32, p. 77

APRIL 7

MASS FOR THE THIRD SCRUTINY

This Mass is celebrated when the Third Scrutiny takes place during the Rite of Christian Initiation of Adults, usually on the Fifth Sunday of Lent.

ENTRANCE ANTIPHON Cf. Ps. 17.5-7

The waves of death rose about me; the pains of the netherworld surrounded me. In my anguish I called to the Lord; and from his holy temple he heard my voice.

→ No. 2, p. 10 (Omit Gloria)

COLLECT

Grant, O Lord, to these chosen ones
that, instructed in the holy mysteries,
they may receive new life at the font of Baptism
and be numbered among the members of your Church.
Through our Lord Jesus Christ, your Son,
who lives and reigns with you in the unity of the Holy
    Spirit,
one God, for ever and ever. ℞. **Amen.** ↓

FIRST READING Ez. 37.12-14

The Lord promises to bring God's people back to their homeland. He will be with them and they will know him.

A reading from the book of the Prophet Ezekiel.

THUS says the Lord God: "I am going to open your graves, and bring you up from your graves, O my people; and I will bring you back to the land of Israel. And you shall know that I am the Lord, when I open your graves, and bring you up from your graves, O my people.

"I will put my spirit within you, and you shall live, and I will place you on your own soil; then you shall know that I, the Lord, have spoken and will act," says the Lord.— The word of the Lord. ℞. **Thanks be to God.** ↓

RESPONSORIAL PSALM Ps. 130   Frank Lynch

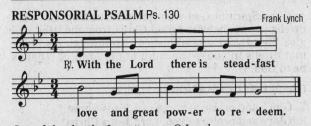

R̹. With the Lord there is stead-fast love and great pow-er to re - deem.

Out of the depths I cry to you, O Lord.
Lord, hear my voice!
Let your ears be attentive
to the voice of my supplications!—R̹.

If you, O Lord, should mark iniquities,
Lord, who could stand?
But there is forgiveness with you,
so that you may be revered.—R̹.

I wait for the Lord,
my soul waits, and in his word I hope;
my soul waits for the Lord
more than watchmen for the morning. —R̹.

For with the Lord there is steadfast love,
and with him is great power to redeem.
It is he who will redeem Israel
from all its iniquities.—R̹. ↓

SECOND READING Rom. 8.8-11

**The followers of Jesus live in the Spirit of God. The same
Spirit who brought Jesus back to life will bring mortal
bodies to life since God's Spirit dwells in them.**

A reading from the Letter of Saint Paul to the Romans.

BROTHERS and sisters: Those who are in the flesh
cannot please God. But you are not in the flesh;
you are in the Spirit, since the Spirit of God dwells in
you. Anyone who does not have the Spirit of Christ
does not belong to him.

But if Christ is in you, though the body is dead because of sin, the Spirit is life because of righteousness.

If the Spirit of God who raised Jesus from the dead dwells in you, he who raised Christ from the dead will give life to your mortal bodies also through his Spirit that dwells in you.—The word of the Lord. ℟. **Thanks be to God.** ↓

GOSPEL ACCLAMATION Jn. 11.25, 26

℣. Glory and praise to you, Lord Jesus Christ!*
℟. **Glory and praise to you, Lord Jesus Christ!**
℣. I am the resurrection and the life, says the Lord; whoever believes in me will never die.
℟. **Glory and praise to you, Lord Jesus Christ!** ↓

GOSPEL Jn. 11.1-45 or 11.3-7, 17, 20-27, 33b-45

Jesus, the resurrection and the life, gave life back to Lazarus, who had died.

[If the "Shorter Form" is used, the indented text in brackets is omitted.]

℣. The Lord be with you. ℟. **And with your spirit.**
✣ A reading from the holy Gospel according to John.
℟. **Glory to you, O Lord.**

[NOW a certain man, Lazarus, was ill. He was from Bethany, the village of Mary and her sister Martha. Mary was the one who anointed the Lord with perfume and wiped his feet with her hair; her brother Lazarus was ill.]

[So] the sisters [of Lazarus] sent a message to Jesus, "Lord, he whom you love is ill." But when Jesus heard this, he said, "This illness does not lead to death; rather it is for God's glory, so that the Son of God may be glorified through it." Accordingly, though Jesus loved Martha and her sister and Lazarus, after having heard that Lazarus was ill, he stayed two days longer in the place where he was.

Then after this he said to the disciples, "Let us go to Judea again."

[The disciples said to him, "Rabbi, the people there were just now trying to stone you, and are you going

---

* *See p. 16 for other Gospel Acclamations.*

there again?" Jesus answered, "Are there not twelve hours of daylight? Those who walk during the day do not stumble, because they see the light of this world. But those who walk at night stumble, because the light is not in them."

After saying this, he told them, "Our friend Lazarus has fallen asleep, but I am going there to awaken him." The disciples said to him, "Lord, if he has fallen asleep, he will be all right." Jesus, however, had been speaking about his death, but they thought that he was referring merely to sleep. Then Jesus told them plainly, "Lazarus is dead. For your sake I am glad I was not there, so that you may believe. But let us go to him." Thomas, who was called the Twin, said to his fellow disciples, "Let us also go, that we may die with him."]

When Jesus arrived, he found that Lazarus had already been in the tomb four days.

[Now Bethany was near Jerusalem, some two miles away, and many Jews had come to Martha and Mary to console them about their brother.]

When Martha heard that Jesus was coming, she went and met him, while Mary stayed at home. Martha said to Jesus, "Lord, if you had been here, my brother would not have died. But even now I know that God will give you whatever you ask of him." Jesus said to her, "Your brother will rise again." Martha said to him, "I know that he will rise again in the resurrection on the last day." Jesus said to her, "I am the resurrection and the life. Whoever believes in me, even though they die, will live, and everyone who lives and believes in me will never die. Do you believe this?" She said to him, "Yes, Lord, I believe that you are the Christ, the Son of God, the one coming into the world."

[When she had said this, she went back and called her sister Mary, and told her privately, "The Teacher is here and is calling for you." And when Mary heard it, she got up quickly and went to him. Now Jesus had not yet come to the village, but was still at the place where Martha had met him. The Jews who were with her in the house, consoling her, saw Mary get up quickly and go out. They followed her because they thought that she was going to the tomb to weep there.

When Mary came where Jesus was and saw him, she knelt at his feet and said to him, "Lord, if you had been here, my brother would not have died." When Jesus saw her weeping, and the Jews who came with her also weeping, he]

[Jesus] was greatly disturbed in spirit and deeply moved. He said, "Where have you laid him?" They said to him, "Lord, come and see." Jesus began to weep. So the Jews said, "See how he loved him!" But some of them said, "Could not he who opened the eyes of the blind man have kept this man from dying?"

Then Jesus, again greatly disturbed, came to the tomb. It was a cave, and a stone was lying against it. Jesus said, "Take away the stone." Martha, the sister of the dead man, said to him, "Lord, already there is a stench because he has been dead four days." Jesus said to her, "Did I not tell you that if you believed, you would see the glory of God?" So they took away the stone. And Jesus looked upward and said, "Father, I thank you for having heard me. I knew that you always hear me, but I have said this for the sake of the crowd standing here, so that they may believe that you sent me."

When he had said this, he cried with a loud voice, "Lazarus, come out!" The dead man came out, his hands and feet bound with strips of cloth, and his face wrapped in a cloth. Jesus said to them, "Unbind him, and let him go."

Many of the Jews therefore, who had come with Mary and had seen what Jesus did, believed in him.—The Gospel of the Lord. ℟. **Praise to you, Lord Jesus Christ.**

➡ No. 15, p. 18

PRAYER OVER THE OFFERINGS

Hear us, almighty God,
and, having instilled in your servants
the first fruits of the Christian faith,
graciously purify them by the working of this sacrifice.
Through Christ our Lord. ℟. **Amen.** ↓

PREFACE (16)

℣. The Lord be with you. ℟. **And with your spirit.**
℣. Lift up your hearts. ℟. **We lift them up to the Lord.**
℣. Let us give thanks to the Lord our God. ℟. **It is right and just.**

It is truly right and just, our duty and our salvation,
always and everywhere to give you thanks,
Lord, holy Father, almighty and eternal God,
through Christ our Lord.

For as true man he wept for Lazarus his friend
and as eternal God raised him from the tomb,
just as, taking pity on the human race,
he leads us by sacred mysteries to new life.

Through him the host of Angels adores your majesty
and rejoices in your presence for ever.
May our voices, we pray, join with theirs
in one chorus of exultant praise, as we acclaim:

➡ No. 23, p. 23

*The commemoration of the godparents in the Eucharistic
Prayers takes place as above (pp. 249, 250) and, if the Roman
Canon is used, the proper form of the* Hanc igitur *(Therefore,
Lord, we pray) is said, as in the First Scrutiny (p. 250).*

The rest follows the Roman Canon, pp. 25-29.

COMMUNION ANTIPHON Cf. Jn. 11.26

**Everyone who lives and believes in me will not die for
ever, says the Lord.** ↓

PRAYER AFTER COMMUNION

May your people be at one, O Lord, we pray,
and in wholehearted submission to you
may they obtain this grace:
that, safe from all distress,
they may readily live out their joy at being saved
and remember in loving prayer those to be reborn.
Through Christ our Lord.
℟. **Amen.**

➡ No. 30, p. 77

Optional Solemn Blessings, p. 97, and Prayers over the People, p. 105

PALM SUNDAY OF THE LORD'S PASSION

"Blessed are you, who have come in your abundant mercy!"

The Commemoration of the Lord's Entrance into Jerusalem

FIRST FORM: THE PROCESSION

At an appropriate hour, a gathering takes place at a smaller church or other suitable place other than inside the church to which the procession will go. The faithful hold branches in their hands.

Wearing the red sacred vestments as for Mass, the Priest and the Deacon, accompanied by other ministers, approach the place where the people are gathered. Instead of the chasuble, the Priest may wear a cope, which he leaves aside when the procession is over, and puts on a chasuble.

Meanwhile, the following antiphon or another appropriate chant is sung.

ANTIPHON Mt. 21.9

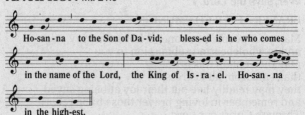

Ho-san-na to the Son of Da-vid; bless-ed is he who comes in the name of the Lord, the King of Is-ra-el. Ho-san-na in the high-est.

OR:

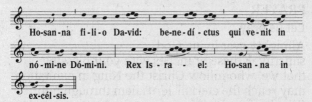

Ho-san-na fi-li-o Da-vid: be-ne-dí-ctus qui ve-nit in
nó-mi-ne Dó-mi-ni.   Rex Is-ra - el: Ho-san-na in
ex-cél-sis.

After this, the Priest and people sign themselves, while the Priest says: In the name of the Father, and of the Son, and of the Holy Spirit. *Then he greets the people in the usual way. A brief address is given, in which the faithful are invited to participate actively and consciously in the celebration of this day, in these or similar words:*

Dear brethren (brothers and sisters),
since the beginning of Lent until now
we have prepared our hearts by penance and
   charitable works.
Today we gather together to herald with the
   whole Church
the beginning of the celebration
of our Lord's Paschal Mystery,
that is to say, of his Passion and Resurrection.
For it was to accomplish this mystery
that he entered his own city of Jerusalem.
Therefore, with all faith and devotion,
let us commemorate
the Lord's entry into the city for our salvation,
following in his footsteps,
so that, being made by his grace partakers of the
   Cross,
we may have a share also in his Resurrection and
   in his life.

After the address, the Priest says one of the following prayers with hands extended.

PRAYER

Let us pray.

Almighty ever-living God,
sanctify ✚ these branches with your blessing,
that we, who follow Christ the King in exultation,
may reach the eternal Jerusalem through him.
Who lives and reigns for ever and ever.
℟. **Amen.** ↓

OR

Increase the faith of those who place their hope in
    you, O God,
and graciously hear the prayers of those who call
    on you,
that we, who today hold high these branches
to hail Christ in his triumph,
may bear fruit for you by good works
    accomplished in him.
Who lives and reigns for ever and ever.
℟. **Amen.** ↓

The Priest sprinkles the branches with holy water without saying anything.

Then a Deacon or, if there is no Deacon, a Priest, proclaims in the usual way the Gospel concerning the Lord's entrance according to one of the four Gospels.

GOSPEL Lk. 19.28-40

> In triumphant glory Jesus comes into Jerusalem. The people spread their cloaks on the ground for him, wave palm branches and sing in his honour.

℣. The Lord be with you. ℟. **And with your spirit.**
✚ A reading from the holy Gospel according to
Luke. ℟. **Glory to you, O Lord.**

JESUS went on ahead, going up to Jerusalem. When he had come near Bethphage and Bethany, at the place called the Mount of Olives, he sent two of the disciples, saying, "Go into the village ahead of you, and as you enter it you will find tied there a colt that has never been ridden. Untie it and bring it here. If anyone asks you, 'Why are you untying it?' just say this, 'The Lord needs it.'"

So those who were sent departed and found it as Jesus had told them. As they were untying the colt, its owners asked them, "Why are you untying the colt?" They said, "The Lord needs it."

Then they brought the colt to Jesus; and after throwing their cloaks on the colt, they set Jesus on it.

As he rode along, people kept spreading their cloaks on the road. As he was now approaching the path down from the Mount of Olives, the whole multitude of the disciples began to praise God joyfully, and with a loud voice, for all the deeds of power that they had seen, saying, "Blessed is the king who comes in the name of the Lord! Peace in heaven, and glory in the highest heaven!"

Some of the Pharisees in the crowd said to him, "Teacher, order your disciples to stop."

Jesus answered, "I tell you, if these were silent, the stones would shout out."—The Gospel of the Lord. ℟. **Praise to you, Lord Jesus Christ.**

After the Gospel, a brief homily may be given. Then, to begin the Procession, an invitation may be given by a

Priest or a Deacon or a lay minister, in these or similar words:

Dear brethren (brothers and sisters),
like the crowds who acclaimed Jesus in Jerusalem,
let us go forth in peace.

OR

Let us go forth in peace.
℟. **In the name of Christ. Amen.**

The Procession to the church where Mass will be celebrated then sets off in the usual way. If incense is used, the thurifer goes first, carrying a thurible with burning incense, then an acolyte or another minister, carrying a cross decorated with palm branches according to local custom, between two ministers with lighted candles. Then follow the Deacon carrying the Book of Gospels, the Priest with the ministers, and, after them, all the faithful carrying branches.

As the Procession moves forward, the following or other suitable chants in honour of Christ the King are sung by the choir and people.

ANTIPHON 1

The children of the Hebrews, carrying olive branches,
went to meet the Lord, crying out and saying:
Hosanna in the highest.

If appropriate, this antiphon is repeated between the strophes (verses) of the following Psalm.

PSALM 23(24)

The LORD's is the earth and its fullness,
the world, and those who dwell in it.
It is he who set it on the seas;
on the rivers he made it firm.

(The antiphon is repeated.)

Who shall climb the mountain of the LORD?
The clean of hands and pure of heart,
whose soul is not set on vain things,
who has not sworn deceitful words.

(The antiphon is repeated.)

Blessings from the LORD shall he receive,
and right reward from the God who saves him.
Such are the people who seek him,
who seek the face of the God of Jacob.

(The antiphon is repeated.)

O gates, lift high your heads;
grow higher, ancient doors.
Let him enter, the king of glory!
Who is this king of glory?
The LORD, the mighty, the valiant;
the LORD, the valiant in war.

(The antiphon is repeated.)

O gates, lift high your heads;
grow higher, ancient doors.
Let him enter, the king of glory!
Who is this king of glory?
He, the LORD of hosts,
he is the king of glory. *(The antiphon is repeated.)*

ANTIPHON 2

The children of the Hebrews spread their
  garments on the road,
crying out and saying: Hosanna to the Son of
  David;
blessed is he who comes in the name of the Lord.

*If appropriate, this antiphon is repeated between the
strophes (verses) of the following Psalm.*

PSALM 46(47)

All peoples, clap your hands.
Cry to God with shouts of joy!
For the LORD, the Most high, is awesome,
the great king over all the earth.

(The antiphon is repeated.)

He humbles peoples under us
and nations under our feet.
Our heritage he chose for us,
the pride of Jacob whom he loves.
God goes up with shouts of joy.
The LORD goes up with trumpet blast.

(The antiphon is repeated.)

Sing praise for God; sing praise!
Sing praise to our king; sing praise!
God is king of all earth.
Sing praise with all your skill.

(The antiphon is repeated.)

God reigns over the nations.
God sits upon his holy throne.
The princes of the peoples are assembled
with the people of the God of Abraham.
The rulers of the earth belong to God,
who is greatly exalted.   *(The antiphon is repeated.)*

Hymn to Christ the King

Chorus:
Glory and honour and praise be to you, Christ,
   King and Redeemer,
to whom young children cried out loving
   Hosannas with joy.

All repeat: **Glory and honour . . .**

Chorus:
Israel's King are you, King David's magnificent offspring;
you are the ruler who come blest in the name of the Lord.

All repeat: **Glory and honour . . .**

Chorus:
Heavenly hosts on high unite in singing your praises;
men and women on earth and all creation join in.

All repeat: **Glory and honour . . .**

Chorus:
Bearing branches of palm, Hebrews came crowding to greet you;
see how with prayers and hymns we come to pay you our vows.

All repeat: **Glory and honour . . .**

Chorus:
They offered gifts of praise to you, so near to your Passion;
see how we sing this song now to you reigning on high.

All repeat: **Glory and honour . . .**

Chorus:
Those you were pleased to accept, now accept our gifts of devotion,
good and merciful King, lover of all that is good.

All repeat: **Glory and honour . . .**

As the procession enters the church, there is sung the following responsory or another chant, which should speak of the Lord's entrance.

RESPONSORY

℟. **As the Lord entered the holy city, the children of the Hebrews proclaimed the resurrection of life. Waving their branches of palm, they cried: Hosanna in the Highest.**

℣. **When the people heard that Jesus was coming to Jerusalem, they went out to meet him. Waving their branches of palm, they cried: Hosanna in the Highest.**

When the Priest arrives at the altar, he venerates it and, if appropriate, incenses it. Then he goes to the chair, where he puts aside the cope, if he has worn one, and puts on the chasuble. Omitting the other Introductory Rites of the Mass and, if appropriate, the Kyrie (Lord, have mercy), *he says the Collect of the Mass, and then continues the Mass in the usual way.*

SECOND FORM: THE SOLEMN ENTRANCE

When a procession outside the church cannot take place, the entrance of the Lord is celebrated inside the church by means of a Solemn Entrance before the principal Mass.

Holding branches in their hands, the faithful gather either outside, in front of the church door, or inside the church itself. The Priest and ministers and a representative group of the faithful go to a suitable place in the church outside the sanctuary, where at least the greater part of the faithful can see the rite.

While the Priest approaches the appointed place, the antiphon Hosanna *or another appropriate chant is sung. Then the blessing of branches and the proclamation of the Gospel of the Lord's entrance into Jerusalem take place as above (pp. 278-279). After the Gospel, the Priest processes solemnly with the ministers and the representative group of the faithful through the church to the sanctuary, while the responsory* As the Lord entered *(above) or another appropriate chant is sung.*

Arriving at the altar, the Priest venerates it. He then goes to the chair and, omitting the Introductory Rites of the Mass and, if appropriate, the Kyrie (Lord, have mercy), *he says the Collect of the Mass, and then continues the Mass in the usual way.*

THIRD FORM: THE SIMPLE ENTRANCE

At all other Masses of this Sunday at which the Solemn Entrance is not held, the memorial of the Lord's entrance into Jerusalem takes place by means of a Simple Entrance.

While the Priest proceeds to the altar, the Entrance Antiphon with its Psalm (below) or another chant on the same theme is sung. Arriving at the altar, the Priest venerates it and goes to the chair. After the Sign of the Cross, he greets the people and continues the Mass in the usual way.

At other Masses, in which singing at the entrance cannot take place, the Priest, as soon as he has arrived at the altar and venerated it, greets the people, reads the Entrance Antiphon, and continues the Mass in the usual way.

ENTRANCE ANTIPHON Cf. Jn. 12.1, 12-13; Ps. 23.9-10

Six days before the Passover, when the Lord came into the city of Jerusalem, the children ran to meet him; in their hands they carried palm branches and with a loud voice cried out: Hosanna in the highest! Blessed are you, who have come in your abundant mercy!

O gates, lift high your heads; grow higher, ancient doors. Let him enter, the king of glory! Who is this king of glory? He, the Lord of hosts, he is the king of glory. Hosanna in the highest! Blessed are you, who have come in your abundant mercy!

AT THE MASS

After the Procession or Solemn Entrance the Priest begins the Mass with the Collect.

COLLECT

Almighty ever-living God,
who as an example of humility for the human race to follow
caused our Saviour to take flesh and submit to the Cross,
graciously grant that we may heed his lesson of patient suffering
and so merit a share in his Resurrection.
Who lives and reigns with you in the unity of the Holy Spirit,
one God, for ever and ever. ℟. **Amen.** ↓

FIRST READING Isa. 50.4-7

The suffering servant was persecuted and struck by his own people; he was spit upon and beaten. He proclaims the true faith and suffers to atone for the sins of his people. Here we see a foreshadowing of the true servant of God.

A reading from the book of the Prophet Isaiah.

THE servant of the Lord said:
"The Lord God has given me the tongue of a teacher,
that I may know how to sustain the weary with a word.
Morning by morning he wakens—
wakens my ear to listen as those who are taught.
The Lord God has opened my ear,
and I was not rebellious,
I did not turn backward.

I gave my back to those who struck me,
and my cheeks to those who pulled out the beard;
I did not hide my face
from insult and spitting.

The Lord God helps me;
therefore I have not been disgraced;
therefore I have set my face like flint,
and I know that I shall not be put to shame."
The word of the Lord. ℟. **Thanks be to God.** ↓

RESPONSORIAL PSALM Ps. 22

John Bouz

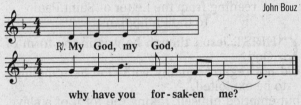

℟. My God, my God, why have you for-sak-en me?

All who see me mock at me;
they make mouths at me, they shake their heads;
"Commit your cause to the Lord; let him deliver;
let him rescue the one in whom he delights!"—℟.

For dogs are all around me;
a company of evildoers encircles me.
My hands and feet have shrivelled;
I can count all my bones.—℟.

They divide my clothes among themselves,
and for my clothing they cast lots.
But you, O Lord, do not be far away!
O my help, come quickly to my aid!—℟.

I will tell of your name to my brothers and sisters;
in the midst of the congregation I will praise you:

You who fear the Lord, praise him!
All you offspring of Jacob, glorify him;
stand in awe of him, all you offspring of Israel!
℟. **My God, my God, why have you forsaken me?** ↓

SECOND READING Phil. 2.6-11

Paul urges us to be humble like Christ. He put off the majesty of his divinity and became man and humbled himself in obedience to an ignominious death on the cross.

A reading from the Letter of Saint Paul
to the Philippians.

CHRIST Jesus, though he was in the form of God,
did not regard equality with God as something
   to be exploited,
but emptied himself, taking the form of a slave,
being born in human likeness.
And being found in human form,
he humbled himself
and became obedient to the point of death—
even death on a cross.

Therefore God highly exalted him
and gave him the name that is above every
   name,
so that at the name of Jesus every knee should
   bend,
in heaven and on earth and under the earth,
and every tongue should confess that Jesus
   Christ is Lord,
to the glory of God the Father.

The word of the Lord. ℟. **Thanks be to God.** ↓

GOSPEL ACCLAMATION Phil. 2.8-9

℣. Praise and honour to you, Lord Jesus Christ!*

℟. **Praise and honour to you, Lord Jesus Christ!**

℣. Christ became obedient for us to death, even death on a Cross.

Therefore God exalted him, and gave him the name above every name.

℟. **Praise and honour to you, Lord Jesus Christ!** ↓

GOSPEL Lk. 22.14—23.56 or 23.1-49

"No one has greater love than this, to lay down one's life for one's friends. You are my friends" (Jn. 15.13-14).

The Passion of the Lord may also be divided into three parts in the traditional manner, the parts being read or sung by three persons. Preferably it is to be proclaimed by a priest or deacons, but in their absence, it may be proclaimed by lectors, the part of Jesus being reserved to a priest.

The Passion begins directly, without introduction.

We participate in the Passion narrative in several ways: by reading it and reflecting on it during the week ahead; by listening with faith as it is proclaimed; by singing acclamations at appropriate places in the text; by respectful posture during the narrative; by reverent silence after the passage about Christ's Death. We do not hold the palms during the reading on Palm Sunday.

Who caused the Death of Jesus? In listening to God's word today, we must remember that our Lord died to save every human person. By our sins we have contributed to his suffering and Death. The authorities of his time bear responsibility for carrying out his execution; this charge must not be laid against all the Jewish people of Jesus' day or of our own. We are all responsible for sin and for our Lord's suffering.

This week we are challenged by the Passion narrative to reflect on the way we are living up to our baptismal promises of dying with Christ to sin and living with him for God.

* See p. 16 for other Gospel Acclamations.

Note: A shorter version (23.1-49) is indicated by asterisks at the beginning and the end (pp. 294-298).

N. THE Passion of our Lord Jesus Christ according to Luke.

AT THE LAST SUPPER

N. WHEN the hour came, Jesus took his place at the table, and the Apostles with him. He said to them, **J.** *"I have eagerly desired to eat this Passover with you before I suffer; for I tell you, I will not eat it until it is fulfilled in the kingdom of God."*

N. Then he took a cup, and after giving thanks he said, **J.** *"Take this and divide it among yourselves; for I tell you that from now on I will not drink of the fruit of the vine until the kingdom of God comes."*

N. Then Jesus took a loaf of bread, and when he had given thanks, he broke it and gave it to them, saying, **J.** *"This is my Body, which is given for you. Do this in remembrance of me."* **N.** And he did the same with the cup after supper, saying, **J.** *"This cup that is poured out for you is the new covenant in my Blood.*

But see, the one who betrays me is with me, and his hand is on the table. For the Son of Man is going as it has been determined, but woe to that one by whom he is betrayed!" **N.** Then they began to ask one another, which one of them it could be who would do this. A dispute also arose among them as to which one of them was to be regarded as the greatest.

But Jesus said to them, **J.** *"The kings of the Gentiles lord it over them; and those in authority over them are called benefactors.*

But not so with you; rather the greatest among you must become like the youngest, and the leader like one who serves. For who is greater, the one who is at the table or the one who serves? Is it not the one at the table? But I am among you as one who serves.

"You are those who have stood by me in my trials; and I confer on you, just as my Father has conferred on me, a kingdom, so that you may eat and drink at my table in my kingdom, and you will sit on thrones judging the twelve tribes of Israel.

Simon, Simon, listen! Satan has demanded to sift all of you like wheat, but I have prayed for you that your own faith may not fail; and you, when once you have turned back, strengthen your brothers." **N.** And Peter said to Jesus, **S. "Lord, I am ready to go with you to prison and to death!"** [**N.** Jesus said,] **J.** *"I tell you, Peter, the cock will not crow this day, until you have denied three times that you know me."*

N. Jesus said to the Apostles, **J.** *"When I sent you out without a purse, bag, or sandals, did you lack anything?"* [**N.** The Apostles said,] **S. "No, not a thing."** [**N.** Jesus said to them,] **J.** *"But now, the one who has a purse must take it, and likewise a bag. And the one who has no sword must sell his cloak and buy one. For I tell you, this Scripture must be fulfilled in me, 'And he was counted among the lawless'; and indeed what is written about me is being fulfilled."*

[**N.** The Apostles said,] **S. "Lord, look, here are two swords."** [**N.** Jesus replied,] **J.** *"It is enough."*

At this point all may join in singing an appropriate acclamation.

JESUS IN THE GARDEN

N. JESUS came out and went, as was his custom, to the Mount of Olives; and the disciples followed him. When he reached the place, he said to his disciples, **J.** *"Pray that you may not come into the time of temptation."*

N. Then Jesus withdrew from them about a stone's throw, knelt down, and prayed, **J.** *"Father, if you are willing, remove this cup from me; yet, not my will but yours be done."*

N. Then an Angel from heaven appeared to Jesus and gave him strength. In his anguish he prayed more earnestly, and his sweat became like great drops of blood falling down on the ground.

When Jesus got up from prayer, he came to the disciples and found them sleeping because of grief, and he said to them, **J.** *"Why are you sleeping? Get up and pray that you may not come into the time of temptation."*

JESUS ARRESTED

N. WHILE Jesus was still speaking, suddenly a crowd came, and the one called Judas, one of the twelve, was leading them. He approached Jesus to kiss him; but Jesus said to him, **J.** *"Judas, is it with a kiss that you are betraying the Son of Man?"*

N. When those who were around Jesus saw what was coming, they asked, **S.** **"Lord, should we strike with the sword?"** **N.** Then one of the disciples struck the slave of the high priest and cut off his right ear. But Jesus said, **J.** *"No more of this!"* **N.** And Jesus touched the slave's ear and healed him.

Then Jesus said to the chief priests, the officers of the temple police, and the elders who had come for him, **J.** *"Have you come out with swords and clubs as if I were a bandit? When I was with you day after day in the temple, you did not lay hands on me. But this is your hour, and the power of darkness!"*

PETER DENIES THE LORD JESUS

N. THEN they seized Jesus and led him away, bringing him into the high priest's house. But Peter was following at a distance.

When they had kindled a fire in the middle of the courtyard and sat down together, Peter sat among them. Then a servant girl, seeing him in the firelight, stared at him and said, **S. "This man also was with him."**

N. But Peter denied it, saying, **S. "Woman, I do not know him."** **N.** A little later someone else, on seeing him, said, **S. "You also are one of them."** **N.** But Peter said, **S. "Man, I am not!"** **N.** Then about an hour later still another kept insisting, **S. "Surely this man also was with him; for he is a Galilean."** **N.** But Peter said, **S. "Man, I do not know what you are talking about!"** **N.** At that moment, while he was still speaking, the cock crowed. The Lord turned and looked at Peter. Then Peter remembered the word of the Lord, how he had said to him, "Before the cock crows today, you will deny me thrèe times." And Peter went out and wept bitterly.

TRIAL IN THE HIGH PRIEST'S HOUSE

N. **N**OW the men who were holding Jesus began to mock him and beat him; they also blindfolded him and kept asking him, **S.** **"Prophesy! Who is it that struck you?"** **N.** They kept heaping many other insults on him.

✻ When day came, the assembly of the elders of the people, both chief priests and scribes, gathered together, and they brought Jesus to their council. They said, **S.** **"If you are the Christ, tell us."** [**N.** Jesus replied,] **J.** *"If I tell you, you will not believe; and if I question you, you will not answer. But from now on the Son of Man will be seated at the right hand of the power of God."* **N.** All of them asked, **S.** **"Are you, then, the Son of God?"** [**N.** Jesus said to them,] *"You say that I am."* [**N.** Then they said,] **S.** **"What further testimony do we need? We have heard it ourselves from his own lips!"**

At this point all may join in singing an appropriate acclamation.

JESUS BEFORE PILATE

N. **T**HEN the assembly rose as a body and brought Jesus before Pilate. They began to accuse him, saying, **S.** **"We found this man perverting our nation, forbidding us to pay taxes to the emperor, and saying that he himself is the Christ, a king."**

N. Then Pilate asked Jesus, **S.** **"Are you the king of the Jews?"** [**N.** He answered,] **J.** *"You say* *so.*" **N.** Then Pilate said to the chief priests and the crowds, **S.** **"I find no basis for an accusation against this man."** **N.** But they were insistent and said, **S.** **"He stirs up the people by teaching throughout all Judea, from Galilee where he began even to this place."** **N.** When Pilate heard this, he asked whether the man was a Galilean. And when he learned that he was under Herod's jurisdiction, he sent him off to Herod, who was himself in Jerusalem at that time.

When Herod saw Jesus, he was very glad, for he had been wanting to see him for a long time, because he had heard about him and was hoping to see Jesus perform some sign. Herod questioned him at some length, but Jesus gave him no answer. The chief priests and the scribes stood by, vehemently accusing him. Even Herod with his soldiers treated him with contempt and mocked him; then he put an elegant robe on him, and sent him back to Pilate. That same day Herod and Pilate became friends with each other; before this they had been enemies.

Pilate then called together the chief priests, the leaders, and the people, and said to them, **S.** **"You brought me this man as one who was perverting the people; and here I have examined him in your presence and have not found this man guilty of any of your charges against him. Neither has Herod, for he sent him back to us. Indeed, he has done nothing to deserve death. I will therefore have him flogged and release him."**

N. Now Pilate was obliged to release someone for them at the festival. Then they all shouted out together, **S. "Away with this fellow! Release Barabbas for us."** **N.** (This was a man who had been put in prison for an insurrection that had taken place in the city, and for murder.) Pilate, wanting to release Jesus, addressed them again; but they kept shouting, **S. "Crucify, crucify him!"** **N.** A third time Pilate said to them, **S. "Why, what evil has he done? I have found in him no ground for the sentence of death; I will therefore have him flogged and then release him."**

N. But they kept urgently demanding with loud shouts that he should be crucified; and their voices prevailed. So Pilate gave his verdict that their demand should be granted. He released the man they asked for, the one who had been put in prison for insurrection and murder, and he handed Jesus over as they wished.

ON THE WAY TO CALVARY

N. AS they led Jesus away, they seized a man, Simon of Cyrene, who was coming from the country, and they laid the Cross on him, and made him carry it behind Jesus.

A great number of the people followed him, and among them were women who were beating their breasts and wailing for him. But Jesus turned to them and said, **J.** *"Daughters of Jerusalem, do not weep for me, but weep for yourselves and for your children. For the days are surely coming when they will say, 'Blessed are the barren, and the wombs that never bore, and the breasts that never nursed.' Then they will begin to say to the*

*mountains, 'Fall on us,' and to the hills, 'Cover us.'
For if they do this when the wood is green, what
will happen when it is dry?"*

*At this point all may join in singing an appropriate ac-
clamation.*

JESUS IS CRUCIFIED AND DIES FOR US

N. TWO others also, who were criminals,
were led away to be put to death with
Jesus. When they came to the place that is
called The Skull, they crucified Jesus there with
the criminals, one on his right and one on his
left.

Then Jesus said, **J.** *"Father, forgive them; for
they do not know what they are doing."* **N.** And
they cast lots to divide his clothing.

And the people stood by, watching; but the
leaders scoffed at him, saying, **S. "He saved
others; let him save himself if he is the Christ of
God, his chosen one!"**

N. The soldiers also mocked Jesus, coming up
and offering him sour wine, and saying, **S. "If
you are the King of the Jews, save yourself!"** N.
There was also an inscription over him, "This is
the King of the Jews."

One of the criminals who were hanged there
kept deriding him and saying, **S. "Are you not
the Christ? Save yourself and us!"** N. But the
other criminal rebuked the first, saying, **S. "Do
you not fear God, since you are under the same
sentence of condemnation? And we indeed have
been condemned justly, for we are getting what
we deserve for our deeds, but this man has done
nothing wrong."** N. Then he said, **S. "Jesus,**

remember me when you come into your kingdom." [N. Jesus replied,] **J.** *"Truly I tell you, today you will be with me in Paradise."*

N. It was now about noon, and darkness came over the whole land until three in the afternoon, while the sun's light failed; and the curtain of the temple was torn in two.

Then Jesus, crying with a loud voice, said, **J.** *"Father, into your hands I commend my spirit."* **N.** Having said this, he breathed his last.

Here all kneel and pause for a short time.

EVENTS AFTER JESUS' DEATH

N. WHEN the centurion saw what had taken place, he praised God and said, **S.** **"Certainly this man was innocent."** **N.** And when all the crowds who had gathered there for this spectacle saw what had taken place, they returned home, beating their breasts.

But all his acquaintances, including the women who had followed him from Galilee, stood at a distance, watching these things.✳

JESUS' BODY IS PLACED IN THE TOMB

N. NOW there was a good and righteous man named Joseph, who, though a member of the council, had not agreed to their plan and action. He came from the Jewish town of Arimathea, and he was waiting expectantly for the kingdom of God. This man went to Pilate and asked for the body of Jesus. Then he took it down, wrapped it in a linen cloth, and laid it in a rock-hewn tomb where no one had ever been laid.

It was the day of Preparation, and the Sabbath was beginning. The women who had come with Jesus from Galilee followed, and they saw the tomb and how his body was laid. Then they returned, and prepared spices and ointments. On the Sabbath these women rested according to the commandment.   → No. 15, p. 18

PRAYER OVER THE OFFERINGS

Through the Passion of your Only Begotten Son, O Lord,
may our reconciliation with you be near at hand,
so that, though we do not merit it by our own deeds,
yet by this sacrifice made once for all,
we may feel already the effects of your mercy.
Through Christ our Lord. ℟. **Amen.** ↓

PREFACE (19)

℣. The Lord be with you. ℟. **And with your spirit.**
℣. Lift up your hearts. ℟. **We lift them up to the Lord.** ℣. Let us give thanks to the Lord our God.
℟. **It is right and just.**

It is truly right and just, our duty and our salvation, always and everywhere to give you thanks,
Lord, holy Father, almighty and eternal God,
through Christ our Lord.

For, though innocent, he suffered willingly for sinners
and accepted unjust condemnation to save the guilty.

His Death has washed away our sins,
and his Resurrection has purchased our
 justification.
And so, with all the Angels,
we praise you, as in joyful celebration we acclaim:
→ No. 23, p. 23

COMMUNION ANTIPHON Mt. 26.42
**Father, if this chalice cannot pass without my
drinking it, your will be done.** ↓

PRAYER AFTER COMMUNION
Nourished with these sacred gifts,
we humbly beseech you, O Lord,
that, just as through the death of your Son
you have brought us to hope for what we believe,
so by his Resurrection
you may lead us to where you call.
Through Christ our Lord.
℟. **Amen.** ↓

*The Deacon or, in his absence, the Priest himself, says
the invitation:* Bow down for the blessing.

PRAYER OVER THE PEOPLE
Look, we pray, O Lord, on this your family,
for whom our Lord Jesus Christ
did not hesitate to be delivered into the hands of
 the wicked
and submit to the agony of the Cross.
Who lives and reigns for ever and ever.
℟. **Amen.** → No. 32, p. 77

——————

"This is my body that is for you.
Do this in remembrance of me."

THE SACRED PASCHAL TRIDUUM

APRIL 18

THURSDAY OF THE LORD'S SUPPER [HOLY THURSDAY]

AT THE EVENING MASS

The Mass of the Lord's Supper is celebrated in the evening, at a convenient time, with the full participation of the whole local community and with all the Priests and ministers exercising their office.

ENTRANCE ANTIPHON Cf. Gal. 6.14

We should glory in the Cross of our Lord Jesus Christ, in whom is our salvation, life and resurrection, through whom we are saved and delivered. → No. 2, p. 10

The Gloria in excelsis (Glory to God in the highest) *is said. While the hymn is being sung, bells are rung, and when it is finished, they remain silent until the* Gloria in excelsis *of the Easter Vigil, unless, if appropriate, the*

Diocesan Bishop has decided otherwise. Likewise, during this same period, the organ and other musical instruments may be used only so as to support the singing.

COLLECT

O God, who have called us to participate
in this most sacred Supper,
in which your Only Begotten Son,
when about to hand himself over to death,
entrusted to the Church a sacrifice new for all
   eternity,
the banquet of his love,
grant, we pray,
that we may draw from so great a mystery,
the fullness of charity and of life.
Through our Lord Jesus Christ, your Son,
who lives and reigns with you in the unity of the
   Holy Spirit,
one God, for ever and ever. ℟. **Amen.** ↓

FIRST READING Ex. 12.1-8, 11-14

**The people are instructed to prepare for the Passover meal.
By the blood of the lamb they are saved from death.**

A reading from the book of Exodus.

THE Lord said to Moses and Aaron in the land
of Egypt: This month shall mark for you the
beginning of months; it shall be the first month of
the year for you. Tell the whole congregation of
Israel that on the tenth of this month they are to
take a lamb for each family, a lamb for each
household. If a household is too small for a whole
lamb, it shall join its closest neighbour in obtaining one; the lamb shall be divided in proportion to
the number of people who eat of it.

Your lamb shall be without blemish, a year-old male; you may take it from the sheep or from the goats. You shall keep it until the fourteenth day of this month; then the whole assembled congregation of Israel shall slaughter it at twilight. They shall take some of the blood and put it on the two doorposts and the lintel of the houses in which they eat it. They shall eat the lamb that same night; they shall eat it roasted over the fire with unleavened bread and bitter herbs.

This is how you shall eat it: your loins girded, your sandals on your feet, and your staff in your hand; and you shall eat it hurriedly. It is the Passover of the Lord. For I will pass through the land of Egypt that night, and I will strike down every firstborn in the land of Egypt, both human beings and animals; on all the gods of Egypt I will execute judgments: I am the Lord. The blood shall be a sign for you on the houses where you live: when I see the blood, I will pass over you, and no plague shall destroy you when I strike the land of Egypt.

This day shall be a day of remembrance for you. You shall celebrate it as a festival to the Lord; throughout your generations you shall observe it as a perpetual ordinance.—The word of the Lord. ℟. **Thanks be to God.** ↓

RESPONSORIAL PSALM Ps. 116

Normand L. Blanchard

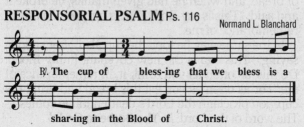

℟. The cup of bless-ing that we bless is a

shar-ing in the Blood of Christ.

What shall I return to the Lord
for all his bounty to me?
I will lift up the cup of salvation
and call on the name of the Lord.

℟. **The cup of blessing that we bless is a sharing
in the Blood of Christ.**

Precious in the sight of the Lord
is the death of his faithful ones.
I am your servant, the son of your serving girl.
You have loosed my bonds.—℟.

I will offer to you a thanksgiving sacrifice
and call on the name of the Lord.
I will pay my vows to the Lord
in the presence of all his people.—℟. ↓

SECOND READING 1 Cor. 11.23-26

Paul recounts the events of the Last Supper which were
handed down to him. The changing of bread and wine
into the body and blood of the Lord proclaims again his
death. It is a sacrificial meal.

A reading from the first Letter of Saint Paul
to the Corinthians.

BROTHERS and sisters: I received from the Lord
what I also handed on to you, that the Lord
Jesus on the night when he was betrayed took a loaf
of bread, and when he had given thanks, he broke it
and said, "This is my Body that is for you. Do this in
remembrance of me."

In the same way he took the cup also, after supper,
saying, "This cup is the new covenant in my Blood.
Do this, as often as you drink it, in remembrance of
me." For as often as you eat this bread and drink the
cup, you proclaim the Lord's death until he comes.—
The word of the Lord. ℟. **Thanks be to God.** ↓

GOSPEL ACCLAMATION Jn. 13.34

℣. Praise to you, Lord Jesus Christ, King of endless glory!*

℟. **Praise to you, Lord Jesus Christ, King of endless glory!**

℣. I give you a new commandment:
love one another as I have loved you.

℟. **Praise to you, Lord Jesus Christ, King of endless glory!** ↓

GOSPEL Jn. 13.1-15

Jesus washes the feet of his disciples to prove to them
his sincere love and great humility which they should
imitate.

℣. The Lord be with you. ℟. **And with your spirit.**
✚ A reading from the holy Gospel according to
John. ℟. **Glory to you, O Lord.**

BEFORE the festival of the Passover, Jesus knew
that his hour had come to depart from this
world and go to the Father. Having loved his own
who were in the world, he loved them to the end.

The devil had already put it into the heart of
Judas, son of Simon Iscariot, to betray him. And
during supper Jesus, knowing that the Father
had given all things into his hands, and that he
had come from God and was going to God, got
up from the table, took off his outer robe, and
tied a towel around himself. Then he poured
water into a basin and began to wash the disciples' feet and to wipe them with the towel that
was tied around him.

See p. 16 for other Gospel Acclamations.

He came to Simon Peter, who said to him, "Lord, are you going to wash my feet?" Jesus answered, "You do not know now what I am doing, but later you will understand." Peter said to him, "You will never wash my feet." Jesus answered, "Unless I wash you, you have no share with me." Simon Peter said to him, "Lord, not my feet only but also my hands and my head!" Jesus said to him, "One who has bathed does not need to wash, except for the feet, but is entirely clean. And you are clean, though not all of you." For he knew who was to betray him; for this reason he said, "Not all of you are clean."

After he had washed their feet, put on his robe, and returned to the table, Jesus said to them, "Do you know what I have done to you? You call me Teacher and Lord—and you are right, for that is what I am. So if I, your Lord and Teacher, have washed your feet, you also ought to wash one another's feet. For I have set you an example, that you also should do as I have done to you."—The Gospel of the Lord. ℟. **Praise to you, Lord Jesus Christ.**

After the proclamation of the Gospel, the Priest gives a homily in which light is shed on the principal mysteries that are commemorated in this Mass, namely, the institution of the Holy Eucharist and of the priestly Order, and the commandment of the Lord concerning fraternal charity.

The Washing of Feet

After the Homily, where a pastoral reason suggests it, the Washing of Feet follows.

Those who are chosen from amongst the people of God are led by the ministers to seats prepared in a suitable place.

Then the Priest (removing his chasuble if necessary) goes to each one, and, with the help of the ministers, pours water over each one's feet and then dries them.

Meanwhile some of the following antiphons or other appropriate chants are sung.

ANTIPHON 1 Cf. Jn. 13.4, 5, 15

**After the Lord had risen from supper,
he poured water into a basin
and began to wash the feet of his disciples:
he left them this example.**

ANTIPHON 2 Cf. Jn. 13.12, 13, 15

**The Lord Jesus, after eating supper with his disciples,
washed their feet and said to them:
Do you know what I, your Lord and Master, have done for you?
I have given you an example, that you should do likewise.**

ANTIPHON 3 Cf. Jn. 13.6, 7, 8

**Lord, are you to wash my feet? Jesus said to him in answer:
If I do not wash your feet, you will have no share with me.**

℣. **So he came to Simon Peter and Peter said to him:**
—**Lord ...**

℣. **What I am doing, you do not know for now,
but later you will come to know.**
—**Lord ...**

ANTIPHON 4 Jn. 13.14

If I, your Lord and Master, have washed your feet, how much more should you wash each other's feet?

ANTIPHON 5 Jn. 13.35

This is how all will know that you are my disciples:
if you have love for one another.

℣. Jesus said to his disciples:
—This is how …

ANTIPHON 6 Jn. 13.34

I give you a new commandment,
that you love one another
as I have loved you, says the Lord.

ANTIPHON 7 1 Cor. 13.13

Let faith, hope and charity, these three, remain among you,
but the greatest of these is charity.

℣. Now faith, hope and charity, these three, remain;
but the greatest of these is charity.
—Let …

After the Washing of Feet, the Priest washes and dries his hands, puts the chasuble back on, and returns to the chair, and from there he directs the Universal Prayer.

The Creed is not said.

The Liturgy of the Eucharist

At the beginning of the Liturgy of the Eucharist, there may be a procession of the faithful in which gifts for the poor may be presented with the bread and wine.

Meanwhile the following, or another appropriate chant, is sung.

Ant. **Where true charity is dwelling, God is present there.**

℣. **By the love of Christ we have been brought together:**

℣. **let us find in him our gladness and our pleasure;**

℣. **may we love him and revere him, God the living,**

℣. **and in love respect each other with sincere hearts.**

Ant. **Where true charity is dwelling, God is present there.**

℣. **So when we as one are gathered all together,**

℣. **let us strive to keep our minds free of division;**

℣. **may there be an end to malice, strife and quarrels,**

℣. **and let Christ our God be dwelling here among us.**

Ant. **Where true charity is dwelling, God is present there.**

℣. **May your face thus be our vision, bright in glory,**

℣. **Christ our God, with all the blessed Saints in heaven:**

℣. **such delight is pure and faultless, joy unbounded,**

℣. **which endures through countless ages world without end. Amen.**   → No. 17, p. 20

PRAYER OVER THE OFFERINGS

Grant us, O Lord, we pray,
that we may participate worthily in these
   mysteries,
for whenever the memorial of this sacrifice is
   celebrated
the work of our redemption is accomplished.
Through Christ our Lord.
℞. **Amen.**   → No. 21, p. 22 (Pref. 47)

*When the Roman Canon is used, this special form of it is
said, with proper formulas for the* Communicantes *(In
communion with those),* Hanc igitur *(Therefore,
Lord, we pray), and* Qui pridie *(On the day before he
was to suffer).*

To you, therefore, most merciful Father,
we make humble prayer and petition
through Jesus Christ, your Son, our Lord:
that you accept
and bless ✛ these gifts, these offerings,
these holy and unblemished sacrifices,
which we offer you firstly
for your holy catholic Church.
Be pleased to grant her peace,
to guard, unite and govern her
throughout the whole world,
together with your servant N. our Pope
and N. our Bishop,
and all those who, holding to the truth,
hand on the catholic and apostolic faith.

Remember, Lord, your servants N. and N.
and all gathered here,
whose faith and devotion are known to you.
For them we offer you this sacrifice of praise
or they offer it for themselves

and all who are dear to them:
for the redemption of their souls,
in hope of health and well-being,
and paying their homage to you,
the eternal God, living and true.

Celebrating the most sacred day
on which our Lord Jesus Christ
was handed over for our sake,
and in communion with those whose memory we
    venerate,
especially the glorious ever-Virgin Mary,
Mother of our God and Lord, Jesus Christ,
and † blessed Joseph, her Spouse,
your blessed Apostles and Martyrs
Peter and Paul, Andrew,
(James, John,
Thomas, James, Philip,
Bartholomew, Matthew, Simon and Jude;
Linus, Cletus, Clement, Sixtus,
Cornelius, Cyprian,
Lawrence, Chrysogonus,
John and Paul,
Cosmas and Damian)
and all your Saints;
we ask that through their merits and prayers,
in all things we may be defended
by your protecting help.
(Through Christ our Lord. Amen.)

Therefore, Lord, we pray:
graciously accept this oblation of our service,
that of your whole family,
which we make to you
as we observe the day
on which our Lord Jesus Christ
handed on the mysteries of his Body and Blood
for his disciples to celebrate;

order our days in your peace,
and command that we be delivered from eternal damnation
and counted among the flock of those you have chosen.
(Through Christ our Lord. Amen.)

Be pleased, O God, we pray,
to bless, acknowledge,
and approve this offering in every respect;
make it spiritual and acceptable,
so that it may become for us
the Body and Blood of your most beloved Son,
our Lord Jesus Christ.

On the day before he was to suffer
for our salvation and the salvation of all,
that is today,
he took bread in his holy and venerable hands,
and with eyes raised to heaven
to you, O God, his almighty Father,
giving you thanks, he said the blessing,
broke the bread
and gave it to his disciples, saying:

Take this, all of you, and eat of it,
for this is my Body,
which will be given up for you.

In a similar way, when supper was ended,
he took this precious chalice
in his holy and venerable hands,
and once more giving you thanks, he said the blessing
and gave the chalice to his disciples, saying:

Take this, all of you, and drink from it,
for this is the chalice of my Blood,
the Blood of the new and eternal covenant,
which will be poured out for you and for many
for the forgiveness of sins.

Do this in memory of me.

The rest follows the Roman Canon, pp. 26-29.

COMMUNION ANTIPHON 1 Cor. 11.24-25

This is the Body that will be given up for you; this is the Chalice of the new covenant in my Blood, says the Lord; do this, whenever you receive it, in memory of me. ↓

After the distribution of Communion, a ciborium with hosts for Communion on the following day is left on the altar. The Priest, standing at the chair, says the Prayer after Communion.

PRAYER AFTER COMMUNION

Grant, almighty God,
that, just as we are renewed
by the Supper of your Son in this present age,
so we may enjoy his banquet for all eternity.
Who lives and reigns for ever and ever. ℟. **Amen.**

The Transfer of the Most Blessed Sacrament

After the Prayer after Communion, the Priest puts incense in the thurible while standing, blesses it and then, kneeling, incenses the Blessed Sacrament three times. Then, having put on a white humeral veil, he rises, takes the ciborium, and covers it with the ends of the veil.

A procession is formed in which the Blessed Sacrament, accompanied by torches and incense, is carried through the church to a place of repose prepared in a part of the church or in a chapel suitably decorated. A lay minister with a cross, standing between two other ministers with lighted candles leads off. Others carrying lighted candles follow. Before the Priest carrying the Blessed Sacrament comes the thurifer with a smoking thurible. Meanwhile, the hymn Pange, lingua *(exclusive of the last two stanzas) or another eucharistic chant is sung.*

When the procession reaches the place of repose, the Priest, with the help of the Deacon if necessary, places the ciborium in the tabernacle, the door of which remains open. Then he puts incense in the thurible and, kneeling, incenses the Blessed Sacrament, while Tantum ergo Sacramentum *or another eucharistic chant is sung. Then the Deacon or the Priest himself places the Sacrament in the tabernacle and closes the door.*

After a period of adoration in silence, the Priest and ministers genuflect and return to the sacristy.

At an appropriate time, the altar is stripped and, if possible, the crosses are removed from the church. It is expedient that any crosses which remain in the church be veiled.

"He bowed his head and gave up his spirit."

APRIL 19

FRIDAY OF THE PASSION OF THE LORD [GOOD FRIDAY]

THE CELEBRATION OF THE PASSION OF THE LORD

This week, on Good Friday and Holy Saturday, the people of God are called to observe a solemn paschal fast. In this way, they are in union with the Christians of every century, and will be ready to receive the joys of the Lord's Resurrection with uplifted and responsive hearts.

The Priest and the Deacon, if a Deacon is present, wearing red vestments as for Mass, go to the altar in silence and, after making a reverence to the altar, prostrate themselves or, if appropriate, kneel and pray in silence for a while. All others kneel.

Then the Priest, with the ministers, goes to the chair where, facing the people, who are standing, he says, with hands extended, one of the following prayers, omitting the invitation Let us pray.

PRAYER

Remember your mercies, O Lord,
and with your eternal protection sanctify your
 servants,

for whom Christ your Son,
by the shedding of his Blood,
established the Paschal Mystery.
Who lives and reigns for ever and ever. ℟. **Amen.**

OR

O God, who by the Passion of Christ your Son,
    our Lord,
abolished the death inherited from ancient sin
by every succeeding generation,
grant that just as, being conformed to him,
we have borne by the law of nature
the image of the man of earth,
so by the sanctification of grace
we may bear the image of the Man of heaven.
Through Christ our Lord. ℟. **Amen.**

FIRST PART: THE LITURGY OF THE WORD

FIRST READING Isa. 52.13—53.12

> **The suffering servant shall be raised up and exalted. The doctrine of expiatory suffering finds supreme expression in these words.**

A reading from the book of the Prophet Isaiah.

SEE, my servant shall prosper;
he shall be exalted and lifted up,
and shall be very high.

Just as there were many who were astonished at
    him
—so marred was his appearance, beyond human
    semblance,
and his form beyond that of the sons of man—
so he shall startle many nations;
kings shall shut their mouths because of him;

for that which had not been told them they shall
see,
and that which they had not heard they shall contemplate.
Who has believed what we have heard?
And to whom has the arm of the Lord been revealed?

For he grew up before the Lord like a young plant,
and like a root out of dry ground;
he had no form or majesty that we should look at
him,
nothing in his appearance that we should desire
him.
He was despised and rejected by men;
a man of suffering and acquainted with infirmity;
and as one from whom others hide their faces
he was despised,
and we held him of no account.

Surely he has borne our infirmities and carried
our diseases;
yet we accounted him stricken,
struck down by God, and afflicted.
But he was wounded for our transgressions,
crushed for our iniquities;
upon him was the punishment that made us
whole,
and by his bruises we are healed.

All we like sheep have gone astray;
each has turned to their own way
and the Lord has laid on him
the iniquity of us all.

He was oppressed, and he was afflicted,
yet he did not open his mouth;

like a lamb that is led to the slaughter,
and like a sheep that before its shearers is silent,
so he did not open his mouth.

By a perversion of justice he was taken away.
Who could have imagined his future?
For he was cut off from the land of the living,
stricken for the transgression of my people.
They made his grave with the wicked
and his tomb with the rich,
although he had done no violence,
and there was no deceit in his mouth.

Yet it was the will of the Lord to crush him with
   pain.
When you make his life an offering for sin,
he shall see his offspring, and shall prolong his
   days;
through him the will of the Lord shall prosper.
Out of his anguish he shall see light;
he shall find satisfaction through his knowledge.
The righteous one, my servant, shall make many
   righteous,
and he shall bear their iniquities.

Therefore I will allot him a portion with the great,
and he shall divide the spoil with the strong;
because he poured out himself to death,
and was numbered with the transgressors;
yet he bore the sin of many,
and made intercession for the transgressors.

The word of the Lord. ℟. **Thanks be to God.** ↓

RESPONSORIAL PSALM Ps. 31

Geoffrey Angeles

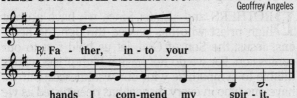

℟. Fa - ther, in - to your hands I com-mend my spir - it.

In you, O Lord, I seek refuge;
do not let me ever be put to shame;
in your righteousness deliver me.
Into your hand I commit my spirit;
you have redeemed me,
O Lord, faithful God.—℟.

I am the scorn of all my adversaries,
a horror to my neighbours,
an object of dread to my acquaintances.
Those who see me in the street flee from me.
I have passed out of mind like one who is dead;
I have become like a broken vessel.—℟.

But I trust in you, O Lord;
I say, "You are my God."
My times are in your hand;
deliver me from the hand of my enemies and
    persecutors.—℟.

Let your face shine upon your servant;
save me in your steadfast love.
Be strong, and let your heart take courage,
all you who wait for the Lord.—℟. ↓

SECOND READING Heb. 4.14-16; 5.7-9

The theme of the compassionate high priest appears
again in this passage. In him Christians can approach
God confidently and without fear.

A reading from the Letter to the Hebrews.

BROTHERS and sisters: Since we have a great high priest who has passed through the heavens, Jesus, the Son of God, let us hold fast to our confession. For we do not have a high priest who is unable to sympathize with our weaknesses, but we have one who in every respect has been tested as we are, yet without sin. Let us therefore approach the throne of grace with boldness, so that we may receive mercy and find grace to help in time of need.

In the days of his flesh, Jesus offered up prayers and supplications, with loud cries and tears, to the one who was able to save him from death, and he was heard because of his reverent submission. Although he was a Son, he learned obedience through what he suffered; and having been made perfect, he became the source of eternal salvation for all who obey him.—The word of the Lord. ℟. **Thanks be to God.** ↓

GOSPEL ACCLAMATION Phil. 2.8-9

℣. Praise and honour to you, Lord Jesus Christ!*
℟. **Praise and honour to you, Lord Jesus Christ!**
℣. Christ became obedient for us to death, even death on a Cross.
Therefore God exalted him and gave him the name above every name.
℟. **Praise and honour to you, Lord Jesus Christ!** ↓

GOSPEL Jn. 18.1—19.42
*The Passion is read in the same way as on the preceding Sunday. The narrator is noted by **N**., the words of Jesus by a **J**. and the words of others by **S**.*

*See p. 16 for other Gospel Acclamations.

It is important for us to understand the meaning of Christ's sufferings today. See the note on p. 289.

The beginning scene is Christ's agony in the garden. Our Lord knows what is to happen. The Scriptures recount the betrayal, the trial, the condemnation, and the crucifixion of Jesus.

N. THE Passion of our Lord Jesus Christ according to John.

JESUS IS ARRESTED

N. AFTER they had eaten the supper, Jesus went out with his disciples across the Kidron valley to a place where there was a garden, which he and his disciples entered. Now Judas, who betrayed him, also knew the place, because Jesus often met there with his disciples. So Judas brought a detachment of soldiers together with police from the chief priests and the Pharisees, and they came there with lanterns and torches and weapons.

Then Jesus, knowing all that was to happen to him, came forward and asked them, **J.** *"Whom are you looking for?"* **N.** They answered, **S. "Jesus of Nazareth."** [**N.** Jesus replied,] **J.** *"I am he."* **N.** Judas, who betrayed him, was standing with them. When Jesus said to them, "I am he," they stepped back and fell to the ground. Again he asked them, **J.** *"Whom are you looking for?"* [**N.** And they said,] **S. "Jesus of Nazareth."** [**N.** Jesus answered,] **J.** *"I told you that I am he. So if you are looking for me, let these men go."* **N.** This was to fulfill the word that he had spoken, "I did not lose a single one of those whom you gave me."

Then Simon Peter, who had a sword, drew it, struck the high priest's slave, and cut off his right ear. The slave's name was Malchus. Jesus said to Peter, **J.** *"Put your sword back into its sheath. Am I not to drink the cup that the Father has given me?"*

TRIAL BEFORE ANNAS

N. **S**O the soldiers, their officer, and the Jewish police arrested Jesus and bound him. First they took him to Annas, who was the father-in-law of Caiaphas, the high priest that year. Caiaphas was the one who had advised the Jews that it was better to have one person die for the people.

Simon Peter and another disciple followed Jesus. Since that disciple was known to the high priest, he went with Jesus into the courtyard of the high priest, but Peter was standing outside at the gate. So the other disciple, who was known to the high priest, went out, spoke to the woman who guarded the gate, and brought Peter in. The woman said to Peter, **S.** **"You are not also one of this man's disciples, are you?"** **N.** Peter said, **S.** **"I am not."** **N.** Now the slaves and the police had made a charcoal fire because it was cold, and they were standing around it and warming themselves. Peter also was standing with them and warming himself.

Then the high priest questioned Jesus about his disciples and about his teaching. Jesus answered, **J.** *"I have spoken openly to the world; I have always taught in synagogues and in the temple, where all the Jews come together. I have* *said nothing in secret. Why do you ask me? Ask those who heard what I said to them; they know what I said."*

N. When he had said this, one of the police standing nearby struck Jesus on the face, saying, **S.** **"Is that how you answer the high priest?"** [**N.** Jesus answered,] **J.** *"If I have spoken wrongly, testify to the wrong. But if I have spoken rightly, why do you strike me?"* **N.** Then Annas sent him bound to Caiaphas the high priest.

PETER DENIES THE LORD JESUS

N. NOW Simon Peter was standing and warming himself. They asked him, **S.** **"You are not also one of his disciples, are you?"** **N.** He denied it and said, **S.** **"I am not."** **N.** One of the slaves of the high priest, a relative of the man whose ear Peter had cut off, asked, **S.** **"Did I not see you in the garden with him?"** **N.** Again Peter denied it, and at that moment the cock crowed.

At this point all may join in singing an acclamation.

TRIAL BEFORE PILATE

N. THEN they took Jesus from Caiaphas to Pilate's headquarters. It was early in the morning. They themselves did not enter the headquarters, so as to avoid ritual defilement and to be able to eat the Passover. So Pilate went out to them and said, **S.** **"What accusation do you bring against this man?"** **N.** They answered, **S.** **"If this man were not a criminal, we**

would not have handed him over to you." N.
Pilate said to them, S. **"Take him yourselves and
judge him according to your law."** N. They
replied, S. **"We are not permitted to put anyone
to death."** N. (This was to fulfill what Jesus had
said when he indicated the kind of death he was
to die.)

Then Pilate entered the headquarters again,
summoned Jesus, and asked him, S. **"Are you the
King of the Jews?"** [N. Jesus answered,] J. *"Do
you ask this on your own, or did others tell you
about me?"* [N. Pilate replied,] S. **"I am not a Jew,
am I? Your own nation and the chief priests have
handed you over to me. What have you done?"**
[N. Jesus answered,] J. *"My kingdom is not from
this world. If my kingdom were from this world,
my followers would be fighting to keep me from
being handed over to the Jews. But as it is, my
kingdom is not from here."* [N. Pilate asked him,]
S. **"So you are a king?"** [N. Jesus answered,] J.
*"You say that I am a king. For this I was born,
and for this I came into the world, to testify to
the truth. Everyone who belongs to the truth listens to my voice."* [N. Pilate asked him,] S. **"What
is truth?"**

N. After he had said this, Pilate went out to
the Jews again and told them, S. **"I find no case
against him. But you have a custom that I release someone for you at the Passover. Do you
want me to release for you the King of the
Jews?"** N. They shouted in reply, S. **"Not this
man, but Barabbas!"** N. Now Barabbas was a
bandit.

Then Pilate took Jesus and had him flogged. And the soldiers wove a crown of thorns and put it on his head, and they dressed him in a purple robe. They kept coming up to him, saying, **S.** **"Hail, King of the Jews!"** **N.** and they struck him on the face.

Pilate went out again and said to them, **S.** **"Look, I am bringing him out to you to let you know that I find no case against him."** **N.** So Jesus came out, wearing the crown of thorns and the purple robe. Pilate said to them, **S.** **"Here is the man!"**

N. When the chief priests and the police saw him, they shouted, **S.** **"Crucify him! Crucify him!"** **N.** Pilate said to them, **S.** **"Take him yourselves and crucify him; I find no case against him."** **N.** They answered him, **S.** **"We have a law, and according to that law he ought to die because he has claimed to be the Son of God."**

N. Now when Pilate heard this, he was more afraid than ever. He entered his headquarters again and asked Jesus, **S.** **"Where are you from?"** **N.** But Jesus gave him no answer. Pilate therefore said to him, **S.** **"Do you refuse to speak to me? Do you not know that I have power to release you, and power to crucify you?"** [**N.** Jesus answered him,] **J.** *"You would have no power over me unless it had been given you from above; therefore the one who handed me over to you is guilty of a greater sin."* **N.** From then on Pilate tried to release him, but the Jews cried out, **S.** **"If you release this man, you are no friend of the emperor. Everyone who**

claims to be a king sets himself against the emperor." **N.** When Pilate heard these words, he brought Jesus outside and sat on the judge's bench at a place called "The Stone Pavement," or in Hebrew "Gabbatha."

Now it was the day of Preparation for the Passover; and it was about noon. Pilate said to the Jews, **S. "Here is your King!" N.** They cried out, **S. "Away with him! Away with him! Crucify him!" N.** Pilate asked them, **S. "Shall I crucify your King?" N.** The chief priests answered, **S. "We have no king but the emperor." N.** Then Pilate handed Jesus over to them to be crucified.

At this point all may join in singing an appropriate acclamation.

JESUS IS CRUCIFIED AND DIES FOR US

N. So they took Jesus; and carrying the Cross by himself, he went out to what is called The Place of the Skull, which in Hebrew is called Golgotha. There they crucified him, and with him two others, one on either side, with Jesus between them.

Pilate also had an inscription written and put on the Cross. It read, "Jesus of Nazareth, the King of the Jews." Many of the people read this inscription, because the place where Jesus was crucified was near the city; and it was written in Hebrew, in Latin, and in Greek. Then the chief priests of the Jews said to Pilate, **S. "Do not write, 'The King of the Jews,' but, 'This man said, I am King of the Jews.'" N.** Pilate answered, **S. "What I have written I have written."**

N. When the soldiers had crucified Jesus, they took his clothes and divided them into four parts, one for each soldier. They also took his tunic; now the tunic was seamless, woven in one piece from the top. So they said to one another, **S. "Let us not tear it, but cast lots for it to see who will get it." N.** This was to fulfill what the Scripture says,

"They divided my clothes among themselves, and for my clothing they cast lots."

And that is what the soldiers did.

Meanwhile, standing near the Cross of Jesus were his mother, and his mother's sister, Mary the wife of Clopas, and Mary Magdalene. When Jesus saw his mother and the disciple whom he loved standing beside her, he said to his mother, **J.** *"Woman, here is your son." ***N.** Then he said to the disciple, **J.** *"Here is your mother." ***N.** And from that hour the disciple took her into his own home.

After this, when Jesus knew that all was now finished, in order to fulfill the Scripture, he said, **J.** *"I am thirsty." ***N.** A jar full of sour wine was standing there. So they put a sponge full of the wine on a branch of hyssop and held it to his mouth. When Jesus had received the wine, he said, **J.** *"It is finished." ***N.** Then he bowed his head and gave up his spirit.

Here all kneel and pause for a short time.

EVENTS AFTER JESUS' DEATH

N. SINCE it was the day of Preparation, the Jews did not want the bodies left on the cross during the Sabbath, especially because that Sabbath was a day of great Solemnity. So they asked Pilate to have the legs of the crucified men broken and the bodies removed.

Then the soldiers came and broke the legs of the first and of the other who had been crucified with him. But when they came to Jesus and saw that he was already dead, they did not break his legs. Instead, one of the soldiers pierced his side with a spear, and at once blood and water came out.

(He who saw this has testified so that you also may believe. His testimony is true, and he knows that he tells the truth.) These things occurred so that the Scripture might be fulfilled, "None of his bones shall be broken." And again another passage of Scripture says, "They will look on the one whom they have pierced."

JESUS' BODY IS PLACED IN THE TOMB

N. **A**FTER these things, Joseph of Arimathea, who was a disciple of Jesus, though a secret one because of his fear of the Jews, asked Pilate to let him take away the body of Jesus. Pilate gave him permission; so he came and removed his body.

Nicodemus, who had at first come to Jesus by night, also came, bringing a mixture of myrrh and aloes, weighing about a hundredweight. They took the body of Jesus and wrapped it with the spices in linen cloths, according to the burial custom of the Jews. Now there was a garden in the place where he was crucified, and in the garden there was a new tomb in which no one had ever been laid. And so, because it was the Jewish day of Preparation, and the tomb was nearby, they laid Jesus there.

After the reading of the Lord's Passion, the Priest gives a brief homily and, at its end, the faithful may be invited to spend a short time in prayer.

THE SOLEMN INTERCESSIONS

The Liturgy of the Word concludes with the Solemn Intercessions, which take place in this way: the Deacon, if a Deacon is present, or if he is not, a lay minister, stands at the ambo, and sings or says the invitation in which the intention is expressed. Then all pray in silence for a while, and afterwards the Priest, standing at the chair or, if appropriate, at the altar, with hands extended, sings or says the prayer.

The faithful may remain either kneeling or standing throughout the entire period of the prayers.

Before the Priest's prayer, in accord with tradition, it is permissible to use the Deacon's invitations Let us kneel — Let us stand, *with all kneeling for silent prayer.*

I. For Holy Church

Let us pray, dearly beloved, for the holy Church of God,
that our God and Lord be pleased to give her peace,
to guard her and to unite her throughout the whole world
and grant that, leading our life in tranquillity and quiet,
we may glorify God the Father almighty.

Prayer in silence. Then the Priest says:

Almighty ever-living God,
who in Christ revealed your glory to all the
  nations,
watch over the works of your mercy,
that your Church, spread throughout all the
  world,
may persevere with steadfast faith in confessing
  your name.
Through Christ our Lord.
℟. **Amen.**

II. For the Pope

Let us pray also for our most Holy Father Pope N.,
that our God and Lord,
who chose him for the Order of Bishops,
may keep him safe and unharmed for the Lord's
  holy Church,
to govern the holy People of God.

Prayer in silence. Then the Priest says:

Almighty ever-living God,
by whose decree all things are founded,
look with favour on our prayers
and in your kindness protect the Pope chosen for us,
that, under him, the Christian people,
governed by you their maker,
may grow in merit by reason of their faith.
Through Christ our Lord.
℟. **Amen.**

III. For all orders and degrees of the faithful

Let us pray also for our Bishop N.,
for all Bishops, Priests, and Deacons of the Church
and for the whole of the faithful people.

Prayer in silence. Then the Priest says:

Almighty ever-living God,
by whose Spirit the whole body of the Church
is sanctified and governed,
hear our humble prayer for your ministers,
that, by the gift of your grace,
all may serve you faithfully.
Through Christ our Lord.
℟. **Amen.**

IV. For catechumens

Let us pray also for (our) catechumens,
that our God and Lord
may open wide the ears of their inmost hearts
and unlock the gates of his mercy,
that, having received forgiveness of all their sins
through the waters of rebirth,
they, too, may be one with Christ Jesus our Lord.

Prayer in silence. Then the Priest says:

Almighty ever-living God,
who make your Church ever fruitful with new
    offspring,
increase the faith and understanding of (our)
    catechumens,
that, reborn in the font of Baptism,
they may be added to the number of your adopted
    children.
Through Christ our Lord.
℟. **Amen.**

V. For the unity of Christians

Let us pray also for all our brothers and sisters
    who believe in Christ,

that our God and Lord may be pleased,
as they live the truth,
to gather them together and keep them in his one
   Church.

Prayer in silence. Then the Priest says:

Almighty ever-living God,
who gather what is scattered
and keep together what you have gathered,
look kindly on the flock of your Son,
that those whom one Baptism has consecrated
may be joined together by integrity of faith
and united in the bond of charity.
Through Christ our Lord.
℞. **Amen.**

VI. For the Jewish people

Let us pray also for the Jewish people,
to whom the Lord our God spoke first,
that he may grant them to advance in love of his
   name
and in faithfulness to his covenant.

Prayer in silence. Then the Priest says:

Almighty ever-living God,
who bestowed your promises on Abraham and
   his descendants,
graciously hear the prayers of your Church,
that the people you first made your own
may attain the fullness of redemption.
Through Christ our Lord.
℞. **Amen.**

VII. For those who do not believe in Christ

Let us pray also for those who do not believe in
    Christ,
that, enlightened by the Holy Spirit,
they, too, may enter on the way of salvation.

Prayer in silence. Then the Priest says:

Almighty ever-living God,
grant to those who do not confess Christ
that, by walking before you with a sincere heart,
they may find the truth
and that we ourselves, being constant in mutual
    love
and striving to understand more fully the mystery
    of your life,
may be made more perfect witnesses to your love
    in the world.
Through Christ our Lord.
℟. **Amen.**

VIII. For those who do not believe in God

Let us pray also for those who do not acknowledge
    God,
that, following what is right in sincerity of heart,
they may find the way to God himself.

Prayer in silence. Then the Priest says:

Almighty ever-living God,
who created all people
to seek you always by desiring you
and, by finding you, come to rest,
grant, we pray,
that, despite every harmful obstacle,
all may recognize the signs of your fatherly love

and the witness of the good works
done by those who believe in you,
and so in gladness confess you,
the one true God and Father of our human race.
Through Christ our Lord.
℟. **Amen.**

IX. For those in public office

Let us pray also for those in public office,
that our God and Lord
may direct their minds and hearts according to
    his will
for the true peace and freedom of all.

Prayer in silence. Then the Priest says:

Almighty ever-living God,
in whose hand lies every human heart
and the rights of peoples,
look with favour, we pray,
on those who govern with authority over us,
that throughout the whole world,
the prosperity of peoples,
the assurance of peace,
and freedom of religion
may through your gift be made secure.
Through Christ our Lord.
℟. **Amen.**

X. For those in tribulation

Let us pray, dearly beloved,
to God the Father almighty,
that he may cleanse the world of all errors,
banish disease, drive out hunger,
unlock prisons, loosen fetters,

granting to travellers safety, to pilgrims return,
health to the sick, and salvation to the dying.

Prayer in silence. Then the Priest says:

Almighty ever-living God,
comfort of mourners, strength of all who toil,
may the prayers of those who cry out in any
   tribulation
come before you,
that all may rejoice,
because in their hour of need
your mercy was at hand.
Through Christ our Lord.
℟. **Amen.**

SECOND PART: THE ADORATION OF THE HOLY CROSS

*After the Solemn Intercessions, the solemn Adoration of
the Holy Cross takes place. Of the two forms of the
showing of the Cross presented here, the more appropriate one, according to pastoral needs, should be chosen.*

The Showing of the Holy Cross

First Form

*The Deacon accompanied by ministers, or another suit-
able minister, goes to the sacristy, from which, in procession, accompanied by two ministers with lighted candles,
he carries the Cross, covered with a violet veil, through
the church to the middle of the sanctuary.*

*The Priest, standing before the altar and facing the peo-
ple, receives the Cross, uncovers a little of its upper part
and elevates it while beginning the* Ecce lignum Crucis
(Behold the wood of the Cross). *He is assisted in
singing by the Deacon or, if need be, by the choir. All respond,* Come, let us adore. *At the end of the singing, all
kneel and for a brief moment adore in silence, while the
Priest stands and holds the Cross raised.*

℣. Behold the wood of the Cross,
on which hung the salvation of the world.

℟. Come, let us a-dore.

Then the Priest uncovers the right arm of the Cross and again, raising up the Cross, begins, Behold the wood of the Cross *and everything takes place as above.*

Finally, he uncovers the Cross entirely and, raising it up, he begins the invitation Behold the wood of the Cross *a third time and everything takes place like the first time.*

Second Form

The Priest or the Deacon accompanied by ministers, or another suitable minister, goes to the door of the church, where he receives the unveiled Cross, and the ministers take lighted candles; then the procession sets off through the church to the sanctuary. Near the door, in the middle of the church and before the entrance of the sanctuary, the one who carries the Cross elevates it, singing, Behold the wood of the Cross, *to which all respond,* Come, let us adore. *After each response all kneel and for a brief moment adore in silence, as above.*

The Adoration of the Holy Cross

Then, accompanied by two ministers with lighted candles, the Priest or the Deacon carries the Cross to the entrance of the sanctuary or to another suitable place and there puts it down or hands it over to the ministers to hold. Candles are placed on the right and left sides of the Cross.

For the Adoration of the Cross, first the Priest Celebrant alone approaches, with the chasuble and his shoes removed, if appropriate. Then the clergy, the lay ministers, and the faithful approach, moving as if in procession, and showing reverence to the Cross by a simple genuflection or by some other sign appropriate to the usage of the region, for example, by kissing the Cross.

Only one Cross should be offered for adoration. If, because of the large number of people, it is not possible for all to approach individually, the Priest, after some of the clergy and faithful have adored, takes the Cross and, standing in the middle before the altar, invites the people in a few words to adore the Holy Cross and afterwards holds the Cross elevated higher for a brief time, for the faithful to adore it in silence.

While the adoration of the Holy Cross is taking place, the antiphon Crucem tuam adoramus *(We adore your Cross, O Lord), the Reproaches, the hymn* Crux fidelis *(Faithful Cross) or other suitable chants are sung, during which all who have already adored the Cross remain seated.*

CHANTS TO BE SUNG DURING THE ADORATION OF THE HOLY CROSS

Antiphon

**We adore your Cross, O Lord,
we praise and glorify your holy Resurrection,
for behold, because of the wood of a tree
joy has come to the whole world.**

**May God have mercy on us and bless us;
may he let his face shed its light upon us
and have mercy on us.**   Cf. Psalm 66.2

And the antiphon is repeated: **We adore . . .**

The Reproaches

Parts assigned to one of the two choirs separately are indicated by the numbers 1 (first choir) and 2 (second choir); parts sung by both choirs together are marked: 1 and 2. Some of the verses may also be sung by two cantors.

I

1 and 2: **My people, what have I done to you?**
    Or how have I grieved you? Answer me!

1:   **Because I led you out of the land of Egypt,**
    you have prepared a Cross for your Saviour.

1:   **Hagios o Theos,**

2:   **Holy is God,**

1:   **Hagios Ischyros,**

2:   **Holy and Mighty,**

1:   **Hagios Athanatos, eleison himas.**

2:   **Holy and Immortal One, have mercy on us.**

1 and 2: **Because I led you out through the desert**
        forty years
    and fed you with manna and brought you into
        a land of plenty,
    you have prepared a Cross for your Saviour.

1:   **Hagios o Theos,**

2:   **Holy is God,**

1:   **Hagios Ischyros,**

2:   **Holy and Mighty,**

1:   **Hagios Athanatos, eleison himas.**

2:   **Holy and Immortal One, have mercy on us.**

1 and 2: **What more should I have done for you**
        and have not done?
    Indeed, I planted you as my most beautiful
        chosen vine
    and you have turned very bitter for me,
    for in my thirst you gave me vinegar to drink
    and with a lance you pierced your Saviour's
        side.

1: **Hagios o Theos,**
2: **Holy is God,**
1: **Hagios Ischyros,**
2: **Holy and Mighty,**
1: **Hagios Athanatos, eleison himas.**
2: **Holy and Immortal One, have mercy on us.**

II

Cantors:
**I scourged Egypt for your sake with its firstborn
    sons,**
and you scourged me and handed me over.

1 and 2 repeat:
My people, what have I done to you?
Or how have I grieved you? Answer me!

Cantors:
**I led you out from Egypt as Pharoah lay sunk in
    the Red Sea,**
and you handed me over to the chief priests.

1 and 2 repeat:
My people . . .

Cantors:
I opened up the sea before you,
and you opened my side with a lance.

1 and 2 repeat:
My people . . .

Cantors:
I went before you in a pillar of cloud,
and you led me into Pilate's palace.

1 and 2 repeat:
My people . . .

Cantors:
I fed you with manna in the desert,
and on me you rained blows and lashes.

1 and 2 repeat:
My people . . .

Cantors:
I gave you saving water from the rock to drink,
and for drink you gave me gall and vinegar.

1 and 2 repeat:
My people . . .

Cantors:
I struck down for you the kings of the Canaanites,
and you struck my head with a reed.

1 and 2 repeat:
My people . . .

Cantors:
I put in your hand a royal sceptre,
and you put on my head a crown of thorns.

1 and 2 repeat:
My people . . .

Cantors:
I exalted you with great power,
and you hung me on the scaffold of the Cross.

1 and 2 repeat:
My people . . .

HYMN

All:

Faithful Cross the Saints rely on,
Noble tree beyond compare!
Never was there such a scion,
Never leaf or flower so rare.
Sweet the timber, sweet the iron,
Sweet the burden that they bear!

Cantors:

Sing, my tongue, in exultation
Of our banner and device!
Make a solemn proclamation
Of a triumph and its price:
How the Savior of creation
Conquered by his sacrifice!

All:

Faithful Cross the Saints rely
    on,
Noble tree beyond compare!
Never was there such a scion,
Never leaf or flower so rare.

Cantors:

For, when Adam first offended,
Eating that forbidden fruit,
Not all hopes of glory ended
With the serpent at the root:
Broken nature would be
    mended
By a second tree and shoot.

All:

Sweet the timber, sweet the
    iron,
Sweet the burden that they
    bear!

Cantors:

Thus the tempter was outwitted
By a wisdom deeper still:
Remedy and ailment fitted,
Means to cure and means to
    kill;
That the world might be acquit-
    ted,
Christ would do his Father's
    will.

All:

Faithful Cross the Saints rely
    on,
Noble tree beyond compare!
Never was there such a scion,
Never leaf or flower so rare.

Cantors:

So the Father, out of pity
For our self-inflicted doom,
Sent him from the heavenly city
When the holy time had come:
He, the Son and the Almighty,
Took our flesh in Mary's womb.

All:

Sweet the timber, sweet the
    iron,
Sweet the burden that they
    bear!

Cantors:

Hear a tiny baby crying,
Founder of the seas and
    strands;
See his virgin Mother tying
Cloth around his feet and hands;
Find him in a manger lying
Tightly wrapped in swaddling-
    bands!

All:

Faithful Cross the Saints rely
    on,
Noble tree beyond compare!
Never was there such a scion,
Never leaf or flower so rare.

Cantors:

So he came, the long-expected,
Not in glory, not to reign;
Only born to be rejected,

Choosing hunger, toil and pain,
Till the scaffold was erected
And the Paschal Lamb was
   slain.

All:

Sweet the timber, sweet the
   iron,
Sweet the burden that they
   bear!

Cantors:

No disgrace was too abhorrent:
Nailed and mocked and
   parched he died;
Blood and water, double war-
   rant,
Issue from his wounded side,
Washing in a mighty torrent
Earth and stars and oceantide.

All:

Faithful Cross the Saints rely
   on,
Noble tree beyond compare!
Never was there such a scion,
Never leaf or flower so rare.

Cantors:

Lofty timber, smooth your
   roughness,
Flex your boughs for blossom-
   ing;
Let your fibers lose their tough-
   ness,
Gently let your tendrils cling;

Lay aside your native gruffness,
Clasp the body of your King!

All:

Sweet the timber, sweet the
   iron,
Sweet the burden that they
   bear!

Cantors:

Noblest tree of all created,
Richly jeweled and embossed:
Post by Lamb's blood conse-
   crated;
Spar that saves the tempest-
   tossed;
Scaffold-beam which, elevated,
Carries what the world has
   cost!

All:

Faithful Cross the Saints rely
   on,
Noble tree beyond compare!
Never was there such a scion,
Never leaf or flower so rare.

*The following conclusion is
never to be omitted:*

All:

Wisdom, power, and adoration
To the blessed Trinity
For redemption and salvation
Through the Paschal Mystery,
Now, in every generation,
And for all eternity. Amen.

*In accordance with local circumstances or popular tradi-
tions and if it is pastorally appropriate, the* Stabat Mater
may be sung, as found in the Graduale Romanum, *or another suitable chant in memory of the compassion of the
Blessed Virgin Mary.*

When the adoration has been concluded, the Cross is carried by the Deacon or a minister to its place at the altar. Lighted candles are placed around or on the altar or near the Cross.

THIRD PART: HOLY COMMUNION

A cloth is spread on the altar, and a corporal and the Missal put in place. Meanwhile the Deacon or, if there is no Deacon, the Priest himself, putting on a humeral veil, brings the Blessed Sacrament back from the place of repose to the altar by a shorter route, while all stand in silence. Two ministers with lighted candles accompany the Blessed Sacrament and place their candlesticks around or upon the altar.

When the Deacon, if a Deacon is present, has placed the Blessed Sacrament upon the altar and uncovered the ciborium, the Priest goes to the altar and genuflects.

Then the Priest, with hands joined, says aloud:

At the Saviour's command
and formed by divine teaching,
we dare to say:

The Priest, with hands extended says, and all present continue:

**Our Father, who art in heaven,
hallowed be thy name;
thy kingdom come,
thy will be done
on earth as it is in heaven.
Give us this day our daily bread,
and forgive us our trespasses,
as we forgive those who trespass against us;
and lead us not into temptation,
but deliver us from evil.**

With hands extended, the Priest continues alone:

Deliver us, Lord, we pray, from every evil,
graciously grant peace in our days,
that, by the help of your mercy,
we may be always free from sin
and safe from all distress,
as we await the blessed hope
and the coming of our Saviour, Jesus Christ.

The people conclude the prayer, acclaiming:

**For the kingdom, the power and the glory are
yours now and for ever.**

Then the Priest, with hands joined, says quietly:

May the receiving of your Body and Blood,
Lord Jesus Christ,
not bring me to judgement and condemnation,
but through your loving mercy
be for me protection in mind and body
and a healing remedy.

*The Priest then genuflects, takes a particle, and, holding
it slightly raised over the ciborium, while facing the people, says aloud:*

Behold the Lamb of God,
behold him who takes away the sins of the world.
Blessed are those called to the supper of the Lamb.

And together with the people he adds once:

**Lord, I am not worthy
that you should enter under my roof,
but only say the word
and my soul shall be healed.**

*And facing the altar, he reverently consumes the Body of
Christ, saying quietly:* May the Body of Christ keep me
safe for eternal life.

He then proceeds to distribute Communion to the faithful. During Communion, Psalm 21 or another appropriate chant may be sung.

When the distribution of Communion has been completed, the ciborium is taken by the Deacon or another suitable minister to a place prepared outside the church or, if circumstances so require, it is placed in the tabernacle.

Then the Priest says: Let us pray, *and, after a period of sacred silence, if circumstances so suggest, has been observed, he says the Prayer after Communion.*

Almighty ever-living God,
who have restored us to life
by the blessed Death and Resurrection of your
   Christ,
preserve in us the work of your mercy,
that, by partaking of this mystery,
we may have a life unceasingly devoted to you.
Through Christ our Lord. ℟. **Amen.**

For the Dismissal the Deacon or, if there is no Deacon, the Priest himself, may say the invitation Bow down for the blessing.

Then the Priest, standing facing the people and extending his hands over them, says this:

PRAYER OVER THE PEOPLE

May abundant blessing, O Lord, we pray,
descend upon your people,
who have honoured the Death of your Son
in the hope of their resurrection:
may pardon come,
comfort be given,
holy faith increase,

and everlasting redemption be made secure.
Through Christ our Lord. ℟. **Amen.**

And all, after genuflecting to the Cross, depart in silence.

After the celebration, the altar is stripped, but the Cross remains on the altar with two or four candlesticks.

APRIL 20

HOLY SATURDAY

On Holy Saturday the Church waits at the Lord's tomb in prayer and fasting, meditating on his Passion and Death and on his Descent into Hell, and awaiting his Resurrection.

The Church abstains from the Sacrifice of the Mass, with the sacred table left bare, until after the solemn Vigil, that is, the anticipation by night of the Resurrection, when the time comes for paschal joys, the abundance of which overflows to occupy fifty days.

"He is not here, but has risen."

APRIL 20

THE EASTER VIGIL IN THE HOLY NIGHT

By most ancient tradition, this is the night of keeping vigil for the Lord (Ex. 12.42), in which, following the Gospel admonition (Lk. 12.35-37), the faithful, carrying lighted lamps in their hands, should be like those looking for the Lord when he returns, so that at his coming he may find them awake and have them sit at his table.

Of this night's Vigil, which is the greatest and most noble of all solemnities, there is to be only one celebration in each church. It is arranged, moreover, in such a way that after the Lucernarium and Easter Proclamation (which constitutes the first part of this Vigil), Holy Church meditates on the wonders the Lord God has done for his people from the beginning, trusting in his word and promise (the second part, that is, the Liturgy of the Word) until, as day approaches, with new members reborn in Baptism (the third part), the Church is called to the table the Lord has prepared for his people, the memorial of his Death and Resurrection until he comes again (the fourth part).

Candles should be prepared for all who participate in the Vigil. The lights of the church are extinguished.

347

FIRST PART:
THE SOLEMN BEGINNING OF THE VIGIL
OR LUCERNARIUM

THE BLESSING OF THE FIRE AND
PREPARATION OF THE CANDLE

A blazing fire is prepared in a suitable place outside the church. When the people are gathered there, the Priest approaches with the ministers, one of whom carries the paschal candle. The processional cross and candles are not carried.

Where, however, a fire cannot be lit outside the church, the rite is carried out as below, p. 350.

The Priest and faithful sign themselves while the Priest says: In the name of the Father, and of the Son, and of the Holy Spirit, *and then he greets the assembled people in the usual way and briefly instructs them about the night vigil in these or similar words:*

Dear brethren (brothers and sisters),
on this most sacred night,
in which our Lord Jesus Christ
passed over from death to life,
the Church calls upon her sons and daughters,
scattered throughout the world,
to come together to watch and pray.
If we keep the memorial
of the Lord's paschal solemnity in this way,
listening to his word and celebrating his mysteries,
then we shall have the sure hope
of sharing his triumph over death
and living with him in God.

Then the Priest blesses the fire, saying with hands extended:

Let us pray.

O God, who through your Son
bestowed upon the faithful the fire of your glory,
sanctify ✠ this new fire, we pray,
and grant that,
by these paschal celebrations,
we may be so inflamed with heavenly desires,
that with minds made pure
we may attain festivities of unending splendour.
Through Christ our Lord.

℟. **Amen.** ↓

After the blessing of the new fire, one of the ministers brings the paschal candle to the Priest, who cuts a cross into the candle with a stylus. Then he makes the Greek letter Alpha above the cross, the letter Omega below, and the four numerals of the current year between the arms of the cross, saying meanwhile:

1. Christ yesterday and today *(he cuts a vertical line)*;
2. the Beginning and the End *(he cuts a horizontal line)*;
3. the Alpha *(he cuts the letter Alpha above the vertical line)*;
4. and the Omega *(he cuts the letter Omega below the vertical line)*.
5. All time belongs to him *(he cuts the first numeral of the current year in the upper left corner of the cross)*;
6. and all the ages *(he cuts the second numeral of the current year in the upper right corner of the cross)*.

7. To him be glory and power *(he cuts the third numeral of the current year in the lower left corner of the cross)*;
8. through every age forever. Amen *(he cuts the fourth numeral of the current year in the lower right corner of the cross).*

```
          A
     2  |  0
    ─────┼─────
     1  |  9
          Ω
```

When the cutting of the cross and of the other signs has been completed, the Priest may insert five grains of incense into the candle in the form of a cross, meanwhile saying:

1. By his holy
2. and glorious wounds,
3. may Christ the Lord
4. guard us
5. and protect us. Amen.

```
          1

     4    2    5

          3
```

Where, because of difficulties that may occur, a fire is not lit, the blessing of fire is adapted to the circumstances. When the people are gathered in the church as on other occasions, the Priest comes to the door of the church, along with the ministers carrying the paschal candle. The people, insofar as it is possible, turn to face the Priest.

The greeting and address take place as above, p. 348; then the fire is blessed and the candle is prepared, as above, pp. 349-350.

The Priest lights the paschal candle from the new fire, saying:

May the light of Christ rising in glory
dispel the darkness of our hearts and minds.

PROCESSION

When the candle has been lit, one of the ministers takes burning coals from the fire and places them in the thuri-

ble, and the Priest puts incense into it in the usual way. The Deacon or, if there is no Deacon, another suitable minister, takes the paschal candle and a procession forms. The thurifer with the smoking thurible precedes the Deacon or other minister who carries the paschal candle. After them follows the Priest with the ministers and the people, all holding in their hands unlit candles.

At the door of the church the Deacon, standing and raising up the candle, sings:

The Light of Christ.

And all reply:

Thanks be to God.

The Priest lights his candle from the flame of the paschal candle.

Then the Deacon moves forward to the middle of the church and, standing and raising up the candle, sings a second time:

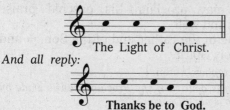

The Light of Christ.

And all reply:

Thanks be to God.

All light their candles from the flame of the paschal candle and continue in procession.

When the Deacon arrives before the altar, he stands facing the people, raises up the candle and sings a third time:

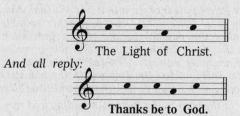

The Light of Christ.

And all reply:

Thanks be to God.

Then the Deacon places the paschal candle on a large candlestand prepared next to the ambo or in the middle of the sanctuary.

And lights are lit throughout the church, except for the altar candles.

THE EASTER PROCLAMATION (EXSULTET)

Arriving at the altar, the Priest goes to his chair, gives his candle to a minister, puts incense into the thurible and blesses the incense as at the Gospel at Mass. The Deacon goes to the Priest and saying, Your blessing, Father, *asks for and receives a blessing from the Priest, who says in a low voice:*

May the Lord be in your heart and on your lips,
that you may proclaim his paschal praise worthily and well,
in the name of the Father and of the Son, ✚ and of the Holy Spirit.

The Deacon replies: Amen. ↓

This blessing is omitted if the Proclamation is made by someone who is not a Deacon.

The Deacon, after incensing the book and the candle, proclaims the Easter Proclamation (Exsultet) at the ambo or at a lectern, with all standing and holding lighted candles in their hands.

The Easter Proclamation may be made, in the absence of a Deacon, by the Priest himself or by another concele-

*brating Priest. If, however, because of necessity, a lay
cantor sings the Proclamation, the words* Therefore,
dearest friends *up to the end of the invitation are omitted, along with the greeting* The Lord be with you.

[*When the Shorter Form is used, omit the italicized parts.*]

Exult, let them exult, the hosts of heaven,
exult, let Angel ministers of God exult,
let the trumpet of salvation
sound aloud our mighty King's triumph!
Be glad, let earth be glad, as glory floods her,
ablaze with light from her eternal King,
let all corners of the earth be glad,
knowing an end to gloom and darkness.
Rejoice, let Mother Church also rejoice,
arrayed with the lightning of his glory,
let this holy building shake with joy,
filled with the mighty voices of the peoples.
(*Therefore, dearest friends,
standing in the awesome glory of this holy light,
invoke with me, I ask you,
the mercy of God almighty,
that he, who has been pleased to number me,
though unworthy, among the Levites,
may pour into me his light unshadowed,
that I may sing this candle's perfect praises*).

(℣. The Lord be with you. ℟. **And with your spirit.**)
℣. Lift up your hearts. ℟. **We lift them up to the
Lord.**
℣. Let us give thanks to the Lord our God. ℟. **It is
right and just.**

It is truly right and just,
with ardent love of mind and heart

and with devoted service of our voice,
to acclaim our God invisible, the almighty Father,
and Jesus Christ, our Lord, his Son, his Only
   Begotten.

Who for our sake paid Adam's debt to the eternal
   Father,
and, pouring out his own dear Blood,
wiped clean the record of our ancient sinfulness.

These then are the feasts of Passover,
in which is slain the Lamb, the one true Lamb,
whose Blood anoints the doorposts of believers.

This is the night,
when once you led our forebears, Israel's children,
from slavery in Egypt
and made them pass dry-shod through the Red
   Sea.

This is the night
that with a pillar of fire
banished the darkness of sin.

This is the night
that even now, throughout the world,
sets Christian believers apart from worldly vices
and from the gloom of sin,
leading them to grace
and joining them to his holy ones.

This is the night,
when Christ broke the prison-bars of death
and rose victorious from the underworld.

Our birth would have been no gain,
had we not been redeemed.
O wonder of your humble care for us!

O love, O charity beyond all telling,
to ransom a slave you gave away your Son!

O truly necessary sin of Adam,
destroyed completely by the Death of Christ!

O happy fault
that earned so great, so glorious a Redeemer!

O truly blessed night,
worthy alone to know the time and hour
when Christ rose from the underworld!

This is the night
of which it is written:
The night shall be as bright as day,
dazzling is the night for me,
and full of gladness.

The sanctifying power of this night
dispels wickedness, washes faults away,
restores innocence to the fallen, and joy to
    mourners,
drives out hatred, fosters concord, and brings
    down the mighty.

On this, your night of grace, O holy Father,
accept this candle, a solemn offering,
the work of bees and of your servants' hands,
an evening sacrifice of praise,
this gift from your most holy Church.

But now we know the praises of this pillar,
which glowing fire ignites for God's honour,
a fire into many flames divided,
yet never dimmed by sharing of its light,
for it is fed by melting wax,
drawn out by mother bees
to build a torch so precious.

O truly blessed night,
when things of heaven are wed to those of earth,
and divine to the human.

Shorter Form only:

On this, your night of grace, O holy Father,
accept this candle, a solemn offering,
the work of bees and of your servants' hands,
an evening sacrifice of praise,
this gift from your most holy Church.

Therefore, O Lord,
we pray you that this candle,
hallowed to the honour of your name,
may persevere undimmed,
to overcome the darkness of this night.
Receive it as a pleasing fragrance,
and let it mingle with the lights of heaven.
May this flame be found still burning
by the Morning Star:
the one Morning Star who never sets,
Christ your Son,
who, coming back from death's domain,
has shed his peaceful light on humanity,
and lives and reigns for ever and ever.

Ry. A - men.

SECOND PART:

THE LITURGY OF THE WORD

*In this Vigil, the mother of all Vigils, nine readings are
provided, namely seven from the Old Testament and two*

from the New (the Epistle and Gospel), all of which should be read whenever this can be done, so that the character of the Vigil, which demands an extended period of time, may be preserved.

Nevertheless, where more serious pastoral circumstances demand it, the number of readings from the Old Testament may be reduced, always bearing in mind that the reading of the Word of God is a fundamental part of this Easter Vigil. At least three readings should be read from the Old Testament, both from the Law and from the Prophets, and their respective Responsorial Psalms should be sung. Never, moreover, should the reading of chapter 14 of Exodus with its canticle be omitted.

After setting aside their candles, all sit. Before the readings begin, the Priest instructs the people in these or similar words:

Dear brethren (brothers and sisters),
now that we have begun our solemn Vigil,
let us listen with quiet hearts to the Word of God.
Let us meditate on how God in times past saved
   his people
and in these, the last days, has sent us his Son as
   our Redeemer.
Let us pray that our God may complete this
   paschal work of salvation
by the fullness of redemption.

Then the readings follow. A reader goes to the ambo and proclaims the reading. Afterwards a psalmist or a cantor sings or says the Psalm, with the people making the response. Then all rise, the Priest says, Let us pray *and, after all have prayed for a while in silence, he says the prayer corresponding to the reading. In place of the Responsorial Psalm a period of sacred silence may be observed, in which case the pause after* Let us pray *is omitted.*

FIRST READING Gen. 1.1—2.2 or 1.1, 26-31a

God created the world and all that is in it, and saw that it was good. This reading from the first book of the Bible shows that God made and loves all that exists.

[If the "Shorter Form" is used, the indented text in brackets is omitted.]

A reading from the book of Genesis.

IN the beginning when God created the heavens and the earth,

[the earth was a formless void and darkness covered the face of the deep, while the spirit of God swept over the face of the waters. Then God said, "Let there be light"; and there was light. And God saw that the light was good; and God separated the light from the darkness. God called the light "Day," and the darkness he called "Night." And there was evening and there was morning, the first day.

And God said, "Let there be a dome in the midst of the waters, and let it separate the waters from the waters." So the Lord made the dome and separated the waters that were under the dome from the waters that were above the dome. And it was so. God called the dome "Sky." And there was evening and there was morning, the second day.

And God said, "Let the waters under the sky be gathered together into one place, and let the dry land appear." And it was so. God called the dry land "Earth," and the waters that were gathered together he called "Seas." And God saw that it was good.

Then God said, "Let the earth put forth vegetation: plants yielding seed, and fruit trees of every kind on earth that bear fruit with the seed in it." And it was so. The earth brought forth vegetation: plants yielding seed of every kind, and trees of every kind bearing fruit with the seed in it. And God saw that it was good. And there was evening and there was morning, the third day.

And God said, "Let there be lights in the dome of the sky to separate the day from the night; and let them be for signs and for seasons and for days and years, and let them be lights in the dome of the sky to give light upon the earth." And it was so.

God made the two great lights—the greater light to rule the day and the lesser light to rule the night—and the stars. God set them in the dome of the sky to give light upon the earth, to rule over the day and over the night, and to separate the light from the darkness. And God saw that it was good. And there was evening and there was morning, the fourth day.

And God said, "Let the waters bring forth swarms of living creatures, and let birds fly above the earth across the dome of the sky." So God created the great sea monsters and every living creature that moves, of every kind, with which the waters swarm, and every winged bird of every kind. And God saw that it was good. God blessed them, saying, "Be fruitful and multiply and fill the waters in the seas, and let birds multiply on the earth." And there was evening and there was morning, the fifth day.

And God said, "Let the earth bring forth living creatures of every kind: cattle and creeping things and wild animals of the earth of every kind." And it was so. God made the wild animals of the earth of every kind, and the cattle of every kind, and everything that creeps upon the ground of every kind. And God saw that it was good.]

[Then] God said, "Let us make man in our image, according to our likeness; and let them have dominion over the fish of the sea, and over the birds of the air, and over the cattle, and over all the wild animals of the earth, and over every creeping thing that creeps upon the earth."

So God created man in his image,
in the image of God he created him;
male and female he created them.

God blessed them, and God said to them, "Be fruitful and multiply, and fill the earth and subdue it; and have dominion over the fish of the sea and over the birds of the air and over every living thing that moves upon the earth." God said, "See, I have given you every plant yielding seed that is upon the face of all the earth, and every tree with seed in its fruit; you shall have them for food. And to every beast of the earth, and to every bird of the air, and to everything that creeps on the earth, everything that has the breath of life, I have given every green plant for food." And it was so. God saw everything that he had made, and indeed, it was very good. And there was evening and there was morning, the sixth day.

[Thus the heavens and the earth were finished, and all their multitude. And on the seventh day God finished the work that he had done, and he rested on the seventh day from all the work that he had done.]

The word of the Lord. ℟. **Thanks be to God.** ↓

RESPONSORIAL PSALM Ps. 104

Geoffrey Angeles

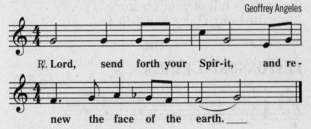

℟. Lord, send forth your Spir-it, and renew the face of the earth.___

Bless the Lord, O my soul.
O Lord my God, you are very great.
You are clothed with honour and majesty,
wrapped in light as with a garment.—℟.

You set the earth on its foundations,
so that it shall never be shaken.
You cover it with the deep as with a garment;
the waters stood above the mountains.—℟.

You make springs gush forth in the valleys;
they flow between the hills.
By the streams the birds of the air have their
   habitation;
they sing among the branches.—℟.

From your lofty abode you water the mountains;
the earth is satisfied with the fruit of your work.
You cause the grass to grow for the cattle,
and plants for people to use, to bring forth food
  from the earth.
℟. **Lord, send forth your Spirit, and renew the
  face of the earth.**

O Lord, how manifold are your works!
In wisdom you have made them all;
the earth is full of your creatures.
Bless the Lord, O my soul.—℟. ↓

OR

RESPONSORIAL PSALM Ps. 33

Leo Marchildon

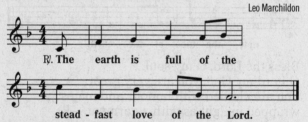

℟. The earth is full of the stead-fast love of the Lord.

The word of the Lord is upright,
and all his work is done in faithfulness.
He loves righteousness and justice;
the earth is full of the steadfast love of the
  Lord.—℟.

By the word of the Lord the heavens were made,
and all their host by the breath of his mouth.
He gathered the waters of the sea as in a bottle;
he put the deeps in storehouses.—℟.

Blessed is the nation whose God is the Lord,
the people whom he has chosen as his heritage.
The Lord looks down from heaven;
he sees all human beings.—℟. ↓

Our soul waits for the Lord;
he is our help and shield.
Let your steadfast love, O Lord, be upon us,
even as we hope in you.—℟. ↓

PRAYER

Let us pray.

Almighty ever-living God,
who are wonderful in the ordering of all your
   works,
may those you have redeemed understand
that there exists nothing more marvellous
than the world's creation in the beginning
except that, at the end of the ages,
Christ our Passover has been sacrificed.
Who lives and reigns for ever and ever.
℟. **Amen.** ↓

OR

PRAYER (On the creation of man)
O God, who wonderfully created human nature
and still more wonderfully redeemed it,
grant us, we pray,
to set our minds against the enticements of sin,
that we may merit to attain eternal joys.
Through Christ our Lord.
℟. **Amen.** ↓

SECOND READING Gen. 22.1-18 or 22.1-2, 9-13, 15-18

> Abraham is obedient to the will of God. Because God
> asks him, without hesitation he prepares to sacrifice his
> son, Isaac. In the new order, God sends the only Son to
> redeem us by his death on the cross.

*[If the "Shorter Form" is used, the indented text in brack-
ets is omitted.]*

A reading from the book of Genesis.

GOD tested Abraham. He said to him, "Abraham!" And Abraham said, "Here I am." God
said, "Take your son, your only son Isaac, whom
you love, and go to the land of Moriah, and offer
him there as a burnt offering on one of the
mountains that I shall show you."

[So Abraham rose early in the morning,
saddled his donkey, and took two of his
young men with him, and his son Isaac; he
cut the wood for the burnt offering, and set
out and went to the place in the distance
that God had shown him.

On the third day Abraham looked up and
saw the place far away. Then Abraham said
to his young men, "Stay here with the donkey; the boy and I will go over there; we
will worship, and then we will come back to
you." Abraham took the wood of the burnt
offering and laid it on his son Isaac, and he
himself carried the fire and the knife. So
the two of them walked on together.

Isaac said to his father Abraham, "Father!"
And Abraham said, "Here I am, my son."
Isaac said, "The fire and the wood are here,

but where is the lamb for a burnt offering?"
Abraham said, "God himself will provide the
lamb for a burnt offering, my son." So the two
of them walked on together.]

When Abraham and Isaac came to the place
that God had shown him, Abraham built an
altar there and laid the wood in order. He bound
his son Isaac, and laid him on the altar, on top
of the wood. Then Abraham reached out his
hand and took the knife to kill his son.

But the Angel of the Lord called to him from
heaven, and said, "Abraham, Abraham!" And he
said, "Here I am." The Angel said, "Do not lay
your hand on the boy or do anything to him; for
now I know that you fear God, since you have
not withheld your son, your only son, from me."
And Abraham looked up and saw a ram, caught
in a thicket by its horns. Abraham went and
took the ram and offered it up as a burnt offering instead of his son.

[So Abraham called that place "The Lord
will provide"; as it is said to this day, "On
the mount of the Lord it shall be provided."]

The Angel of the Lord called to Abraham a second time from heaven, and said, "By myself I have
sworn, says the Lord: Because you have done this,
and have not withheld your son, your only son, I
will indeed bless you, and I will make your offspring as numerous as the stars of heaven, and as
the sand that is on the seashore. And your offspring shall possess the gate of their enemies, and
by your offspring shall all the nations of the earth

gain blessing for themselves, because you have obeyed my voice."—The word of the Lord.
℟. **Thanks be to God.** ↓

RESPONSORIAL PSALM Ps. 16

David McIsaac

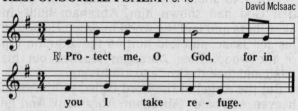

℟. Pro - tect me, O God, for in you I take re - fuge.

The Lord is my chosen portion and my cup;
you hold my lot.
I keep the Lord always before me;
because he is at my right hand, I shall not be
   moved.—℟.

Therefore my heart is glad, and my soul rejoices;
my body also rests secure.
For you do not give me up to Sheol,
or let your faithful one see the Pit.—℟.

You show me the path of life.
In your presence there is fullness of joy;
in your right hand are pleasures
forevermore.—℟. ↓

PRAYER

Let us pray.

O God, supreme Father of the faithful,
who increase the children of your promise
by pouring out the grace of adoption

throughout the whole world
and who through the Paschal Mystery
make your servant Abraham father of nations,
as once you swore,
grant, we pray,
that your peoples may enter worthily
into the grace to which you call them.
Through Christ our Lord. ℟. **Amen.** ↓

THIRD READING Ex. 14.15-31; 15.20, 1

God saved the chosen people from slavery and death by
leading them through the waters of the sea; now our
God saves us by leading us through the waters of baptism, by which we come to share in the death and rising
of Jesus.

A reading from the book of Exodus.

THE Lord said to Moses, "Why do you cry out to
me? Tell the children of Israel to go forward.
But you, lift up your staff, and stretch out your
hand over the sea and divide it, that the children
of Israel may go into the sea on dry ground. Then I
will harden the hearts of the Egyptians so that
they will go in after them; and so I will gain glory
for myself over Pharaoh and all his army, his chariots, and his chariot drivers. And the Egyptians
shall know that I am the Lord, when I have gained
glory for myself over Pharaoh, his chariots, and
his chariot drivers."

The Angel of God who was going before the Is-
raelite army moved and went behind them; and
the pillar of cloud moved from in front of them
and took its place behind them. It came between
the army of Egypt and the army of Israel. And so

the cloud was there with the darkness, and it lit up the night; one did not come near the other all night.

Then Moses stretched out his hand over the sea. The Lord drove the sea back by a strong east wind all night, and turned the sea into dry land; and the waters were divided. The children of Israel went into the sea on dry ground, the waters forming a wall for them on their right and on their left.

The Egyptians pursued, and went into the sea after them, all of Pharaoh's horses, chariots, and chariot drivers. At the morning watch, the Lord in the pillar of fire and cloud looked down upon the Egyptian army, and threw the Egyptian army into panic. He clogged their chariot wheels so that they turned with difficulty. The Egyptians said, "Let us flee from the children of Israel, for the Lord is fighting for them against Egypt."

Then the Lord said to Moses, "Stretch out your hand over the sea, so that the water may come back upon the Egyptians, upon their chariots and chariot drivers." So Moses stretched out his hand over the sea, and at dawn the sea returned to its normal depth. As the Egyptians fled before it, the Lord tossed the Egyptians into the sea. The waters returned and covered the chariots and the chariot drivers, the entire army of Pharaoh that had followed them into the sea; not one of them remained.

But the children of Israel walked on dry ground through the sea, the waters forming a wall for them on their right and on their left. Thus the Lord saved Israel that day from the Egyptians; and Israel saw the Egyptians dead on the seashore. Israel saw the great work that the Lord did against the Egyptians. So the people feared the Lord and believed in the Lord and in his servant Moses.

The Prophet Miriam, Aaron's sister, took a tambourine in her hand; and all the women went out after her with tambourines and with dancing. Moses and the children of Israel sang this song to the Lord: ↓

RESPONSORIAL PSALM Ex. 15

Geoffrey Angeles

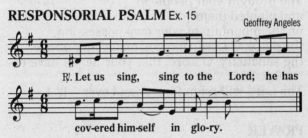

℟. Let us sing, sing to the Lord; he has cov-ered him-self in glo-ry.

I will sing to the Lord, for he has triumphed gloriously;
horse and rider he has thrown into the sea.
The Lord is my strength and my might,
and he has become my salvation;
this is my God, and I will praise him,
my father's God, and I will exalt him. —℟.

The Lord is a warrior;
the Lord is his name.
Pharaoh's chariots and his army he cast into the sea;
his picked officers were sunk in the Red Sea.
The floods covered them;
they went down into the depths like a stone.—℟.

Your right hand, O Lord, glorious in power;
your right hand, O Lord, shattered the enemy.
In the greatness of your majesty
you overthrew your adversaries;
you sent out your fury,
it consumed them like stubble.
℟. **Let us sing to the Lord; he has covered himself in glory.**

You brought your people in
and planted them
on the mountain of your own possession,
the place, O Lord, that you made your abode,
the sanctuary, O Lord, that your hands have established.
The Lord will reign forever and ever.—℟. ↓

PRAYER

Let us pray.

O God, whose ancient wonders
remain undimmed in splendour even in our day,
for what you once bestowed on a single people,
freeing them from Pharaoh's persecution
by the power of your right hand,
now you bring about as the salvation of the nations
through the waters of rebirth,
grant, we pray, that the whole world
may become children of Abraham
and inherit the dignity of Israel's birthright.
Through Christ our Lord.
℟. **Amen.** ↓

OR

PRAYER

O God, who by the light of the New Testament
have unlocked the meaning
of wonders worked in former times,
so that the Red Sea prefigures the sacred font
and the nation delivered from slavery
foreshadows the Christian people,
grant, we pray, that all nations,
obtaining the privilege of Israel by merit of faith,
may be reborn by partaking of your Spirit.
Through Christ our Lord.
℟. **Amen.** ↓

FOURTH READING Isa. 54.5-14

> For a time, God hid from the chosen people, but God's
> love for this people is everlasting. God takes pity on
> them and promises them prosperity.

A reading from the book of the Prophet Isaiah.

THUS says the Lord, the God of hosts.
Your Maker is your husband,
the Lord of hosts is his name;
the Holy One of Israel is your Redeemer,
the God of the whole earth he is called.
For the Lord has called you
like a wife forsaken and grieved in spirit,
like the wife of a man's youth when she is cast
  off,
says your God.
For a brief moment I abandoned you,
but with great compassion I will gather you.

In overflowing wrath for a moment
I hid my face from you,
but with everlasting love I will have compassion
    on you,
says the Lord, your Redeemer.

This is like the days of Noah to me:
Just as I swore that the waters of Noah
would never again go over the earth,
so I have sworn that I will not be angry with you
    and will not rebuke you.
For the mountains may depart
and the hills be removed,
but my steadfast love shall not depart from you,
and my covenant of peace shall not be removed,
says the Lord, who has compassion on you.

O afflicted one, storm-tossed, and not comforted,
I am about to set your stones in antimony,
and lay your foundations with sapphires.
I will make your pinnacles of rubies,
your gates of jewels,
and all your walls of precious stones.

All your children shall be taught by the Lord,
and great shall be the prosperity of your
    children.
In righteousness you shall be established;
you shall be far from oppression, for you shall
    not fear;
and from terror, for it shall not come near you.

The word of the Lord. ℟. **Thanks be to God.** ↓

RESPONSORIAL PSALM Ps. 30

Normand L. Blanchard

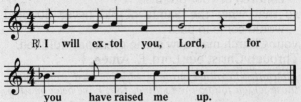

℟. I will ex-tol you, Lord, for you have raised me up.

I will extol you, O Lord, for you have drawn me up,
and did not let my foes rejoice over me.
O Lord, you brought up my soul from Sheol,
restored me to life from among those gone
    down to the Pit.—℟.

Sing praises to the Lord, O you his faithful ones,
and give thanks to his holy name.
For his anger is but for a moment;
his favour is for a lifetime.
Weeping may linger for the night,
but joy comes with the morning.—℟.

Hear, O Lord, and be gracious to me!
O Lord, be my helper!
You have turned my mourning into dancing.
O Lord my God, I will give thanks to you for-
    ever.—℟. ↓

PRAYER

Let us pray.

Almighty ever-living God,
surpass, for the honour of your name,
what you pledged to the Patriarchs by reason of
    their faith,

and through sacred adoption increase the
    children of your promise,
so that what the Saints of old never doubted
    would come to pass
your Church may now see in great part fulfilled.
Through Christ our Lord. ℟. **Amen.** ↓

*Alternatively, other prayers may be used from among
those which follow the readings that have been omitted.*

FIFTH READING Isa. 55.1-11

**God is a loving Father, calling all people to come back.
Our God promises an everlasting covenant with them.
God is merciful, generous, and forgiving.**

A reading from the book of the Prophet Isaiah.

THUS says the Lord:
    "Everyone who thirsts,
come to the waters;
and you that have no money,
come, buy and eat!
Come, buy wine and milk
without money and without price.
Why do you spend your money for that which is
    not bread,
and your labour for that which does not satisfy?
Listen carefully to me, and eat what is good,
and delight yourselves in rich food.
Incline your ear, and come to me;
listen, so that you may live.
I will make with you an everlasting covenant,
my steadfast, sure love for David.
See, I made him a witness to the peoples,
a leader and commander for the peoples.

See, you shall call nations that you do not know,
and nations that do not know you shall run to you,
because of the Lord your God, the Holy One of
    Israel,
for he has glorified you.

Seek the Lord while he may be found,
call upon him while he is near;
let the wicked person forsake their way,
and the unrighteous person their thoughts;
let that person return to the Lord that he may have
    mercy on them,
and to our God, for he will abundantly pardon.

For my thoughts are not your thoughts,
nor are your ways my ways, says the Lord.
For as the heavens are higher than the earth,
so are my ways higher than your ways
and my thoughts than your thoughts.

For as the rain and the snow come down from
    heaven,
and do not return there until they have watered
    the earth,
making it bring forth and sprout,
giving seed to the sower and bread to the one
    who eats,
so shall my word be that goes out from my
    mouth;
it shall not return to me empty,
but it shall accomplish that which I purpose,
and succeed in the thing for which I sent it."

The word of the Lord.

℟. **Thanks be to God.** ↓

RESPONSORIAL PSALM Isa. 12

Normand L. Blanchard

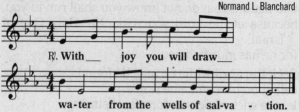

R̸. With___ joy you will draw___ wa-ter from the wells of sal-va - tion.

Surely God is my salvation;
I will trust, and will not be afraid,
for the Lord God is my strength and my might;
he has become my salvation.
With joy you will draw water
from the wells of salvation.—R̸.

Give thanks to the Lord,
call on his name;
make known his deeds among the nations;
proclaim that his name is exalted.—R̸.

Sing praises to the Lord,
for he has done gloriously;
let this be known in all the earth.
Shout aloud and sing for joy, O royal Zion,
for great in your midst
is the Holy One of Israel.—R̸. ↓

PRAYER

Let us pray.

Almighty ever-living God,
sole hope of the world,
who by the preaching of your Prophets
unveiled the mysteries of this present age,

graciously increase the longing of your people,
for only at the prompting of your grace
do the faithful progress in any kind of virtue.
Through Christ our Lord.
℟. **Amen.** ↓

SIXTH READING Bar. 3.9-15, 32—4.4

Baruch tells the people of Israel to walk in the ways of God. They have to learn prudence, wisdom, understanding. Then they will have peace forever.

A reading from the book of the Prophet Baruch.

HEAR the commandments of life, O Israel;
give ear, and learn wisdom!
Why is it, O Israel,
why is it that you are in the land of your enemies,
that you are growing old in a foreign country,
that you are defiled with the dead,
that you are counted among those in Hades?
You have forsaken the fountain of wisdom.
If you had walked in the way of God,
you would be living in peace forever.

Learn where there is wisdom,
where there is strength,
where there is understanding,
so that you may at the same time discern
where there is length of days, and life,
where there is light for the eyes, and peace.
Who has found her place?
And who has entered her storehouses?

But the one who knows all things knows her,
he found her by his understanding.
The one who prepared the earth for all time
filled it with four-footed creatures;

the one who sends forth the light, and it goes;
he called it, and it obeyed him, trembling;
the stars shone in their watches, and were glad;
he called them, and they said, "Here we are!"
They shone with gladness for him who made them.

This is our God;
no other can be compared to him.
He found the whole way to knowledge,
and gave her to his servant Jacob
and to Israel, whom he loved.
Afterward she appeared on earth
and lived with humanity.

She is the book of the commandments of God,
the law that endures forever.
All who hold her fast will live,
and those who forsake her will die.

Turn, O Jacob, and take her;
walk toward the shining of her light.
Do not give your glory to another,
or your advantages to an alien people.

Happy are we, O Israel,
for we know what is pleasing to God.

The word of the Lord. ℟. **Thanks be to God.** ↓

RESPONSORIAL PSALM Ps. 19

Frank Lynch

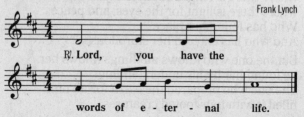

℟. Lord, you have the words of e-ter-nal life.

The law of the Lord is perfect,
reviving the soul;
the decrees of the Lord are sure,
making wise the simple.—℟.

The precepts of the Lord are right,
rejoicing the heart;
the commandment of the Lord is clear,
enlightening the eyes.—℟.

The fear of the Lord is pure,
enduring forever;
the ordinances of the Lord are true
and righteous altogether.—℟.

More to be desired are they than gold,
even much fine gold;
sweeter also than honey,
and drippings of the honeycomb.—℟. ↓

PRAYER

Let us pray.

O God, who constantly increase your Church
by your call to the nations,
graciously grant
to those you wash clean in the waters of Baptism
the assurance of your unfailing protection.
Through Christ our Lord.
℟. **Amen.** ↓

SEVENTH READING Ez. 36.16-17a, 18-28

God wants the chosen people to respect God's holy
name. All shall know the holiness of God, who will
cleanse this people from idol worship and bring them
home again.

A reading from the book of the Prophet Ezekiel.

THE word of the Lord came to me: Son of man, when the house of Israel lived on their own soil, they defiled it with their ways and their deeds; their conduct in my sight was unclean. So I poured out my wrath upon them for the blood that they had shed upon the land, and for the idols with which they had defiled it. I scattered them among the nations, and they were dispersed through the countries; in accordance with their conduct and their deeds I judged them.

But when they came to the nations, wherever they came, they profaned my holy name, in that it was said of them, "These are the people of the Lord, and yet they had to go out of his land."

But I had concern for my holy name, which the house of Israel had profaned among the nations to which they came. Therefore say to the house of Israel, Thus says the Lord God: It is not for your sake, O house of Israel, that I am about to act, but for the sake of my holy name, which you have profaned among the nations to which you came.

I will sanctify my great name, which has been profaned among the nations, and which you have profaned among them; and the nations shall know that I am the Lord, says the Lord God, when through you I display my holiness before their eyes.

I will take you from the nations, and gather you from all the countries, and bring you into your own land.

I will sprinkle clean water upon you, and you shall be clean from all your uncleanness, and from all your idols I will cleanse you.

A new heart I will give you, and a new spirit I will put within you; and I will remove from your body the heart of stone and give you a heart of flesh. I will put my spirit within you, and make you follow my statutes and be careful to observe my ordinances. Then you shall live in the land that I gave to your ancestors; and you shall be my people, and I will be your God.—The word of the Lord. ℟. **Thanks be to God.** ↓

When Baptism is celebrated, the following Responsorial Psalm is used.

RESPONSORIAL PSALM Ps. 42; 43

Michel Guimont

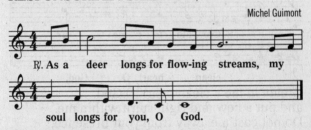

℟. As a deer longs for flow-ing streams, my soul longs for you, O God.

My soul thirsts for God, for the living God.
When shall I come and behold the face of
    God?—℟.

I went with the throng,
and led them in procession to the house of God,
with glad shouts and songs of thanksgiving,
a multitude keeping festival.—℟.

O send out your light and your truth;
let them lead me;
let them bring me to your holy mountain
and to your dwelling.—℟.

Then I will go to the altar of God,
to God my exceeding joy;
and I will praise you with the harp,
O God, my God.

℟. **As a deer longs for flowing streams, my soul
longs for you, O God.** ↓

OR

*When Baptism is not celebrated, the Responsorial Psalm
after the Fifth Reading (Isa. 12) as above, p. 376, may be
used; or the following:*

RESPONSORIAL PSALM Ps. 51

David Szanto

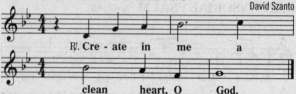

℟. Cre - ate in me a clean heart, O God.

Create in me a clean heart, O God,
and put a new and right spirit within me.
Do not cast me away from your presence,
and do not take your holy spirit from me.—℟.

Restore to me the joy of your salvation,
and sustain in me a willing spirit.
Then I will teach transgressors your ways,
and sinners will return to you.—℟.

For you have no delight in sacrifice;
if I were to give a burnt offering, you would not
be pleased.
The sacrifice acceptable to God
is a broken spirit;
a broken and contrite heart, O God,
you will not despise.—℟. ↓

PRAYER

Let us pray.

O God of unchanging power and eternal light,
look with favour on the wondrous mystery of the
  whole Church
and serenely accomplish the work of human
  salvation,
which you planned from all eternity;
may the whole world know and see
that what was cast down is raised up,
what had become old is made new,
and all things are restored to integrity through
  Christ,
just as by him they came into being.
Who lives and reigns for ever and ever.
℟. **Amen.** ↓

OR

PRAYER

O God, who by the pages of both Testaments
instruct and prepare us to celebrate the Paschal
  Mystery,
grant that we may comprehend your mercy,
so that the gifts we receive from you this night
may confirm our hope of the gifts to come.
Through Christ our Lord. ℟. **Amen.** ↓

*After the last reading from the Old Testament with its
Responsorial Psalm and its prayer, the altar candles are
lit, and the Priest intones the hymn* Gloria in excelsis
Deo *(Glory to God in the highest), which is taken up
by all, while bells are rung, according to local custom.*

*When the hymn is concluded, the Priest says the Collect
in the usual way.*

COLLECT

Let us pray.

O God, who make this most sacred night radiant
with the glory of the Lord's Resurrection,
stir up in your Church a spirit of adoption,
so that, renewed in body and mind,
we may render you undivided service.
Through our Lord Jesus Christ, your Son,
who lives and reigns with you in the unity of the
  Holy Spirit,
one God, for ever and ever. ℟. **Amen.** ↓

Then the reader proclaims the reading from the Apostle.

EPISTLE Rom. 6.3-11

In baptism we are united to Christ, and we begin to be
formed in him. Christ has died; we will die. Christ is
risen; we will rise.

A reading from the Letter of Saint Paul
to the Romans.

BROTHERS and sisters: Do you not know that
all of us who have been baptized into Christ
Jesus were baptized into his death? Therefore we
have been buried with him by baptism into death,
so that, just as Christ was raised from the dead by
the glory of the Father, so we too might walk in
newness of life. For if we have been united with
him in a death like his, we will certainly be united
with him in a resurrection like his.

We know that our old self was crucified with
him so that the body of sin might be destroyed,
and we might no longer be enslaved to sin. For
whoever has died is freed from sin. But if we have
died with Christ, we believe that we will also live
with him.

We know that Christ, being raised from the dead, will never die again; death no longer has dominion over him. The death he died, he died to sin, once for all; but the life he lives, he lives to God. So you also must consider yourselves dead to sin and alive to God in Christ Jesus.—The word of the Lord. ℟. **Thanks be to God.** ↓

After the Epistle has been read, all rise, then the Priest solemnly intones the Alleluia *three times, raising his voice by a step each time, with all repeating it. If necessary, the psalmist intones the* Alleluia.

RESPONSORIAL PSALM – SOLEMN ALLELUIA Ps. 118

Geoffrey Angeles

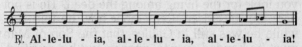

℟. **Al-le-lu - ia, al-le-lu - ia, al-le-lu - ia!**

O give thanks to the Lord, for he is good;
his steadfast love endures forever.
Let Israel say,
"His steadfast love endures forever."—℟.

"The right hand of the Lord is exalted;
the right hand of the Lord does valiantly."
I shall not die, but I shall live,
and recount the deeds of the Lord.—℟.

The stone that the builders rejected
has become the chief cornerstone.
This is the Lord's doing;
it is marvellous in our eyes.—℟. ↓

GOSPEL Lk. 24.1-12

Christ has died, Christ has risen, Christ will come again! God's mercy brings us forgiveness and salvation.

℣. The Lord be with you. ℟. **And with your spirit.**
✠ A reading from the holy Gospel according to
Luke. ℟. **Glory to you, O Lord.**

ON the first day of the week, at early dawn, the
women who had accompanied Jesus from
Galilee came to the tomb, taking the spices that
they had prepared. They found the stone rolled
away from the tomb, but when they went in, they
did not find the body.

While they were perplexed about this, suddenly
two men in dazzling clothes stood beside them.
The women were terrified and bowed their faces
to the ground, but the men said to them, "Why do
you look for the living among the dead? He is not
here, but has risen. Remember how he told you,
while he was still in Galilee, that the Son of Man
must be handed over to sinners, and be crucified,
and on the third day rise again."

Then the women remembered Jesus' words, and
returning from the tomb, they told all this to the
eleven and to all the rest. Now it was Mary Magdalene, Joanna, Mary the mother of James, and
the other women with them who told this to the
Apostles.

These words seemed to the Apostles an idle
tale, and they did not believe the women. But Peter
got up and ran to the tomb; stooping and looking
in, he saw the linen cloths by themselves; then he
went home, amazed at what had happened.—The
Gospel of the Lord. ℟. **Praise to you, Lord Jesus
Christ.**

*After the Gospel, the Homily, even if brief, is not to be
omitted.*

Then the Liturgy of the Sacraments of Initiation begins.

THIRD PART:
THE LITURGY OF THE SACRAMENTS OF INITIATION

The following is adapted from the Rite of Christian Initiation of Adults.

Celebration of Baptism

PRESENTATION OF THE CANDIDATES

An assisting Deacon or other minister calls the candidates for Baptism forward and their godparents present them. The Invitation to Prayer and the Litany of the Saints follow.

INVITATION TO PRAYER

The Priest addresses the following or a similar invitation for the assembly to join in prayer for the candidates for Baptism.

Dearly beloved,
with one heart and one soul, let us by our prayers
come to the aid of these our brothers and sisters
    in their blessed hope,
so that, as they approach the font of rebirth,
the almighty Father may bestow on them
all his merciful help.

LITANY OF THE SAINTS

The singing of the Litany of the Saints is led by cantors and may include, at the proper place, names of other Saints (for example, The Titular Saint of the church, the Patron Saints of the place or of those to be baptized) or petitions suitable to the occasion.

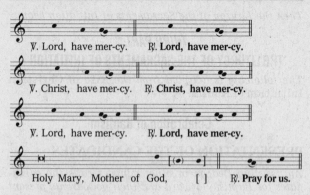

℣. Lord, have mer-cy. ℟. **Lord, have mer-cy.**

℣. Christ, have mer-cy. ℟. **Christ, have mer-cy.**

℣. Lord, have mer-cy. ℟. **Lord, have mer-cy.**

Holy Mary, Mother of God, [ ] ℟. **Pray for us.**

Saint Michael,*
Holy Angels of God,
Saint John the Baptist,
Saint Joseph,
Saint Peter and Saint Paul,
Saint Andrew,
Saint John,
Saint Mary Magdalene,
Saint Stephen,
Saint Ignatius of Antioch,
Saint Lawrence,
Saint Perpetua and Saint Felicity,
Saint Agnes,
Saint Gregory,
Saint Augustine,
Saint Athanasius,
Saint Basil,
Saint Martin,
Saint Benedict,
Saint Francis and Saint Dominic,
Saint Francis Xavier,

Repeat Pray for us *after each invocation.*

Saint John Vianney,
Saint Catherine of Siena,
Saint Teresa of Jesus,
All holy men and women, Saints of God,

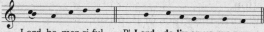

Lord, be mer-ci-ful, ℟. **Lord, de-liv-er us, we pray.**

From all evil,*
From every sin,
From everlasting death,
By your Incarnation,
By your Death and Resurrection,
By the outpouring of the Holy Spirit,

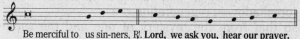

Be merciful to us sin-ners, ℟. **Lord, we ask you, hear our prayer.**

Bring these chosen ones to new birth through the grace of Baptism, **Lord, we ask you, hear our prayer.**
Jesus, Son of the living God, **Lord, we ask you, hear our prayer.**

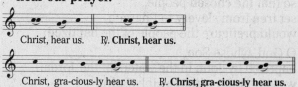

Christ, hear us. ℟. **Christ, hear us.**

Christ, gra-cious-ly hear us. ℟. **Christ, gra-cious-ly hear us.**

BLESSING OF BAPTISMAL WATER

The Priest then blesses the baptismal water, saying the following prayer with hands extended:

---

* Repeat Lord, deliver us, we pray *after each invocation.*

O God, who by invisible power
accomplish a wondrous effect
through sacramental signs
and who in many ways have prepared water, your
   creation,
to show forth the grace of Baptism;

O God, whose Spirit
in the first moments of the world's creation
hovered over the waters,
so that the very substance of water
would even then take to itself the power to
   sanctify;

O God, who by the outpouring of the flood
foreshadowed regeneration,
so that from the mystery of one and the same
   element of water
would come an end to vice and a beginning of
   virtue;

O God, who caused the children of Abraham
to pass dry-shod through the Red Sea,
so that the chosen people,
set free from slavery to Pharaoh,
would prefigure the people of the baptized;

O God, whose Son,
baptized by John in the waters of the Jordan,
was anointed with the Holy Spirit,
and, as he hung upon the Cross,
gave forth water from his side along with blood,
and after his Resurrection, commanded his
   disciples:
"Go forth, teach all nations, baptizing them

in the name of the Father and of the Son and of
  the Holy Spirit,"
look now, we pray, upon the face of your Church
and graciously unseal for her the fountain of
  Baptism.

May this water receive by the Holy Spirit
the grace of your Only Begotten Son,
so that human nature, created in your image
and washed clean through the Sacrament of
  Baptism
from all the squalor of the life of old,
may be found worthy to rise to the life of
  newborn children
through water and the Holy Spirit.

And, if appropriate, lowering the paschal candle into the
water either once or three times, he continues:

May the power of the Holy Spirit,
O Lord, we pray,
come down through your Son
into the fullness of this font,

and, holding the candle in the water, he continues:

so that all who have been buried with Christ
by Baptism into death
may rise again to life with him.
Who lives and reigns with you in the unity of the
  Holy Spirit,
one God, for ever and ever.

℟. **A-men.**

Then the candle is lifted out of the water, as the people
acclaim:

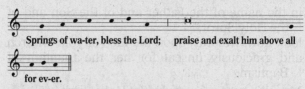

Springs of wa-ter, bless the Lord;   praise and exalt him above all

for ev-er.

THE BLESSING OF WATER

If no one present is to be baptized and the font is not to be blessed, the Priest introduces the faithful to the blessing of water, saying:

Dear brothers and sisters,
let us humbly beseech the Lord our God
to bless this water he has created,
which will be sprinkled upon us
as a memorial of our Baptism.
May he graciously renew us,
that we may remain faithful to the Spirit
whom we have received.

And after a brief pause in silence, he proclaims the following prayer, with hands extended:

Lord our God,
in your mercy be present to your people
who keep vigil on this most sacred night,
and, for us who recall the wondrous work of our
    creation
and the still greater work of our redemption,
graciously bless this water.
For you created water to make the fields fruitful
and to refresh and cleanse our bodies.
You also made water the instrument of your
    mercy:
for through water you freed your people from
    slavery

and quenched their thirst in the desert;
through water the Prophets proclaimed the new
  covenant
you were to enter upon with the human race;
and last of all,
through water, which Christ made holy in the
  Jordan,
you have renewed our corrupted nature
in the bath of regeneration.

Therefore, may this water be for us
a memorial of the Baptism we have received,
and grant that we may share
in the gladness of our brothers and sisters,
who at Easter have received their Baptism.
Through Christ our Lord.
℟. **Amen.**

RENUNCIATION OF SIN AND PROFESSION OF FAITH

If there are baptismal candidates, the Priest, in a series of questions to which the candidates reply, **I do**, *asks the candidates to renounce sin and profess their faith.*

BAPTISM

The Priest baptizes each candidate either by immersion or by the pouring of water.

N., I baptize you in the name of the Father, and of the Son, and of the Holy Spirit.

EXPLANATORY RITES

The celebration of Baptism continues with the explanatory rites, after which the celebration of Confirmation normally follows.

ANOINTING AFTER BAPTISM

If the Confirmation of those baptized is separated from their Baptism, the Priest anoints them with chrism immediately after Baptism.

The God of power and Father of our Lord Jesus
   Christ
has freed you from sin
and brought you to new life
through water and the Holy Spirit.

He now anoints you with the chrism of salvation,
so that, united with his people,
you may remain for ever a member of Christ
who is Priest, Prophet, and King.

Newly baptized: **Amen.**

In silence each of the newly baptized is anointed with chrism on the crown of the head.

CLOTHING WITH THE BAPTISMAL GARMENT

The garment used in this Rite may be white or of a colour that conforms to local custom. If circumstances suggest, this Rite may be omitted.

N. and N., you have become a new creation
and have clothed yourselves in Christ.
Receive this baptismal garment
and bring it unstained to the judgment seat of
   our Lord Jesus Christ,
so that you may have everlasting life.

Newly baptized: **Amen.**

PRESENTATION OF A LIGHTED CANDLE

The Priest takes the Easter candle in his hands or touches it, saying:

Godparents, please come forward to give to the newly baptized the light of Christ.

A godparent of each of the newly baptized goes to the Priest, lights a candle from the Easter candle, then presents it to the newly baptized.

You have been enlightened by Christ.
Walk always as children of the light
and keep the flame of faith alive in your hearts.
When the Lord comes, may you go out to meet him
with all the saints in the heavenly kingdom.

Newly baptized: **Amen.**

The Renewal of Baptismal Promises

INVITATION

After the celebration of Baptism, the Priest addresses the community, in order to invite those present to the renewal of their baptismal promises; the candidates for reception into full communion join the rest of the community in this renunciation of sin and profession of faith. All stand and hold lighted candles.

The Priest addresses the faithful in these or similar words.

Dear brethren (brothers and sisters), through the Paschal Mystery
we have been buried with Christ in Baptism,
so that we may walk with him in newness of life.
And so, now that our Lenten observance is concluded,
let us renew the promises of Holy Baptism,
by which we once renounced Satan and his works
and promised to serve God in the holy Catholic Church.
And so I ask you:

A

Priest: Do you renounce Satan?

All: **I do.**

Priest: And all his works?

All: **I do.**

Priest: And all his empty show?

All: **I do.**

B

Priest: Do you renounce sin,
so as to live in the freedom of the children of
God?

All: **I do.**

Priest: Do you renounce the lure of evil,
so that sin may have no mastery over you?

All: **I do.**

Priest: Do you renounce Satan,
the author and prince of sin?

All: **I do.**

PROFESSION OF FAITH

Then the Priest continues:

Priest: Do you believe in God,
the Father almighty,
Creator of heaven and earth?

All: **I do.**

Priest: Do you believe in Jesus Christ, his only
Son, our Lord,
who was born of the Virgin Mary,
suffered death and was buried,
rose again from the dead
and is seated at the right hand of the Father?

All: **I do.**

Priest: Do you believe in the Holy Spirit,
   the holy catholic Church,
   the communion of saints,
   the forgiveness of sins,
   the resurrection of the body,
   and life everlasting?

All: **I do.**

And the Priest concludes:

And may almighty God, the Father of our Lord
   Jesus Christ,
who has given us new birth by water and the
   Holy Spirit
and bestowed on us forgiveness of our sins,
keep us by his grace,
in Christ Jesus our Lord,
for eternal life.

All: **Amen.**

SPRINKLING WITH BAPTISMAL WATER

The Priest sprinkles all the people with the blessed baptismal water, while all sing the following song or any other that is baptismal in character.

ANTIPHON

I saw water flowing from the Temple,
from its right-hand side, alleluia;
and all to whom this water came were saved
and shall say: Alleluia, alleluia.

Celebration of Reception

INVITATION

If Baptism has been celebrated at the font, the Priest, the assisting ministers, and the newly baptized with their godparents proceed to the sanctuary. As they do so the assembly may sing a suitable song.

Then in the following or similar words the Priest invites the candidates for reception, along with their sponsors, to come into the sanctuary and before the community to make a profession of faith.

N. and N., of your own free will you have asked to be received into the full communion of the Catholic Church. You have made your decision after careful thought under the guidance of the Holy Spirit. I now invite you to come forward with your sponsors and in the presence of this community to profess the Catholic faith. In this faith you will be one with us for the first time at the eucharistic table of the Lord Jesus, the sign of the Church's unity.

PROFESSION BY THE CANDIDATES

When the candidates for reception and their sponsors have taken their places in the sanctuary, the Priest asks the candidates to make the following profession of faith. The candidates say:

I believe and profess all that the holy Catholic Church believes, teaches, and proclaims to be revealed by God.

ACT OF RECEPTION

Then the candidates with their sponsors go individually to the Priest, who says to each candidate (laying his right hand on the head of any candidate who is not to receive Confirmation):

N., the Lord receives you into the Catholic Church. His loving kindness has led you here, so that in the unity of the Holy Spirit you may have full communion with us in the faith that you have professed in the presence of his family.

Celebration of Confirmation

INVITATION

The newly baptized with their godparents and, if they have not received the Sacrament of Confirmation, the newly received with their sponsors, stand before the Priest. He first speaks briefly to the newly baptized and the newly received in these or similar words.

My dear candidates for Confirmation, by your Baptism you have been born again in Christ and you have become members of Christ and of his priestly people. Now you are to share in the outpouring of the Holy Spirit among us, the Spirit sent by the Lord upon his apostles at Pentecost and given by them and their successors to the baptized.

The promised strength of the Holy Spirit, which you are to receive, will make you more like Christ and help you to be witnesses to his suffering, death, and resurrection. It will strengthen you to be active members of the Church and to build up the Body of Christ in faith and love.

My dear friends, let us pray to God our Father, that he will pour out the Holy Spirit on these candidates for Confirmation to strengthen them with his gifts and anoint them to be more like Christ, the Son of God.

All pray briefly in silence.

LAYING ON OF HANDS

The Priest holds his hands outstretched over the entire group of those to be confirmed and says the following prayer.

Almighty God, Father of our Lord Jesus Christ,
Who brought these your servants to new birth
by water and the Holy Spirit,
freeing them from sin:
send upon them, O Lord, the Holy Spirit, the Paraclete;
give them the spirit of wisdom and understanding,
the spirit of counsel and fortitude,
the spirit of knowledge and piety;
fill them with the spirit of the fear of the Lord.
Through Christ our Lord.
℟. **Amen.**

ANOINTING WITH CHRISM

Either or both godparents and sponsors place the right hand on the shoulder of the candidate; and a godparent or a sponsor of the candidate gives the candidate's name to the minister of the sacrament. During the conferral of the sacrament an appropriate song may be sung.

The minister of the sacrament dips his right thumb in the chrism and makes the Sign of the Cross on the forehead of the one to be confirmed as he says:

N., be sealed with the Gift of the Holy Spirit.
Newly confirmed: **Amen.**

Minister: Peace be with you.
Newly confirmed: **And with your spirit.**

After all have received the sacrament, the newly confirmed as well as the godparents and sponsors are led to their places in the assembly.

[Since the Profession of Faith is not said, the Universal Prayer (no. 16, p. 19) begins immediately and for the first time the neophytes take part in it.]

FOURTH PART:
THE LITURGY OF THE EUCHARIST

The Priest goes to the altar and begins the Liturgy of the Eucharist in the usual way.

It is desirable that the bread and wine be brought forward by the newly baptized or, if they are children, by their parents or godparents.

PRAYER OVER THE OFFERINGS

Accept, we ask, O Lord,
the prayers of your people
with the sacrificial offerings,
that what has begun in the paschal mysteries
may, by the working of your power,
bring us to the healing of eternity.
Through Christ our Lord.
℟. **Amen.**

→ No. 21, p. 22 (Pref. 21: on this night above all)

In the Eucharistic Prayer, a commemoration is made of the baptized and their godparents in accord with the formulas which are found in the Roman Missal and Roman Ritual for each of the Eucharistic Prayers.

COMMUNION ANTIPHON 1 Cor. 5.7-8

Christ our Passover has been sacrificed; therefore let us keep the feast with the unleavened bread of purity and truth, alleluia. ↓

Psalm 117 may appropriately be sung.

PRAYER AFTER COMMUNION

Pour out on us, O Lord, the Spirit of your love,
and in your kindness make those you have
   nourished
by this paschal Sacrament
one in mind and heart.
Through Christ our Lord. ℟. **Amen.** ↓

SOLEMN BLESSING

May almighty God bless you
through today's Easter Solemnity
and, in his compassion,
defend you from every assault of sin.
℟. **Amen.**

And may he, who restores you to eternal life
in the Resurrection of his Only Begotten,
endow you with the prize of immortality.
℟. **Amen.**

Now that the days of the Lord's Passion have
   drawn to a close,
may you who celebrate the gladness of the
   Paschal Feast
come with Christ's help, and exulting in spirit,
to those feasts that are celebrated in eternal joy.
℟. **Amen.**

And may the blessing of almighty God,
the Father, and the Son, ✜ and the Holy Spirit,

come down on you and remain with you for ever.
℟. **Amen.**

The final blessing formula from the Rite of Baptism of Adults or of Children may also be used, according to circumstances.

To dismiss the people the Deacon or, if there is no Deacon, the Priest himself sings or says:

Go forth, the Mass is ended, alleluia, alleluia.

OR

Go in peace, alleluia, alleluia.

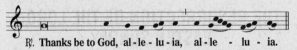

℟. **Thanks be to God, al - le - lu - ia, al - le - lu - ia.**

This practice is observed throughout the Octave of Easter.

"I have risen, and I am with you still."

APRIL 21

THE RESURRECTION OF THE LORD: EASTER SUNDAY

ENTRANCE ANTIPHON Cf. Ps. 138.18, 5-6

I have risen, and I am with you still, alleluia. You have laid your hand upon me, alleluia. Too wonderful for me, this knowledge, alleluia, alleluia.

→ No. 2, p. 10

OR Lk. 24.34; cf. Rev. 1.6

The Lord is truly risen, alleluia. To him be glory and power for all the ages of eternity, alleluia, alleluia.

→ No. 2, p. 10

COLLECT

O God, who on this day,
through your Only Begotten Son,
have conquered death
and unlocked for us the path to eternity,
grant, we pray, that we who keep
the solemnity of the Lord's Resurrection

may, through the renewal brought by your Spirit,
rise up in the light of life.
Through our Lord Jesus Christ, your Son,
who lives and reigns with you in the unity of the
   Holy Spirit,
one God, for ever and ever. ℟. **Amen.** ↓

FIRST READING Acts 10.34a, 37-43

In his sermon Peter sums up the good news, the Gospel.
Salvation comes through Christ, the beloved Son of the
Father, and the anointed of the Holy Spirit.

A reading from the Acts of the Apostles.

PETER began to speak: "You know the message that spread throughout Judea, beginning
in Galilee after the baptism that John announced:
how God anointed Jesus of Nazareth with the
Holy Spirit and with power; how he went about
doing good and healing all who were oppressed
by the devil, for God was with him.

We are witnesses to all that he did both in
Judea and in Jerusalem. They put him to death
by hanging him on a tree; but God raised him
on the third day and allowed him to appear, not
to all the people but to us who were chosen by
God as witnesses, and who ate and drank with
him after he rose from the dead.

He commanded us to preach to the people
and to testify that he is the one ordained by God
as judge of the living and the dead. All the
Prophets testify about him that everyone who
believes in him receives forgiveness of sins
through his name."—The word of the Lord.
℟. **Thanks be to God.** ↓

RESPONSORIAL PSALM Ps. 118

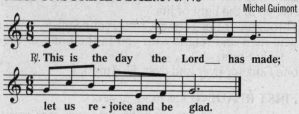

Michel Guimont

℞. This is the day the Lord___ has made;
let us re - joice and be glad.

Or: ℞. Alleluia! Alleluia! Alleluia!

O give thanks to the Lord, for he is good;
his steadfast love endures forever.
Let Israel say,
"His steadfast love endures forever."—℞.

"The right hand of the Lord is exalted;
the right hand of the Lord does valiantly."
I shall not die, but I shall live,
and recount the deeds of the Lord.—℞.

The stone that the builders rejected
has become the chief cornerstone.
This is the Lord's doing;
it is marvellous in our eyes.—℞. ↓

*One of the following texts may be chosen as the Second
Reading.*

SECOND READING Col. 3.1-4

Look to the glory of Christ in which we share because our
lives are hidden in him through baptism, and we are destined to share in his glory.

A reading from the Letter of Saint Paul
to the Colossians.

BROTHERS and sisters: If you have been raised with Christ, seek the things that are above, where Christ is, seated at the right hand of God. Set your minds on things that are above, not on things that are on earth, for you have died, and your life is hidden with Christ in God. When Christ who is your life is revealed, then you also will be revealed with him in glory.— The word of the Lord. ℟. **Thanks be to God.** ↓

OR

SECOND READING 1 Cor. 5.6b-8

Turn away from your old ways, from sin. Have a change of heart; be virtuous.

A reading from the first Letter of Saint Paul to the Corinthians.

DO you not know that a little yeast leavens the whole batch of dough? Clean out the old yeast so that you may be a new batch, as you really are unleavened. For our paschal lamb, Christ, has been sacrificed. Therefore, let us celebrate the festival, not with the old yeast, the yeast of malice and evil, but with the unleavened bread of sincerity and truth.—The word of the Lord. ℟. **Thanks be to God.** ↓

SEQUENCE *(Victimae paschali laudes)*

1. **Christians, praise the paschal victim!**
   Offer thankful sacrifice!
2. **Christ the Lamb has saved the sheep,**
   Christ the just one paid the price,
   Reconciling sinners to the Father.

3. **Death and life fought bitterly**
   For this wondrous victory;
   The Lord of life who died reigns glorified!

4. **"O Mary, come and say**
   what you saw at break of day."

5. **"The empty tomb of my living Lord!**
   I saw Christ Jesus risen and adored!

6. **"Bright Angels testified,**
   Shroud and grave clothes side by side!

7. **"Yes, Christ my hope rose gloriously.**
   He goes before you into Galilee."

8. **Share the Good News, sing joyfully:**
   His death is victory!
   Lord Jesus, Victor King, show us mercy. ↓

GOSPEL ACCLAMATION 1 Cor. 5.7-8

℣. Alleluia. ℟. **Alleluia.**
℣. Christ, our Paschal Lamb, has been sacrificed;
let us feast with joy in the Lord.
℟. **Alleluia.** ↓

(FOR MORNING MASS)

GOSPEL Jn. 20.1-18 or 20.1-9

> Let us ponder this mystery of Christ's rising, and like
> Christ's first followers be strengthened in our faith.

[If the "Shorter Form" is used, the indented text in brack-
ets is omitted.]

℣. The Lord be with you. ℟. **And with your spirit.**
✠ A reading from the holy Gospel according to
John. ℟. **Glory to you, O Lord.**

EARLY on the first day of the week, while it
was still dark, Mary Magdalene came to the

tomb and saw that the stone had been removed from the tomb. So she ran and went to Simon Peter and the other disciple, the one whom Jesus loved, and said to them, "They have taken the Lord out of the tomb, and we do not know where they have laid him."

Then Peter and the other disciple set out and went toward the tomb. The two were running together, but the other disciple outran Peter and reached the tomb first. He bent down to look in and saw the linen wrappings lying there, but he did not go in.

Then Simon Peter came, following him, and went into the tomb. He saw the linen wrappings lying there, and the cloth that had been on Jesus' head, not lying with the linen wrappings but rolled up in a place by itself. Then the other disciple, who reached the tomb first, also went in, and he saw and believed; for as yet they did not understand the Scripture, that he must rise from the dead.

[Then the disciples returned to their homes. But Mary Magdalene stood weeping outside the tomb. As she wept, she bent over to look into the tomb; and she saw two Angels in white, sitting where the body of Jesus had been lying, one at the head and the other at the feet. They said to her, "Woman, why are you weeping?" She said to them, "They have taken away my Lord, and I do not know where they have laid him."

When she had said this, she turned around and saw Jesus standing there, but she did not know that it was Jesus. Jesus said to her, "Woman, why are you weeping? Whom are you looking for?" Supposing him to be the gardener, she said to him, "Sir, if you have carried him away, tell me where you have laid him, and I will take him away."

Jesus said to her, "Mary!" She turned and said to him in Hebrew, "Rabbouni!" which means Teacher. Jesus said to her, "Do not hold on to me, because I have not yet ascended to the Father. But go to my brothers and say to them, 'I am ascending to my Father and your Father, to my God and your God.'"

Mary Magdalene went and announced to the disciples, "I have seen the Lord," and she told them that he had said these things to her.]

The Gospel of the Lord. ℟. **Praise to you, Lord Jesus Christ.**   ➔ No. 15, p. 18

In Easter Sunday Masses which are celebrated with a congregation, the rite of the renewal of baptismal promises may take place after the Homily, according to the text used at the Easter Vigil (p. 395). In that case the Creed is omitted.

OR

(The Gospel from the Easter Vigil noted below may be used.)

GOSPEL Lk. 24.1-12

See p. 385.

(FOR AN AFTERNOON OR EVENING MASS)

GOSPEL Lk. 24.13-35

Let us accept the testimony of these two witnesses, that our hearts may burn with the fire of faith.

℣. The Lord be with you. ℟. **And with your spirit.**
✛ A reading from the holy Gospel according to
Luke. ℟. **Glory to you, O Lord.**

ON the first day of the week, two of the disciples were going to a village called Emmaus,
about eleven kilometres from Jerusalem, and
talking with each other about all these things
that had happened. While they were talking and
discussing, Jesus himself came near and went
with them, but their eyes were kept from recognizing him.

And he said to them, "What are you discussing
with each other while you walk along?" They
stood still, looking sad. Then one of them, whose
name was Cleopas, answered him, "Are you the
only stranger in Jerusalem who does not know the
things that have taken place there in these days?"

He asked them, "What things?" They replied,
"The things about Jesus of Nazareth, who was a
Prophet mighty in deed and word before God and
all the people, and how our chief priests and leaders handed him over to be condemned to death
and crucified him. But we had hoped that he was
the one to redeem Israel. Yes, and besides all this,
it is now the third day since these things took
place. Moreover, some women of our group as-
tounded us. They were at the tomb early this
morning, and when they did not find his body
there, they came back and told us that they had
indeed seen a vision of Angels who said that he
was alive. Some of those who were with us went

to the tomb and found it just as the women had said; but they did not see him."

Then he said to them, "Oh, how foolish you are, and how slow of heart to believe all that the Prophets have declared! Was it not necessary that the Christ should suffer these things and then enter into his glory?"

Then beginning with Moses and all the Prophets, he interpreted to them the things about himself in all the Scriptures. As they came near the village to which they were going, he walked ahead as if he were going on. But they urged him strongly, saying, "Stay with us, because it is almost evening and the day is now nearly over." So he went in to stay with them.

When he was at the table with them, he took bread, blessed and broke it, and gave it to them. Then their eyes were opened, and they recognized him; and he vanished from their sight.

They said to each other, "Were not our hearts burning within us while he was talking to us on the road, while he was opening the Scriptures to us?"

That same hour they got up and returned to Jerusalem; and they found the eleven and their companions gathered together. These were saying, "The Lord has risen indeed, and he has appeared to Simon!"

Then they told what had happened on the road, and how he had been made known to them in the breaking of the bread.—The Gospel of the Lord.
℟. **Praise to you, Lord Jesus Christ.** → No. 15, p. 18

*However, in Easter Sunday Masses which are celebrated
with a congregation, the rite of the renewal of baptismal
promises may take place after the Homily, according to
the text used at the Easter Vigil (p. 395). In that case the
Creed is omitted.*

PRAYER OVER THE OFFERINGS

Exultant with paschal gladness, O Lord,
we offer the sacrifice
by which your Church
is wondrously reborn and nourished.
Through Christ our Lord. ℟. **Amen.**

→ No. 21, p. 22 (Pref. 21: on this day above all)

When the Roman Canon is used, the proper forms of the
Communicantes (In communion with those) *and*
Hanc igitur (Therefore, Lord, we pray) *are said.*

COMMUNION ANTIPHON 1 Cor. 5.7-8

**Christ our Passover has been sacrificed, alleluia;
therefore let us keep the feast with the unleavened bread of purity and truth, alleluia, alleluia.** ↓

PRAYER AFTER COMMUNION

Look upon your Church, O God,
with unfailing love and favour,
so that, renewed by the paschal mysteries,
she may come to the glory of the resurrection.
Through Christ our Lord. ℟. **Amen.** → No. 30, p. 77

*To impart the blessing at the end of Mass, the Priest may
appropriately use the formula of Solemn Blessing for the
Mass of the Easter Vigil, p. 402.*

Dismissal: see p. 403.

"Thomas answered him, 'My Lord and my God!'"

APRIL 28

2nd SUNDAY OF EASTER
(or of DIVINE MERCY)

ENTRANCE ANTIPHON 1 Pet. 2.2

Like newborn infants, you must long for the pure, spiritual milk, that in him you may grow to salvation, alleluia. → No. 2, p. 10

OR 4 Esdr. 2.36-37

Receive the joy of your glory, giving thanks to God, who has called you into the heavenly Kingdom, alleluia. → No. 2, p. 10

COLLECT

God of everlasting mercy,
who in the very recurrence of the paschal feast
kindle the faith of the people you have made your
    own,
increase, we pray, the grace you have bestowed,
that all may grasp and rightly understand
in what font they have been washed,

by whose Spirit they have been reborn,
by whose Blood they have been redeemed.
Through our Lord Jesus Christ, your Son,
who lives and reigns with you in the unity of the
   Holy Spirit,
one God, for ever and ever. ℟. **Amen.** ↓

FIRST READING Acts 5.12-16

**Through signs and wonders—miracles—the Lord supports
the work of the apostles and leads people to the Faith.**

A reading from the Acts of the Apostles.

MANY signs and wonders were done among
the people through the Apostles. And the
believers were all together in Solomon's Portico.
None of the rest dared to join them, but the people held them in high esteem.

Yet more than ever believers were added to the
Lord, great numbers of both men and women, so
that they even carried out the sick into the streets,
and laid them on cots and mats, in order that
Peter's shadow might fall on some of them as he
came by. A great number of people would also
gather from the towns around Jerusalem, bringing the sick and those tormented by unclean spirits, and they were all cured.—The word of the
Lord. ℟. **Thanks be to God.** ↓

RESPONSORIAL PSALM Ps. 118

Leo Marchildon

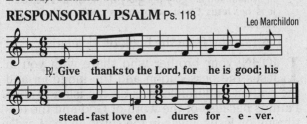

℟. Give   thanks to the Lord, for   he is good; his
stead-fast love en - dures for - e - ver.

Or: ℟. **Alleluia!**

Let Israel say,
"His steadfast love endures forever."
Let the house of Aaron say,
"His steadfast love endures forever."
Let those who fear the Lord say,
"His steadfast love endures forever."

℞. **Give thanks to the Lord, for he is good; his
steadfast love endures forever.**

The stone that the builders rejected
has become the chief cornerstone.
This is the Lord's doing;
it is marvellous in our eyes.
This is the day that the Lord has made;
let us rejoice and be glad in it.—℞.

Save us, we beseech you, O Lord!
O Lord, we beseech you, give us success!
Blessed is the one who comes in the name of the
Lord.
We bless you from the house of the Lord.
The Lord is God,
and he has given us light.—℞. ↓

SECOND READING Rev. 1.9-11a, 12-13, 17-19

In symbol and allegory the glory of the Lord is depicted.
It is he, Jesus Christ, who shares power with God the
Father.

A reading from the book of Revelation.

I, JOHN, your brother who share with you in
Jesus the persecution and the kingdom and
the patient endurance, was on the island called
Patmos because of the word of God and the testimony of Jesus. I was in the spirit on the Lord's

day, and I heard behind me a loud voice like a trumpet saying, "Write in a book what you see and send it to the seven Churches."

Then I turned to see whose voice it was that spoke to me, and on turning I saw seven golden lampstands, and in the midst of the lampstands I saw one like the Son of Man, clothed with a long robe and with a golden sash across his chest.

When I saw him, I fell at his feet as though dead. But he placed his right hand on me, saying, "Do not be afraid; I am the first and the last, and the living one. I was dead, but see, I am alive forever and ever; and I have the keys of Death and of Hades. Now write what you have seen, what is, and what is to take place after this."—The word of the Lord. ℟. **Thanks be to God.** ↓

GOSPEL ACCLAMATION See Jn. 20.29

℣. Alleluia. ℟. **Alleluia.**
℣. You believed, Thomas, because you have seen me;
blessed are those who have not seen, and yet believe.
℟. **Alleluia.** ↓

GOSPEL Jn. 20.19-31

> Jesus is risen; he comes and stands before his disciples. He encourages them and strengthens their faith.

℣. The Lord be with you. ℟. **And with your spirit.**
✠ A reading from the holy Gospel according to John. ℟. **Glory to you, O Lord.**

IT was evening on the day Jesus rose from the dead, the first day of the week, and the doors of the house where the disciples had met were locked for fear of the Jews. Jesus came and stood among them and said, "Peace be with you." After he said this, he showed them his hands and his side. Then the disciples rejoiced when they saw the Lord.

Jesus said to them again, "Peace be with you. As the Father has sent me, so I send you." When he had said this, he breathed on them and said to them, "Receive the Holy Spirit. If you forgive the sins of any, they are forgiven them; if you retain the sins of any, they are retained."

But Thomas, who was called the Twin, one of the twelve, was not with them when Jesus came. So the other disciples told him, "We have seen the Lord." But he said to them, "Unless I see the mark of the nails in his hands, and put my finger in the mark of the nails and my hand in his side, I will not believe."

After eight days his disciples were again in the house, and Thomas was with them. Although the doors were shut, Jesus came and stood among them and said, "Peace be with you." Then he said to Thomas, "Put your finger here and see my hands. Reach out your hand and put it in my side. Do not doubt but believe." Thomas answered him, "My Lord and my God!"

Jesus said to him, "Have you believed because you have seen me? Blessed are those who have not seen and yet have come to believe."

Now Jesus did many other signs in the presence of his disciples, which are not written in this book. But these are written so that you may come to believe that Jesus is the Christ, the Son of God, and that through believing you may have life in his name.—The Gospel of the Lord. ℟. **Praise to you, Lord Jesus Christ.** → No. 15, p. 18

PRAYER OVER THE OFFERINGS

Accept, O Lord, we pray,
the oblations of your people
(and of those you have brought to new birth),
that, renewed by confession of your name and by
   Baptism,
they may attain unending happiness.
Through Christ our Lord. ℟. **Amen.**
→ No. 21, p. 22 (Pref. 21: on this day above all)

When the Roman Canon is used, the proper forms of the Communicantes *(In communion with those) and* Hanc igitur *(Therefore, Lord, we pray) are said.*

·COMMUNION ANTIPHON Cf. Jn. 20.27

Bring your hand and feel the place of the nails, and do not be unbelieving but believing, alleluia. ↓

PRAYER AFTER COMMUNION

Grant, we pray, almighty God,
that our reception of this paschal Sacrament
may have a continuing effect
in our minds and hearts.
Through Christ our Lord.
℟. **Amen.**   → No. 30, p. 77

Optional Solemn Blessings, p. 97, and Prayers over the People, p. 105
Dismissal: see p. 403.

"Cast the net to the right side of the boat,"
Jesus suggested.

MAY 5

3rd SUNDAY OF EASTER

ENTRANCE ANTIPHON Cf. Ps. 65.1-2

Cry out with joy to God, all the earth; O sing to the glory of his name. O render him glorious praise, alleluia. ➔ No. 2, p. 10

COLLECT

May your people exult for ever, O God,
in renewed youthfulness of spirit,
so that, rejoicing now in the restored glory of our
    adoption,
we may look forward in confident hope
to the rejoicing of the day of resurrection.
Through our Lord Jesus Christ, your Son,
who lives and reigns with you in the unity of the
    Holy Spirit,
one God, for ever and ever. ℟. **Amen.** ↓

FIRST READING Acts 5.28-32, 40b-41

With a strong faith the apostles persevere in the mission that Christ gave them.

A reading from the Acts of the Apostles.

IN those days: The high priest questioned the Apostles, saying, "We gave you strict orders not to teach in this name, yet here you have filled Jerusalem with your teaching and you are determined to bring this man's blood on us."

But Peter and the Apostles answered, "We must obey God rather than human beings. The God of our ancestors raised up Jesus, whom you had killed by hanging him on a tree. God exalted him at his right hand as Leader and Saviour that he might give repentance to Israel and forgiveness of sins. And we are witnesses to these things, and so is the Holy Spirit whom God has given to those who obey him."

Then the council ordered the Apostles not to speak in the name of Jesus, and let them go. As they left the council, they rejoiced that they were considered worthy to suffer dishonour for the sake of the name.—The word of the Lord. ℟. **Thanks be to God.** ↓

RESPONSORIAL PSALM Ps. 30

Normand L. Blanchard

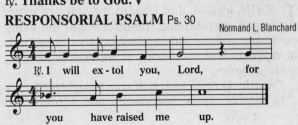

℟. I will ex-tol you, Lord, for you have raised me up.

Or: ℟. **Alleluia!**

I will extol you, O Lord, for you have drawn me up,
and did not let my foes rejoice over me.
O Lord, you brought up my soul from Sheol,
restored me to life from among those gone
    down to the Pit.

R̸. **I will extol you, Lord, for you have raised
me up.**

Sing praises to the Lord, O you his faithful ones,
and give thanks to his holy name.
For his anger is but for a moment;
his favour is for a lifetime.
Weeping may linger for the night,
but joy comes with the morning.—R̸.

Hear, O Lord, and be gracious to me!
O Lord, be my helper!
You have turned my mourning into dancing.
O Lord my God, I will give thanks to you for-
    ever.—R̸. ↓

SECOND READING Rev. 5.11-14

**The power and the glory of God are acclaimed by all cre-
ation.**

A reading from the book of Revelation.

I, JOHN, looked, and I heard the voice of many
Angels surrounding the throne and the living
creatures and the elders; they numbered myriads
of myriads and thousands of thousands, singing
with full voice,

"Worthy is the Lamb that was slaughtered
  to receive power and wealth and wisdom and
      might
  and honour and glory and blessing!"

Then I heard every creature in heaven and on earth and under the earth and in the sea, and all that is in them, singing,

"To the one seated on the throne and to the Lamb

be blessing and honour and glory and might forever and ever!"

And the four living creatures said, "Amen!" And the elders fell down and worshipped.—The word of the Lord. ℟. **Thanks be to God.** ↓

GOSPEL ACCLAMATION

℣. Alleluia. ℟. **Alleluia.**
℣. Christ is risen, the Lord of all creation;
he has shown pity on all people.
℟. **Alleluia.** ↓

GOSPEL Jn. 21.1-19

Again the risen Saviour appears to his disciples in a very human way. Peter in three affirmations rejects his triple denial and again hears the call "Follow me."

℣. The Lord be with you. ℟. **And with your spirit.**
✠ A reading from the holy Gospel according to John. ℟. **Glory to you, O Lord.**

JESUS showed himself again to the disciples by the Sea of Tiberias; and he showed himself in this way. Gathered there together were Simon Peter, Thomas called the Twin, Nathanael of Cana in Galilee, the sons of Zebedee, and two others of his disciples. Simon Peter said to them, "I am going fishing." They said to him, "We will go with you." They went out and got into the boat, but that night they caught nothing.

Just after daybreak, Jesus stood on the beach; but the disciples did not know that it was Jesus. Jesus said to them, "Children, you have no fish, have you?" They answered him, "No." He said to them, "Cast the net to the right side of the boat, and you will find some." So they cast it, and now they were not able to haul it in because there were so many fish.

That disciple whom Jesus loved said to Peter, "It is the Lord!" When Simon Peter heard that it was the Lord, he put on some clothes, for he was naked, and jumped into the sea. But the other disciples came in the boat, dragging the net full of fish, for they were not far from the land, only about ninety metres off.

When they had gone ashore, they saw a charcoal fire there, with fish on it, and bread.

Jesus said to them, "Bring some of the fish that you have just caught." So Simon Peter went aboard and hauled the net ashore, full of large fish, a hundred fifty-three of them; and though there were so many, the net was not torn. Jesus said to them, "Come and have breakfast." Now none of the disciples dared to ask him, "Who are you?" because they knew it was the Lord. Jesus came and took the bread and gave it to them, and did the same with the fish. This was now the third time that Jesus appeared to the disciples after he was raised from the dead.

When they had finished breakfast, Jesus said to Simon Peter, "Simon son of John, do you love me more than these?" He said to him, "Yes, Lord; you know that I love you." Jesus said to him, "Feed my lambs."

A second time he said to him, "Simon son of John, do you love me?" He said to him, "Yes, Lord; you know that I love you." Jesus said to him, "Tend my sheep."

He said to him the third time, "Simon son of John, do you love me?" Peter felt hurt because he said to him the third time, "Do you love me?" And he said to him, "Lord, you know everything; you know that I love you." Jesus said to him, "Feed my sheep.

Very truly, I tell you, when you were younger, you used to fasten your own belt and to go wherever you wished. But when you grow old, you will stretch out your hands, and someone else will fasten a belt around you and take you where you do not wish to go."

(He said this to indicate the kind of death by which he would glorify God.) After this he said to him, "Follow me."—The Gospel of the Lord. ℟. **Praise to you, Lord Jesus Christ.** → No. 15, p. 18

PRAYER OVER THE OFFERINGS

Receive, O Lord, we pray,
these offerings of your exultant Church,
and, as you have given her cause for such great
     gladness,
grant also that the gifts we bring
may bear fruit in perpetual happiness.
Through Christ our Lord.
℟. **Amen.**   → No. 21, p. 22 (Pref. 21-25)

COMMUNION ANTIPHON Cf. Lk. 24.35

The disciples recognized the Lord Jesus in the breaking of the bread, alleluia. ↓

OR Lk. 24.46-47

The Christ had to suffer and on the third day rise from the dead; in his name repentance and remission of sins must be preached to all the nations, alleluia. ↓

PRAYER AFTER COMMUNION

Look with kindness upon your people, O Lord,
and grant, we pray,
that those you were pleased to renew by eternal
　mysteries
may attain in their flesh
the incorruptible glory of the resurrection.
Through Christ our Lord.
℟. **Amen.**　　　　　　　　→ No. 30, p. 77

Optional Solemn Blessings, p. 97, and Prayers over the People, p. 105

"My sheep hear my voice."

MAY 12

4th SUNDAY OF EASTER

ENTRANCE ANTIPHON Cf. Ps. 32.5-6

The merciful love of the Lord fills the earth; by the word of the Lord the heavens were made, alleluia.
→ No. 2, p. 10

COLLECT

Almighty ever-living God,
lead us to a share in the joys of heaven,
so that the humble flock may reach
where the brave Shepherd has gone before.
Who lives and reigns with you in the unity of the
Holy Spirit,
one God, for ever and ever. ℟. **Amen.** ↓

FIRST READING Acts 13.14, 43-52

As missionaries, Paul and Barnabas meet with some success and encounter strong opposition. Steadfastness in faith is a source of joy.

427

A reading from the Acts of the Apostles.

PAUL and Barnabas went on from Perga and came to Antioch in Pisidia. On the Sabbath day they went into the synagogue and sat down. When the meeting of the synagogue broke up, many Jews and devout converts to Judaism followed Paul and Barnabas, who spoke to them and urged them to continue in the grace of God.

The next Sabbath almost the whole city gathered to hear the word of the Lord. But when the Jewish officials saw the crowds, they were filled with jealousy; and blaspheming, they contradicted what was spoken by Paul.

Then both Paul and Barnabas spoke out boldly, saying, "It was necessary that the word of God should be spoken first to you. Since you reject it and judge yourselves to be unworthy of eternal life, we are now turning to the Gentiles. For so the Lord has commanded us, saying, 'I have set you to be a light for the Gentiles, so that you may bring salvation to the ends of the earth.'" When the Gentiles heard this, they were glad and praised the word of the Lord; and as many as had been destined for eternal life became believers.

Thus the word of the Lord spread throughout the region. But the officials incited the devout women of high standing and the leading men of the city, and stirred up persecution against Paul and Barnabas, and drove them out of their region. So they shook the dust off their feet in protest against them, and went to Iconium. And the disciples were filled with joy and with the Holy Spirit.—The word of the Lord. ℞. **Thanks be to God.** ↓

RESPONSORIAL PSALM Ps. 100

Kathrine Bellamy

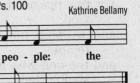

℟. We   are   his   peo - ple: the

sheep   of   his   pas - ture.

Or: ℟. **Alleluia!**

Make a joyful noise to the Lord, all the earth.
Worship the Lord with gladness;
come into his presence with singing.—℟.

Know that the Lord is God.
It is he that made us, and we are his;
we are his people, and the sheep of his pasture.—℟.

For the Lord is good;
his steadfast love endures forever,
and his faithfulness to all generations.—℟. ↓

SECOND READING Rev. 7.9, 14b-17

Those who remain faithful despite severe persecution will find their reward is to be with God and restored to peace.

A reading from the book of Revelation.

AFTER this I, John, looked, and there was a great multitude that no one could count, from every nation, from all tribes and peoples and languages, standing before the throne and before the Lamb, robed in white, with palm branches in their hands.

And one of the elders then said to me, "These are they who have come out of the great ordeal; they have washed their robes and made them white in the blood of the Lamb.

For this reason they are before the throne of God,

and worship him day and night within his temple,

and the one who is seated on the throne will shelter them.

They will hunger no more, and thirst no more; the sun will not strike them, nor any scorching heat;

for the Lamb at the centre of the throne will be their shepherd,

and he will guide them to springs of the water of life,

and God will wipe away every tear from their eyes."

The word of the Lord. ℟. **Thanks be to God.** ↓

GOSPEL ACCLAMATION Jn. 10.14

℣. Alleluia. ℟. **Alleluia.**
℣. I am the good shepherd, says the Lord;
I know my sheep, and my own know me.
℟. **Alleluia.** ↓

GOSPEL Jn. 10.27-30

Jesus proclaims his oneness with the Father. His love for us is so great that he brings us eternal life.

℣. The Lord be with you. ℟. **And with your spirit.**
✛ A reading from the holy Gospel according to John. ℟. **Glory to you, O Lord.**

JESUS said: "My sheep hear my voice. I know them, and they follow me. I give them eternal life, and they will never perish. No one will snatch them out of my hand. What my Father has given me is greater than all else, and no one can snatch it out of the Father's hand. The Father and I are one."—The Gospel of the Lord. ℟. **Praise to you, Lord Jesus Christ.**   ➙ No. 15, p. 18

PRAYER OVER THE OFFERINGS

Grant, we pray, O Lord,
that we may always find delight in these paschal
    mysteries,
so that the renewal constantly at work within us
may be the cause of our unending joy.
Through Christ our Lord.
℟. **Amen.**   ➙ No. 21, p. 22 (Pref. 21-25)

COMMUNION ANTIPHON

The Good Shepherd has risen, who laid down his life for his sheep and willingly died for his flock, alleluia. ↓

PRAYER AFTER COMMUNION

Look upon your flock, kind Shepherd,
and be pleased to settle in eternal pastures
the sheep you have redeemed
by the Precious Blood of your Son.
Who lives and reigns for ever and ever.
℟. **Amen.**   ➙ No. 30, p. 77

Optional Solemn Blessings, p. 97, and Prayers over the People, p. 105

"I give you a new commandment. . . . Just as I have loved you, you also should love one another."

MAY 19

5th SUNDAY OF EASTER

ENTRANCE ANTIPHON Cf. Ps. 97.1-2

O sing a new song to the Lord, for he has worked wonders; in the sight of the nations he has shown his deliverance, alleluia. → No. 2, p. 10

COLLECT

Almighty ever-living God,
constantly accomplish the Paschal Mystery within us,
that those you were pleased to make new in Holy Baptism
may, under your protective care, bear much fruit
and come to the joys of life eternal.
Through our Lord Jesus Christ, your Son,
who lives and reigns with you in the unity of the Holy Spirit,
one God, for ever and ever. ℟. **Amen.** ↓

FIRST READING Acts 14.21b-27

The life we have through faith is not easy; we must struggle against many difficulties, even temptations, on our journey to eternal life.

A reading from the Acts of the Apostles.

PAUL and Barnabas returned to Lystra, then on to Iconium and Antioch. There they strengthened the souls of the disciples and encouraged them to continue in the faith, saying, "It is through many persecutions that we must enter the kingdom of God." And after they had appointed elders for them in each Church, with prayer and fasting they entrusted them to the Lord in whom they had come to believe.

Then they passed through Pisidia and came to Pamphylia. When they had spoken the word in Perga, they went down to Attalia. From there they sailed back to Antioch, where they had been commended to the grace of God for the work that they had completed.

When they arrived, they called the Church together and related all that God had done with them, and how he had opened a door of faith for the Gentiles.—The word of the Lord. ℟. **Thanks be to God.** ↓

RESPONSORIAL PSALM Ps. 145   Normand L. Blanchard

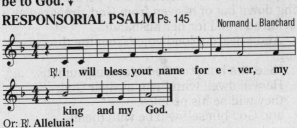

℟. I will bless your name for e - ver, my king and my God.

Or: ℟. **Alleluia!**

The Lord is gracious and merciful,
slow to anger and abounding in steadfast love.
The Lord is good to all,
and his compassion is over all that he has made.
℟. **I will bless your name for ever, my king and
   my God.**

All your works shall give thanks to you, O Lord,
and all your faithful shall bless you.
They shall speak of the glory of your kingdom,
and tell of your power.—℟.

To make known to human beings your mighty
   deeds,
and the glorious splendour of your kingdom.
Your kingdom is an everlasting kingdom,
and your dominion endures throughout all generations.—℟. ↓

SECOND READING Rev. 21.1-5a

In the Kingdom of God all things are made new.

A reading from the book of Revelation.

THEN I, John, saw a new heaven and a new
earth; for the first heaven and the first earth
had passed away, and the sea was no more.

I saw the holy city, the new Jerusalem, coming down out of heaven from God, prepared as a
bride adorned for her husband.

And I heard a loud voice from the throne saying,
   "See, the home of God is among humans.
   He will dwell with them as their God;
   they will be his peoples,
   and God himself will be with them;

he will wipe every tear from their eyes.
Death will be no more;
mourning and crying and pain will be no
    more,
for the first things have passed away."
And the one who was seated on the throne
    said,
"See, I am making all things new."

The word of the Lord. ℟. **Thanks be to God.** ↓

GOSPEL ACCLAMATION See Jn. 13.34

℣. Alleluia. ℟. **Alleluia.**
℣. I give you a new commandment:
love one another just as I have loved you.
℟. **Alleluia.** ↓

GOSPEL Jn. 13.1, 31-33a, 34-35

**Jesus is about to be betrayed yet he teaches us the way
to glory—the way he will go. It is the way of love.**

℣. The Lord be with you. ℟. **And with your spirit.**
✝ A reading from the holy Gospel according to
John. ℟. **Glory to you, O Lord.**

BEFORE the festival of the Passover, Jesus
knew that his hour had come to depart from
this world and go to the Father. Having loved his
own who were in the world, he loved them to
the end.

During the supper, when Judas had gone out,
Jesus said, "Now the Son of Man has been glorified, and God has been glorified in him. If God
has been glorified in him, God will also glorify
him in himself and will glorify him at once.

Little children, I am with you only a little longer. I give you a new commandment, that you love one another. Just as I have loved you, you also should love one another. By this everyone will know that you are my disciples, if you have love for one another."—The Gospel of the Lord. ℟. **Praise to you, Lord Jesus Christ.**   → No. 15, p. 18

PRAYER OVER THE OFFERINGS

O God, who by the wonderful exchange effected in this sacrifice
have made us partakers of the one supreme Godhead,
grant, we pray,
that, as we have come to know your truth,
we may make it ours by a worthy way of life.
Through Christ our Lord.
℟. **Amen.**   → No. 21, p. 22 (Pref. 21-25)

COMMUNION ANTIPHON Cf. Jn. 15.1, 5

I am the true vine and you are the branches, says the Lord. Whoever remains in me, and I in him, bears fruit in plenty, alleluia. ↓

PRAYER AFTER COMMUNION

Graciously be present to your people, we pray, O Lord,
and lead those you have imbued with heavenly mysteries
to pass from former ways to newness of life.
Through Christ our Lord.
℟. **Amen.**   → No. 30, p. 77

Optional Solemn Blessings, p. 97, and Prayers over the People, p. 105

"The Advocate, the Holy Spirit, whom the Father will send in my name. . . ."

MAY 26

6th SUNDAY OF EASTER

ENTRANCE ANTIPHON Cf. Isa. 48.20

Proclaim a joyful sound and let it be heard; proclaim to the ends of the earth: The Lord has freed his people, alleluia. → No. 2, p. 10

COLLECT

Grant, almighty God,
that we may celebrate with heartfelt devotion
    these days of joy,
which we keep in honour of the risen Lord,
and that what we relive in remembrance
we may always hold to in what we do.
Through our Lord Jesus Christ, your Son,
who lives and reigns with you in the unity of the
    Holy Spirit,
one God, for ever and ever. ℞. **Amen.** ↓

FIRST READING Acts 15.1-2, 22-29

The Church faces its first test caused by inner dissensions and shows how, guided by the Spirit, charity will prevail.

A reading from the Acts of the Apostles.

CERTAIN individuals came down from Judea and were teaching the brothers, "Unless you are circumcised according to the custom of Moses, you cannot be saved." And after Paul and Barnabas had no small dissension and debate with them, Paul and Barnabas and some of the others were appointed to go up to Jerusalem to discuss this question with the Apostles and the elders.

Then the Apostles and the elders, with the consent of the whole Church, decided to choose men from among their members and to send them to Antioch with Paul and Barnabas.

They sent Judas called Barsabbas, and Silas, leaders among the brothers, with the following letter:

"The brothers, both the Apostles and the elders, to the believers of Gentile origin in Antioch and Syria and Cilicia, greetings. Since we have heard that certain persons who have gone out from us, though with no instructions from us, have said things to disturb you and have unsettled your minds, we have decided unanimously to choose representatives and send them to you, along with our beloved Barnabas and Paul, who have risked their lives for the sake of our Lord Jesus Christ. We have therefore sent Judas and Silas, who themselves will tell you the same things by word of mouth. For it has seemed good to the Holy Spirit and to us to impose on you no further burden than these essentials: that you abstain from what has been sacrificed to idols, and from blood and from what is strangled, and from fornication. If you keep yourselves from these, you will do well. Farewell."—The word of the Lord. ℟. **Thanks be to God.** ↓

RESPONSORIAL PSALM Ps. 67   Normand L. Blanchard

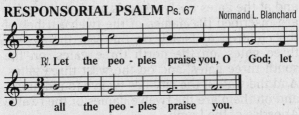

℟. Let the peo - ples praise you, O God; let all the peo - ples praise you.

Or: ℟. **Alleluia!**

May God be gracious to us and bless us
and make his face to shine upon us,
that your way may be known upon earth,
your saving power among all nations.—℟.

Let the nations be glad and sing for joy,
for you judge the peoples with equity
and guide the nations upon earth.
Let the peoples praise you, O God;
let all the peoples praise you.—℟.

The earth has yielded its increase;
God, our God, has blessed us.
May God continue to bless us;
let all the ends of the earth revere him.—℟. ↓

SECOND READING Rev. 21.10-14, 22-23

In symbolic language the Church is depicted as a wonderful glorious city, caught up in the glory of God.

A reading from the book of Revelation.

IN the spirit the Angel carried me away to a
great, high mountain and showed me the holy
city Jerusalem coming down out of heaven from
God. It has the glory of God and a radiance like
a very rare jewel, like jasper, clear as crystal.

It has a great, high wall with twelve gates,
and at the gates twelve Angels, and on the gates
are inscribed the names of the twelve tribes of
the children of Israel; on the east there were
three gates, on the north three gates, on the
south three gates, and on the west three gates.
And the wall of the city has twelve foundations,
and on them are the twelve names of the twelve
Apostles of the Lamb.

I saw no temple in the city, for its temple is
the Lord God the Almighty and the Lamb. And
the city has no need of sun or moon to shine on
it, for the glory of God is its light, and its lamp is
the Lamb.—The word of the Lord. ℞. **Thanks be
to God.** ↓

GOSPEL ACCLAMATION Jn. 14.23

℣. Alleluia. ℞. **Alleluia.**
℣. Whoever loves me will keep my word,
and my Father will love him, and we will come to
　him.
℞. **Alleluia.** ↓

GOSPEL Jn. 14.23-29

In saying farewell, Jesus has not deserted us. In his name,
the Father sends the Holy Spirit, that we may drink in his
power and live in peace.

℣. The Lord be with you. ℟. **And with your spirit.**
✛ A reading from the holy Gospel according to
John. ℟. **Glory to you, O Lord.**

JESUS said to his disciples: "Whoever loves me
will keep my word, and my Father will love
him, and we will come to him and make our home
with him. Whoever does not love me does not
keep my words; and the word that you hear is not
mine, but is from the Father who sent me.

I have said these things to you while I am still
with you. But the Advocate, the Holy Spirit, whom
the Father will send in my name, will teach you
everything, and remind you of all that I have said
to you.

Peace I leave with you; my peace I give to you. I
do not give to you as the world gives. Do not let
your hearts be troubled, and do not let them be
afraid.

You heard me say to you, 'I am going away,
and I am coming to you.' If you loved me, you
would rejoice that I am going to the Father, because the Father is greater than I. And now I
have told you this before it occurs, so that when
it does occur, you may believe."—The Gospel of
the Lord. ℟. **Praise to you, Lord Jesus Christ.**

➥ No. 15, p. 18

PRAYER OVER THE OFFERINGS

May our prayers rise up to you, O Lord,
together with the sacrificial offerings,
so that, purified by your graciousness,
we may be conformed to the mysteries of your
    mighty love.

Through Christ our Lord.
℟. **Amen.**   ➙ No. 21, p. 22 (Pref. 21-25)

COMMUNION ANTIPHON Jn. 14.15-16

If you love me, keep my commandments, says the Lord, and I will ask the Father and he will send you another Paraclete, to abide with you for ever, alleluia. ↓

PRAYER AFTER COMMUNION

Almighty ever-living God,
who restore us to eternal life in the Resurrection
   of Christ,
increase in us, we pray, the fruits of this paschal
   Sacrament
and pour into our hearts the strength of this
   saving food.
Through Christ our Lord.
℟. **Amen.**   ➙ No. 30, p. 77

Optional Solemn Blessings, p. 97, and Prayers over the People, p. 105

"Go and teach all people my gospel."

JUNE 2

THE ASCENSION OF THE LORD

Solemnity

AT THE VIGIL MASS (June 1)

ENTRANCE ANTIPHON Ps. 67.33, 35

You kingdoms of the earth, sing to God; praise the Lord, who ascends above the highest heavens; his majesty and might are in the skies, alleluia.

→ No. 2, p. 10

COLLECT

O God, whose Son today ascended to the heavens
as the Apostles looked on,
grant, we pray, that, in accordance with his
    promise,
we may be worthy for him to live with us always
    on earth,
and we with him in heaven.

443

Who lives and reigns with you in the unity of the
 Holy Spirit,
one God, for ever and ever. ℟. **Amen.** ↓

*The readings for this Mass can be found beginning on
p. 445.*

PRAYER OVER THE OFFERINGS

O God, whose Only Begotten Son, our High Priest,
is seated ever-living at your right hand to
 intercede for us,
grant that we may approach with confidence the
 throne of grace
and there obtain your mercy.
Through Christ our Lord.
℟. **Amen.**   ➔ No. 21, p. 22 (Pref. 26-27)

When the Roman Canon is used, the proper form of the
Communicantes (In communion with those) *is said.*

COMMUNION ANTIPHON Cf. Heb. 10.12

**Christ, offering a single sacrifice for sins, is seated
for ever at God's right hand, alleluia.** ↓

PRAYER AFTER COMMUNION

May the gifts we have received from your altar,
 Lord,
kindle in our hearts a longing for the heavenly
 homeland
and cause us to press forward, following in the
 Saviour's footsteps,
to the place where for our sake he entered
 before us.
Who lives and reigns for ever and ever.
℟. **Amen.**   ➔ No. 30, p. 77

Optional Solemn Blessings, p. 97, and Prayers over the People, p. 105

AT THE MASS DURING THE DAY

ENTRANCE ANTIPHON Acts 1.11

Men of Galilee, why gaze in wonder at the heavens? This Jesus whom you saw ascending into heaven will return as you saw him go, alleluia.

➔ No. 2, p. 10

COLLECT

Gladden us with holy joys, almighty God,
and make us rejoice with devout thanksgiving,
for the Ascension of Christ your Son
is our exaltation,
and, where the Head has gone before in glory,
the Body is called to follow in hope.
Through our Lord Jesus Christ, your Son,
who lives and reigns with you in the unity of the
    Holy Spirit,
one God, for ever and ever. R̸. **Amen.** ↓

OR

Grant, we pray, almighty God,
that we, who believe that your Only Begotten
    Son, our Redeemer,
ascended this day to the heavens,
may in spirit dwell already in heavenly realms.
Who lives and reigns with you in the unity of the
    Holy Spirit,
one God, for ever and ever. R̸. **Amen.** ↓

FIRST READING Acts 1.1-11

Christ is divine! He will come again! Our faith affirms
this for us. We live in the era of the Holy Spirit.

A reading from the Acts of the Apostles.

IN the first book, Theophilus, I wrote about all that Jesus did and taught from the beginning until the day when he was taken up to heaven, after giving instructions through the Holy Spirit to the Apostles whom he had chosen. After his suffering he presented himself alive to them by many convincing proofs, appearing to them during forty days and speaking about the kingdom of God.

While staying with them, he ordered them not to leave Jerusalem, but to wait there for the promise of the Father. "This," he said, "is what you have heard from me; for John baptized with water, but you will be baptized with the Holy Spirit not many days from now."

So when they had come together, they asked him, "Lord, is this the time when you will restore the kingdom to Israel?" He replied, "It is not for you to know the times or periods that the Father has set by his own authority. But you will receive power when the Holy Spirit has come upon you; and you will be my witnesses in Jerusalem, in all Judea and Samaria, and to the ends of the earth."

When he had said this, as they were watching, he was lifted up, and a cloud took him out of their sight. While he was going and they were gazing up toward heaven, suddenly two men in white robes stood by them. They said, "Men of Galilee, why do you stand looking up toward heaven? This Jesus, who has been taken up from you into heaven, will come in the same way as you saw him go into heaven."—The word of the Lord. ℟. **Thanks be to God.** ↓

RESPONSORIAL PSALM Ps. 47

Michel Guimont

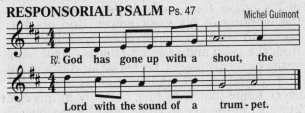

R̸. **God has gone up with a shout, the Lord with the sound of a trum-pet.**

Or: R̸. **Alleluia!**

Clap your hands, all you peoples;
shout to God with loud songs of joy.
For the Lord, the Most High, is awesome,
a great king over all the earth.—R̸.

God has gone up with a shout,
the Lord with the sound of a trumpet.
Sing praises to God, sing praises;
sing praises to our King, sing praises.—R̸.

For God is the king of all the earth;
sing praises with a Psalm.
God is king over the nations;
God sits on his holy throne.—R̸. ↓

SECOND READING Eph. 1.17-23

Paul speaks of Jesus as the Father of glory who is ready to hear our prayers, to grant wisdom and knowledge.

A reading from the Letter of Saint Paul
to the Ephesians.

BROTHERS and sisters: I pray that the God of
our Lord Jesus Christ, the Father of glory,
may give you a spirit of wisdom and revelation
as you come to know him, so that, with the eyes
of your heart enlightened, you may know what
is the hope to which he has called you, what are
the riches of his glorious inheritance among the
saints, and what is the immeasurable greatness

of his power for us who believe, according to the working of his great power. God put this power to work in Christ when he raised him from the dead and seated him at his right hand in the heavenly places, far above all rule and authority and power and dominion, and above every name that is named, not only in this age but also in the age to come. And he has put all things under his feet and has made him the head over all things for the Church, which is his body, the fullness of him who fills all in all.— The word of the Lord. ℟. **Thanks be to God.** ↓

OR Heb. 9.24-28; 10.19-23

Christ has entered the heavenly sanctuary, where he is now our Intercessor. Through him, we have confident access to the Father. We should approach with sincerity, faith, and hope.

A reading from the Letter to the Hebrews.

CHRIST did not enter a sanctuary made by human hands, a mere copy of the true one, but he entered into heaven itself, now to appear in the presence of God on our behalf. Nor was it to offer himself again and again, as the high priest enters the Holy Place year after year with blood that is not his own; for then he would have had to suffer again and again since the foundation of the world. But as it is, he has appeared once for all at the end of the age to remove sin by the sacrifice of himself.

And just as it is appointed for human beings to die once, and after that comes the judgment, so Christ, having been offered once to bear the sins of many, will appear a second time, not to deal with sin, but to save those who are eagerly waiting for him.

Therefore, brothers and sisters, since we have confidence to enter the sanctuary by the blood of Jesus, by the new and living way that he opened for us through the curtain, that is, through his flesh, and since we have a great priest over the house of God, let us approach with a true heart in full assurance of faith, with our hearts sprinkled clean from an evil conscience and our bodies washed with pure water. Let us hold fast to the confession of our hope without wavering, for he who has promised is faithful.—The word of the Lord. ℟. **Thanks be to God.** ↓

GOSPEL ACCLAMATION Mt. 28.19, 20

℣. Alleluia. ℟. **Alleluia.**
℣. Go, make disciples of all nations;
I am with you always, to the end of the age.
℟. **Alleluia.** ↓

GOSPEL Lk. 24.46-53

We are called to penance for the remission of sins.

℣. The Lord be with you. ℟. **And with your spirit.**
✣ A reading from the holy Gospel according to Luke. ℟. **Glory to you, O Lord.**

JESUS said to the disciples, "These are my words that I spoke to you while I was still with you—that everything written about me in the Law of Moses, the Prophets, and the Psalms must be fulfilled."

Then he opened their minds to understand the Scriptures, and he said to them, "Thus it is written, that the Christ is to suffer and to rise from the dead on the third day, and that repentance and forgiveness of sins is to be proclaimed in his name to all nations, beginning from Jerusalem. You are witnesses of these things. And see, I am sending upon you what

my Father promised; so stay here in the city until you
have been clothed with power from on high."

Then he led them out as far as Bethany, and,
lifting up his hands, he blessed them. While he
was blessing them, he withdrew from them and
was carried up into heaven. And they worshipped him, and returned to Jerusalem with
great joy; and they were continually in the temple blessing God.—The Gospel of the Lord.
℟. **Praise to you, Lord Jesus Christ.**→ No. 15, p. 18

PRAYER OVER THE OFFERINGS

We offer sacrifice now in supplication, O Lord,
to honour the wondrous Ascension of your Son:
grant, we pray,
that through this most holy exchange
we, too, may rise up to the heavenly realms.
Through Christ our Lord.
℟. **Amen.**   → No. 21, p. 22 (Pref. 26-27)

When the Roman Canon is used, the proper form of the
Communicantes *(In communion with those) is said.*

COMMUNION ANTIPHON Mt. 28.20

**Behold, I am with you always, even to the end of
the age, alleluia.** ↓

PRAYER AFTER COMMUNION

Almighty ever-living God,
who allow those on earth to celebrate divine
   mysteries,
grant, we pray,
that Christian hope may draw us onward
to where our nature is united with you.
Through Christ our Lord. ℟. **Amen.** → No. 30, p. 77

Optional Solemn Blessings, p. 97, and Prayers over the People, p. 105

"All of them were filled with the Holy Spirit."

JUNE 9

PENTECOST SUNDAY

Solemnity

AT THE VIGIL MASS (Simple Form) (June 8)

ENTRANCE ANTIPHON Rom. 5.5; cf. 8.11

The love of God has been poured into our hearts through the Spirit of God dwelling within us, alleluia. ➙ No. 2, p. 10

COLLECT

Almighty ever-living God,
who willed the Paschal Mystery
to be encompassed as a sign in fifty days,
grant that from out of the scattered nations
the confusion of many tongues
may be gathered by heavenly grace
into one great confession of your name.
Through our Lord Jesus Christ, your Son,

who lives and reigns with you in the unity of the
   Holy Spirit,
one God, for ever and ever. ℟. **Amen.** ↓

OR

Grant, we pray, almighty God,
that the splendour of your glory
may shine forth upon us
and that, by the bright rays of the Holy Spirit,
the light of your light may confirm the hearts
of those born again by your grace.
Through our Lord Jesus Christ, your Son,
who lives and reigns with you in the unity of the
   Holy Spirit,
one God, for ever and ever. ℟. **Amen.** ↓

FIRST READING

A Gen. 11.1-9

**Those who put their trust in pride and human ability are
bound to fail.**

   A reading from the book of Genesis.

Now the whole earth had one language and
the same words. And as people migrated
from the east, they came upon a plain in the land
of Shinar and settled there. And they said to one
another, "Come, let us make bricks, and burn
them thoroughly." And they had brick for stone,
and bitumen for mortar. Then they said, "Come,
let us build ourselves a city, and a tower with its
top in the heavens, and let us make a name for
ourselves; otherwise we shall be scattered abroad
upon the face of the whole earth." The Lord came

down to see the city and the tower, which the children of Adam had built. And the Lord said, "Look, they are one people, and they have all one language; and this is only the beginning of what they will do; nothing that they propose to do will now be impossible for them. Come, let us go down, and confuse their language there, so that they will not understand one another's speech." So the Lord scattered them abroad from there over the face of all the earth, and they left off building the city. Therefore it was called Babel, because there the Lord confused the language of all the earth; and from there the Lord scattered them abroad over the face of all the earth.—The word of the Lord. ℟. **Thanks be to God.** ↓

OR

B Ex. 19.3-8a, 16-20b

The Lord God covenants with the Israelites—they are to be a holy nation, a princely Kingdom.

A reading from the book of Exodus.

MOSES went up to God; the Lord called to him from the mountain, saying, "Thus you shall say to the house of Jacob, and tell the children of Israel: 'You have seen what I did to the Egyptians, and how I bore you on eagles' wings and brought you to myself. Now therefore, if you obey my voice and keep my covenant, you shall be my treasured possession out of all the peoples. Indeed, the whole earth is mine, but you shall be for me a priestly kingdom and a holy nation.' These are the words that you shall speak to the children of Israel." So Moses came, summoned the elders of

the people, and set before them all these words
that the Lord had commanded him. The people all
answered as one: "Everything that the Lord has
spoken we will do."

On the morning of the third day there was thunder and lightning, as well as a thick cloud on the
mountain, and a blast of a trumpet so loud that all
the people who were in the camp trembled. Moses
brought the people out of the camp to meet God.
They took their stand at the foot of the mountain.
Now Mount Sinai was wrapped in smoke, because
the Lord had descended upon it in fire; the smoke
went up like the smoke of a kiln, while the whole
mountain shook violently. As the blast of the trumpet grew louder and louder, Moses would speak
and God would answer him in thunder. When the
Lord descended upon Mount Sinai, to the top of
the mountain, the Lord summoned Moses to the
top of the mountain, and Moses went up.—The
word of the Lord. ℟. **Thanks be to God.** ↓

OR

C Ez. 37.1-14

The prophet, in a vision, sees the power of God—the band
of the living and the dead, as he describes the resurrection
of the dead.

A reading from the book of the Prophet Ezekiel.

THE hand of the Lord came upon me, and he
brought me out by the spirit of the Lord and
set me down in the middle of a valley; it was full
of bones. He led me all around them; there were
very many lying in the valley, and they were very
dry. He said to me, "Son of man, can these bones

live?" I answered, "O Lord God, you know." Then he said to me, "Prophesy to these bones, and say to them: O dry bones, hear the word of the Lord. Thus says the Lord God to these bones: I will cause breath to enter you, and you shall live. I will lay sinews on you, and will cause flesh to come upon you, and cover you with skin, and put spirit in you, and you shall live; and you shall know that I am the Lord." So I prophesied as I had been commanded; and as I prophesied, suddenly there was a noise, a rattling, and the bones came together, bone to its bone. I looked, and there were sinews on them, and flesh had come upon them, and skin had covered them; but there was no spirit in them. Then he said to me, "Prophesy to the spirit, prophesy, son of man, and say to the breath: Thus says the Lord God: Come from the four winds, and breathe upon these slain, that they may live." I prophesied as he commanded me, and the spirit came into them, and they lived, and stood on their feet, a vast multitude. Then he said to me, "Son of man, these bones are the whole house of Israel. They say, 'Our bones are dried up, and our hope is lost; we are cut off completely.' Therefore prophesy, and say to them, Thus says the Lord God: I am going to open your graves, and bring you up from your graves, O my people; and I will bring you back to the land of Israel. And you shall know that I am the Lord, when I open your graves, and bring you up from your graves, O my people. I will put my spirit within you, and you shall live, and I will place you on your own soil; then you shall know that I, the

Lord, have spoken and will act," says the Lord.—
The word of the Lord. ℟. **Thanks be to God.** ↓

OR

D Joel 2.28-32

At the end of time, the Day of the Lord, Judgment Day, those who persevere in faith will be saved.

A reading from the book of the Prophet Joel.

THUS says the Lord:
I will pour out my spirit on all flesh;
your sons and your daughters shall prophesy,
    your elders shall dream dreams,
    and your young people shall see visions.
Even on the male and female slaves,
    in those days, I will pour out my spirit.
I will show portents in the heavens and on the
        earth,
    blood and fire and columns of smoke.
The sun shall be turned to darkness,
    and the moon to blood,
        before the great and terrible day of the
        Lord comes.
Then everyone who calls on the name of the
        Lord shall be saved;
for in Mount Zion and in Jerusalem
    there shall be those who escape, as the
        Lord has said,
and among the survivors shall be those whom the
        Lord calls.

The word of the Lord. ℟. **Thanks be to God.** ↓

RESPONSORIAL PSALM Ps. 104   Normand L. Blanchard

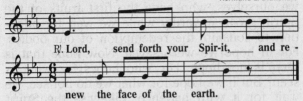

℟. Lord, send forth your Spir-it,___ and re-new the face of the earth.

Or: ℟. Alleluia!

Bless the Lord, O my soul.
O Lord my God, you are very great.
You are clothed with honour and majesty,
wrapped in light as with a garment.—℟.

O Lord, how manifold are your works!
In wisdom you have made them all;
the earth is full of your creatures,
living things both small and great.—℟.

These all look to you
to give them their food in due season;
when you give to them, they gather it up;
when you open your hand, they are filled with
    good things.—℟.

When you take away their breath,
they die and return to their dust.
When you send forth your spirit, they are created;
and you renew the face of the earth.—℟. ↓

SECOND READING Rom. 8.22-27

Be patient and have hope. The Spirit intercedes for us.

A reading from the Letter of Saint Paul
to the Romans.

BROTHERS and sisters: we know that the
whole creation has been groaning in labour

pains until now; and not only the creation, but we ourselves, who have the first fruits of the Spirit, groan inwardly while we wait for adoption to sonship, the redemption of our bodies. For in hope we were saved. Now hope that is seen is not hope. For who hopes for what is seen? But if we hope for what we do not see, we wait for it with patience. Likewise the Spirit helps us in our weakness; for we do not know how to pray as we ought, but that very Spirit intercedes with sighs too deep for words. And God, who searches the heart, knows what is the mind of the Spirit, because the Spirit intercedes for the saints according to the will of God.—The word of the Lord. ℟. **Thanks be to God.** ↓

GOSPEL ACCLAMATION
℣. Alleluia. ℟. **Alleluia.**
℣. Come, Holy Spirit, fill the hearts of your faithful and kindle in them the fire of your love.
℟. **Alleluia.** ↓

GOSPEL Jn. 7.37-39

Jesus indicates that the Holy Spirit will bear witness to the good news. He will guide Christians to the truth and teach about things to come.

℣. The Lord be with you. ℟. **And with your spirit.**
✤ A reading from the holy Gospel according to John. ℟. **Glory to you, O Lord.**

ON the last day of the festival, the great day, while Jesus was standing in the temple, he cried out, "Let anyone who is thirsty come to me and drink. As the Scripture has said, 'Out of the heart of the one who believes in me shall flow rivers of living water.'" Now he said this about the Spirit, which believers in him were to receive; for as yet there was no Spirit, because Jesus was not yet glorified.—The Gospel of the Lord. ℟. **Praise to you, Lord Jesus Christ.**

➙ No. 15, p. 18

PRAYER OVER THE OFFERINGS

Pour out upon these gifts the blessing of your
    Spirit,
we pray, O Lord,
so that through them your Church may be
    imbued with such love
that the truth of your saving mystery
may shine forth for the whole world.
Through Christ our Lord.
℟. **Amen.**

➙ Pref. 28, p. 467

When the Roman Canon is used, the proper form of the
Communicantes (In communion with those) *is said.*

COMMUNION ANTIPHON Jn. 7.37

On the last day of the festival, Jesus stood and cried out: If anyone is thirsty, let him come to me and drink, alleluia. ↓

PRAYER AFTER COMMUNION

May these gifts we have consumed
benefit us, O Lord,
that we may always be aflame with the same
    Spirit,
whom you wondrously poured out on your
    Apostles.

Through Christ our Lord.

℟. **Amen.** → No. 30, p. 77

Optional Solemn Blessings, p. 97, and Prayers over the People, p. 105

(*At the end of the Dismissal the people respond:* "**Thanks be to God, alleluia, alleluia.**")

AT THE MASS DURING THE DAY

ENTRANCE ANTIPHON Wis. 1.7

The Spirit of the Lord has filled the whole world and that which contains all things understands what is said, alleluia. → No. 2, p. 10

OR Rom. 5.5; cf. 8.11

The love of God has been poured into our hearts through the Spirit of God dwelling within us, alleluia. → No. 2, p. 10

COLLECT

O God, who by the mystery of today's great feast
sanctify your whole Church in every people and
 nation,
pour out, we pray, the gifts of the Holy Spirit
across the face of the earth
and, with the divine grace that was at work
when the Gospel was first proclaimed,
fill now once more the hearts of believers.
Through our Lord Jesus Christ, your Son,
who lives and reigns with you in the unity of the
 Holy Spirit,
one God, for ever and ever. ℟. **Amen.** ↓

FIRST READING Acts 2.1-11

As promised by Jesus, the Holy Spirit fills the faithful, and, inspired, they proclaim the good news.

A reading from the Acts of the Apostles.

WHEN the day of Pentecost had come, they were all together in one place. And suddenly from heaven there came a sound like the rush of a violent wind, and it filled the entire house where they were sitting. Divided tongues, as of fire, appeared among them, and a tongue rested on each of them. All of them were filled with the Holy Spirit and began to speak in other languages, as the Spirit gave them ability.

Now there were devout Jews from every nation under heaven living in Jerusalem. And at this sound the crowd gathered and was bewildered, because each one heard them speaking in their own language. Amazed and astonished, they asked, "Are not all these who are speaking Galileans? And how is it that we hear, each of us, in our own language? Parthians, Medes, Elamites, and residents of Mesopotamia, Judea and Cappadocia, Pontus and Asia, Phrygia and Pamphylia, Egypt and the parts of Libya belonging to Cyrene, and visitors from Rome, both Jews and converts, Cretans and Arabs—in our own languages we hear them speaking about God's deeds of power."—The word of the Lord. ℟. **Thanks be to God.** ↓

RESPONSORIAL PSALM Ps. 104

Kathrine Bellamy

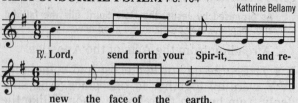

℟. Lord, send forth your Spir-it,___ and re-new the face of the earth.

Or: ℟. Alleluia!

Bless the Lord, O my soul.
O Lord my God, you are very great.
O Lord, how manifold are your works!
The earth is full of your creatures.—℟.

When you take away their breath,
they die and return to their dust.
When you send forth your spirit, they are created;
and you renew the face of the earth.—℟.

May the glory of the Lord endure forever;
may the Lord rejoice in his works.
May my meditation be pleasing to him,
for I rejoice in the Lord.—℟. ↓

SECOND READING 1 Cor. 12.3b-7, 12-13

The gifts of the Spirit are not exclusive but for all. The Spirit brings a radical unity to the body of Christ.

A reading from the first Letter of Saint Paul
to the Corinthians.

BROTHERS and sisters: No one can say
"Jesus is Lord" except by the Holy Spirit.
Now there are varieties of gifts, but the same
Spirit; and there are varieties of services, but

the same Lord; and there are varieties of activities, but it is the same God who activates all of them in everyone. To each is given the manifestation of the Spirit for the common good.

For just as the body is one and has many members, and all the members of the body, though many, are one body, so it is with Christ. For in the one Spirit we were all baptized into one body—Jews or Greeks, slaves or free—and we were all made to drink of one Spirit.—The word of the Lord. ℟. **Thanks be to God.** ↓

OR

Rom. 8.8-17

We should live by the Spirit. For those who are led by the Spirit are children of God, heirs of God and joint heirs with Christ.

A reading from the Letter of Saint Paul
to the Romans.

BROTHERS and sisters: Those who are in the flesh cannot please God. But you are not in the flesh; you are in the Spirit, since the Spirit of God dwells in you. Anyone who does not have the Spirit of Christ does not belong to him.

But if Christ is in you, though the body is dead because of sin, the Spirit is life because of righteousness. If the Spirit of God who raised Jesus from the dead dwells in you, he who raised Christ from the dead will give life to your mortal bodies also through his Spirit that dwells in you.

So then, brothers and sisters, we are debtors, not to the flesh, to live according to the flesh—

for if you live according to the flesh, you will die; but if by the Spirit you put to death the deeds of the body, you will live.

For all who are led by the Spirit of God are sons and daughters of God. For you did not receive a spirit of slavery to fall back into fear, but you have received a spirit of adoption to sonship. When we cry, "Abba! Father!" it is that very Spirit bearing witness with our spirit that we are children of God, and if children, then heirs, heirs of God and joint heirs with Christ—if, in fact, we suffer with him so that we may also be glorified with him.—The word of the Lord. ℟. **Thanks be to God.** ↓

SEQUENCE *(Veni, Sancte Spiritus)*

1. Holy Spirit, Lord divine,
   Come, from heights of heav'n and shine,
   Come with blessed radiance bright!

2. Come, O Father of the poor,
   Come, whose treasured gifts ensure,
   Come, our heart's unfailing light!

3. Of consolers, wisest, best,
   And our soul's most welcome guest,
   Sweet refreshment, sweet repose.

4. In our labour rest most sweet,
   Pleasant coolness in the heat,
   Consolation in our woes.

5. Light most blessed, shine with grace
   In our heart's most secret place,
   Fill your faithful through and through.

6. Left without your presence here,
   Life itself would disappear,
   Nothing thrives apart from you!

7. Cleanse our soiled hearts of sin,
   Arid souls refresh within,
   Wounded lives to health restore.

8. Bend the stubborn heart and will,
   Melt the frozen, warm the chill,

Guide the wayward home once more!

9. On the faithful who are true
   And profess their faith in you,
   In your sev'nfold gift descend!

10. Give us virtue's sure reward,
    Give us your salvation, Lord,
    Give us joys that never end! ↓

GOSPEL ACCLAMATION

℣. Alleluia. ℟. **Alleluia.**
℣. Come, Holy Spirit, fill the hearts of your faithful
and kindle in them the fire of your love.
℟. **Alleluia.** ↓

GOSPEL Jn. 20.19-23

Jesus gives the blessing of peace, and bestows his authority on the disciples as he confers on them the Holy Spirit.

℣. The Lord be with you. ℟. **And with your spirit.**
✠ A reading from the holy Gospel according to John. ℟. **Glory to you, O Lord.**

IT was evening on the day Jesus rose from the dead, the first day of the week, and the doors of the house where the disciples had met were locked for fear of the Jews. Jesus came and stood among them and said, "Peace be with you." After he said this, he showed them his hands and his side. Then the disciples rejoiced when they saw the Lord. Jesus said to them again, "Peace be with you. As the Father has sent me, so I send you." When he had said this, he breathed on them and said to them, "Receive the Holy Spirit. If you forgive the sins of any, they are forgiven them; if you retain the sins of any, they are retained."—The Gospel of the Lord. ℟. **Praise to you, Lord Jesus Christ.**

➜ No. 15, p. 18

OR

Jn. 14.15-16, 23b-26

The Holy Spirit, whom the Father will send in the name of Jesus, will teach Christians everything. He will be their Advocate forever.

℣. The Lord be with you. ℟. **And with your spirit.** ✠ A reading from the holy Gospel according to John. ℟. **Glory to you, O Lord.**

JESUS said to the disciples: "If you love me, you will keep my commandments. And I will ask the Father, and he will give you another Advocate, to be with you forever.

Whoever loves me will keep my word, and my Father will love him, and we will come to him and make our home with him. Whoever does not love me does not keep my words; and the word that you hear is not mine, but is from the Father who sent me.

I have said these things to you while I am still with you. But the Advocate, the Holy Spirit, whom the Father will send in my name, will teach you everything, and remind you of all that I have said to you."—The Gospel of the Lord. ℟. **Praise to you, Lord Jesus Christ.** ➜ No. 15, p. 18

PRAYER OVER THE OFFERINGS

Grant, we pray, O Lord,
that, as promised by your Son,
the Holy Spirit may reveal to us more abundantly
the hidden mystery of this sacrifice
and graciously lead us into all truth.
Through Christ our Lord. ℟. **Amen.** ↓

PREFACE (28)

℣. The Lord be with you. ℟. **And with your spirit.**
℣. Lift up your hearts. ℟. **We lift them up to the Lord.** ℣. Let us give thanks to the Lord our God.
℟. **It is right and just.**

It is truly right and just, our duty and our salvation,
always and everywhere to give you thanks,
Lord, holy Father, almighty and eternal God.

For, bringing your Paschal Mystery to completion,
you bestowed the Holy Spirit today
on those you made your adopted children
by uniting them to your Only Begotten Son.

This same Spirit, as the Church came to birth,
opened to all peoples the knowledge of God
and brought together the many languages of the
    earth
in profession of the one faith.

Therefore, overcome with paschal joy,
every land, every people exults in your praise
and even the heavenly Powers, with the angelic
    hosts,

sing together the unending hymn of your glory,
as they acclaim: → No. 23, p. 23

When the Roman Canon is used, the proper form of the
Communicantes (In communion with those) *is said.*

COMMUNION ANTIPHON Acts 2.4, 11
**They were all filled with the Holy Spirit and
spoke of the marvels of God, alleluia.** ↓

PRAYER AFTER COMMUNION
O God, who bestow heavenly gifts upon your
   Church,
safeguard, we pray, the grace you have given,
that the gift of the Holy Spirit poured out upon
   her
may retain all its force
and that this spiritual food
may gain her abundance of eternal redemption.
Through Christ our Lord.
℟. **Amen.** → No. 30, p. 77

Optional Solemn Blessings, p. 97, and Prayers over the People, p. 105

(At the end of the Dismissal, the people respond: **"Thanks
be to God, alleluia, alleluia."***)*

"Glory to the Father, the Son, and the Holy Spirit."

JUNE 16

THE MOST HOLY TRINITY

Solemnity

ENTRANCE ANTIPHON

Blest be God the Father, and the Only Begotten Son of God, and also the Holy Spirit, for he has shown us his merciful love. → No. 2, p. 10

COLLECT

God our Father, who by sending into the world
the Word of truth and the Spirit of sanctification
made known to the human race your wondrous
   mystery,
grant us, we pray, that in professing the true faith,
we may acknowledge the Trinity of eternal glory
and adore your Unity, powerful in majesty.
Through our Lord Jesus Christ, your Son,
who lives and reigns with you in the unity of the
   Holy Spirit,
one God, for ever and ever. ℟. **Amen.** ↓

FIRST READING Prov. 8.22-31

In a messianic application, the "Wisdom of God" who speaks in this reading foreshadows the revelation of the Second Person of the Trinity.

A reading from the book of Proverbs.

THUS says the Wisdom of God:
"The Lord created me at the beginning of his work,
the first of his acts of long ago.
Ages ago I was set up,
at the first, before the beginning of the earth.
When there were no depths I was brought forth,
when there were no springs abounding with water.

Before the mountains had been shaped,
before the hills, I was brought forth—
when he had not yet made earth and fields,
or the world's first bits of soil.

When he established the heavens, I was there,
when he drew a circle on the face of the deep,
when he made firm the skies above,
when he established the fountains of the deep,
when he assigned to the sea its limit,
so that the waters might not transgress his command,
when he marked out the foundations of the earth,
then I was beside him, like a master worker;
and I was daily his delight,
rejoicing before him always,
rejoicing in his inhabited world
and delighting in the children of Adam."

The word of the Lord. ℟. **Thanks be to God.** ↓

RESPONSORIAL PSALM Ps. 8

Normand L. Blanchard

℟. O Lord, our God, how ma-jes-tic is your name in

all the earth!

When I look at your heavens, the work of your
    fingers,
the moon and the stars that you have established;
what is a man that you are mindful of him,
or the son of man that you care for him?—℟.

Yet you have made him a little lower than the
    Angels,
and crowned him with glory and honour.
You have given him dominion over the works of
    your hands;
you have put all things under his feet.—℟.

All sheep and oxen,
and also the beasts of the field,
the birds of the air, and the fish of the sea,
whatever passes along the paths of the seas.—℟. ↓

SECOND READING Rom. 5.1-5

Our hope, our faith, will be fulfilled because the Holy
Spirit has been given to us.

A reading from the Letter of Saint Paul
to the Romans.

BROTHERS and sisters: Since we are justified
by faith, we have peace with God through our
Lord Jesus Christ, through whom we have ob-

tained access to this grace in which we stand; and we boast in our hope of sharing the glory of God.

And not only that, but we also boast in our sufferings, knowing that suffering produces endurance, and endurance produces character, and character produces hope, and hope does not disappoint us, because God's love has been poured into our hearts through the Holy Spirit that has been given to us.—The word of the Lord. ℟. **Thanks be to God.** ↓

GOSPEL ACCLAMATION See Rev. 1.8

℣. Alleluia. ℟. **Alleluia.**
℣. Glory to the Father, the Son, and the Holy Spirit:
to God who is, who was, and who is to come.
℟. **Alleluia.** ↓

GOSPEL Jn. 16.12-15

All that the Father has belongs to Jesus. The Spirit of truth will guide us and announce to us the things to come.

℣. The Lord be with you. ℟. **And with your spirit.**
✝ A reading from the holy Gospel according to John. ℟. **Glory to you, O Lord.**

JESUS said to his disciples: "I still have many things to say to you, but you cannot bear them now. When the Spirit of truth comes, he will guide you into all the truth; for he will not speak on his own, but will speak whatever he hears, and he will declare to you the things that are to come. He will glorify me, because he will take what is mine and declare it to you. All that

the Father has is mine. For this reason I said
that he will take what is mine and declare it to
you."—The Gospel of the Lord. ℟. **Praise to you,
Lord Jesus Christ.**   → No. 15, p. 18

PRAYER OVER THE OFFERINGS

Sanctify by the invocation of your name,
we pray, O Lord our God,
this oblation of our service,
and by it make of us an eternal offering to you.
Through Christ our Lord. ℟. **Amen.** ↓

PREFACE (43)

℣. The Lord be with you. ℟. **And with your spirit.**
℣. Lift up your hearts. ℟. **We lift them up to the
Lord.** ℣. Let us give thanks to the Lord our God.
℟. **It is right and just.**

It is truly right and just, our duty and our salvation,
always and everywhere to give you thanks,
Lord, holy Father, almighty and eternal God.

For with your Only Begotten Son and the Holy
    Spirit
you are one God, one Lord:
not in the unity of a single person,
but in a Trinity of one substance.

For what you have revealed to us of your glory
we believe equally of your Son
and of the Holy Spirit,
so that, in the confessing of the true and eternal
    Godhead,
you might be adored in what is proper to each
    Person,

their unity in substance,
and their equality in majesty.

For this is praised by Angels and Archangels,
Cherubim, too, and Seraphim,
who never cease to cry out each day,
as with one voice they acclaim: → No. 23, p. 23

COMMUNION ANTIPHON Gal. 4.6

Since you are children of God, God has sent into your hearts the Spirit of his Son, the Spirit who cries out: Abba, Father. ↓

PRAYER AFTER COMMUNION

May receiving this Sacrament, O Lord our God,
bring us health of body and soul,
as we confess your eternal holy Trinity and
  undivided Unity.
Through Christ our Lord.
R̸. **Amen.** → No. 30, p. 77

Optional Solemn Blessings, p. 97, and Prayers over the People, p. 105

"Jesus . . . looked up to heaven, and blessed
and broke [the loaves]."

JUNE 23

THE MOST HOLY
BODY AND BLOOD OF CHRIST
(CORPUS CHRISTI)

Solemnity

ENTRANCE ANTIPHON Cf. Ps. 80.17
**He fed them with the finest wheat and satisfied
them with honey from the rock.** → No. 2, p. 10

COLLECT
O God, who in this wonderful Sacrament
have left us a memorial of your Passion,
grant us, we pray,
so to revere the sacred mysteries of your Body
   and Blood
that we may always experience in ourselves
the fruits of your redemption.

Who live and reign with God the Father
in the unity of the Holy Spirit,
one God, for ever and ever. ℟. **Amen.** ↓

FIRST READING Gen. 14.18-20

Sharing bread and wine, a foreshadowing of the eucharistic elements, Abram is blessed and God is praised.

A reading from the book of Genesis.

IN those days: After Abram's return King Melchizedek of Salem brought out bread and wine; he was priest of God Most High. He blessed Abram and said,
"Blessed be Abram by God Most High,
    maker of heaven and earth;
and blessed be God Most High,
    who has delivered your enemies into your
        hand!"
And Abram gave him one tenth of everything.—

The word of the Lord. ℟. **Thanks be to God.** ↓

RESPONSORIAL PSALM Ps. 110

Normand L. Blanchard

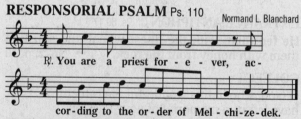

℟. You are a priest for - e - ver, according to the or - der of Mel - chi - ze - dek.

The Lord says to my lord,
"Sit at my right hand
until I make your enemies your footstool."—℟.

The Lord sends out from Zion
your mighty sceptre.
Rule in the midst of your foes.—℟.

Your people will offer themselves willingly
on the day you lead your forces on the holy
mountains.
From the womb of the morning, like dew, your
youth will come to you.—℟.

The Lord has sworn and will not change his mind,
"You are a priest forever
according to the order of Melchizedek."—℟. ↓

SECOND READING 1 Cor. 11.23-26

When we eat this bread and drink this cup, we proclaim your glory, Lord Jesus, until you come again.

A reading from the first Letter of Saint Paul
to the Corinthians.

BROTHERS and sisters: I received from the
Lord what I also handed on to you, that the
Lord Jesus on the night when he was betrayed
took a loaf of bread, and when he had given
thanks, he broke it and said, "This is my Body
that is for you. Do this in remembrance of me."

In the same way he took the cup also, after
supper, saying, "This cup is the new covenant in
my Blood. Do this, as often as you drink it, in remembrance of me." For as often as you eat this
bread and drink the cup, you proclaim the
Lord's death until he comes.—The word of the
Lord. ℟. **Thanks be to God.** ↓

SEQUENCE

*This optional sequence is intended to be sung; otherwise it
is better omitted. The shorter version begins at the asterisk.*

1. Laud, O Sion, your salvation,
laud with hymns of exultation

Christ, your King and Shepherd
true:

Bring him all the praise you
  know,
He is more than you bestow;
never can you reach his due.

2. Wondrous theme for glad
  thanksgiving
is the living and life-giving
Bread today before you set,
from his hands of old partaken,
As we know, by faith un-
  shaken,
where the Twelve at supper
  met.

3. Full and clear ring out your
  chanting,
let not joy nor grace be wanting.
From your heart let praises
  burst.
For this day the Feast is holden,
When the institution olden
of that Supper was rehearsed.

4. Here the new law's new
  oblation,
by the new King's revelation,
Ends the forms of ancient rite.
Now the new the old effaces,
Substance now the shadow
  chases,
light of day dispels the night.

5. What he did at supper
  seated,
Christ ordained to be repeated,
His remembrance not to cease.
And his rule for guidance taking,
Bread and wine we hallow,
  making,
thus, our sacrifice of peace.

6. This the truth each Christian
  learns:
bread into his own flesh Christ
  turns,
To his precious Blood the wine.
Sight must fail, no thought con-
  ceives,
But a steadfast faith believes,
resting on a power divine.

7. Here beneath these signs are
  hidden
priceless things to sense forbidden.
Signs alone, not things, we see:
Blood and flesh as wine, bread
  broken;
Yet beneath each wondrous
  token,
Christ entire we know to be.

8. All who of this great food
  partake,
they sever not the Lord, nor
  break:
Christ is whole to all that taste.
Be one or be a thousand fed
They eat alike that living Bread,
eat of him who cannot waste.

9. Good and guilty likewise
  sharing,
though their different ends pre-
  paring:
timeless death, or blessed life.
Life to these, to those damnation,
Even like participation
is with unlike outcomes rife.

10. When the sacrament is broken,
doubt not, but believe as spoken,

That each severed outward
token
does the very whole contain.
None that precious gift divides,
breaking but the sign betides.
Jesus still the same abides,
still unbroken he remains.
*11. Hail, the food of Angels
given
to the pilgrim who has striven,
to the child as bread from
heaven,
food alone for spirit meant:
Now the former types fulfilling—
Isaac bound, a victim willing,
Paschal Lamb, its life-blood
spilling,
manna to the ancients sent.

12. Bread yourself, good Shepherd, tend us;
Jesus, with your love befriend
us.
You refresh us and defend us;
to your lasting goodness send us
That the land of life we see.
Lord, who all things both rule
and know,
who on this earth such food bestow,
Grant that with your saints we
follow
to that banquet ever hallow,
With them heirs and guests to
be. ↓

GOSPEL ACCLAMATION Jn. 6.51

℣. Alleluia. ℟. **Alleluia.**
℣. I am the living bread of heaven, says the Lord;
whoever eats of this bread will live forever.
℟. **Alleluia.** ↓

GOSPEL Lk. 9.11b-17

The compassion of Jesus is limitless. He pronounces a blessing and gives nourishment to the crowd. In the eucharist he
gives us his Body and Blood and unites us to himself.

℣. The Lord be with you. ℟. **And with your spirit.**
✠ A reading from the holy Gospel according to
Luke. ℟. **Glory to you, O Lord.**

JESUS spoke to the crowds about the kingdom
of God, and healed those who needed to be
cured.

The day was drawing to a close, and the twelve came to him and said, "Send the crowd away, so that they may go into the surrounding villages and countryside, to lodge and get provisions; for we are here in a deserted place."

But Jesus said to them, "You give them something to eat." They said, "We have no more than five loaves and two fish—unless we are to go and buy food for all these people." For there were about five thousand men. And Jesus said to his disciples, "Make the people sit down in groups of about fifty each." They did so and made them all sit down.

And taking the five loaves and the two fish, he looked up to heaven, and blessed and broke them, and gave them to the disciples to set before the crowd.

And all ate and were filled. What was left over was gathered up, twelve baskets of broken pieces.—The Gospel of the Lord. ℟. **Praise to you, Lord Jesus Christ.**

→ No. 15, p. 18

PRAYER OVER THE OFFERINGS

Grant your Church, O Lord, we pray,
the gifts of unity and peace,
whose signs are to be seen in mystery
in the offerings we here present.
Through Christ our Lord.
℟. **Amen.**

→ No. 21, p. 22 (Pref. 47-48)

COMMUNION ANTIPHON Jn. 6.57

Whoever eats my flesh and drinks my blood remains in me and I in him, says the Lord. ↓

PRAYER AFTER COMMUNION

Grant, O Lord, we pray,
that we may delight for all eternity
in that share in your divine life,
which is foreshadowed in the present age
by our reception of your precious Body and
  Blood.
℟. **Amen.**   ➜ No. 30, p. 77

Optional Solemn Blessings, p. 97, and Prayers over the People, p. 105

"No one who puts a hand to the plough and looks back
is fit for the kingdom of God."

JUNE 30

13th SUNDAY IN ORDINARY TIME

ENTRANCE ANTIPHON Ps. 46.2

**All peoples, clap your hands. Cry to God with
shouts of joy!** → No. 2, p. 10

COLLECT

O God, who through the grace of adoption
chose us to be children of light,
grant, we pray,
that we may not be wrapped in the darkness of
    error
but always be seen to stand in the bright light of
    truth.
Through our Lord Jesus Christ, your Son,
who lives and reigns with you in the unity of the
    Holy Spirit,
one God, for ever and ever. ℟. **Amen.** ↓

FIRST READING 1 Kgs. 19.16b, 19-21

> Elisha receives the divine call and leaves all his posses-
> sions. Our dedication should also be total.

A reading from the first book of Kings.

THE Lord spoke to the Prophet Elijah and
said, "You shall anoint Elisha, son of
Shaphat, as Prophet in your place."

So Elijah set out from there, and found Elisha,
who was ploughing. There were twelve yoke of
oxen ahead of him, and he was with the twelfth.

Elijah passed by Elisha and threw his mantle
over him. Elisha left the oxen, ran after Elijah,
and said, "Let me kiss my father and my mother,
and then I will follow you."

Then Elijah said to him, "Go back again; for
what have I done to you?" Elisha returned from
following Elijah, took the yoke of oxen, and
slaughtered them; using the equipment from the
oxen, he boiled their flesh, and gave it to the
people, and they ate. Then Elisha set out and
followed Elijah, and became his servant.—The
word of the Lord. ℟. **Thanks be to God.** ↓

RESPONSORIAL PSALM Ps. 16

David MacIsaac

℟. **You   are   my   cho - sen
        por - tion,   O   Lord.**

Protect me, O God, for in you I take refuge.
I say to the Lord, "You are my Lord;

I have no good apart from you."
The Lord is my chosen portion and my cup; you
hold my lot.

℟. **You are my chosen portion, O Lord.**

I bless the Lord who gives me counsel;
in the night also my heart instructs me.
I keep the Lord always before me;
because he is at my right hand, I shall not be
moved.—℟.

Therefore my heart is glad, and my soul rejoices;
my body also rests secure.
For you do not give me up to Sheol,
or let your faithful one see the Pit.—℟.

You show me the path of life.
In your presence there is fullness of joy;
in your right hand are pleasures forevermore.
—℟. ↓

SECOND READING Gal. 5.1, 13-18

We are called to be at one another's service and to love
others as we love ourselves.

A reading from the Letter of Saint Paul
to the Galatians.

BROTHERS and sisters: For freedom Christ
has set us free. Stand firm, therefore, and do
not submit again to a yoke of slavery. For you
were called to freedom, brothers and sisters;
only do not use your freedom as an opportunity
for self-indulgence, but through love become
slaves to one another.

For the whole law is summed up in a single
commandment, "You shall love your neighbour

as yourself." If, however, you bite and devour one another, take care that you are not consumed by one another.

Live by the Spirit, I say, and do not gratify the desires of the flesh. For what the flesh desires is opposed to the Spirit, and what the Spirit desires is opposed to the flesh; for these are opposed to each other, to prevent you from doing what you want. But if you are led by the Spirit, you are not subject to the law.—The word of the Lord. ℟. **Thanks be to God.** ↓

GOSPEL ACCLAMATION 1 Sam. 3.9; Jn. 6.69b

℣. Alleluia. ℟. **Alleluia.**
℣. Speak, O Lord, for your servant is listening; you have the words of eternal life.
℟. **Alleluia.** ↓

GOSPEL Lk. 9.51-62

To follow Jesus we must be ready to give of ourselves totally.

℣. The Lord be with you. ℟. **And with your spirit.**
✣ A reading from the holy Gospel according to Luke. ℟. **Glory to you, O Lord.**

WHEN the days drew near for him to be taken up, Jesus set his face to go to Jerusalem.

And he sent messengers ahead of him. On their way they entered a village of the Samaritans to make ready for Jesus; but the Samaritans did not receive him, because his face was set toward Jerusalem.

When his disciples James and John saw it, they said, "Lord, do you want us to command fire to come down from heaven and consume them?" But Jesus turned and rebuked them. Then they went on to another village.

As they were going along the road, someone said to him, "I will follow you wherever you go." And Jesus said to him, "Foxes have holes, and birds of the air have nests; but the Son of Man has nowhere to lay his head."

To another Jesus said, "Follow me." But he replied, "Lord, first let me go and bury my father." But Jesus said to him, "Let the dead bury their own dead; but as for you, go and proclaim the kingdom of God."

Another said, "I will follow you, Lord; but let me first say farewell to those at my home." Jesus said to him, "No one who puts a hand to the plough and looks back is fit for the kingdom of God."—The Gospel of the Lord. ℟. **Praise to you, Lord Jesus Christ.**   → No. 15, p. 18

PRAYER OVER THE OFFERINGS

O God, who graciously accomplish
the effects of your mysteries,
grant, we pray,
that the deeds by which we serve you
may be worthy of these sacred gifts.
Through Christ our Lord.
℟. **Amen.**   → No. 21, p. 22 (Pref. 29-36)

COMMUNION ANTIPHON Cf. Ps. 102.1

Bless the Lord, O my soul, and all within me, his holy name. ↓

OR Jn. 17.20-21

O Father, I pray for them, that they may be one in us, that the world may believe that you have sent me, says the Lord. ↓

PRAYER AFTER COMMUNION

May this divine sacrifice we have offered and
    received
fill us with life, O Lord, we pray,
so that, bound to you in lasting charity,
we may bear fruit that lasts for ever.
Through Christ our Lord.
℟. **Amen.**

→ No. 30, p. 77

Optional Solemn Blessings, p. 97, and Prayers over the People, p. 105

"He said to them, 'The harvest is plentiful,
but the labourers are few.'"

JULY 7

14th SUNDAY IN ORDINARY TIME

ENTRANCE ANTIPHON Cf. Ps. 47.10-11

**Your merciful love, O God, we have received in
the midst of your temple. Your praise, O God, like
your name, reaches the ends of the earth; your
right hand is filled with saving justice.**

➥ No. 2, p. 10

COLLECT

O God, who in the abasement of your Son
have raised up a fallen world,
fill your faithful with holy joy,
for on those you have rescued from slavery to sin
you bestow eternal gladness.
Through our Lord Jesus Christ, your Son,

who lives and reigns with you in the unity of the
   Holy Spirit,
one God, for ever and ever. ℟. **Amen.** ↓

FIRST READING Isa. 66.10-14

**We may apply this reading to the Church. The Church is
Jerusalem, a loving, protecting mother, who receives the
blessing of God.**

A reading from the book of the Prophet Isaiah.

REJOICE with Jerusalem,
   and be glad for her,
all you who love her;
rejoice with her in joy,
all you who mourn over her—
that you may nurse and be satisfied
from her consoling breast;
that you may drink deeply with delight
from her glorious bosom.

For thus says the Lord:
"I will extend prosperity to her like a river,
and the wealth of the nations like an overflowing stream;
and you shall nurse and be carried on her arm,
and dandled on her knees.
As a mother comforts her child,
so I will comfort you;
you shall be comforted in Jerusalem.

You shall see, and your heart shall rejoice;
your bodies shall flourish like the grass;
and it shall be known
that the hand of the Lord is with his servants."

The word of the Lord. ℟. **Thanks be to God.** ↓

RESPONSORIAL PSALM Ps. 66

Scott Knarr

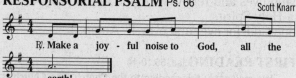

℟. Make a joy - ful noise to God, all the earth!

Make a joyful noise to God, all the earth;
sing the glory of his name;
give to him glorious praise.
Say to God, "How awesome are your deeds!"—℟.

"All the earth worships you;
they sing praises to you, sing praises to your name."
Come and see what God has done:
he is awesome in his deeds among the children
    of Adam.—℟.

He turned the sea into dry land;
they passed through the river on foot.
There we rejoiced in him,
who rules by his might forever.—℟.

Come and hear, all you who fear God,
and I will tell what he has done for me.
Blessed be God, because he has not rejected my
    prayer
or removed his steadfast love from me.—℟. ↓

SECOND READING Gal. 6.14-18

Through the cross of Christ we are created anew.

A reading from the Letter of Saint Paul
to the Galatians.

BROTHERS and sisters: May I never boast of
anything except the Cross of our Lord Jesus
Christ, by which the world has been crucified to
me, and I to the world. For neither circumcision

nor uncircumcision is anything; but a new creation is everything!

As for those who will follow this rule—peace be upon them, and mercy, and upon the Israel of God. From now on, let no one make trouble for me; for I carry the marks of Jesus branded on my body.

May the grace of our Lord Jesus Christ be with your spirit, brothers and sisters. Amen.— The word of the Lord. ℟. **Thanks be to God. ↓**

GOSPEL ACCLAMATION Col. 3.15a,16a

℣. Alleluia. ℟. **Alleluia.**
℣. Let the peace of Christ rule in your hearts, let the word of Christ dwell in you richly.
℟. **Alleluia. ↓**

GOSPEL Lk. 10.1-12, 17-20 or 10.1-9

Even though our good works may be fruitful, we rejoice not in them but in our perseverance in grace.

[If the "Shorter Form" is used, the indented text in brackets is omitted.]

℣. The Lord be with you. ℟. **And with your spirit.**
✚ A reading from the holy Gospel according to Luke. ℟. **Glory to you, O Lord.**

THE Lord appointed seventy others and sent them on ahead of him in pairs to every town and place where he himself intended to go.

He said to them, "The harvest is plentiful, but the labourers are few; therefore ask the Lord of the harvest to send out labourers into his harvest. Go on your way. See, I am sending you out like lambs into the midst of wolves. Carry no purse, no bag, no sandals; and greet no one on the road.

Whatever house you enter, first say, 'Peace to this house!' And if someone of peace is there, your peace will rest on that person; but if not, it will return to you. Remain in the same house, eating and drinking whatever they provide, for the labourer deserves his wage. Do not move about from house to house.

Whenever you enter a town and its people welcome you, eat what is set before you; cure the sick who are there, and say to them, 'The kingdom of God has come near to you.'

[But whenever you enter a town and they do not welcome you, go out into its streets and say, 'Even the dust of your town that clings to our feet, we wipe off in protest against you. Yet know this: the kingdom of God has come near.' I tell you, on that day it will be more tolerable for Sodom than for that town."

The seventy returned with joy, saying, "Lord, in your name even the demons submit to us!" Jesus said to them, "I watched Satan fall from heaven like a flash of lightning. See, I have given you authority to tread on snakes and scorpions, and over all the power of the enemy; and nothing will hurt you.

Nevertheless, do not rejoice at this, that the spirits submit to you, but rejoice that your names are written in heaven."]

The Gospel of the Lord. ℟. **Praise to you, Lord Jesus Christ.**
➔ No. 15, p. 18

PRAYER OVER THE OFFERINGS

May this oblation dedicated to your name
purify us, O Lord,
and day by day bring our conduct
closer to the life of heaven.
℟. **Amen.**   ➔ No. 21, p. 22 (Pref. 29-36)

COMMUNION ANTIPHON Ps. 33.9

Taste and see that the Lord is good; blessed the man who seeks refuge in him. ↓

OR Mt 11.28

Come to me, all who labour and are burdened, and I will refresh you, says the Lord. ↓

PRAYER AFTER COMMUNION

Grant, we pray, O Lord,
that, having been replenished by such great gifts,
we may gain the prize of salvation
and never cease to praise you.
Through Christ our Lord.
℟. **Amen.**   ➔ No. 30, p. 77

Optional Solemn Blessings, p. 97, and Prayers over the People, p. 105

"He went to him and bandaged his wounds."

JULY 14

15th SUNDAY IN ORDINARY TIME

ENTRANCE ANTIPHON Cf. Ps. 16.15

As for me, in justice I shall behold your face; I shall be filled with the vision of your glory.

→ No. 2, p. 10

COLLECT

O God, who show the light of your truth
to those who go astray,
so that they may return to the right path,
give all who for the faith they profess
are accounted Christians
the grace to reject whatever is contrary to the
    name of Christ
and to strive after all that does it honour.
Through our Lord Jesus Christ, your Son,
who lives and reigns with you in the unity of the
    Holy Spirit,
one God, for ever and ever. ℟. **Amen.** ↓

FIRST READING Deut. 30.10-14

We heed the word of the Lord by keeping the commandments. God's word is not foreign to us.

A reading from the book of Deuteronomy.

MOSES spoke to the people, saying, "Obey the Lord your God by observing his commandments and decrees that are written in this book of the Law; turn to the Lord your God with all your heart and with all your soul.

Surely this commandment that I am commanding you today is not too hard for you, nor is it too far away. It is not in heaven, that you should say, 'Who will go up to heaven for us, and get it for us so that we may hear it and observe it?'

Neither is it beyond the sea, that you should say, 'Who will cross to the other side of the sea for us, and get it for us so that we may hear it and observe it?'

No, the word is very near to you; it is in your mouth and in your heart for you to observe."— The word of the Lord. R̸. **Thanks be to God.** ↓

RESPONSORIAL PSALM Ps. 69

R̸. **Seek God in your need, and let your hearts revive.**

As for me, my prayer is to you, O Lord.
At an acceptable time, O God,
in the abundance of your steadfast love, answer me.
With your steadfast help, rescue me.
Answer me, O Lord, for your steadfast love is good;
according to your abundant mercy, turn to me.
    —R̸.

But I am lowly and in pain;
let your salvation, O God, protect me.
I will praise the name of God with a song;
I will magnify him with thanksgiving.
℟. **Seek God in your need, and let your hearts revive.**

Let the oppressed see it and be glad;
you who seek God, let your hearts revive.—℟.

For God will save Zion
and rebuild the cities of Judah;
the children of his servants shall inherit it,
those who love his name shall live in it.—℟. ↓

OR

RESPONSORIAL PSALM Ps. 19

Michel Guimont

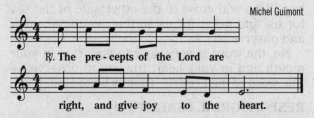

℟. The pre-cepts of the Lord are right, and give joy to the heart.

The law of the Lord is perfect,
reviving the soul;
the decrees of the Lord are sure,
making wise the simple.—℟.

The precepts of the Lord are right,
rejoicing the heart;
the commandment of the Lord is clear,
enlightening the eyes.—℟.

The fear of the Lord is pure,
enduring forever;
the ordinances of the Lord are true
and righteous altogether.—℟.

More to be desired are they than gold,
even much fine gold;
sweeter also than honey,
and drippings of the honeycomb.—℟. ↓

SECOND READING Col. 1.15-20

The glory of Christ is proclaimed for all to know.

A reading from the Letter of Saint Paul
to the Colossians.

CHRIST is the image of the invisible God, the
firstborn of all creation; for in him all things in
heaven and on earth were created, things visible
and invisible, whether thrones or dominions or
rulers or powers—all things have been created
through him and for him.

Christ is before all things, and in him all things
hold together.

He is the head of the body, the Church; he is the
beginning, the firstborn from the dead, so that he
might come to have first place in everything.

For in Christ all the fullness of God was pleased
to dwell, and through him God was pleased to reconcile to himself all things, whether on earth or in
heaven, by making peace through the blood of his
Cross.—The word of the Lord. ℟. **Thanks be to
God.** ↓

GOSPEL ACCLAMATION Jn. 6.63, 68

℣. Alleluia. ℟. **Alleluia.**
℣. Your words, Lord, are spirit and life;

you have the words of eternal life.
℟. **Alleluia.** ↓

GOSPEL Lk. 10.25-37

> A man is mugged. Who cares? How do we love others as we love ourselves?

℣. The Lord be with you. ℟. **And with your spirit.**
✠ A reading from the holy Gospel according to Luke. ℟. **Glory to you, O Lord.**

A LAWYER stood up to test Jesus. "Teacher," he said, "what must I do to inherit eternal life?"

Jesus said to him, "What is written in the Law? What do you read there?" The lawyer answered, "You shall love the Lord your God with all your heart, and with all your soul, and with all your strength, and with all your mind; and your neighbour as yourself."

And Jesus said to him, "You have given the right answer; do this, and you will live." But wanting to justify himself, the lawyer asked Jesus, "And who is my neighbour?"

Jesus replied, "A man was going down from Jerusalem to Jericho, and fell into the hands of robbers, who stripped him, beat him, and went away, leaving him half dead.

Now by chance a priest was going down that road; and when he saw him, he passed by on the other side. So likewise a Levite, when he came to the place and saw him, passed by on the other side.

But a Samaritan while travelling came near him; and when he saw him, he was moved with pity. He went to him and bandaged his wounds, having poured oil and wine on them. Then he put him on his own animal, brought him to an inn, and took care of him.

The next day the Samaritan took out two denarii, gave them to the innkeeper, and said, 'Take care of him; and when I come back, I will repay you whatever more you spend.'"

Jesus asked, "Which of these three, do you think, was a neighbour to the man who fell into the hands of the robbers?" The lawyer said, "The one who showed him mercy." Jesus said to him, "Go and do likewise."—The Gospel of the Lord. ℟. **Praise to you, Lord Jesus Christ.** → No. 15, p. 18

PRAYER OVER THE OFFERINGS

Look upon the offerings of the Church, O Lord,
as she makes her prayer to you,
and grant that, when consumed by those who
   believe,
they may bring ever greater holiness.
Through Christ our Lord.
℟. **Amen.**   → No. 21, p. 22 (Pref. 29-36)

COMMUNION ANTIPHON Cf. Ps. 83.4-5

The sparrow finds a home, and the swallow a nest for her young: by your altars, O Lord of hosts, my King and my God. Blessed are they who dwell in your house, for ever singing your praise. ↓

OR Jn. 6.57

Whoever eats my flesh and drinks my blood remains in me and I in him, says the Lord. ↓

PRAYER AFTER COMMUNION

Having consumed these gifts, we pray, O Lord,
that, by our participation in this mystery,
its saving effects upon us may grow.
Through Christ our Lord.
R/. **Amen.**

➡ No. 30, p. 77

Optional Solemn Blessings, p. 97, and Prayers over the People, p. 105

"Mary has chosen the better part, which will
not be taken away from her."

JULY 21

16th SUNDAY IN ORDINARY TIME

ENTRANCE ANTIPHON Ps. 53.6, 8

See, I have God for my help. The Lord sustains
my soul. I will sacrifice to you with willing heart,
and praise your name, O Lord, for it is good.

➡ No. 2, p. 10

COLLECT

Show favour, O Lord, to your servants
and mercifully increase the gifts of your grace,
that, made fervent in hope, faith and charity,
they may be ever watchful in keeping your
    commands.
Through our Lord Jesus Christ, your Son,
who lives and reigns with you in the unity of the
    Holy Spirit,
one God, for ever and ever. ℟. **Amen.** ↓

FIRST READING Gen. 18.1-10a

**Abraham extends hospitality and the Lord reveals that the
promise to Abraham will be fulfilled.**

A reading from the book of Genesis.

THE Lord appeared to Abraham by the oaks
    of Mamre, as Abraham sat at the entrance of
his tent in the heat of the day. Abraham looked
up and saw three men standing near him. When
he saw them, he ran from the tent entrance to
meet them, and bowed down to the ground.

He said, "My lord, if I find favour with you, do
not pass by your servant. Let a little water be
brought, and wash your feet, and rest yourselves under the tree. Let me bring a little bread,
that you may refresh yourselves, and after that
you may pass on—since you have come to your
servant." So they said, "Do as you have said."

And Abraham hastened into the tent to
Sarah, and said, "Make ready quickly three
measures of choice flour, knead it, and make

cakes." Abraham ran to the herd, and took a calf, tender and good, and gave it to the servant, who hastened to prepare it. Then he took curds and milk and the calf that he had prepared, and set it before them; and he stood by them under the tree while they ate.

They said to Abraham, "Where is your wife Sarah?" And he said, "There, in the tent."

Then one said, "I will surely return to you in due season, and your wife Sarah shall have a son."—The word of the Lord. ℟. **Thanks be to God.** ↓

RESPONSORIAL PSALM Ps. 15

Frank Lynch

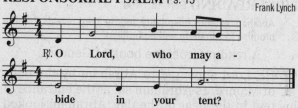

℟. O Lord, who may abide in your tent?

Whoever walks blamelessly, and does what is right,
and speaks the truth from their heart;
whoever does not slander with their tongue.—℟.

Whoever does no evil to a friend,
nor takes up a reproach against a neighbour;
in whose eyes the wicked one is despised,
but who honours those who fear the Lord.—℟.

Whoever stands by their oath even to their hurt;
who does not lend money at interest,
and does not take a bribe against the innocent.
One who does these things shall never be moved.—℟. ↓

SECOND READING Col. 1.24-28

The word of God in its fullness is now revealed in the mystery of Christ.

A reading from the Letter of Saint Paul
to the Colossians.

Brothers and sisters: I am now rejoicing in my sufferings for your sake, and in my flesh I am completing what is lacking in Christ's afflictions for the sake of his body, that is, the Church.

I became its servant according to God's commission that was given to me for you, to make the word of God fully known, the mystery that has been hidden throughout the ages and generations but has now been revealed to his saints.

To them God chose to make known how great among the Gentiles are the riches of the glory of this mystery, which is Christ in you, the hope of glory. It is Christ whom we proclaim, warning every person and teaching every person in all wisdom, so that we may present every person mature in Christ.—The word of the Lord.
℟. **Thanks be to God.** ↓

GOSPEL ACCLAMATION Lk. 8.15

℣. Alleluia. ℟. **Alleluia.**
℣. Blessed are they who hold fast to God's word in an honest and good heart,
and bear fruit with patient endurance.
℟. **Alleluia.** ↓

GOSPEL Lk. 10.38-42

Strive for a sense of proportion—maintain a balance in all things.

℣. The Lord be with you. ℟. **And with your spirit.**
✚ A reading from the holy Gospel according to Luke. ℟. **Glory to you, O Lord.**

NOW as Jesus and his disciples went on their way, he entered a certain village, where a woman named Martha welcomed him into her home. She had a sister named Mary, who sat at the Lord's feet and listened to what he was saying.

But Martha was distracted by her many tasks; so she came to Jesus and asked, "Lord, do you not care that my sister has left me to do all the work by myself? Tell her then to help me."

But the Lord answered her, "Martha, Martha, you are worried and distracted by many things; there is need of only one thing. Mary has chosen the better part, which will not be taken away from her."—The Gospel of the Lord. ℟. **Praise to you, Lord Jesus Christ.**   → No. 15, p. 18

PRAYER OVER THE OFFERINGS

O God, who in the one perfect sacrifice
brought to completion varied offerings of the law,
accept, we pray, this sacrifice from your faithful
    servants
and make it holy, as you blessed the gifts of Abel,
so that what each has offered to the honour of
    your majesty
may benefit the salvation of all.
Through Christ our Lord.
℟. **Amen.**   → No. 21, p. 22 (Pref. 29-36)

COMMUNION ANTIPHON Ps. 110.4-5

The Lord, the gracious, the merciful, has made a memorial of his wonders; he gives food to those who fear him. ↓

OR Rev. 3.20

Behold, I stand at the door and knock, says the Lord. If anyone hears my voice and opens the door to me, I will enter his house and dine with him, and he with me. ↓

PRAYER AFTER COMMUNION

Graciously be present to your people, we pray,
    O Lord,
and lead those you have imbued with heavenly
    mysteries
to pass from former ways to newness of life.
Through Christ our Lord.
℟. **Amen.**   → No. 30, p. 77

Optional Solemn Blessings, p. 97, and Prayers over the People, p. 105

"Lord, teach us to pray, as John taught his disciples."

JULY 28

17th SUNDAY IN ORDINARY TIME

ENTRANCE ANTIPHON Cf. Ps. 67.6-7, 36

God is in his holy place, God who unites those who dwell in his house; he himself gives might and strength to his people. ➔ No. 2, p. 10

COLLECT

O God, protector of those who hope in you,
without whom nothing has firm foundation,
   nothing is holy,
bestow in abundance your mercy upon us
and grant that, with you as our ruler and guide,
we may use the good things that pass
in such a way as to hold fast even now
to those that ever endure.
Through our Lord Jesus Christ, your Son,

who lives and reigns with you in the unity of the
    Holy Spirit,
one God, for ever and ever. ℟. **Amen.** ↓

FIRST READING Gen. 18.20-32

**The Lord is just and merciful. He will hear our prayers
and give us strength to handle any situation in life.**

A reading from the book of Genesis.

THE Lord said: "How great is the outcry
against Sodom and Gomorrah and how very
grave their sin! I must go down and see whether
they have done altogether according to the outcry that has come to me; and if not, I will know."

So the men turned from there, and went toward Sodom, while Abraham remained standing before the Lord. Then Abraham came near
and said, "Will you indeed sweep away the
righteous with the wicked? Suppose there are
fifty righteous within the city; will you then
sweep away the place and not forgive it for the
fifty righteous who are in it? Far be it from you
to do such a thing, to slay the righteous with the
wicked, so that the righteous fare as the wicked!
Far be that from you! Shall not the Judge of all
the earth do what is just?" And the Lord said, "If
I find at Sodom fifty righteous in the city, I will
forgive the whole place for their sake."

Abraham answered, "Let me take it upon myself to speak to the Lord, I who am but dust and
ashes. Suppose five of the fifty righteous are
lacking? Will you destroy the whole city for lack
of five?" And the Lord said, "I will not destroy it
if I find forty-five there."

Again Abraham spoke to the Lord, "Suppose forty are found there." He answered, "For the sake of forty I will not do it."

Then Abraham said, "Oh do not let the Lord be angry if I speak. Suppose thirty are found there." The Lord answered, "I will not do it, if I find thirty there."

Abraham said, "Let me take it upon myself to speak to the Lord. Suppose twenty are found there." The Lord answered, "For the sake of twenty I will not destroy it."

Then Abraham said, "Oh do not let the Lord be angry if I speak just once more. Suppose ten are found there." The Lord answered, "For the sake of ten I will not destroy it."—The word of the Lord. ℟. **Thanks be to God.** ↓

RESPONSORIAL PSALM Ps. 138

Leo Marchildon

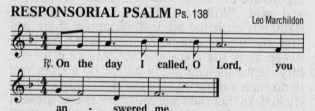

℟. On the day I called, O Lord, you answered me.

I give you thanks, O Lord, with my whole heart;
before the Angels I sing your praise;
I bow down toward your holy temple,
and give thanks to your name
for your steadfast love and your faithfulness.—℟.

For you have exalted your name
and your word above everything.
On the day I called, you answered me,
you increased my strength of soul.—℟.

For though the Lord is high, he regards the
   lowly;
but the haughty he perceives from far away.
Though I walk in the midst of trouble,
you preserve me against the wrath of my enemies.—℟.

You stretch out your hand and your right hand
   delivers me.
The Lord will fulfill his purpose for me;
your steadfast love, O Lord, endures forever.
Do not forsake the work of your hands.—℟. ↓

SECOND READING Col. 2.12-14

**The merciful Lord cancels our debt, pardons all our sins.
He has given us new life in Christ.**

A reading from the Letter of Saint Paul
to the Colossians.

BROTHERS and sisters, when you were
buried with Christ in baptism, you were also
raised with him through faith in the power of
God, who raised Christ from the dead.

And when you were dead in trespasses and
the uncircumcision of your flesh, God made you
alive together with him, when he forgave us all
our trespasses, erasing the record that stood
against us with its legal demands. He set this
aside, nailing it to the Cross.—The word of the
Lord. ℟. **Thanks be to God.** ↓

GOSPEL ACCLAMATION Rom. 8.15

℣. Alleluia. ℟. **Alleluia.**
℣. You have received a Spirit of adoption,

in whom we cry, Abba! Father!
℟. **Alleluia.** ↓

GOSPEL Lk. 11.1-13

> In the Lord's Prayer Jesus urges us to persevere in prayer
> and trust in the goodness of our loving Father.

℣. The Lord be with you. ℟. **And with your spirit.**
✠ A reading from the holy Gospel according to
Luke. ℟. **Glory to you, O Lord.**

JESUS was praying in a certain place, and
after he had finished, one of his disciples said
to him, "Lord, teach us to pray, as John taught
his disciples."

He said to them, "When you pray, say:
'Father, hallowed be your name.
  Your kingdom come.
  Give us each day our daily bread.
  And forgive us our sins,
    for we ourselves forgive everyone indebted
      to us.
  And lead us not into temptation.'"

And Jesus said to the disciples, "Suppose one
of you has a friend, and you go to him at mid-
night and say to him, 'Friend, lend me three
loaves of bread; for a friend of mine has arrived,
and I have nothing to set before him.' And your
friend answers from within, 'Do not bother me;
the door has already been locked, and my children are with me in bed; I cannot get up and
give you anything.'

I tell you, even though he will not get up and
give him anything because he is his friend, at

least because of his persistence he will get up and give him whatever he needs.

So I say to you: Ask, and it will be given you; search, and you will find; knock, and the door will be opened for you. For everyone who asks receives, and everyone who searches finds, and for everyone who knocks, the door will be opened.

Is there any father among you who, if your child asks for a fish, will give the child a snake instead of a fish? Or if the child asks for an egg, will give a scorpion?

If you then, who are evil, know how to give good gifts to your children, how much more will the heavenly Father give the Holy Spirit to those who ask him!"—The Gospel of the Lord. ℟. **Praise to you, Lord Jesus Christ.**   → No. 15, p. 18

PRAYER OVER THE OFFERINGS

Accept, O Lord, we pray, the offerings
which we bring from the abundance of your gifts,
that through the powerful working of your grace
these most sacred mysteries may sanctify our
    present way of life
and lead us to eternal gladness.
Through Christ our Lord.
℟. **Amen.**   → No. 21, p. 22 (Pref. 29-36)

COMMUNION ANTIPHON Ps. 102.2

Bless the Lord, O my soul, and never forget all his benefits. ↓

OR Mt. 5.7-8

Blessed are the merciful, for they shall receive mercy. Blessed are the clean of heart, for they shall see God. ↓

PRAYER AFTER COMMUNION

We have consumed, O Lord, this divine Sacrament,
the perpetual memorial of the Passion of your Son;
grant, we pray, that this gift,
which he himself gave us with love beyond all
    telling,
may profit us for salvation.
Through Christ our Lord.
℟. **Amen.**

→ No. 30, p. 77

Optional Solemn Blessings, p. 97, and Prayers over the People, p. 105

"Be on your guard against all kinds of greed. . . ."

AUGUST 4

18th SUNDAY IN ORDINARY TIME

ENTRANCE ANTIPHON Ps. 69.2, 6

O God, come to my assistance; O Lord, make haste to help me! You are my rescuer, my help; O Lord, do not delay. → No. 2, p. 10

COLLECT

Draw near to your servants, O Lord,
and answer their prayers with unceasing
　　kindness,
that, for those who glory in you as their Creator
　　and guide,
you may restore what you have created
and keep safe what you have restored.
Through our Lord Jesus Christ, your Son,
who lives and reigns with you in the unity of the
　　Holy Spirit,
one God, for ever and ever. ℟. **Amen.** ↓

FIRST READING Eccl. 1.2; 2.21-23

Without our faith, all our strivings lead to nothing.

A reading from the book of Ecclesiastes.

VANITY of vanities, says the Teacher,
   vanity of vanities! All is vanity.
Sometimes one who has toiled with wisdom and
   knowledge and skill
must leave all to be enjoyed by another
who did not toil for it.
This also is vanity and a great evil.

What does a person get from all their toil and
   strain,
their toil under the sun?
For their days are full of pain,
and their work is a vexation;
even at night their mind does not rest.
This also is vanity.

The word of the Lord. ℟. **Thanks be to God.** ↓

RESPONSORIAL PSALM Ps. 90

Frank Lynch

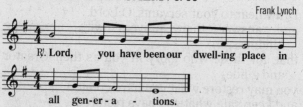

℟. Lord, you have been our dwelling place in all gen-er-a-tions.

You turn man back to dust, and say,
"Turn back, you children of Adam."
For a thousand years in your sight
are like yesterday when it is past,
or like a watch in the night.—℟.

You sweep them away; they are like a dream,
like grass that is renewed in the morning;
in the morning it flourishes and is renewed;
in the evening it fades and withers.—℟.

So teach us to count our days
that we may gain a wise heart.
Turn, O Lord! How long?
Have compassion on your servants!—℟.

Satisfy us in the morning with your steadfast
    love,
so that we may rejoice and be glad all our days.
Let the favour of the Lord our God be upon us,
and prosper for us the work of our hands.—℟. ↓

SECOND READING Col. 3.1-5, 9-11

In baptism the Christian is to die to the old self and to sin
in order to live with Christ. When he appears, all who
have been faithful will appear with him in glory.

A reading from the Letter of Saint Paul
to the Colossians.

BROTHERS and sisters: If you have been raised
with Christ, seek the things that are above,
where Christ is, seated at the right hand of God.

Set your minds on things that are above, not on
things that are on earth, for you have died, and
your life is hidden with Christ in God. When
Christ who is your life is revealed, then you also
will be revealed with him in glory.

Put to death, therefore, whatever in you is
earthly: fornication, impurity, passion, evil desire,
and greed, which is idolatry.

Do not lie to one another, seeing that you have stripped off the old self with its practices and have clothed yourselves with the new self, which is being renewed in knowledge according to the image of its creator.

In that renewal there is no longer Greek and Jew, circumcised and uncircumcised, barbarian, Scythian, slave and free; but Christ is all and in all!—The word of the Lord. ℟. **Thanks be to God.** ↓

GOSPEL ACCLAMATION Mt. 5.3

℣. Alleluia. ℟. **Alleluia.**
℣. Blessed are the poor in spirit,
for theirs is the kingdom of heaven!
℟. **Alleluia.** ↓

GOSPEL Lk. 12.13-21

How foolish and vain are those who put all their trust in their own devices.

℣. The Lord be with you. ℟. **And with your spirit.**
✠ A reading from the holy Gospel according to Luke. ℟. **Glory to you, O Lord.**

SOMEONE in the crowd said to Jesus, "Teacher, tell my brother to divide the family inheritance with me." But Jesus said to him, "Friend, who set me to be a judge or arbitrator over you?"

And Jesus said to the crowd, "Take care! Be on your guard against all kinds of greed; for one's life does not consist in the abundance of possessions."

Then Jesus told them a parable: "The land of a rich man produced abundantly. And he thought to himself, 'What should I do, for I have no place to store my crops?' Then he said, 'I will do this: I will pull down my barns and build larger ones, and there I will store all my grain and my goods. And I will say to my soul, "Soul, you have ample goods laid up for many years; relax, eat, drink, be merry."

But God said to him, 'You fool! This very night your life is being demanded of you. And the things you have prepared, whose will they be?' So it is with those who store up treasures for themselves but are not rich toward God."— The Gospel of the Lord. ℟. **Praise to you, Lord Jesus Christ.**   → No. 15, p. 18

PRAYER OVER THE OFFERINGS

Graciously sanctify these gifts, O Lord, we pray, and, accepting the oblation of this spiritual sacrifice,
make of us an eternal offering to you.
Through Christ our Lord.
℟. **Amen.**   → No. 21, p. 22 (Pref. 29-36)

COMMUNION ANTIPHON Wis. 16.20

You have given us, O Lord, bread from heaven, endowed with all delights and sweetness in every taste. ↓

OR Jn. 6.35

I am the bread of life, says the Lord; whoever comes to me will not hunger and whoever believes in me will not thirst. ↓

PRAYER AFTER COMMUNION

Accompany with constant protection, O Lord,
those you renew with these heavenly gifts
and, in your never-failing care for them,
make them worthy of eternal redemption.
Through Christ our Lord.
℟. **Amen.**   ➜ No. 30, p. 77

Optional Solemn Blessings, p. 97, and Prayers over the People, p. 105

"Be dressed for action and have your lamps lit."

AUGUST 11

19th SUNDAY IN ORDINARY TIME

ENTRANCE ANTIPHON Cf. Ps. 73.20, 19, 22, 23

Look to your covenant, O Lord, and forget not
the life of your poor ones for ever. Arise, O God,
and defend your cause, and forget not the cries of
those who seek you.   ➜ No. 2, p. 10

COLLECT

Almighty ever-living God,
whom, taught by the Holy Spirit,
we dare to call our Father,
bring, we pray, to perfection in our hearts
the spirit of adoption as your sons and daughters,
that we may merit to enter into the inheritance
which you have promised.
Through our Lord Jesus Christ, your Son,
who lives and reigns with you in the unity of the
    Holy Spirit,
one God, for ever and ever. ℟. **Amen.** ↓

FIRST READING Wis. 18.6-9

**The first Passover is recalled, when the faithful people of
God prayed behind closed doors, and the angel of death
struck at the firstborn of Egypt.**

A reading from the book of Wisdom.

THE night of the deliverance from Egypt
    was made known beforehand to our ances-
    tors,
so that they might rejoice in sure knowledge of the
    oaths
in which they trusted.

The deliverance of the righteous
and the destruction of their enemies
were expected by your people.
For by the same means
by which you punished our enemies
you called us to yourself and glorified us.

For in secret
the holy children of good people offered sacrifices,

and with one accord agreed to the divine law,
so that the saints would share alike the same
   things,
both blessings and dangers;
and already they were singing the praises of the
   ancestors.

The word of the Lord. ℟. **Thanks be to God.** ↓

RESPONSORIAL PSALM Ps. 33

Kathrine Bellamy

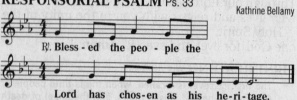

℟. Bless - ed   the peo - ple   the
Lord   has   chos-en   as   his   he-ri-tage.

Rejoice in the Lord, O you righteous.
Praise befits the upright.
Blessed is the nation whose God is the Lord,
the people whom he has chosen as his heritage.—℟.

Truly the eye of the Lord is on those who fear him,
on those who hope in his steadfast love,
to deliver their soul from death,
and to keep them alive in famine.—℟.

Our soul waits for the Lord;
he is our help and shield.
Let your steadfast love, O Lord, be upon us,
even as we hope in you.—℟. ↓

SECOND READING Heb. 11.1-2, 8-19 or 11.1-2, 8-12

Abraham, our father in faith, relies on the confident assurance of what he hopes for. May we take courage from
his example.

[If the "Shorter Form" is used, the indented text in brackets is omitted.]

A reading from the Letter to the Hebrews.

BROTHERS and sisters: Faith is the assurance of things hoped for, the conviction of things not seen. Indeed, by faith our ancestors received approval.

By faith Abraham obeyed when he was called to set out for a place that he was to receive as an inheritance; and he set out, not knowing where he was going. By faith he stayed for a time in the land he had been promised, as in a foreign land, living in tents, as did Isaac and Jacob, who were heirs with him of the same promise.

For Abraham looked forward to the city that has foundations, whose architect and builder is God. By faith Sarah herself, though barren, received power to conceive, even when she was too old, because she considered him faithful who had promised.

Therefore from one person, and this one as good as dead, descendants were born, "as many as the stars of heaven and as the innumerable grains of sand by the seashore."

[All of these died in faith without having received the promises, but from a distance they saw and greeted them. They confessed that they were strangers and foreigners on the earth, for people who speak in this way make it clear that they are seeking a homeland. If they had been thinking of the land that they had left behind, they would have had opportunity to return.

But as it is, they desire a better country, that is, a heavenly one. Therefore God is not ashamed to be called their God; indeed, he has prepared a city for them.

By faith Abraham, when put to the test, offered up Isaac. He who had received the promises was ready to offer up his only-begotten son, of whom he had been told, "It is through Isaac that descendants shall be named for you." Abraham considered the fact that God is able even to raise someone from the dead—and figuratively speaking, he did receive Isaac back.]

The word of the Lord. ℟. **Thanks be to God.** ↓

GOSPEL ACCLAMATION Mt. 24.42, 44

℣. Alleluia. ℟. **Alleluia.**
℣. Keep awake and be ready,
for you know not when the Son of Man is coming.
℟. **Alleluia.** ↓

GOSPEL Lk. 12.32-48 or 12.35-40

As the faithful people of God, we must act in accordance with our faith. We must be constant.

[If the "Shorter Form" is used, the indented text in brackets is omitted.]

℣. The Lord be with you. ℟. **And with your spirit.**
✠ A reading from the holy Gospel according to Luke. ℟. **Glory to you, O Lord.**

JESUS said to his disciples,
    ["Do not be afraid, little flock, for it is
your Father's good pleasure to give you the
kingdom. Sell your possessions, and give
alms. Make purses for yourselves that do not
wear out, an unfailing treasure in heaven,
where no thief comes near and no moth de-
stroys. For where your treasure is, there your
heart will be also.]

"Be dressed for action and have your lamps
lit; be like those who are waiting for their master to return from the wedding banquet, so that
they may open the door for him as soon as he
comes and knocks. Blessed are those slaves
whom the master finds alert when he comes;
truly I tell you, he will fasten his belt and have
them sit down to eat, and he will come and
serve them.

If he comes during the middle of the night, or
near dawn, and finds them so, blessed are those
slaves.

But know this: if the owner of the house had
known at what hour the thief was coming, he
would not have let his house be broken into.

You also must be ready, for the Son of Man is
coming at an unexpected hour."

    [Peter said, "Lord, are you telling this para-
ble for us or for everyone?" And the Lord said,
"Who then is the faithful and prudent manager whom his master will put in charge of
his slaves, to give them their allowance of
food at the proper time? Blessed is that slave
whom his master will find at work when he

arrives. Truly I tell you, he will put that one in charge of all his possessions. But if that slave says to himself, 'My master is delayed in coming,' and if he begins to beat the other slaves, men and women, and to eat and drink and get drunk, the master of that slave will come on a day when he does not expect him and at an hour that he does not know, and will cut him in pieces, and put him with the unfaithful.

That slave who knew what his master wanted, but did not prepare himself or do what was wanted, will receive a severe beating. But the one who did not know and did what deserved a beating will receive a light beating.

From everyone to whom much has been given, much will be required; and from the one to whom much has been entrusted, even more will be demanded."]

The Gospel of the Lord. ℟. **Praise to you, Lord Jesus Christ.**

→ No. 15, p. 18

PRAYER OVER THE OFFERINGS

Be pleased, O Lord, to accept the offerings of your
  Church,
for in your mercy you have given them to be
  offered
and by your power you transform them
into the mystery of our salvation.
Through Christ our Lord.
℟. **Amen.**

→ No. 21, p. 22 (Pref. 29-36)

COMMUNION ANTIPHON Ps. 146.12, 14

O Jerusalem, glorify the Lord, who gives you your fill of finest wheat. ↓

OR Cf. Jn. 6.51

The bread that I will give, says the Lord, is my flesh for the life of the world. ↓

PRAYER AFTER COMMUNION

May the communion in your Sacrament
that we have consumed, save us, O Lord,
and confirm us in the light of your truth.
Through Christ our Lord.
℞. **Amen.**   → No. 30, p. 77

Optional Solemn Blessings, p. 97, and Prayers over the People, p. 105

"I came to bring fire to the earth. . . ."

AUGUST 18

20th SUNDAY IN ORDINARY TIME

ENTRANCE ANTIPHON Ps. 83.10-11

Turn your eyes, O God, our shield; and look on the face of your anointed one; one day within your courts is better than a thousand elsewhere.

→ No. 2, p. 10

COLLECT

O God, who have prepared for those who love you
good things which no eye can see,
fill our hearts, we pray, with the warmth of your love,
so that, loving you in all things and above all things,
we may attain your promises,
which surpass every human desire.

Through our Lord Jesus Christ, your Son,
who lives and reigns with you in the unity of the
   Holy Spirit,
one God, for ever and ever. ℟. **Amen.** ↓

FIRST READING   Jer. 38.4-6, 8-10

In a symbolic way, the Prophet's experience is a resurrection. He is buried in the cistern and later drawn up from it.

A reading from the book of the Prophet Jeremiah.

THE officials said to the king, "This man ought to be put to death, because he is discouraging the soldiers who are left in this city, and all the people, by speaking such words to them. For this man is not seeking the welfare of this people, but their harm."

King Zedekiah said, "Here he is; he is in your hands; for the king is powerless against you."

So they took Jeremiah and threw him into the cistern of Malchiah, the king's son, which was in the court of the guard, letting Jeremiah down by ropes. Now there was no water in the cistern, but only mud, and Jeremiah sank in the mud.

So Ebed-melech the Ethiopian, an officer in the king's house, left the king's house and spoke to the king, "My lord king, these men have acted wickedly in all they did to the Prophet Jeremiah by throwing him into the cistern to die there of hunger, for there is no bread left in the city." Then the king commanded Ebed-melech the Ethiopian, "Take three men with you from here, and pull the Prophet Jeremiah up from the cis-

tern before he dies."—The word of the Lord.
℟. **Thanks be to God.** ↓

RESPONSORIAL PSALM Ps. 40

Paul McKay

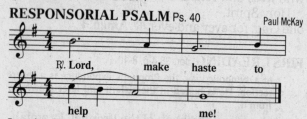

℟. Lord, make haste to help me!

I waited patiently for the Lord;
he inclined to me and heard my cry.—℟.

He drew me up from the desolate pit,
out of the miry bog,
and set my feet upon a rock,
making my steps secure.—℟.

He put a new song in my mouth,
a song of praise to our God.
Many will see and fear,
and put their trust in the Lord.—℟.

As for me, I am poor and needy,
but the Lord takes thought for me.
You are my help and my deliverer;
do not delay, O my God.—℟. ↓

SECOND READING Heb. 12.1-4

**Take courage from the example of Christ. Do not lose
sight of the eternal reward.**

A reading from the Letter to the Hebrews.

Brothers and sisters: since we are surrounded by so great a cloud of witnesses, let
us also lay aside every weight and the sin that
clings so closely, and let us run with perseverance
the race that is set before us, looking to Jesus the

pioneer and perfecter of our faith, who for the sake of the joy that was set before him endured the Cross, disregarding its shame, and has taken his seat at the right hand of the throne of God.

Consider Jesus who endured such hostility against himself from sinners, so that you may not grow weary or lose heart. In your struggle against sin you have not yet resisted to the point of shedding your blood.—The word of the Lord. ℟. **Thanks be to God.** ↓

GOSPEL ACCLAMATION Jn. 10.27

℣. Alleluia. ℟. **Alleluia.**

℣. My sheep hear my voice, says the Lord;
I know them, and they follow me.
℟. **Alleluia.** ↓

GOSPEL Lk. 12.49-53

Many cannot find peace because they do not accept Christ. To them his coming is the cause of division.

℣. The Lord be with you. ℟. **And with your spirit.**
✛ A reading from the holy Gospel according to Luke. ℟. **Glory to you, O Lord.**

JESUS said to his disciples: "I came to bring fire to the earth, and how I wish it were already kindled! I have a baptism with which to be baptized, and what stress I am under until it is completed!

Do you think that I have come to bring peace to the earth? No, I tell you, but rather division! From now on five in one household will be divided, three against two and two against three; they will be divided: father against son and son

against father, mother against daughter and
daughter against mother, mother-in-law against
her daughter-in-law and daughter-in-law against
mother-in-law."—The Gospel of the Lord.
℟. **Praise to you, Lord Jesus Christ.** ➔ No. 15, p. 18

PRAYER OVER THE OFFERINGS

Receive our oblation, O Lord,
by which is brought about a glorious exchange,
that, by offering what you have given,
we may merit to receive your very self.
Through Christ our Lord.
℟. **Amen.**   ➔ No. 21, p. 22 (Pref. 29-36)

COMMUNION ANTIPHON Ps 129.7

**With the Lord there is mercy; in him is plentiful
redemption.** ↓

OR Jn. 6.51

**I am the living bread that came down from
heaven, says the Lord. Whoever eats of this
bread will live for ever.** ↓

PRAYER AFTER COMMUNION

Made partakers of Christ through these Sacraments,
we humbly implore your mercy, Lord,
that, conformed to his image on earth,
we may merit also to be his co-heirs in heaven.
Who lives and reigns for ever and ever.
℟. **Amen.**   ➔ No. 30, p. 77

Optional Solemn Blessings, p. 97, and Prayers over the People, p. 105

"Strive to enter through the narrow door; for many . . .
will try to enter and will not be able."

AUGUST 25

21st SUNDAY IN ORDINARY TIME

ENTRANCE ANTIPHON Cf. Ps. 85.1-3

**Turn your ear, O Lord, and answer me; save the
servant who trusts in you, my God. Have mercy
on me, O Lord, for I cry to you all the day long.**

→ No. 2, p. 10

COLLECT

O God, who cause the minds of the faithful
to unite in a single purpose,
grant your people to love what you command
and to desire what you promise,
that, amid the uncertainties of this world,
our hearts may be fixed on that place
where true gladness is found.
Through our Lord Jesus Christ, your Son,

who lives and reigns with you in the unity of the Holy Spirit,
one God, for ever and ever. ℟. **Amen.**↓

FIRST READING Isa. 66.18-21

Salvation is offered to all and will embrace all, even the alien, some of whom will receive the sacred duty to minister the Holy Mysteries.

A reading from the book of the Prophet Isaiah.

THUS says the Lord: "For I know their works and their thoughts, and I am coming to gather all nations and tongues; and they shall come and shall see my glory, and I will set a sign among them.

From them I will send survivors to the nations, to Tarshish, Put, and Lud—which draw the bow—to Tubal and Javan, to the coastlands far away that have not heard of my fame or seen my glory; and they shall declare my glory among the nations.

They shall bring all your kindred from all the nations as an offering to the Lord, on horses, and in chariots, and in litters, and on mules, and on dromedaries, to my holy mountain Jerusalem," says the Lord, "just as the children of Israel bring a grain offering in a clean vessel to the house of the Lord.

And I will also take some of them as priests and as Levites," says the Lord.—The word of the Lord. ℟. **Thanks be to God.** ↓

RESPONSORIAL PSALM Ps. 117

Leo Marchildon

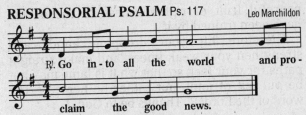

℟. Go in-to all the world and pro-claim the good news.

Or: ℟. **Alleluia!**

Praise the Lord, all you nations!
Extol him, all you peoples!—℟.

For great is his steadfast love toward us,
and the faithfulness of the Lord endures forever.—℟. ↓

SECOND READING Heb. 12.5-7, 11-13

Look beyond trials and tribulations, remain steadfast in
faith, and rely on the goodness and love of God. For he
disciplines those he loves.

A reading from the Letter to the Hebrews.

BROTHERS and sisters: You have forgotten the
exhortation that addresses you as children—
"My son, do not regard lightly the discipline of
the Lord,
or lose heart when you are punished by him;
for the Lord disciplines the one whom he loves,
and chastises every son whom he accepts."
Endure trials for the sake of discipline. God
is treating you as sons; for what son is there
whom a father does not discipline?
Now, discipline always seems painful rather
than pleasant at the time, but later it yields the

peaceful fruit of righteousness to those who have been trained by it.

Therefore lift your drooping hands and strengthen your weak knees, and make straight paths for your feet, so that what is lame may not be put out of joint, but rather be healed.—The word of the Lord. ℟. **Thanks be to God.** ↓

GOSPEL ACCLAMATION Jn. 14.6

℣. Alleluia. ℟. **Alleluia.**

℣. I am the way, the truth, and the life, says the Lord;

no one comes to the Father, except through me.

℟. **Alleluia.** ↓

GOSPEL Lk. 13.22-30

The kingdom of God will extend to people from all over, but all who have rejected the Word will find themselves as outcasts.

℣. The Lord be with you. ℟. **And with your spirit.**

✠ A reading from the holy Gospel according to Luke. ℟. **Glory to you, O Lord.**

JESUS went through one town and village after another, teaching as he made his way to Jerusalem.

Someone asked him, "Lord, will only a few be saved?" Jesus said to them, "Strive to enter through the narrow door; for many, I tell you, will try to enter and will not be able.

When once the owner of the house has got up and shut the door, and you begin to stand outside and to knock at the door, saying, 'Lord, open to us,' then in reply he will say to you, 'I do not know where you come from.'

Then you will begin to say, 'We ate and drank with you, and you taught in our streets.' But the Lord will say, 'I do not know where you come from; go away from me, all you evildoers!'

There will be weeping and gnashing of teeth when you see Abraham and Isaac and Jacob and all the Prophets in the kingdom of God, and you yourselves thrown out. Then people will come from east and west, from north and south, and will eat in the kingdom of God.

Indeed, some are last who will be first, and some are first who will be last."—The Gospel of the Lord. ℟. **Praise to you, Lord Jesus Christ.**

→ No. 15, p. 18

PRAYER OVER THE OFFERINGS

O Lord, who gained for yourself a people by
   adoption
through the one sacrifice offered once for all,
bestow graciously on us, we pray,
the gifts of unity and peace in your Church.
Through Christ our Lord.
℟. **Amen.**   → No. 21, p. 22 (Pref. 29-36)

COMMUNION ANTIPHON Cf. Ps 103.13-15

The earth is replete with the fruits of your work, O Lord; you bring forth bread from the earth and wine to cheer the heart. ↓

OR Cf. Jn. 6.54

Whoever eats my flesh and drinks my blood has

eternal life, says the Lord, and I will raise him up on the last day. ↓

PRAYER AFTER COMMUNION

Complete within us, O Lord, we pray,
the healing work of your mercy
and graciously perfect and sustain us,
so that in all things we may please you.
Through Christ our Lord.

R̸. **Amen.**

→ No. 30, p. 77

Optional Solemn Blessings, p. 97, and Prayers over the People, p. 105

"All who exalt themselves will be humbled. . . ."

SEPTEMBER 1

22nd SUNDAY IN ORDINARY TIME

ENTRANCE ANTIPHON Cf. Ps. 85.3, 5

Have mercy on me, O Lord, for I cry to you all
the day long. O Lord, you are good and forgiving,
full of mercy to all who call to you.   → No. 2, p. 10

COLLECT

God of might, giver of every good gift,
put into our hearts the love of your name,
so that, by deepening our sense of reverence,
you may nurture in us what is good
and, by your watchful care,
keep safe what you have nurtured.
Through our Lord Jesus Christ, your Son,
who lives and reigns with you in the unity of the
　　Holy Spirit,
one God, for ever and ever. ℟. **Amen.** ↓

FIRST READING　Sir. 3.17-20, 28-29

Know your own limitations. Live within your own capabilities.

A reading from the book of Sirach.

M Y child, perform your tasks with humility;
then you will be loved by those whom God
　accepts.
The greater you are,
the more you must humble yourself;
so you will find favour in the sight of the Lord.
Many are lofty and renowned,
but to the humble the Lord reveals his secrets.
For great is the might of the Lord;
but by the humble he is glorified.

When calamity befalls someone proud,
there is no healing,
for an evil plant has taken root in them.

The mind of the intelligent appreciates proverbs,
and an attentive ear is the desire of the wise.

The word of the Lord. ℟. **Thanks be to God.** ↓

RESPONSIVE PSALM Ps. 68

Leo Marchildon

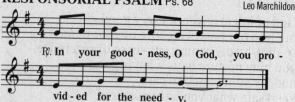

R). In your good-ness, O God, you pro-
vid-ed for the need-y.

Let the righteous be joyful;
let them exult before God;
let them be jubilant with joy.
Sing to God, sing praises to his name;
his name is the Lord,
be exultant before him.—R).

Father of orphans and protector of widows
is God in his holy habitation.
God gives the desolate a home to live in;
he leads out the prisoners to prosperity.—R).

Rain in abundance, O God,
you showered abroad;
you restored your heritage when it languished;
your flock found a dwelling in it;
in your goodness, O God,
you provided for the needy.—R). ↓

SECOND READING Heb. 12.18-19, 22-24a

**We are drawn to God who loves us and gives us faith.
We are not driven to God out of fear.**

A reading from the Letter to the Hebrews.

BROTHERS and sisters: You have not come to
something that can be touched, a blazing
fire, and darkness, and gloom, and a tempest,
and the sound of a trumpet, and a voice whose

words made the hearers beg that not another word be spoken to them.

But you have come to Mount Zion and to the city of the living God, the heavenly Jerusalem, and to innumerable Angels in festal gathering, and to the assembly of the firstborn who are enrolled in heaven, and to God the judge of all, and to the spirits of the righteous made perfect, and to Jesus, the mediator of a new covenant.—The word of the Lord. ℟. **Thanks be to God.** ↓

GOSPEL ACCLAMATION Mt. 11.29

℣. Alleluia. ℟. **Alleluia.**
℣. Take my yoke upon you, and learn from me, for I am gentle and humble in heart.
℟. **Alleluia.** ↓

GOSPEL Lk. 14.1, 7-14

Act in true humility. Do not be frustrated by trying to create an "image" for yourself.

℣. The Lord be with you. ℟. **And with your spirit.**
✝ A reading from the holy Gospel according to Luke. ℟. **Glory to you, O Lord.**

ON one occasion when Jesus was going to the house of a leader of the Pharisees to eat a meal on the Sabbath, the lawyers and Pharisees were watching him closely. When Jesus noticed how the guests chose the places of honour, he told them a parable.

"When you are invited by someone to a wedding banquet, do not sit down at the place of honour, in case someone more distinguished than you has been invited by your host; and the host who invited both of you may come and say to you, 'Give this person your place,' and then in disgrace you would start to take the lowest place.

But when you are invited, go and sit down at the lowest place, so that when your host comes, he may say to you, 'Friend, move up higher'; then you will be honoured in the presence of all who sit at the table with you. For whoever exalts himself will be humbled, and whoever humbles himself will be exalted."

Jesus said also to the Pharisee who had invited him, "When you give a luncheon or a dinner, do not invite your friends or your brothers or sisters or your relatives or rich neighbours, in case they may invite you in return, and you would be repaid. But when you give a banquet, invite the poor, the crippled, the lame, and the blind. And you will be blessed, because they cannot repay you, for you will be repaid at the resurrection of the righteous."—The Gospel of the Lord. ℟. **Praise to you, Lord Jesus Christ.**

→ No. 15, p. 18

PRAYER OVER THE OFFERINGS

May this sacred offering, O Lord,
confer on us always the blessing of salvation,
that what it celebrates in mystery
it may accomplish in power.
Through Christ our Lord.
℟. **Amen.**

→ No. 21, p. 22 (Pref. 29-36)

COMMUNION ANTIPHON Ps. 30(31).20

How great is the goodness, Lord, that you keep for those who fear you. ↓

OR Mt. 5.9-10

Blessed are the peacemakers, for they shall be called children of God. Blessed are they who are persecuted for the sake of righteousness, for theirs is the Kingdom of Heaven. ↓

PRAYER AFTER COMMUNION

Renewed by this bread from the heavenly table,
we beseech you, Lord,
that, being the food of charity,
it may confirm our hearts
and stir us to serve you in our neighbour.
Through Christ our Lord.
℟. **Amen.**

→ No. 30, p. 77

Optional Solemn Blessings, p. 97, and Prayers over the People, p. 105

"Whoever does not carry the cross and follow me cannot be my disciple."

SEPTEMBER 8

23rd SUNDAY IN ORDINARY TIME

ENTRANCE ANTIPHON Ps. 118.137, 124

You are just, O Lord, and your judgement is right; treat your servant in accord with your merciful love.

→ No. 2, p. 10

COLLECT

O God, by whom we are redeemed and receive adoption,

look graciously upon your beloved sons and daughters,

that those who believe in Christ

may receive true freedom

and an everlasting inheritance.

Through our Lord Jesus Christ, your Son,

who lives and reigns with you in the unity of the
Holy Spirit,
one God, for ever and ever. ℟. **Amen.** ↓

FIRST READING Wis. 9.13-18

**Our human knowledge (science) alone cannot reach the
heights attained by faith.**

A reading from the book of Wisdom.

FOR who can learn the counsel of God?
Or who can discern what the Lord wills?
For the reasoning of mortals is worthless,
and our designs are likely to fail;
for a perishable body weighs down the soul,
and this earthly tent burdens the thoughtful mind.

We can hardly guess at what is on earth,
and what is at hand we find with labour;
but who has traced out what is in the heavens?
Who has learned your counsel,
unless you have given wisdom
and sent your holy spirit from on high?

And thus the paths of those on earth were set
right,
and people were taught what pleases you,
and were saved by wisdom.

The word of the Lord. ℟. **Thanks be to God.** ↓

RESPONSORIAL PSALM Ps. 90

Michel Guimont

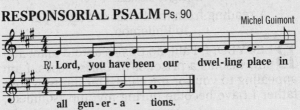

℟. Lord, you have been our   dwel-ling place in
all gen-er-a - tions.

You turn man back to dust, and say,
"Turn back, you children of Adam."
For a thousand years in your sight
are like yesterday when it is past,
or like a watch in the night.

℟. **Lord, you have been our dwelling place in all
generations.**

You sweep them away; they are like a dream,
like grass that is renewed in the morning;
in the morning it flourishes and is renewed;
in the evening it fades and withers.—℟.

So teach us to count our days
that we may gain a wise heart.
Turn, O Lord! How long?
Have compassion on your servants!—℟.

Satisfy us in the morning with your steadfast
love,
so that we may rejoice and be glad all our days.
Let the favour of the Lord our God be upon us,
and prosper for us the work of our hands.—℟. ↓

SECOND READING Philem. 9b-10, 12-17

**Paul has converted a runaway slave, and he asks the
slave's master to forgive the man.**

A reading from the Letter of Saint Paul
to Philemon.

BELOVED: I, Paul, do this as an old man, and
now also as a prisoner of Christ Jesus. I am
appealing to you for my child, Onesimus, whose
father I have become during my imprisonment.

I am sending him, that is, my own heart, back to you. I wanted to keep him with me, so that he might be of service to me in your place during my imprisonment for the Gospel; but I preferred to do nothing without your consent, in order that your good deed might be voluntary and not something forced.

Perhaps this is the reason he was separated from you for a while, so that you might have him back forever, no longer as a slave but more than a slave, a beloved brother—especially to me but how much more to you, both in the flesh and in the Lord.

So if you consider me your partner, welcome him as you would welcome me.—The word of the Lord. ℟. **Thanks be to God.** ↓

GOSPEL ACCLAMATION Ps. 119.135

℣. Alleluia. ℟. **Alleluia.**
℣. Make your face shine upon your servant,
and teach me your statutes.
℟. **Alleluia.** ↓

GOSPEL Lk. 14.25-33

We are all careful to estimate the cost of worldly ventures. We must also be willing to sacrifice whatever is necessary to preserve our faith.

℣. The Lord be with you. ℟. **And with your spirit.**
✝ A reading from the holy Gospel according to Luke. ℟. **Glory to you, O Lord.**

LARGE crowds were travelling with Jesus; and he turned and said to them, "Whoever comes to me and does not hate their father and mother, spouse and children, brothers and sisters, yes, and even their life itself, cannot be my disciple. Whoever does not carry their cross and follow me cannot be my disciple.

For which of you, intending to build a tower, does not first sit down and estimate the cost, to see whether he has enough to complete it? Otherwise, when he has laid a foundation and is not able to finish, all who see it will begin to ridicule him, saying, 'This fellow began to build and was not able to finish.'

Or what king, going out to wage war against another king, will not sit down first and consider whether he is able with ten thousand to oppose the one who comes against him with twenty thousand? If he cannot, then, while the other is still far away, he sends a delegation and asks for the terms of peace.

So therefore, whoever of you does not give up all their possessions cannot be my disciple."—The Gospel of the Lord. ℟. **Praise to you, Lord Jesus Christ.**

→ No. 15, p. 18

PRAYER OVER THE OFFERINGS

O God, who give us the gift of true prayer and of
    peace,
graciously grant that, through this offering,
we may do fitting homage to your divine majesty
and, by partaking of the sacred mystery,
we may be faithfully united in mind and heart.
Through Christ our Lord.
℟. **Amen.**

→ No. 21, p. 22 (Pref. 29-36)

COMMUNION ANTIPHON Cf. Ps. 41.2-3

Like the deer that yearns for running streams, so my soul is yearning for you, my God; my soul is thirsting for God, the living God. ↓

OR Jn. 8.12

I am the light of the world, says the Lord; whoever follows me will not walk in darkness, but will have the light of life. ↓

PRAYER AFTER COMMUNION

Grant that your faithful, O Lord,
whom you nourish and endow with life
through the food of your Word and heavenly
   Sacrament,
may so benefit from your beloved Son's great
   gifts
that we may merit an eternal share in his life.
Who lives and reigns for ever and ever.
℟. **Amen.**   → No. 30, p. 77

Optional Solemn Blessings, p. 97, and Prayers over the People, p. 105

"Rejoice with me, for I have found my sheep. . . ."

SEPTEMBER 15

24th SUNDAY IN ORDINARY TIME

ENTRANCE ANTIPHON Cf. Sir. 36.18

Give peace, O Lord, to those who wait for you, that your prophets be found true. Hear the prayers of your servant, and of your people Israel.

➔ No. 2, p. 10

COLLECT

Look upon us, O God,
Creator and ruler of all things,
and, that we may feel the working of your mercy,
grant that we may serve you with all our heart.
Through our Lord Jesus Christ, your Son,
who lives and reigns with you in the unity of the
   Holy Spirit,
one God, for ever and ever.
℟. **Amen.** ↓

FIRST READING Ex. 32.7-11, 13-14

Despite the unfaithfulness of his people, the Lord remains true to his covenant.

A reading from the book of Exodus.

THE Lord said to Moses, "Go down at once! Your people, whom you brought up out of the land of Egypt, have acted perversely; they have been quick to turn aside from the way that I commanded them; they have cast for themselves an image of a calf, and have worshipped it and sacrificed to it, and said, 'These are your gods, O Israel, who brought you up out of the land of Egypt!'"

The Lord said to Moses, "I have seen this people, how stiff-necked they are. Now let me alone, so that my wrath may burn hot against them and I may consume them; and of you I will make a great nation."

But Moses implored the Lord his God, and said, "O Lord, why does your wrath burn hot against your people, whom you brought out of the land of Egypt with great power and with a mighty hand? Remember Abraham, Isaac, and Israel, your servants, how you swore to them by your own self, saying to them, 'I will multiply your descendants like the stars of heaven, and all this land that I have promised I will give to your descendants, and they shall inherit it forever.'"

And the Lord changed his mind about the disaster that he planned to bring on his people.— The word of the Lord. ℟. **Thanks be to God.** ↓

RESPONSORIAL PSALM Ps. 51.

Leo Marchildon

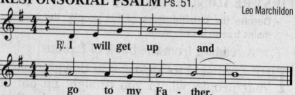

R̷. I will get up and go to my Fa - ther.

Have mercy on me, O God,
according to your steadfast love;
according to your abundant mercy
blot out my transgressions.
Wash me thoroughly from my iniquity,
and cleanse me from my sin.—R̷.

Create in me a clean heart, O God,
and put a new and right spirit within me.
Do not cast me away from your presence,
and do not take your holy spirit from me.—R̷.

O Lord, open my lips,
and my mouth will declare your praise.
The sacrifice acceptable to God
is a broken spirit;
a broken and contrite heart, O God,
you will not despise.—R̷. ↓

SECOND READING 1 Tim. 1.12-17

Christ has come to bring salvation to sinners. We have
but to turn to him and we will receive grace in overflowing measure.

A reading from the first Letter of Saint Paul
to Timothy.

BELOVED: I am grateful to Christ Jesus our
Lord, who has strengthened me, because he
judged me faithful and appointed me to his ser-

vice, even though I was formerly a blasphemer, a persecutor, and a man of violence.

But I received mercy because I had acted ignorantly in unbelief, and the grace of our Lord overflowed for me with the faith and love that are in Christ Jesus.

The saying is sure and worthy of full acceptance, that Christ Jesus came into the world to save sinners—of whom I am the foremost.

But for that very reason I received mercy, so that in me, as the foremost, Jesus Christ might display the utmost patience, making me an example to those who would come to believe in him for eternal life.

To the King of the ages, immortal, invisible, the only God, be honour and glory forever and ever. Amen.—The word of the Lord. ℟. **Thanks be to God.** ↓

GOSPEL ACCLAMATION 2 Cor. 5.19

℣. Alleluia. ℟. **Alleluia.**

℣. In Christ God was reconciling the world to himself,
and entrusting the message of reconciliation to us.

℟. **Alleluia.** ↓

GOSPEL Lk. 15.1-32 or 15.1-10

Repentance, turning away from sin, brings joy to all. Not only the one who repents, but all who love and care.

[If the "Shorter Form" is used, the indented text in brackets is omitted.]

℣. The Lord be with you. ℟. **And with your spirit.**
✠ A reading from the holy Gospel according to
Luke. ℟. **Glory to you, O Lord.**

ALL the tax collectors and sinners were coming near to listen to Jesus. And the Pharisees
and the scribes were grumbling and saying,
"This fellow welcomes sinners and eats with
them."

So he told them a parable: "Which one of you,
having a hundred sheep and losing one of them,
does not leave the ninety-nine in the wilderness
and go after the one that is lost until he finds it?
When he has found it, he lays it on his shoulders and rejoices. And when he comes home, he
calls together his friends and neighbours, saying to them, 'Rejoice with me, for I have found
my sheep that was lost.' Just so, I tell you, there
will be more joy in heaven over one sinner who
repents than over ninety-nine righteous persons
who need no repentance.

Or what woman having ten silver coins, if she
loses one of them, does not light a lamp, sweep
the house, and search carefully until she finds
it? When she has found it, she calls together her
friends and neighbours, saying, 'Rejoice with
me, for I have found the coin that I had lost.'

Just so, I tell you, there is joy in the presence of
the Angels of God over one sinner who repents."

[Then Jesus said, "There was a man who
had two sons. The younger of them said to
his father, 'Father, give me the share of the
property that will belong to me.' So the
father divided his property between them.

A few days later the younger son gathered all he had and travelled to a distant country, and there he squandered his property in dissolute living. When he had spent everything, a severe famine took place throughout that country, and he began to be in need. So he went and hired himself out to one of the citizens of that country, who sent him to his fields to feed the pigs. The young man would gladly have filled himself with the pods that the pigs were eating; and no one gave him anything.

But when he came to himself he said, 'How many of my father's hired hands have bread enough and to spare, but here I am dying of hunger! I will get up and go to my father, and I will say to him, "Father, I have sinned against heaven and before you; I am no longer worthy to be called your son; treat me like one of your hired hands."'

So he set off and went to his father. But while he was still far off, his father saw him and was filled with compassion; he ran and put his arms around him and kissed him. Then the son said to him, 'Father, I have sinned against heaven and before you; I am no longer worthy to be called your son.'

But the father said to his slaves, 'Quickly, bring out a robe—the best one—and put it on him; put a ring on his finger and sandals on his feet. And get the fatted calf and kill it, and let us eat and celebrate; for this son of mine was dead and is alive again; he was lost and is found!' And they began to celebrate.

Now his elder son was in the field; and when he came and approached the house, he heard music and dancing. He called one of the slaves and asked what was going on. The slave replied, 'Your brother has come, and your father has killed the fatted calf, because he has got him back safe and sound.' Then the elder son became angry and refused to go in. His father came out and began to plead with him. But he answered his father, 'Listen! For all these years I have been working like a slave for you, and I have never disobeyed your command; yet you have never given me even a young goat so that I might celebrate with my friends. But when this son of yours came back, who has devoured your property with prostitutes, you killed the fatted calf for him!'

Then the father said to him, 'Son, you are always with me, and all that is mine is yours. But we had to celebrate and rejoice, because this brother of yours was dead and has come to life; he was lost and has been found.'"]

The Gospel of the Lord. ℟. **Praise to you, Lord Jesus Christ.**   ➡ No. 15, p. 18

PRAYER OVER THE OFFERINGS

Look with favour on our supplications, O Lord,
and in your kindness accept these, your servants' offerings,
that what each has offered to the honour of your name

may serve the salvation of all.
Through Christ our Lord.
℟. **Amen.**   ➔ No. 21, p. 22 (Pref. 29-36)

COMMUNION ANTIPHON Cf. Ps. 35.8

**How precious is your mercy, O God! The children
of men seek shelter in the shadow of your wings.** ↓

OR See 1 Cor. 10.16

**The chalice of blessing that we bless is a commu-
nion in the Blood of Christ; and the bread that we
break is a sharing in the Body of the Lord.** ↓

PRAYER AFTER COMMUNION

May the working of this heavenly gift, O Lord, we
    pray,
take possession of our minds and bodies,
so that its effects, and not our own desires,
may always prevail in us.
Through Christ our Lord.
℟. **Amen.**   ➔ No. 30, p. 77

Optional Solemn Blessings, p. 97, and Prayers over the People, p. 105

"Give me an accounting of your management. . . ."

SEPTEMBER 22

25th SUNDAY IN ORDINARY TIME

ENTRANCE ANTIPHON

I am the salvation of the people, says the Lord.
Should they cry to me in any distress, I will hear
them, and I will be their Lord for ever.

→ No. 2, p. 10

COLLECT

O God, who founded all the commands of your
    sacred Law
upon love of you and of our neighbour,
grant that, by keeping your precepts,
we may merit to attain eternal life.
Through our Lord Jesus Christ, your Son,
who lives and reigns with you in the unity of the
    Holy Spirit,
one God, for ever and ever. ℟. **Amen.** ↓

FIRST READING Amos 8.4-7

The Lord will punish those who cheat and oppress the poor.
There is no place for the gouger, the con artist, the greedy.

A reading from the book of the Prophet Amos.

HEAR this, you that trample on the needy,
and bring to ruin the poor of the land,
saying, "When will the new moon be over so
that we may sell grain;
and the Sabbath, so that we may offer wheat for
sale?
We will measure out less and charge more,
and tamper with the scales,
buying the poor for silver
and the needy for a pair of sandals,
and selling the sweepings of the wheat."

The Lord has sworn by the pride of Jacob:
"Surely I will never forget any of their deeds."

The word of the Lord. ℟. **Thanks be to God.** ↓

RESPONSORIAL PSALM Ps. 113

Leo Marchildon

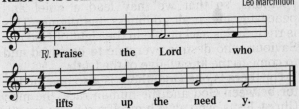

℟. **Praise   the   Lord   who   lifts   up   the   need - y.**

Or: ℟. **Alleluia!**

Praise, O servants of the Lord;
praise the name of the Lord.
Blessed be the name of the Lord
from this time on and forevermore.—℟.

The Lord is high above all nations,
and his glory above the heavens.
Who is like the Lord our God, who is seated on
  high,
who looks far down on the heavens and the earth?
℞. **Praise the Lord who lifts up the needy.**

The Lord raises the poor from the dust,
and lifts the needy from the ash heap,
to make them sit with princes,
with the princes of his people.—℞. ↓

SECOND READING 1 Tim. 2.1-7

We should pray with a pure heart and blameless hands.
Our prayers of the faithful in this Mass continue our
prayer for all.

A reading from the first Letter of Saint Paul
to Timothy.

BELOVED: I urge that supplications, prayers,
intercessions, and thanksgivings be made
for everyone, for kings and all who are in high
positions, so that we may lead a quiet and
peaceable life in all godliness and dignity. This
is right and is acceptable in the sight of God our
Saviour, who desires everyone to be saved and
to come to the knowledge of the truth.

For there is one God; there is also one mediator between God and the human race, the man
Christ Jesus, who gave himself a ransom for all;
this was attested at the right time.

For this I was appointed a herald and an
apostle, a teacher of the Gentiles in faith and
truth. I am telling the truth, I am not lying.—The
word of the Lord. ℞. **Thanks be to God.** ↓

GOSPEL ACCLAMATION 2 Cor. 8.9

℣. Alleluia. ℟. **Alleluia.**

℣. Though Jesus Christ was rich, yet he became poor,

so that by his poverty you might become rich.

℟. **Alleluia.** ↓

GOSPEL Lk. 16.1-13 or 16.10-13

If we are shrewd in an evil way, we may be admired by other evil people for our cleverness. But we cannot win in the long run. We cannot divide ourselves between God and worldly gain.

[If the "Shorter Form" is used, the indented text in brackets is omitted.]

℣. The Lord be with you. ℟. **And with your spirit.**

✛ A reading from the holy Gospel according to Luke. ℟. **Glory to you, O Lord.**

JESUS said to the disciples,

["There was a rich man who had a manager, and charges were brought to him that the manager was squandering his property.

So the rich man summoned him and said to him, 'What is this that I hear about you? Give me an accounting of your management, because you cannot be my manager any longer.'

Then the manager said to himself, 'What will I do, now that my master is taking the position away from me? I am not strong enough to dig, and I am ashamed to beg. I have decided what to do so that, when I am dismissed as manager, people may welcome me into their homes.'

So, summoning his master's debtors one by one, he asked the first, 'How much do you owe my master?' He answered, 'A hundred jugs of olive oil.' He said to him, 'Take your bill, sit down quickly, and make it fifty.' Then he asked another, 'And how much do you owe?' He replied, 'A hundred containers of wheat.' He said to him, 'Take your bill and make it eighty.'

And his master commended the dishonest manager because he had acted shrewdly; for the children of this age are more shrewd in dealing with their own generation than are the children of light.

And I tell you, make friends for yourselves by means of dishonest wealth so that when it is gone, they may welcome you into the eternal homes.]

Whoever is faithful in a very little is faithful also in much; and whoever is dishonest in a very little is dishonest also in much. If then you have not been faithful with the dishonest wealth, who will entrust to you the true riches? And if you have not been faithful with what belongs to another, who will give you what is your own?

No slave can serve two masters; for a slave will either hate the one and love the other, or be devoted to the one and despise the other. You cannot serve God and wealth."—The Gospel of the Lord. ℟. **Praise to you, Lord Jesus Christ.**

→ No. 15, p. 18

PRAYER OVER THE OFFERINGS

Receive with favour, O Lord, we pray,
the offerings of your people,

that what they profess with devotion and faith
may be theirs through these heavenly mysteries.
Through Christ our Lord.
℟. **Amen.**   → No. 21, p. 22 (Pref. 29-36)

COMMUNION ANTIPHON Ps. 118.4-5

**You have laid down your precepts to be carefully
kept; may my ways be firm in keeping your
statutes.** ↓

OR Jn. 10.14

**I am the Good Shepherd, says the Lord; I know
my sheep, and mine know me.** ↓

PRAYER AFTER COMMUNION

Graciously raise up, O Lord,
those you renew with this Sacrament,
that we may come to possess your redemption
both in mystery and in the manner of our life.
Through Christ our Lord.
℟. **Amen.**   → No. 30, p. 77

Optional Solemn Blessings, p. 97, and Prayers over the People, p. 105

"He . . . saw Abraham far away with Lazarus by his side."

SEPTEMBER 29

26th SUNDAY IN ORDINARY TIME

ENTRANCE ANTIPHON Dan. 3.31, 29, 30, 43, 42

All that you have done to us, O Lord, you have done with true judgement, for we have sinned against you and not obeyed your commandments. But give glory to your name and deal with us according to the bounty of your mercy.

➜ No. 2, p. 10

COLLECT

O God, who manifest your almighty power
above all by pardoning and showing mercy,
bestow, we pray, your grace abundantly upon us
and make those hastening to attain your promises
heirs to the treasures of heaven.
Through our Lord Jesus Christ, your Son,

who lives and reigns with you in the unity of the
   Holy Spirit,
one God, for ever and ever. ℟. **Amen.** ↓

FIRST READING Amos 6.1a, 4-7

**The prophet Amos castigates those who sit in the lap of
luxury and pay no attention to the needs of others.**

A reading from the book of the Prophet Amos.

THUS says the Lord, the God of hosts:
   "Alas for those who are at ease in Zion,
and for those who feel secure on Mount Samaria!

Alas for those who lie on beds of ivory,
and lounge on their couches,
and eat lambs from the flock,
and calves from the stall;
who sing idle songs to the sound of the harp,
and like David improvise on instruments of music;
who drink wine from bowls,
and anoint themselves with the finest oils,
but are not grieved over the ruin of Joseph!

Therefore they shall now be the first to go into
   exile,
and the revelry of those who lie in ease shall pass
   away."

The word of the Lord. ℟. **Thanks be to God.** ↓

RESPONSORIAL PSALM Ps. 146   Geoffrey Angeles

℟. Praise the Lord, O my soul, O my soul!

Or: ℟. **Alleluia!**

It is the Lord who keeps faith forever,
who executes justice for the oppressed;
who gives food to the hungry.
The Lord sets the prisoners free.
℟. **Praise the Lord, O my soul!**

The Lord opens the eyes of the blind
and lifts up those who are bowed down;
the Lord loves the righteous
and watches over the strangers.—℟.

The Lord upholds the orphan and the widow,
but the way of the wicked he brings to ruin.
The Lord will reign forever,
your God, O Zion, for all generations.—℟. ↓

SECOND READING 1 Tim. 6.11-16

In faith is salvation. Be positive and steadfast; hold firm,
for the Lord Jesus will come again.

A reading from the first Letter of Saint Paul
to Timothy.

AS for you, man of God; pursue righteousness, godliness, faith, love, endurance, gentleness. Fight the good fight of the faith; take
hold of the eternal life, to which you were called
and for which you made the good confession in
the presence of many witnesses.

In the presence of God, who gives life to all
things, and of Christ Jesus, who in his testimony
before Pontius Pilate made the good confession,
I charge you to keep the commandment without
spot or blame until the manifestation of our
Lord Jesus Christ, which he will bring about at

the right time. He is the blessed and only Sovereign, the King of kings and Lord of lords.

It is he alone who has immortality and dwells in unapproachable light, whom no human being has ever seen or can see; to him be honour and eternal dominion. Amen.—The word of the Lord.
℟. **Thanks be to God.** ↓

GOSPEL ACCLAMATION 2 Cor. 8.9

℣. Alleluia. ℟. **Alleluia.**
℣. Though Jesus Christ was rich, yet he became poor,
so that by his poverty you might become rich.
℟. **Alleluia.** ↓

GOSPEL Lk. 16.19-31

Even the richest person cannot buy salvation. This comes from being faithful to the Word of God.

℣. The Lord be with you. ℟. **And with your spirit.**
✠ A reading from the holy Gospel according to Luke. ℟. **Glory to you, O Lord.**

JESUS told this parable to those among the Pharisees who loved money: "There was a rich man who was dressed in purple and fine linen and who feasted sumptuously every day. And at his gate lay a poor man named Lazarus, covered with sores, who longed to satisfy his hunger with what fell from the rich man's table; even the dogs would come and lick his sores.

The poor man died and was carried away by the Angels to be with Abraham. The rich man also died and was buried. In Hades, where he was being tormented, he looked up and saw

Abraham far away with Lazarus by his side. He called out, 'Father Abraham, have mercy on me, and send Lazarus to dip the tip of his finger in water and cool my tongue; for I am in agony in these flames.'

But Abraham said, 'Child, remember that during your lifetime you received your good things, and Lazarus in like manner evil things; but now he is comforted here, and you are in agony. Besides all this, between you and us a great chasm has been fixed, so that those who might want to pass from here to you cannot do so, and no one can cross from there to us.'

The man who had been rich said, 'Then, father, I beg you to send Lazarus to my father's house— for I have five brothers—that he may warn them, so that they will not also come into this place of torment.'

Abraham replied, 'They have Moses and the Prophets; they should listen to them.' He said, 'No, father Abraham; but if someone goes to them from the dead, they will repent.' Abraham said to him, 'If they do not listen to Moses and the Prophets, neither will they be convinced even if someone rises from the dead.'"—The Gospel of the Lord. ℟. **Praise to you, Lord Jesus Christ.**

→ No. 15, p. 18

PRAYER OVER THE OFFERINGS

Grant us, O merciful God,
that this our offering may find acceptance with
    you
and that through it the wellspring of all blessing

may be laid open before us.
Through Christ our Lord.
℟. **Amen.**   ➔ No. 21, p. 22 (Pref. 29-36)

COMMUNION ANTIPHON Cf. Ps. 118.49-50

Remember your word to your servant, O Lord, by which you have given me hope. This is my comfort when I am brought low. ↓

OR 1 Jn. 3.16

By this we came to know the love of God: that Christ laid down his life for us; so we ought to lay down our lives for one another. ↓

PRAYER AFTER COMMUNION

May this heavenly mystery, O Lord,
restore us in mind and body,
that we may be co-heirs in glory with Christ,
to whose suffering we are united
whenever we proclaim his Death.
Who lives and reigns for ever and ever.
℟. **Amen.**   ➔ No. 30, p. 77

Optional Solemn Blessings, p. 97, and Prayers over the People, p. 105

"If you had faith the size of a mustard seed, you could
say to this mulberry tree, 'Be uprooted. . . .'"

OCTOBER 6

27th SUNDAY IN ORDINARY TIME

ENTRANCE ANTIPHON Cf. Est. 4.17

**Within your will, O Lord, all things are estab-
lished, and there is none that can resist your will.
For you have made all things, the heaven and the
earth, and all that is held within the circle of
heaven; you are the Lord of all.**   → No. 2, p. 10

COLLECT

Almighty ever-living God,
who in the abundance of your kindness
surpass the merits and the desires of those who
    entreat you,
pour out your mercy upon us
to pardon what conscience dreads
and to give what prayer does not dare to ask.
Through our Lord Jesus Christ, your Son,
who lives and reigns with you in the unity of the
    Holy Spirit,
one God, for ever and ever. ℟. **Amen.** ↓

FIRST READING Hab. 1.2-3; 2.2-4

> We might become discouraged. But let us take heart; in God's own time the Lord will save us.

A reading from the book of the Prophet Habakkuk.

"O LORD, how long shall I cry for help,
and you will not listen?
Or cry to you 'Violence!'
and you will not save?
Why do you make me see wrongdoing
and look at trouble?
Destruction and violence are before me;
strife and contention arise."

Then the Lord answered me and said:
"Write the vision;
make it plain on tablets,
so that a runner may read it.
For there is still a vision for the appointed time;
it speaks of the end, and does not lie.
If it seems to tarry, wait for it;
it will surely come, it will not delay.
Look at the proud person!
Their spirit is not right in them,
but the righteous person lives by their faith."

The word of the Lord. ℟. **Thanks be to God.** ↓

RESPONSORIAL PSALM Ps. 95

Leo Marchildon

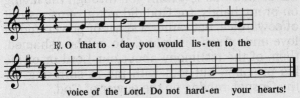

℟. O that to - day you would lis-ten to the voice of the Lord. Do not hard-en your hearts!

O come, let us sing to the Lord;
let us make a joyful noise to the rock of our sal-
     vation!
Let us come into his presence with thanksgiving;
let us make a joyful noise to him with songs of
     praise!

℟. **O that today you would listen to the voice of
the Lord. Do not harden your hearts!**

O come, let us worship and bow down,
let us kneel before the Lord, our Maker!
For he is our God, and we are the people of his
     pasture,
and the sheep of his hand.—℟.

O that today you would listen to his voice!
Do not harden your hearts, as at Meribah,
as on the day at Massah in the wilderness,
when your ancestors tested me,
and put me to the proof,
though they had seen my work.—℟. ↓

SECOND READING 2 Tim. 1.6-8, 13-14

Be firm in faith despite all adversity. The Holy Spirit, the
spirit of strength, dwells in us.

A reading from the second Letter of Saint Paul
to Timothy.

BELOVED: I remind you to rekindle the gift
of God that is within you through the laying
on of my hands; for God did not give us a spirit
of cowardice, but rather a spirit of power and of
love and of self-discipline. Do not be ashamed,
then, of the testimony about our Lord or of me
his prisoner, but join with me in suffering for
the Gospel, relying on the power of God.

Hold to the standard of sound teaching that you have heard from me, in the faith and love that are in Christ Jesus. Guard the good treasure entrusted to you, with the help of the Holy Spirit living in us.—The word of the Lord. ℟. **Thanks be to God.** ↓

GOSPEL ACCLAMATION 1 Pet. 1.25

℣. Alleluia. ℟. **Alleluia.**
℣. The word of the Lord endures for ever;
that word is the good news announced to you.
℟. **Alleluia.** ↓

GOSPEL Lk. 17.5-10

Our faith is to be lived. We cannot be satisfied with merely doing no more than our duty. We must strive to excel.

℣. The Lord be with you. ℟. **And with your spirit.**
✠ A reading from the holy Gospel according to Luke. ℟. **Glory to you, O Lord.**

THE Apostles said to the Lord, "Increase our faith!" The Lord replied, "If you had faith the size of a mustard seed, you could say to this mulberry tree, 'Be uprooted and planted in the sea,' and it would obey you.

Who among you would say to your slave who has just come in from ploughing or tending sheep in the field, 'Come here at once and take your place at the table'? Would you not rather say to him, 'Prepare supper for me, put on your apron and serve me while I eat and drink; later you may eat and drink'? Do you thank the slave for doing what was commanded? So you also, when you have done all that you were ordered to do, say, 'We

are worthless slaves; we have done only what we ought to have done!'"—The Gospel of the Lord.
℟. **Praise to you, Lord Jesus Christ.** → No. 15, p. 18

PRAYER OVER THE OFFERINGS

Accept, O Lord, we pray,
the sacrifices instituted by your commands
and, through the sacred mysteries,
which we celebrate with dutiful service,
graciously complete the sanctifying work
by which you are pleased to redeem us.
Through Christ our Lord.
℟. **Amen.**   → No. 21, p. 22 (Pref. 29-36)

COMMUNION ANTIPHON Lam. 3.25

The Lord is good to those who hope in him, to the soul that seeks him. ↓

OR Cf. 1 Cor. 10.17

Though many, we are one bread, one body, for we all partake of the one Bread and one Chalice. ↓

PRAYER AFTER COMMUNION

Grant us, almighty God,
that we may be refreshed and nourished
by the Sacrament which we have received,
so as to be transformed into what we consume.
Through Christ our Lord.
℟. **Amen.**   → No. 30, p. 77

Optional Solemn Blessings, p. 97, and Prayers over the People, p. 105

"Get up . . . ; your faith has made you well."

OCTOBER 13

28th SUNDAY IN ORDINARY TIME

ENTRANCE ANTIPHON Ps. 129.3-4

If you, O Lord, should mark iniquities, Lord, who could stand? But with you is found forgiveness, O God of Israel. → No. 2, p. 10

COLLECT

May your grace, O Lord, we pray,
at all times go before us and follow after
and make us always determined
to carry out good works.
Through our Lord Jesus Christ, your Son,
who lives and reigns with you in the unity of the
   Holy Spirit,
one God, for ever and ever.
℟. **Amen.** ↓

FIRST READING 2 Kgs. 5.14-17

The healing power of God comes to a man who does not belong to the chosen people, and he proclaims his faith in the Lord.

A reading from the second book of Kings.

NAAMAN the Syrian went down and immersed himself seven times in the Jordan, according to the word of the man of God; his flesh was restored like the flesh of a young boy, and he was clean.

Then he returned to the man of God, he and all his company; Naaman came and stood before Elisha and said, "Now I know that there is no God in all the earth except in Israel; please accept a present from your servant."

But Elisha said, "As the Lord lives, whom I serve, I will accept nothing!" Naaman urged Elisha to accept, but he refused.

Then Naaman said, "If not, please let two mule-loads of earth be given to your servant; for your servant will no longer offer burnt offering or sacrifice to any god except the Lord."—The word of the Lord. ℟. **Thanks be to God.** ↓

RESPONSORIAL PSALM Ps. 98

Frank Lynch

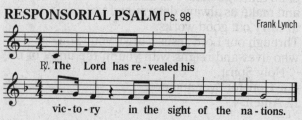

℟. The Lord has re‑vealed his vic‑to‑ry in the sight of the na‑tions.

O sing to the Lord a new song,
for he has done marvellous things.

His right hand and his holy arm
have brought him victory.—R̶⃨.

The Lord has made known his victory;
he has revealed his vindication in the sight of
   the nations.
He has remembered his steadfast love
and faithfulness to the house of Israel.—R̶⃨.

All the ends of the earth have seen
the victory of our God.
Make a joyful noise to the Lord, all the earth;
break forth into joyous song and sing praises.
   —R̶⃨. ↓

SECOND READING 2 Tim. 2.8-13

**In Christ we have died. Through Christ we are to rise, and
with him we shall reign.**

A reading from the second Letter of Saint Paul
to Timothy.

BELOVED: Remember Jesus Christ, raised
   from the dead, a descendant of David—that
is my Gospel, for which I suffer hardship, even
to the point of being chained like a criminal. But
the word of God is not chained.

   Therefore I endure everything for the sake of
the elect, so that they may also obtain the salvation that is in Christ Jesus, with eternal glory.

   The saying is sure:
If we have died with him,
we will also live with him;
   if we endure,
   we will also reign with him;
   if we deny him,

he will also deny us;
if we are faithless,
he remains faithful—
for he cannot deny himself.

The word of the Lord. ℟. **Thanks be to God.** ↓

GOSPEL ACCLAMATION 1 Thess. 5.18

℣. Alleluia. ℟. **Alleluia.**
℣. Give thanks in all circumstances;
for this is the will of God in Christ Jesus for you.
℟. **Alleluia.** ↓

GOSPEL Lk. 17.11-19

> The healing power of God comes through Christ, even to a man who does not belong to the chosen people. This man's faith prompts his thankfulness.

℣. The Lord be with you. ℟. **And with your spirit.**
✤ A reading from the holy Gospel according to Luke. ℟. **Glory to you, O Lord.**

ON the way to Jerusalem Jesus was going through the region between Samaria and Galilee.

As he entered a village, ten lepers approached him. Keeping their distance, they called out, saying, "Jesus, Master, have mercy on us!"

When Jesus saw them, he said to them, "Go and show yourselves to the priests." And as they went, they were made clean. Then one of them, when he saw that he was healed, turned back, praising God with a loud voice. He prostrated himself at Jesus' feet and thanked him. And he was a Samaritan.

Then Jesus asked, "Were not ten made clean? But the other nine, where are they? Was none of them found to return and give praise to God except this foreigner?"

Then Jesus said to the Samaritan, "Get up and go on your way; your faith has made you well."—The Gospel of the Lord. ℟. **Praise to you, Lord Jesus Christ.**   ➜ No. 15, p. 18

PRAYER OVER THE OFFERINGS

Accept, O Lord, the prayers of your faithful
with the sacrificial offerings,
that, through these acts of devotedness,
we may pass over to the glory of heaven.
Through Christ our Lord.
℟. **Amen.**   ➜ No. 21, p. 22 (Pref. 29-36)

COMMUNION ANTIPHON Cf. Ps. 33.11

The rich suffer want and go hungry, but those who seek the Lord lack no blessing. ↓

OR 1 Jn. 3.2

When the Lord appears, we shall be like him, for we shall see him as he is. ↓

PRAYER AFTER COMMUNION

We entreat your majesty most humbly, O Lord,
that, as you feed us with the nourishment
which comes from the most holy Body and Blood
   of your Son,
so you may make us sharers of his divine nature.
Who lives and reigns for ever and ever.
℟. **Amen.**   ➜ No. 30, p. 77

Optional Solemn Blessings, p. 97, and Prayers over the People, p. 105

"Will not God grant justice to his chosen ones
who cry to him day and night?"

OCTOBER 20

29th SUNDAY IN ORDINARY TIME

ENTRANCE ANTIPHON Cf. Ps. 16.6, 8

To you I call; for you will surely heed me, O God;
turn your ear to me; hear my words. Guard me as
the apple of your eye; in the shadow of your
wings protect me. → No. 2, p. 10

COLLECT

Almighty ever-living God,
grant that we may always conform our will to
    yours
and serve your majesty in sincerity of heart.
Through our Lord Jesus Christ, your Son,
who lives and reigns with you in the unity of the
    Holy Spirit,
one God, for ever and ever. ℟. **Amen.** ↓

FIRST READING Ex. 17.8-13

Moses prays without ceasing, not losing heart despite physical fatigue.

A reading from the book of Exodus.

AMALEK came and fought with Israel at Rephidim. Moses said to Joshua, "Choose some men for us and go out, fight with Amalek. Tomorrow I will stand on the top of the hill with the staff of God in my hand."

So Joshua did as Moses told him, and fought with Amalek, while Moses, Aaron, and Hur went up to the top of the hill.

Whenever Moses held up his hands, Israel prevailed; and whenever he lowered his hands, Amalek prevailed. But Moses' hands grew weary; so they took a stone and put it under him, and he sat on it. Aaron and Hur held up his hands, one on one side, and the other on the other side; so his hands were steady until the sun set.

And Joshua defeated Amalek and his people with the sword.—The word of the Lord. ℟. **Thanks be to God.** ↓

RESPONSORIAL PSALM Ps. 121

Leo Marchildon

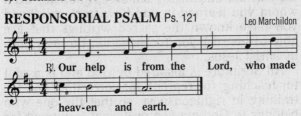

℟. Our help is from the Lord, who made heav-en and earth.

I lift up my eyes to the hills—
from where will my help come?
My help comes from the Lord,
who made heaven and earth.—℟.

The Lord will not let your foot be moved;
he who keeps you will not slumber.
He who keeps Israel
will neither slumber nor sleep.

℟. **Our help is from the Lord, who made heaven
and earth.**

The Lord is your keeper;
the Lord is your shade at your right hand.
The sun shall not strike you by day,
nor the moon by night.—℟.

The Lord will keep you from all evil;
he will keep your life.
The Lord will keep your going out and your
   coming in
from this time on and forevermore.—℟. ↓

SECOND READING 2 Tim. 3.14—4.2

**The Bible is the source of teaching, the safe guide for the
people of God in every good work.**

A reading from the second Letter of Saint Paul
to Timothy.

BELOVED: Continue in what you have
learned and firmly believed, knowing from
whom you learned it, and how from childhood
you have known the sacred writings that are
able to instruct you for salvation through faith
in Christ Jesus.

   All Scripture is inspired by God and is useful
for teaching, for reproof, for correction, and for
training in righteousness, so that the one who
belongs to God may be proficient, equipped for
every good work.

   In the presence of God and of Christ Jesus,
who is to judge the living and the dead, and in

view of his appearing and his kingdom, I solemnly urge you: proclaim the message; be persistent whether the time is favourable or unfavourable; convince, rebuke, and encourage, with the utmost patience in teaching.—The word of the Lord. ℞. **Thanks be to God.** ↓

GOSPEL ACCLAMATION Heb. 4.12

℣. Alleluia. ℞. **Alleluia.**
℣. The word of God is living and active;
it judges the thoughts and intentions of the heart.
℞. **Alleluia.** ↓

GOSPEL Lk. 18.1-8

Jesus urges us to pray without ceasing and to have faith in the goodness of God.

℣. The Lord be with you. ℞. **And with your spirit.**
✛ A reading from the holy Gospel according to Luke. ℞. **Glory to you, O Lord.**

JESUS told the disciples a parable about their need to pray always and not to lose heart.

He said, "In a certain city there was a judge who neither feared God nor had respect for any human being. In that city there was a widow who kept coming to him and saying, 'Grant me justice against my opponent.'

For a while the judge refused; but later he said to himself, 'Though I have no fear of God and no respect for any human being, yet because this widow keeps bothering me, I will grant her justice, so that she may not wear me out by continually coming."

And the Lord said, "Listen to what the unjust judge says. Will not God grant justice to his chosen ones who cry to him day and night? Will he delay long in helping them? I tell you, God will quickly grant justice to them. And yet, when the Son of Man comes, will he find faith on earth?"—The Gospel of the Lord. ℟. **Praise to you, Lord Jesus Christ.**   ➔ No. 15, p. 18

PRAYER OVER THE OFFERINGS

Grant us, Lord, we pray,
a sincere respect for your gifts,
that, through the purifying action of your grace,
we may be cleansed by the very mysteries we
    serve.
Through Christ our Lord.
℟. **Amen.**   ➔ No. 21, p. 22 (Pref. 29-36)

COMMUNION ANTIPHON Cf. Ps. 32.18-19

Behold, the eyes of the Lord are on those who fear him, who hope in his merciful love, to rescue their souls from death, to keep them alive in famine. ↓

OR Mk. 10.45

The Son of Man has come to give his life as a ransom for many. ↓

PRAYER AFTER COMMUNION

Grant, O Lord, we pray,
that, benefiting from participation in heavenly
    things,

we may be helped by what you give in this present
  age
and prepared for the gifts that are eternal.
Through Christ our Lord.
℟. **Amen.**   ➜ No. 30, p. 77

Optional Solemn Blessings, p. 97, and Prayers over the People, p. 105

"God, I thank you that I am not like other people."

OCTOBER 27

30th SUNDAY IN ORDINARY TIME

ENTRANCE ANTIPHON Cf. Ps. 104.3-4

**Let the hearts that seek the Lord rejoice; turn to
the Lord and his strength; constantly seek his
face.**   ➜ No. 2, p. 10

COLLECT

Almighty ever-living God,
increase our faith, hope and charity,
and make us love what you command,
so that we may merit what you promise.

Through our Lord Jesus Christ, your Son,
who lives and reigns with you in the unity of the
   Holy Spirit,
one God, for ever and ever. ℟. **Amen.** ↓

FIRST READING Sir. 35.15-17, 20-22

No one is unimportant in the sight of God. If we serve willingly, God will receive our prayers.

   A reading from the book of Sirach.

THE Lord is the judge,
   and with him there is no partiality.
He will not show partiality to the poor
but he will listen to the prayer of one who is
   wronged.
The Lord will not ignore the supplication of the
   orphan,
or the widow when she pours out her complaint.

The person whose service is pleasing to the
   Lord will be accepted,
and their prayer will reach to the clouds.

The prayer of the humble pierces the clouds,
and it will not rest until it reaches its goal;
it will not desist until the Most High responds
and does justice for the righteous,
and executes judgment.
Indeed, the Lord will not delay.

The word of the Lord. ℟. **Thanks be to God.** ↓

RESPONSORIAL PSALM Ps. 34

Leo Marchildon

℟. The   poor   one   called   and   the

Lord   heard.

I will bless the Lord at all times;
his praise shall continually be in my mouth.
My soul makes its boast in the Lord;
let the humble hear and be glad.—R̹.

The face of the Lord is against evildoers,
to cut off the remembrance of them from the
    earth.
When the righteous cry for help, the Lord hears,
and rescues them from all their troubles.—R̹.

The Lord is near to the brokenhearted,
and saves the crushed in spirit.
The Lord redeems the life of his servants;
none of those who take refuge in him will be
    condemned.—R̹. ↓

SECOND READING 2 Tim. 4.6-8, 16-18

**Paul sees time running out and his life drawing to a
close. He is comforted by faith in God's just judgment.**

A reading from the second Letter of Saint Paul
to Timothy.

BELOVED: I am already being poured out as
a libation, and the time of my departure has
come. I have fought the good fight, I have finished the race, I have kept the faith.

From now on there is reserved for me the
crown of righteousness, which the Lord, the
righteous judge, will give me on that day, and

not only to me but also to all who have longed for his appearing.

At my first defence no one came to my support, but all deserted me. May it not be counted against them!

But the Lord stood by me and gave me strength, so that through me the message might be fully proclaimed and all the Gentiles might hear it. So I was rescued from the lion's mouth.

The Lord will rescue me from every evil attack and save me for his heavenly kingdom. To him be the glory forever and ever. Amen.—The word of the Lord. ℟. **Thanks be to God.** ↓

GOSPEL ACCLAMATION 2 Cor. 5.19

℣. Alleluia. ℟. **Alleluia.**

℣. In Christ God was reconciling the world to himself,

and entrusting the message of reconciliation to us. ℟. **Alleluia.** ↓

GOSPEL Lk. 18.9-14

Pride brings no true reward but only projects an "image." In humility true values are seen.

℣. The Lord be with you. ℟. **And with your spirit.**
✤ A reading from the holy Gospel according to Luke. ℟. **Glory to you, O Lord.**

JESUS told this parable to some who trusted in themselves that they were righteous, and regarded others with contempt:

"Two men went up to the temple to pray, one a Pharisee and the other a tax collector. The

Pharisee, standing by himself, was praying thus, 'God, I thank you that I am not like other people: thieves, rogues, adulterers, or even like this tax collector. I fast twice a week; I give a tenth of all my income.'

But the tax collector, standing far off, would not even look up to heaven, but was beating his breast and saying, 'God, be merciful to me, a sinner!'

I tell you, this man went down to his home justified rather than the other; for whoever exalts himself will be humbled, but whoever humbles himself will be exalted."—The Gospel of the Lord. ℟. **Praise to you, Lord Jesus Christ.** → No. 15, p. 18

PRAYER OVER THE OFFERINGS

Look, we pray, O Lord,
on the offerings we make to your majesty,
that whatever is done by us in your service
may be directed above all to your glory.
Through Christ our Lord.
℟. **Amen.**   → No. 21, p. 22 (Pref. 29-36)

COMMUNION ANTIPHON Cf. Ps. 19.6

We will ring out our joy at your saving help and exult in the name of our God. ↓

OR Eph. 5.2

Christ loved us and gave himself up for us, as a fragrant offering to God. ↓

PRAYER AFTER COMMUNION

May your Sacraments, O Lord, we pray,
perfect in us what lies within them,

that what we now celebrate in signs
we may one day possess in truth.
Through Christ our Lord.
℟. **Amen.**

➜ No. 30, p. 77

Optional Solemn Blessings, p. 97, and Prayers over the People, p. 105

Zacchaeus "climbed a sycamore tree to see Jesus. . . ."

NOVEMBER 3

31st SUNDAY IN ORDINARY TIME

ENTRANCE ANTIPHON Cf. Ps. 37.22-23

**Forsake me not, O Lord, my God; be not far from
me! Make haste and come to my help, O Lord,
my strong salvation!**

➜ No. 2, p. 10

COLLECT

Almighty and merciful God,
by whose gift your faithful offer you
right and praiseworthy service,
grant, we pray,

that we may hasten without stumbling
to receive the things you have promised.
Through our Lord Jesus Christ, your Son,
who lives and reigns with you in the unity of the
    Holy Spirit,
one God, for ever and ever. ℟. **Amen.** ↓

FIRST READING Wis. 11.22—12.2

**The Lord is the greatest. Everything else is insignificant;
everything else depends on him.**

A reading from the book of Wisdom.

THE whole world before you, O Lord,
    is like a speck that tips the scales,
and like a drop of morning dew that falls on the
    ground.
But you are merciful to all,
for you can do all things,
and you overlook people's sins,
so that they may repent.

Lord, you love all things that exist,
and detest none of the things that you have
    made,
for you would not have made anything if you
    had hated it.
How would anything have endured
if you had not willed it?
Or how would anything not called forth by you
have been preserved?
You spare all things, for they are yours, O Lord,
you who love the living.

For your immortal spirit is in all things.
Therefore you correct little by little those who
    trespass,

and you remind and warn them of the things
  through which they sin,
so that they may be freed from wickedness
and put their trust in you, O Lord.

The word of the Lord. ℞. **Thanks be to God.** ↓

RESPONSORIAL PSALM Ps. 145

Leo Marchildon

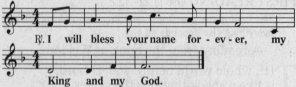

℞. I will bless your name for - ev - er, my King and my God.

I will extol you, my God and King,
and bless your name forever and ever.
Every day I will bless you,
and praise your name forever and ever.—℞.

The Lord is gracious and merciful,
slow to anger and abounding in steadfast love.
The Lord is good to all,
and his compassion is over all that he has made.—℞.

All your works shall give thanks to you, O Lord,
and all your faithful shall bless you.
They shall speak of the glory of your kingdom,
and tell of your power.—℞.

The Lord is faithful in all his words,
and gracious in all his deeds.
The Lord upholds all who are falling,
and raises up all who are bowed down.—℞. ↓

SECOND READING 2 Thess. 1.11—2.2

**The Lord will come again. Do not be misled by false pre-
dictions; rather strive to be worthy of his call.**

A reading from the second Letter of Saint Paul to the Thessalonians.

BROTHERS and sisters: We always pray for you, asking that our God will make you worthy of his call and will fulfill by his power every good resolve and work of faith, so that the name of our Lord Jesus may be glorified in you, and you in him, according to the grace of our God and the Lord Jesus Christ.

As to the coming of our Lord Jesus Christ and our being gathered together to him, we beg you, brothers and sisters, not to be quickly shaken in mind or alarmed, either by spirit or by word or by letter, as though from us, to the effect that the day of the Lord is already here.—The word of the Lord. ℟. **Thanks be to God.** ↓

GOSPEL ACCLAMATION Jn. 3.16

℣. Alleluia. ℟. **Alleluia.**

℣. God so loved the world that he gave his only-begotten Son,

that everyone who believes in him may have eternal life.

℟. **Alleluia.** ↓

GOSPEL Lk. 19.1-10

No one is so evil, so bad, that he or she cannot be saved. God's love will bring his forgiveness and reunite all who repent.

℣. The Lord be with you. ℟. **And with your spirit.**

✝ A reading from the holy Gospel according to Luke. ℟. **Glory to you, O Lord.**

JESUS entered Jericho and was passing through it. A man was there named Zacchaeus; he was a chief tax collector and was rich. He was trying to see who Jesus was, but on account of the crowd he could not, because he was short in stature.

So he ran ahead and climbed a sycamore tree to see Jesus, because he was going to pass that way. When Jesus came to the place, he looked up and said to him, "Zacchaeus, hurry and come down; for I must stay at your house today."

So Zacchaeus hurried down and was happy to welcome Jesus. All who saw it began to grumble and said, "He has gone to be the guest of one who is a sinner."

Zacchaeus stood there and said to the Lord, "Look, half of my possessions, Lord, I will give to the poor; and if I have defrauded anyone of anything, I will pay back four times as much."

Then Jesus said of him, "Today salvation has come to this house, because Zacchaeus too is a son of Abraham. For the Son of Man came to seek out and to save the lost."—The Gospel of the Lord. ℟. **Praise to you, Lord Jesus Christ.**

→ No. 15, p. 18

PRAYER OVER THE OFFERINGS

May these sacrificial offerings, O Lord,
become for you a pure oblation,
and for us a holy outpouring of your mercy.
Through Christ our Lord.
℟. **Amen.**

→ No. 21, p. 22 (Pref. 29-36)

COMMUNION ANTIPHON Cf. Ps. 15.11

You will show me the path of life, the fullness of joy in your presence, O Lord. ↓

OR Jn. 6.58

Just as the living Father sent me and I have life because of the Father, so whoever feeds on me shall have life because of me, says the Lord. ↓

PRAYER AFTER COMMUNION

May the working of your power, O Lord,
increase in us, we pray,
so that, renewed by these heavenly Sacraments,
we may be prepared by your gift
for receiving what they promise.
Through Christ our Lord.
℟. **Amen.**   → No. 30, p. 77

Optional Solemn Blessings, p. 97, and Prayers over the People, p. 105

"He is God not of the dead, but of the living."

NOVEMBER 10

32nd SUNDAY IN ORDINARY TIME

ENTRANCE ANTIPHON Cf. Ps. 87.3

Let my prayer come into your presence. Incline
your ear to my cry for help, O Lord. → No. 2, p. 10

COLLECT

Almighty and merciful God,
graciously keep from us all adversity,
so that, unhindered in mind and body alike,
we may pursue in freedom of heart
the things that are yours.
Through our Lord Jesus Christ, your Son,
who lives and reigns with you in the unity of the
    Holy Spirit,
one God, for ever and ever.
℟. **Amen.** ↓

FIRST READING 2 Macc. 7.1-2, 9-14

Faith in the resurrection, a belief held even before the coming of Christ, gives strength to endure all trials.

A reading from the second book of Maccabees.

IT happened that seven brothers and their mother were arrested and were being compelled by King Antiochus, under torture with whips and thongs, to partake of unlawful swine's flesh. One of the brothers, speaking for all, said, "What do you intend to ask and learn from us? For we are ready to die rather than transgress the laws of our ancestors."

After the first brother had died, they brought forward the second for their sport. And when he was at his last breath, he said to the king, "You accursed wretch, you dismiss us from this present life, but the King of the universe will raise us up to an everlasting renewal of life, because we have died for his laws."

After him, the third was the victim of their sport. When it was demanded, he quickly put out his tongue and courageously stretched forth his hands, and said nobly, "I got these from Heaven, and because of God's laws I disdain them, and from God I hope to get them back again."

As a result the king himself and those with him were astonished at the young man's spirit, for he regarded his sufferings as nothing.

After the third brother too had died, they maltreated and tortured the fourth in the same way.

When he was near death, he said to his torturers, "One cannot but choose to die at the hands of humans and to cherish the hope God gives of being raised by him. But for you, there will be no resurrection to life!"—The word of the Lord. ℟. **Thanks be to God.** ↓

RESPONSORIAL PSALM Ps. 17

David Szanto

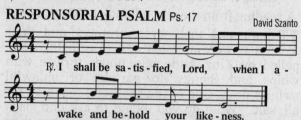

℟. I shall be sa-tis-fied, Lord, when I a-wake and be-hold your like-ness.

Hear a just cause, O Lord;
attend to my cry;
give ear to my prayer
from lips free of deceit.—℟.

My steps have held fast to your paths;
my feet have not slipped.
I call upon you, for you will answer me, O God;
incline your ear to me, hear my words.—℟.

Guard me as the apple of the eye;
hide me in the shadow of your wings,
As for me, I shall behold your face in righteousness;
when I awake I shall be satisfied, beholding
your likeness.—℟. ↓

SECOND READING 2 Thess. 2.16—3.5

Have faith, fear no evil, the Lord is constant. He is our strength.

A reading from the second Letter of Saint Paul
to the Thessalonians.

BROTHERS and sisters: May our Lord Jesus
Christ himself and God our Father, who loved
us and through grace gave us eternal comfort and

good hope, comfort your hearts and strengthen them in every good work and word.

Brothers and sisters, pray for us, so that the word of the Lord may spread rapidly and be glorified everywhere, just as it is among you, and that we may be rescued from wicked and evil people; for not all have faith.

But the Lord is faithful; he will strengthen you and guard you from the evil one. And we have confidence in the Lord concerning you, that you are doing and will go on doing the things that we command. May the Lord direct your hearts to the love of God and to the stead-fastness of Christ.—The word of the Lord. ℟. **Thanks be to God.** ↓

GOSPEL ACCLAMATION Rev. 1.5-6

℣. Alleluia. ℟. **Alleluia.**
℣. Jesus Christ is the firstborn of the dead;
to him be glory and dominion for ever and ever.
℟. **Alleluia.** ↓

GOSPEL Lk. 20.27-38 or 20.27, 34-38

Our God is God of the living who reveals the mystery of resurrection.

[If the "Shorter Form" is used, the indented text in brackets is omitted.]

℣. The Lord be with you. ℟. **And with your spirit.**
✜ A reading from the holy Gospel according to Luke. ℟. **Glory to you, O Lord.**

SOME Sadducees, those who say there is no resurrection, came to Jesus [and asked him a question, "Teacher, Moses wrote for us that if a man's brother dies, leaving a wife but no children, the man shall marry the widow and raise up children for his brother. Now there were seven brothers; the first married, and died childless; then the second and the third married her, and so in the same way all seven died childless.

Finally the woman also died. In the resurrection, therefore, whose wife will the woman be?—for the seven had married her."]

Jesus said to them, "The children of this age marry and are given in marriage; but those who are considered worthy of a place in that age and in the resurrection from the dead neither marry nor are given in marriage. Indeed they cannot die any more, because they are like Angels and are sons and daughters of God, being children of the resurrection.

And the fact that the dead are raised Moses himself showed in the story about the bush, where he speaks of the Lord as the God of Abraham, the God of Isaac, and the God of Jacob. Now he is God not of the dead, but of the living; for to him all of them are alive."—The Gospel of the Lord. ℟. **Praise to you, Lord Jesus Christ.**

→ No. 15, p. 18

PRAYER OVER THE OFFERINGS

Look with favour, we pray, O Lord,
upon the sacrificial gifts offered here,
that, celebrating in mystery the Passion of your
  Son,

we may honour it with loving devotion.
Through Christ our Lord.
R). **Amen.**   → No. 21, p. 22 (Pref. 29-36)

COMMUNION ANTIPHON Cf. Ps. 22.1-2

**The Lord is my shepherd; there is nothing I shall
want. Fresh and green are the pastures where
he gives me repose, near restful waters he leads
me.** ↓

OR Cf. Lk. 24.35

**The disciples recognized the Lord Jesus in the
breaking of bread.** ↓

PRAYER AFTER COMMUNION

Nourished by this sacred gift, O Lord,
we give you thanks and beseech your mercy,
that, by the pouring forth of your Spirit,
the grace of integrity may endure
in those your heavenly power has entered.
Through Christ our Lord.
R). **Amen.**   → No. 30, p. 77

Optional Solemn Blessings, p. 97, and Prayers over the People, p. 105

"The days will come when not one stone will be left upon another; all will be thrown down."

NOVEMBER 17

33rd SUNDAY IN ORDINARY TIME

ENTRANCE ANTIPHON Jer. 29.11, 12, 14

The Lord said: I think thoughts of peace and not of affliction. You will call upon me, and I will answer you, and I will lead back your captives from every place.
➔ No. 2, p. 10

COLLECT

Grant us, we pray, O Lord our God,
the constant gladness of being devoted to you,
for it is full and lasting happiness
to serve with constancy
the author of all that is good.
Through our Lord Jesus Christ, your Son,
who lives and reigns with you in the unity of the
    Holy Spirit,
one God, for ever and ever. ℟. **Amen.** ↓

FIRST READING Mal. 4.1-2

The time of judgment is coming. For the faithful it will be a day of glory.

A reading from the book of the Prophet Malachi.

"SEE, the day is coming, burning like an oven,

when all the arrogant and all evildoers will be stubble;

the day that comes shall burn them up," says the Lord of hosts,

"so that it will leave them neither root nor branch.

But for you who revere my name
the sun of righteousness shall rise,
with healing in its wings."

The word of the Lord. ℟. **Thanks be to God.** ↓

RESPONSORIAL PSALM Ps. 98

Scott Knarr

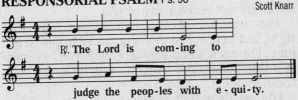

℟. The Lord is coming to judge the peoples with equity.

Sing praises to the Lord with the lyre,
with the lyre and the sound of melody.
With trumpets and the sound of the horn
make a joyful noise before the King, the Lord.—℟.

Let the sea roar, and all that fills it;
the world and those who live in it.
Let the floods clap their hands;
let the hills sing together for joy at the presence
of the Lord.—℟.

For the Lord is coming,
coming to judge the earth.
He will judge the world with righteousness,
and the peoples with equity.

℟. **The Lord is coming to judge the peoples with equity.** ↓

SECOND READING 2 Thess. 3.7-12

We must all work together and cooperate with one another. No one can sit back and enjoy the fruits of another's labour.

A reading from the second Letter of Saint Paul
to the Thessalonians.

BROTHERS and sisters, you yourselves know
how you ought to imitate us; we were not
idle when we were with you, and we did not eat
anyone's bread without paying for it; but with
toil and labour we worked night and day, so that
we might not burden any of you.

This was not because we do not have that
right, but in order to give you an example to imitate. For even when we were with you, we gave
you this command: "Anyone unwilling to work
should not eat."

For we hear that some of you are living in
idleness, mere busybodies, not doing any work.
Now such persons we command and exhort in
the Lord Jesus Christ to do their work quietly
and to earn their own living.—The word of the
Lord. ℟. **Thanks be to God.** ↓

GOSPEL ACCLAMATION Lk. 21.28

℣. Alleluia. ℟. **Alleluia.**

℣. Stand up and raise your heads,

because your redemption is drawing near.
℟. **Alleluia.** ↓

GOSPEL Lk. 21.5-19

Nothing in this world will last for ever, and we can be sure of trials and tribulations. But if we put our trust and hope in Christ, we will find life.

℣. The Lord be with you. ℟. **And with your spirit.**
✛ A reading from the holy Gospel according to Luke. ℟. **Glory to you, O Lord.**

WHEN some were speaking about the temple, how it was adorned with beautiful stones and gifts dedicated to God, Jesus said, "As for these things that you see, the days will come when not one stone will be left upon another; all will be thrown down."

They asked him, "Teacher, when will this be, and what will be the sign that this is about to take place?"

And Jesus said, "Beware that you are not led astray; for many will come in my name and say, 'I am he!' and, 'The time is near!' Do not go after them.

"When you hear of wars and insurrections, do not be terrified; for these things must take place first, but the end will not follow immediately."

Then Jesus said to them, "Nation will rise against nation, and kingdom against kingdom; there will be great earthquakes, and in various places famines and plagues; and there will be dreadful portents and great signs from heaven.

But before all this occurs, they will arrest you and persecute you; they will hand you over to

synagogues and prisons, and you will be brought
before kings and governors because of my name.

This will give you an opportunity to testify. So
make up your minds not to prepare your defence
in advance; for I will give you words and a wisdom that none of your opponents will be able to
withstand or contradict.

You will be betrayed even by parents, by brothers and sisters, and by relatives and friends; and
they will put some of you to death. You will be
hated by all because of my name. But not a hair of
your head will perish. By your endurance you will
gain your souls."—The Gospel of the Lord.
℟. **Praise to you, Lord Jesus Christ.** → No. 15, p. 18

PRAYER OVER THE OFFERINGS

Grant, O Lord, we pray,
that what we offer in the sight of your majesty
may obtain for us the grace of being devoted to
   you
and gain us the prize of everlasting happiness.
Through Christ our Lord.
℟. **Amen.**   → No. 21, p. 22 (Pref. 29-36)

COMMUNION ANTIPHON Ps. 72.28

**To be near God is my happiness, to place my
hope in God the Lord.** ↓

OR Mk. 11.23-24

**Amen, I say to you: Whatever you ask in prayer,
believe that you will receive, and it shall be given
to you, says the Lord.** ↓

PRAYER AFTER COMMUNION

We have partaken of the gifts of this sacred
    mystery,
humbly imploring, O Lord,
that what your Son commanded us to do
in memory of him
may bring us growth in charity.
Through Christ our Lord.
℞. **Amen.**   ➝ No. 30, p. 77

Optional Solemn Blessings, p. 97, and Prayers over the People, p. 105

"The Lord will reign for ever."

NOVEMBER 24

OUR LORD JESUS CHRIST, KING OF THE UNIVERSE
(34th SUNDAY IN ORDINARY TIME)
Solemnity

ENTRANCE ANTIPHON Rev. 5.12; 1.6
How worthy is the Lamb who was slain, to receive power and divinity, and wisdom and

strength and honour. To him belong glory and
power for ever and ever. → No. 2, p. 10

COLLECT

Almighty ever-living God,
whose will is to restore all things
in your beloved Son, the King of the universe,
grant, we pray,
that the whole creation, set free from slavery,
may render your majesty service
and ceaselessly proclaim your praise.
Through our Lord Jesus Christ, your Son,
who lives and reigns with you in the unity of the
   Holy Spirit,
one God, for ever and ever. ℟. **Amen.** ↓

FIRST READING 2 Sam. 5.1-3

**David is anointed to be king in fulfillment of the promise
of the Lord.**

A reading from the second book of Samuel.

ALL the tribes of Israel came to David at
Hebron, and said, "Look, we are your bone
and flesh. For some time, while Saul was king
over us, it was you who led out Israel and
brought it in. The Lord said to you: 'It is you
who shall be shepherd of my people Israel, you
who shall be ruler over Israel.'"

So all the elders of Israel came to the king at
Hebron; and King David made a covenant with
them at Hebron before the Lord, and they
anointed David king over Israel.—The word of
the Lord. ℟. **Thanks be to God.** ↓

PRAYER AFTER COMMUNION

Having received the food of immortality,
we ask, O Lord,
that, glorying in obedience
to the commands of Christ, the King of the
    universe,
we may live with him eternally in his heavenly
    Kingdom.
Who lives and reigns for ever and ever.
R̷. **Amen.**   ➜ No. 30, p. 77

Optional Solemn Blessings, p. 97, and Prayers over the People, p. 105

HYMNAL

1

O Come, O Come, Emmanuel

Tr. J. M. Neale, 1816-66
and others

Veni Emmanuel
Melody adapted by
T. Helmore, 1811-90

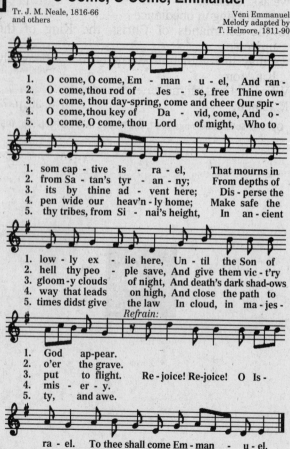

1. O come, O come, Em - man - u - el, And ran -
2. O come, thou rod of Jes - se, free Thine own
3. O come, thou day-spring, come and cheer Our spir -
4. O come, thou key of Da - vid, come, And o -
5. O come, O come, thou Lord of might, Who to

1. som cap - tive Is - ra - el, That mourns in
2. from Sa - tan's tyr - an - ny; From depths of
3. its by thine ad - vent here; Dis - perse the
4. pen wide our heav'n - ly home; Make safe the
5. thy tribes, from Si - nai's height, In an - cient

1. low - ly ex - ile here, Un - til the Son of
2. hell thy peo - ple save, And give them vic - t'ry
3. gloom - y clouds of night, And death's dark shad - ows
4. way that leads on high, And close the path to
5. times didst give the law In cloud, in ma - jes -

Refrain:

1. God ap - pear.
2. o'er the grave.
3. put to flight. Re - joice! Re - joice! O Is -
4. mis - er - y.
5. ty, and awe.

ra - el. To thee shall come Em - man - u - el.

612

Hark, a Mystic Voice Is Sounding

2

Tr. E. Caswall, 1849

En Clara Vox
R.L. de Pearsall, 1795-1856

1.

Hark, a mystic voice is sounding;
"Christ is nigh," It seems to
say;
"Cast away the dreams of
darkness,
O ye children of the day."

2.

Startled at the solemn warning,
Let the earthbound soul arise;

Christ her sun, all sloth dis-
pelling,
Shines upon the morning
skies.

3.

Lo, the Lamb so long ex-
pected
Comes with pardon down
from heav'n;
Let us haste, with tears of sorrow,
One and all, to be forgiv'n.

The Coming of Our God

3

1.

The coming of our Lord
Our thought must now employ;
Then let us meet him on the
road.
With song of holy joy.

2.

The co-eternal Son
A maiden's offspring see;

A servant's form Christ put-
teth on;
To set his people free.

3.

Daughter of Sion, rise
To greet thine Infant King;
Not let thy thankless heart de-
spise
The pardon he doth bring.

O Come, Divine Messiah

4

Anne Pellegrin, 1663-1745
Sr. St. Mary of St. Philip

Venez Divin Messie
16th Century French
Harm. G. Ridout, 1971

O come, divine Messiah!
The world in silence waits the
day
When hope shall sing its tri-
umph,
And sadness flee away.

Chorus: Sweet Saviour, haste,
Come, come to earth:
Dispel the night, and show
thy face,
And bid us hail the dawn of
grace.
O come, divine Messiah,
The world in silence waits
the day
When hope shall sing its tri-
umph,
And sadness flee away.

5   Hark! The Herald Angels Sing

1. Hark! The herald angels sing,
   "Glory to the newborn King.
   Peace on earth, and mercy mild,
   God and sinners reconciled."
   Joyful, all ye nations, rise,
   Join the triumph of the skies.
   With th'angelic host proclaim,
   "Christ is born in Bethlehem."

   —Refrain. Hark! The herald angels sing,
   "Glory to the newborn King."

2. Christ, by highest heav'n adored,
   Christ, the everlasting Lord.
   Late in time behold him come,
   Offspring of a virgin's womb.
   Veiled in flesh, the Godhead see;
   Hail th'incarnate Deity!
   Pleased as Man with men to appear,
   Jesus, our Emmanuel. *—Refrain*

6   Silent Night

Silent night, holy night!
  All is calm, all is bright.
'Round yon Virgin Mother and
  Child.
  Holy Infant so tender and
  mild:
Sleep in heavenly peace,
  Sleep in heavenly peace!

Silent night, holy night!
  Shepherds quake at the
  sight!
Glories stream from heaven
  afar.
Heav'nly hosts sing Alleluia:
Christ, the Saviour is born,
  Christ, the Saviour is born!

7   We Three Kings

1. We three kings of Orient are
   Bearing gifts we traverse afar,
   Field and fountain, moor and mountain,
   Following yonder Star.

   Refrain: O Star of wonder, Star of night,
   Star with royal beauty bright,
   Westward leading, still proceeding,
   Guide us to thy perfect light.

2. Born a king on Bethlehem's plain,
   Gold I bring to crown Him again,
   King forever, ceasing never,
   Over us all to reign. *—Refrain*

O Come, All Ye Faithful

8

1. O come, all ye faithful, joyful and triumphant,
   O come ye, O come ye to Bethlehem;
   Come and behold him born the King of angels.

   —*Refrain:* O come, let us adore him,
   O come, let us adore him,
   O come, let us adore him, Christ the Lord.

2. Sing choirs of angels, Sing in exultation,
   Sing all ye citizens of Heav'n above;
   Glory to God in the highest. —*Refrain*

3. See how the shepherd summoned to his cradle,
   Leaving their flocks draw nigh with lowly fear;
   We too will thither bend our joyful footsteps. —*Refrain*

The First Noel

9

1. The first Noel the angel did say,
   Was to certain poor shepherds in fields as they lay;
   In fields where they lay keeping their sheep
   On a cold winter's night that was so deep.

   —*Refrain:* Noel, Noel, Noel, Noel,
   Born is the King of Israel.

2. They looked up and saw a star,
   Shining in the east, beyond them far,
   And to the earth it gave great light,
   And so it continued both day and night. —*Refrain*

3. This star drew nigh to the northwest,
   O'er Bethlehem it took its rest,
   And there it did both stop and stay,
   Right over the place where Jesus lay. —*Refrain*

4. Then entered in those wise men three,
   Full reverently upon their knee,
   And offered there in his presence,
   Their gold and myrrh and frankincense. —*Refrain*

10   Angels We Have Heard on High

1. Angels we have heard on high,
   Sweetly singing o'er the plain,
   And the mountains in reply
   Echoing their joyous strain.

   Refrain: Gloria in excelsis Deo. (Repeat)

2. Shepherds, why this jubilee,
   Why your joyous strains prolong?
   Say, what may the tidings be
   Which inspire your heav'nly song? —*Refrain*

3. Come to Bethlehem and see
   Him whose birth the angels sing;
   Come, adore on bended knee
   Christ the Lord, the newborn King. —*Refrain*

11   Joy to the World

1.
Joy to the world! The Lord is
   come;
Let earth receive her King;
Let every heart prepare him
   room,
And heav'n and nature sing,
And heav'n and nature sing,
   And heaven, and heaven
   and nature sing.

2.
Joy to the world! the Saviour
   reigns;
Let men their songs employ,
While fields and floods,
   Rocks, hills, and plains,
Repeat the sounding joy,
   Repeat the sounding joy,
Repeat, repeat the sounding
   joy.

12   O Sing a Joyous Carol

1. O sing a joyous carol
   Unto the Holy Child,
   And praise with gladsome
      voices
   His mother undefiled.
   Our gladsome voices greet-
      ing
   Shall hail our Infant King;
   And our sweet Lady listens
   When joyful voices sing.

2. Who is there meekly lying
   In yonder stable poor?
   Dear children, it is Jesus;
   He bids you now adore.
   Who is there kneeling by
      him?
   In Virgin beauty fair?
   It is our Mother Mary,
   She bids you all draw
   near.

616

Lord, Who throughout These 40 Days

1. Lord, Who throughout these forty days
   For us did fast and pray,
   Teach us to overcome our sins
   And close by you to stay.

2. As you with Satan did contend
   And did the vic'try win,
   O give us strength in you to fight,
   In you to conquer sin.

3. As you did hunger and did thirst,
   So teach us, gracious Lord,
   To die to self and so to live
   By your most holy word.

O Faithful Cross

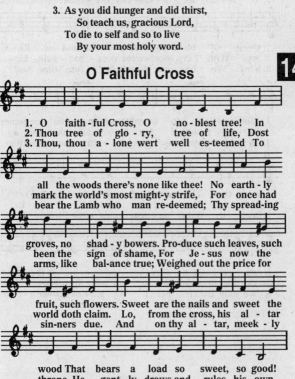

1. O faith-ful Cross, O no-blest tree! In
   all the woods there's none like thee! No earth-ly
   groves, no shad-y bowers. Pro-duce such leaves, such
   fruit, such flowers. Sweet are the nails and sweet the
   wood That bears a load so sweet, so good!

2. Thou tree of glo-ry, tree of life, Dost
   mark the world's most might-y strife, For once had
   been the sign of shame, For Je-sus now the
   world doth claim. Lo, from the cross, his al-tar
   throne, He gent-ly draws and rules his own.

3. Thou, thou a-lone wert well es-teemed To
   bear the Lamb who man re-deemed; Thy spread-ing
   arms, like bal-ance true; Weighed out the price for
   sin-ners due. And on thy al-tar, meek-ly
   laid, The lamb of God a-tone-ment made.

O Sacred Head, Surrounded

H.W. Baker, 1861
A.T. Russell, 1851, alt.

Passion Chorale
H. L. Hassler, 1601
Adapted, J.S. Bach, 1685-1750

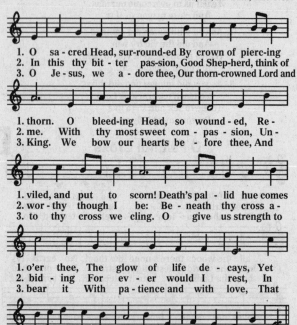

1. O sa-cred Head, sur-round-ed By crown of pierc-ing thorn. O bleed-ing Head, so wound-ed, Re-viled, and put to scorn! Death's pal-lid hue comes o'er thee, The glow of life de-cays, Yet an-gel hosts a-dore thee, And trem-ble as they gaze.

2. In this thy bit-ter pas-sion, Good Shep-herd, think of me. With thy most sweet com-pas-sion, Un-wor-thy though I be: Be-neath thy cross a-bid-ing For ev-er would I rest, In thy dear love con-fid-ing, And with thy pre-sence blest.

3. O Je-sus, we a-dore thee, Our thorn-crowned Lord and King. We bow our hearts be-fore thee, And to thy cross we cling. O give us strength to bear it With pa-tience and with love, That we may tru-ly mer-it A glo-rious crown a-bove.

All Glory, Laud and Honour

St. Theodulph of Orleans, c. 820
Tr. J.M. Neale, 1854, alt.

St. Theodulph
M. Teachner, 1615

16

1. All glo-ry, laud, and hon-our To thee, Re-deem-er,

1. King, To whom the lips of chil-dren Made

Fine

1. sweet ho-san-nas ring. 2. Thou art the King of
3. The com-pa-ny of
4. The peo-ple of the
5. To thee be-fore thy
6. Thou didst ac-cept their

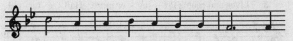

2. Is-rael, Thou Da-vid's roy-al Son. Who
3. an-gels Are prais-ing thee on high, And
4. He-brews With palms be-fore thee went; Our
5. pas-sion They sang their hymns of praise; To
6. prais-es, Ac-cept the pray'rs we bring, Who

D.C.

2. in the Lord's name com-est, The King and bles-sed One.
3. mor-tal men and all things Cre-a-ted make re-ply.
4. praise and pray'r and an-thems Be-fore thee we pre-sent.
5. thee now high ex-alt-ed Our mel-o-dy we raise.
6. in all good de-light-est, Thou good and gra-cious King.

619

Christ the Lord Is Ris'n Today

Jane E. Leeson, c. 1851,
based on Victimae Paschali

Victimae Paschali
Traditional

1. Christ, the Lord is   ris'n to - day, Chris-tians, haste your
2. Christ, the vic-tim   un - de-filed, Man to God has
3. Christ, who once for   sin - ners bled, Now the first - born

1. vows to pay;   Of - fer ye your prais - es meet
2. rec - on - ciled; When in strange and aw - ful strife
3. from the dead, Thron'd in end - less might   and pow'r

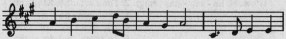

1. At the pas - chal   vic-tim's feet. For the sheep the
2. Met to - geth - er   death and life; Chris-tians, on this
3. Lives and reigns for   ev - er more. Hail, e - ter - nal

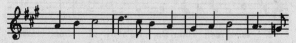

1. Lamb has bled, Sin-less in the sinners' stead; Christ, the
2. hap - py day Haste with joy your vows to pay. Christ, the
3. hope on high! Hail, thou King of vic - to - ry!   Hail, thou

1. Lord, is   ris'n   on high, Now he lives, no more to die!
2. Lord, is   ris'n   on high, Now he lives, no more to die!
3. Prince of life a-dored! Help and save us, gra-cious Lord.

The Strife is O'er

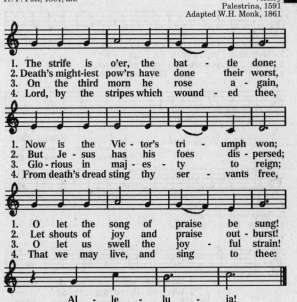

Tr. F. Pott, 1861, alt.

Victory
Palestrina, 1591
Adapted W.H. Monk, 1861

18

1. The strife is o'er, the bat - tle done;
2. Death's might-iest pow'rs have done their worst,
3. On the third morn he rose a - gain,
4. Lord, by the stripes which wound - ed thee,

1. Now is the Vic - tor's tri - umph won;
2. But Je - sus has his foes dis - persed;
3. Glo - rious in maj - es - ty to reign;
4. From death's dread sting thy ser - vants free,

1. O let the song of praise be sung!
2. Let shouts of joy and praise out - burst!
3. O let us swell the joy - ful strain!
4. That we may live, and sing to thee:

Al - le - lu - ia!

O God, Our Help in Ages Past

19

1.

O God, our help in ages past,
　Our hope for years to come,
Our shelter from the stormy blast,
　And our eternal home.

2.

Beneath the shadow of Thy throne,
　Thy saints have dwelt se-cure,
Sufficient is Thine arm alone,
　And our defence is sure.

3.

Before the hills in order stood,
　Or earth received her frame,
From everlasting Thou art God,
　To endless years the same.

4.

A thousand ages in Thy sight,
　Are like an evening gone.
Short as the watch that ends the night,
　Before the rising sun.

621

Jesus Christ Is Ris'n Today

1. Je - sus Christ is ris'n to - day,
2. Hymns of praise then let us sing,
3. But the pains which he en - dured,
4. Sing we to our God a - bove,

Al - -

- le - lu - ia!

1. Our tri - um - phant
2. Un - to Christ our
3. Our sal - va - tion
4. Praise e - ter - nal

1. ho - ly day,
2. heav'n - ly King,
3. have pro - cured;
4. as his love.

Al - - le -

1. Who did once up - on the cross,
2. Who en - dured the cross and grave,
3. Now a - bove the sky he's King,
4. Praise him, all ye heav'nly host,

lu - ia!

Al - - le - lu - ia!

1. Suf - fer to re - deem our loss.
2. Sin - ners to re - deem and save.
3. Where the an - gels ev - er sing.
4. Fa - ther, Son and Ho - ly Ghost.

Al - - le - lu - ia!

That Eastertide with Joy was Bright

Verses 1, 2: tr. J.M. Neale, 1851
Verse 3: tr. J. Chambers, 1857, alt.

Lasst Uns Erfreuen
Geistliches Kirchengesang, 1623

21

1. That East-er-tide with joy was bright, The
2. He showed to them his hands, his side, Where
3. To God the Fa-ther let us sing, To

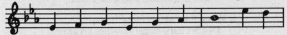

1. sun shone out with fair-er light, Al-le-
2. yet those glo-rious wounds a-bide, Al-le-
3. God the Son, our ris-en King, Al-le-

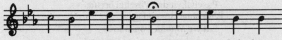

1. lu-ia, al-le-lu-ia, When, to their long-
2. lu-ia, al-le-lu-ia, The to-kens true
3. lu-ia, al-le-lu-ia, And e-qual-ly

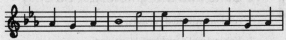

1. ing eyes re-stored, The glad a-pos-tles saw their
2. which made it plain. Their Lord in-deed was ris'n a-
3. let us a-dore The Ho-ly Spir-it ev-er-

1. Lord, Al-le-lu-ia, al-le-lu-ia, Al-le-
2. gain, Al-le-lu-ia, al-le-lu-ia, Al-le-
3. more, Al-le-lu-ia, al-le-lu-ia, Al-le-

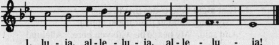

1. lu-ia, al-le-lu-ia, al-le-lu-ia!
2. lu-ia, al-le-lu-ia, al-le-lu-ia!
3. lu-ia, al-le-lu-ia, al-le-lu-ia!

623

22 At the Lamb's High Feast We Sing

1. At the Lamb's high feast we sing
   Praise to our victor'ous King.
   He has washed us in the tide
   Flowing from his opened side;
   Praise we him whose love divine
   Gives his sacred Blood for wine,
   Gives his Body for the feast,
   Christ the Victim, Christ the Priest.

2. When the Paschal blood is poured,
   Death's dark Angel sheathes his sword;
   Israel's hosts triumphant go
   Through the wave that drowns the foe.
   Christ the Lamb, whose Blood was shed,
   Paschal victim, Paschal bread;
   With sincerity and love
   Eat we Manna from above.

23 Ye Sons and Daughters, Let Us Sing

Alleluia! Alleluia! Alleluia!

1. Ye sons and daughters, let us sing!
   The King of heav'n, our glorious King,
   From death today rose triumphing. Alleluia!

2. That Easter morn, at break of day,
   The faithful women went their way
   To seek the tomb where Jesus lay. Alleluia!

3. An angel clothed in white they see,
   Who sat and spoke unto the three,
   "Your Lord has gone to Galilee." Alleluia!

4. That night th'apostles met in fear,
   And Christ did in their midst appear.
   And said, "My peace be with you here." Alleluia!

5. How blest are they who have not seen
   And yet whose faith has constant been,
   For they eternal life shall win. Alleluia!

O Holy Spirit, Lord of Peace

Tr. J. Chandler, 1806-76, alt.

Jeremiah Clark, 1709

1. O Ho - ly Spir - it, Lord of grace, E -
2. As thou in bond of love dost join The
3. All glo - ry to the Fa - ther be, All

1. ter - nal fount of love, In - flame, we pray, our
2. Fa - ther and the Son, So fill us all with
3. glo - ry to the Son, And Ho - ly Spir - it

1. in-most hearts With fire from heav'n a - bove.
2. mu-tual love, U - nite our hearts as one.
3. ev - er more While end - less a - ges run.

Creator Spirit, Lord of Grace

25

1. Creator Spirit, Lord of grace
   Make thou our hearts thy dwelling place
   And with thy might celestial, aid
   The souls of those whom thou hast made.

2. O to our souls thy light impart;
   And give thy love to every heart;
   Turn all our weakness into might,
   O thou the source of life and light.

3. To God the Father let us sing
   To God the Son, our risen king;
   And equally with thee adore
   The Spirit, God forevermore.

26 Praise God from Whom All Blessings Flow

1. Praise God, from whom all blessings flow;
   Praise him, all creatures here below;
   Praise him above, ye heav'nly host;
   Praise Father, Son, and Holy Ghost.

2. All people that on earth do dwell,
   Sing to the Lord with cheerful voice;
   Him serve with mirth, his praise forth tell,
   Come ye before him and rejoice.

3. Know that the Lord is God indeed:
   Without our aid he did us make;
   We are his folk, he doth us feed,
   And for his sheep he doth us take.

4. O enter then his gates with praise,
   Approach with joy his courts unto;
   Praise, laud, and bless his name always,
   For it is seemly so to do.

27 Come, Holy Ghost

1. Come, Holy Ghost, Creator blest,
   And in our hearts take up your rest;
   Come with your grace and heav'nly aid
   To fill the hearts which you have made,
   To fill the hearts which you have made.

2. O Comforter, to you we cry,
   The heav'nly gift of God most high;
   The fount of life and fire of love,
   And sweet anointing from above,
   And sweet anointing from above.

3. To every sense your light impart,
   And shed your love in ev'ry heart.
   To our weak flesh, your strength supply:
   Unfailing courage from on high,
   Unfailing courage from on high.

4. O grant that we through you may come
   To know the Father and the Son,
   And hold with firm, unchanging faith,
   That you are Spirit of them both,
   That you are Spirit of them both.

Holy, Holy, Holy

R. Heber, 1826, alt,

Nicaea
J. B. Dykes, 1861

1. Ho - ly, ho - ly, ho - ly! Lord God Al -
2. Ho - ly, ho - ly, ho - ly! an - gel hosts a -
3. Ho - ly, ho - ly, ho - ly! though the dark-ness
4. Ho - ly, ho - ly, ho - ly! Lord God Al -

1. might - y! Ear - ly in the morn - ing our
2. dore thee, Cast - ing down their gol - den crowns a -
3. hide thee, Though the eye of sin - ful man thy
4. might - y All thy works shall praise thy name, in

1. song shall rise to thee; Ho - ly, ho - ly
2. round the glas - sy sea. Che - ru - bim and
3. glo - ry may not see, On - ly thou art
4. earth, and sky, and sea; Ho - ly, ho - ly

1. ho - ly! mer - ci - ful and might - y:
2. sera - phim fall - ing down be - fore thee:
3. ho - ly! there is none be - side thee:
4. ho - ly! mer - ci - ful and might - y:

1. God in three Per - sons, bless-ed Trin - i - ty:
2. Which wert, and art, and ev - er more shall be.
3. Per - fect in pow'r, in love, and pur - i - ty:
4. God in three Per - sons, bless-ed Trin - i - ty:

Now Thank We All Our God

M. Rinkart, 1586-1649
Tr. Catherine Winkworth, 1858

Nun Danket
J. Crüger, 1647

1. Now thank we all our God, With heart, and hand, and
2. O may this boun-teous God Through all our life be
3. All praise and thanks to God The Fa-ther now be

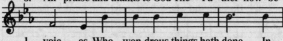

1. voic-es, Who won-drous things hath done, In
2. near us! With ev-er joy-ful hearts And
3. giv-en, The Son, and him who reigns With

1. whom his world re-joic-es; Who from our moth-er's
2. bless-ed peace to cheer us; And keep us in his
3. them in high-est heav-en, The one e-ter-nal

1. arms Hath blessed us on our way With
2. grace, And guide us when per-plex'd And
3. God, Whom heav'n and earth a-dore; For

1. count-less gifts of love, And still is ours to-day.
2. free us from all ills In this world and the next.
3. thus it was, is now, And shall be, ev-er-more.

We Gather Together

1. We gather together to ask the Lord's blessing;
   He chastens and hastens his will to make known;
   The wicked oppressing now cease from distressing:
   Sing praises to his name; he forgets not his own.

2. Beside us to guide us, our God with us joining,
   Ordaining, maintaining his kingdom divine;
   So from the beginning the fight we were winning:
   Thou, Lord, wast at our side; all glory be thine.

To Jesus Christ, Our Sovereign King

31

M.B. Hellriegel

Ich Glaub An Gott
Mainz, 1900

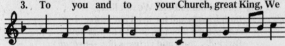

1. To Je - sus Christ, our sov-'reign King, Who
2. Your reign ex - tend, O King be - nign, To
3. To you and to your Church, great King, We

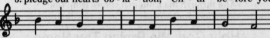

1. is the world's sal - va - tion, All praise and hom - age
2. ev - 'ry land and na - tion; For in your king-dom,
3. pledge our hearts' ob - la - tion; Un - til be - fore your

1. do we bring And thanks and ad - o - ra - tion.
2. Lord di - vine, A - lone we find sal - va - tion.
3. throne we sing In end - less ju - bi - la - tion:

Refrain:

Christ, Je - sus, Vic - tor! Christ, Je - sus, Rul - er!

Christ, Je - sus, Lord and Re - deem - er!

O Lord, I Am Not Worthy

32

1. O Lord, I am not worthy,
   That thou shouldst come to me,
   But speak the word of comfort:
   My spirit healed shall be.

2. And humbly I'll receive thee,
   The bridegroom of my soul,
   No more by sin to grieve thee
   Or fly thy sweet control.

3. O Sacrament most holy,
   O Sacrament divine,
   All praise and all thanksgiving
   Be every moment thine.

629

33   Faith of Our Fathers

1. Faith of our fathers, living still,
   In spite of dungeon, fire and sword;
   O how our hearts beat high with joy
   When'ver we hear that glorious word!

   Refrain: Faith of our fathers, holy faith,
             We will be true to thee til death.

2. Faith of our fathers! We will love
   Both friends and foe in all our strife.
   And preach thee too, as love knows how,
   By kindly word and virtuous life. —*Refrain*

3. Faith of our fathers! Mary's pray'r
   Shall keep our country close to thee;
   And through the truth that comes from God
   Mankind shall prosper and be free. —*Refrain*

34   Holy God, We Praise Thy Name

1. Holy God, we praise thy name!
   Lord of all, we bow before thee!
   All on earth thy sceptre claim,
   All in heaven above adore thee.
   Infinite thy vast domain,
   Everlasting is thy reign. *Repeat last two lines*

2. Hark! the loud celestial hymn
   Angel choirs above are raising;
   Cherubim and seraphim,
   In unceasing chorus praising,
   Fill the heavens with sweet accord;
   Holy, holy, holy Lord! *Repeat last two lines*

35   Redeemer, King and Saviour

1.

Redeemer, King and Saviour
Your death we celebrate
So good, yet born our brother,
You live in human state.
O Saviour, in your dying
You do your Father's will,
Give us the strength to suffer
To live for others still.

2.

Your dying and your rising
Give hope and life to all.
Your faithful way of giving
Embraces great and small.
Help us to make our journey,
to walk your glorious way,
And from the night of dying
To find a joy-filled day.

Taste and See

Tune: James E. Moore, Jr., b. 1951

Text: Psalm 34;
James E. Moore, Jr., b. 1951

Refrain

Taste and see, taste and see the good-ness of the Lord. O taste and see, taste and see the good - ness of the Lord, of the Lord.

Verses

1. I will bless the Lord at all times.
2. Glo - ri - fy the Lord with me,
3. Wor-ship the Lord, all you peo-ple.

Praise shall al-ways be on my lips;
To-geth-er let us all praise God's name.
You'll want for noth-ing if you ask.

my soul shall glo-ry in the Lord
I called the Lord who an - swered me;
Taste and see that the Lord is good;

D.C.

for God has been so good to me.
from all my trou-bles I was set free.
in God we need put all our trust.

Crown Him with Many Crowns

M. Bridges, 1851
and others

Diademata
G.J. Elvey, 1868

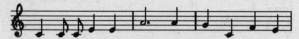

1. Crown him with man-y crowns. The Lamb up-on his
2. Crown him the Lord of Lords, Who o-ver all doth
3. Crown him the Lord of heav'n En-throned in worlds a-

1. throne: Hark, how the heav'n-ly an-them drowns All
2. reign, Who once on earth th'in-car-nate Word, For
3. bove; Crown him the King, to whom is giv'n The

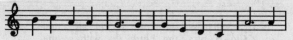

1. mu-sic but its own! A-wake my soul, and sing Of
2. ran-somed sin-ners slain, Now lives in realms of light, Where
3. won-drous name of Love. Crown him with man-y crowns. As

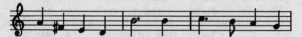

1. him who died for thee. And hail him as thy
2. saints with an-gels sing Their songs be-fore him
3. thrones be-fore him fall. Crown him, ye kings, with

1. match-less King Through all e-ter-ni-ty.
2. day and night, Their God, Re-deem-er, King.
3. man-y crowns, For he is King of all.

632

Immaculate Mary

38

Anon.

Lourdes
Traditional Lourdes Melody

1. Im - mac - u - late Ma - ry, your prais - es we
2. In heav - en, the bless - ed your glo - ry pro -
3. Your name is our pow - er, your vir - tues our
4. We pray for our moth - er, the Church up - on

1. sing, You reign now in heav-en with Je - sus our King.
2. claim; On earth, we your chil-dren in - voke your fair name.
3. light, Your love is our com - fort, your plead-ing our might.
4. earth, And bless, dear-est la - dy, the land of our birth.

Refrain:

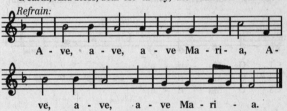

A - ve, a - ve, a - ve Ma - ri - a, A -

ve, a - ve, a - ve Ma - ri - a.

Hail, O Star of Ocean

39

1. Hail, O Star of Ocean,
   Portal of the sky!
   Ever Virgin Mother
   Of the Lord most high.

2. O by Gabriel's Ave
   Uttered long ago,
   Eva's name reversing
   Brought us peace below.

40 Hail, Holy Queen, Enthroned Above

Traditional

Salve Regina Caelitum
Traditional

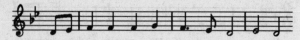

1. Hail, ho - ly Queen en - throned a - bove, O Ma -
2. Our life, our sweet-ness here be - low, O Ma -
3. We hon - our you for Christ, your son, O Ma -

1. ri - a! Hail, moth-er of mer - cy and of love,
2. ri - a! Our hope in sor - row and in woe,
3. ri - a! Who has for us re - demp-tion won,

Refrain:

1. O Ma - ri - a!
2. O Ma - ri - a! Tri - umph all ye
3. O Ma - ri - a!

che - ru - bim, Sing with us, ye se - ra - phim,

Heav'n and earth re - sound the hymn: Sal - ve,

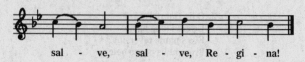

sal - ve, sal - ve, Re - gi - na!

634

For All the Saints

W.W. How, 1864

Sine Nomine
R. Vaughan Williams, 1906

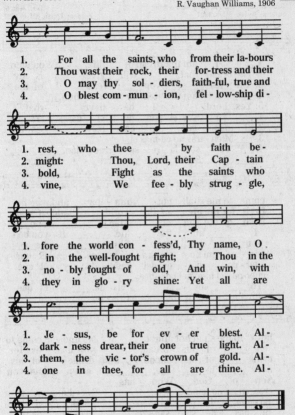

1. For all the saints, who from their la-bours
2. Thou wast their rock, their for-tress and their
3. O may thy sol - diers, faith-ful, true and
4. O blest com - mun - ion, fel - low-ship di -

1. rest, who thee by faith be -
2. might: Thou, Lord, their Cap - tain
3. bold, Fight as the saints who
4. vine, We fee - bly strug - gle,

1. fore the world con - fess'd, Thy name, O
2. in the well-fought fight; Thou in the
3. no - bly fought of old, And win, with
4. they in glo - ry shine: Yet all are

1. Je - sus, be for ev - er blest. Al -
2. dark - ness drear, their one true light. Al -
3. them, the vic - tor's crown of gold. Al -
4. one in thee, for all are thine. Al -

1-4 le - lu - ia, al - le - lu - ia!

Music from the English Hymnal,
used by permission of Oxford University Press

I Am the Bread of Life

Tune: BREAD OF LIFE, Irreg. with refrain;
Suzanne Toolan, SM, b. 1927

Text: John 6;
Suzanne Toolan, SM, b. 1927

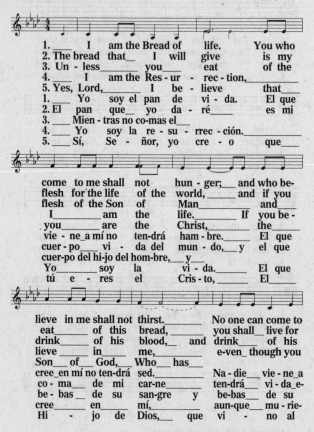

me   un - less   the__ Fa - ther   beck-ons.
ev - er,_____ you shall__ live   for   ev - er.
blood,_____ you shall not have life with - in you.
die,_____ you shall__ live   for   ev - er.
come   in - to_____ the____   world.___
mí_____ mien-tras el Pa - dre   lla - me.
ter - na,_____ ten - drá   vi - da_e   ter - na.
san - gre,   no ten - drá   vi - da   en ti.
ra,_____ ten - drá vi - da e -   ter - na.
mun-do_____ pa-ra sal-var-nos.

And   I will raise   you up,   and I will
Yo   le re - su - ci - ta - ré,   Yo lo re -

raise   you up,   and I will raise   you
su - ci - ta - ré,   Yo lo re - su - ci - ta -

up   on   the last   day.
ré   el   di - a   de_El.

O Most Holy One

43

1. O most holy one, O most lowly one,
   Loving virgin, Maria!
   Mother, maid of fairest love,
   Lady, queen of all above,
   Ora, ora pro nobis.

2. Virgin ever fair, Mother, hear our prayer,
   Look upon us, Maria!
   Bring to us your treasure,
   Grace beyond all measure,
   Ora, ora pro nobis.

English text from the New St. Basil Hymnal
by permission of The Basillian Press, Toronto.

637

44 Send Us Your Spirit

Tune: David Haas, b. 1957
acc. by Jeanne Cotter, b. 1964

Text: David Haas, b. 1957

Refrain

Come Lord Je-sus, send us your Spir-it, re-new the face of the earth. Come Lord Je-sus, send us your Spir-it, re-new the face of the earth.

Verses

1. Come to us, Spir-it of God, breathe in us now, we sing to-geth-er. Spir-it of hope and of light, fill our lives, come to us, Spir-it of God.

2. Fill us with the fire of your love, burn in us now, bring us to-geth-er. Come to us, dwell in us, change our lives, O Lord, come to us, Spir-it of God.

3. Send us the wings of new birth, fill all the earth with the love you have taught us. Let all cre-a-tion now be shak-en with love, come to us, Spir-it of God.

May be sung in canon.

Praise to the Lord, the Almighty

J. Neander, 1950-80
Tr. Catherine Winkworth, 1863, alt.

Lobe Den Herren
Stralsund Gesangbuch, 1665

45

1. Praise to the Lord, the Al - might - y, the King of cre -
2. Praise to the Lord, let us of - fer our gifts at the
3. Praise to the Lord, who does pros-per our work and de -
4. Praise to the Lord, O let all that is in us a -

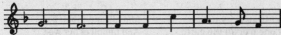

1. a - tion! O my soul, praise him for
2. al - tar. Let not our sins and of -
3. fend us; Sure - ly his good - ness and
4. dore him. All that has life and breath

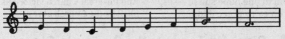

1. he is your health and sal - va - tion.
2. fen - ces now cause us to fal - ter.
3. mer - cy here dai - ly at - tend us;
4. come now re - joi - cing be - fore him.

1. All you who hear, now to the al - tar draw
2. Christ the high priest, bids us all join in the
3. Pon - der a - new what the Al - might - y can
4. Let the A - men sound from his peo - ple a -

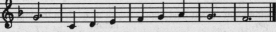

1. near; Join in pro - found ad - o - ra - tion.
2. feast, Vic - tims with him on the al - tar.
3. do, If with his love he be - friends us.
4. gain, As we here wor-ship be - fore him.

639

The Church's One Foundation

1.

The Church's one foundation
Is Jesus Christ her Lord.
She is his new creation,
By water and the Word;
From heav'n he came and sought her,
To be his holy bride;
With his own blood he bought her,
And for her life he died.

2.

Elect from ev'ry nation,
Yet one o'er all the earth.
Her charter of salvation,
One Lord, one faith, one birth;
One holy Name she blesses,
Partakes one holy food;
And to one hope she presses,
With ev'ry grace endued.

3.

Mid toil and tribulation,
And tumult of her war.
She waits the consummation
Of peace for evermore;
Till with the vision glorious
Her loving eyes are blest,
And the great Church victorious
Shall be the Church at rest.

Sing, My Tongue, the Saviour's Glory

1.

Sing, my tongue, the Saviour's
glory,
Of his flesh the myst'ry sing;
Of the Blood, all price exceed-
ing,
Shed by our immortal King,
Destined for the world's re-
demption,
From a noble womb to spring.

2.

Of a pure and spotless Virgin
Born for us on earth below,
He, as Man, with man convers-
ing,
Stayed, the seeds of truth to
sow;
Then he closed in solemn order
Wondrously his life of woe.

3.

On the night of that Last Sup-
per,
Seated with his chosen band,
He the Paschal victim eating,
First fulfils the Law's com-
mand;
Then as food to his Apostles
Gives himself with his own
Hand.

4.

Word made flesh the bread of
nature
By his word to Flesh he turns;
Wine into his blood he changes
What though sense no change
discerns?
Only be the heart in earnest,
Faith its lesson quickly learns.

5.

Down in adoration falling
Lo! the sacred Host we hail;
Lo! o'er ancient forms depart-
ing,
Newer rites of grace prevail;
Faith for all defects supplying,
Where the feeble senses fail.

6.

To the Everlasting Father,
And the Son who reigns on
high,
With the Holy Ghost proceed-
ing
Forth from each eternally
Be salvation, honour, blessing,
Might and endless majesty.
Amen.

Lord, Dismiss Us with Thy Blessing   48

1.

Lord, dismiss us with thy
blessing;
Fill our hearts with joy and
peace;
May we all, thy love possess-
ing,
Triumph in redeeming grace:
O refresh us, O refresh us,
And the world its turmoil
cease.

2.

Thanks to thee and adoration
For the scriptures' joyful
sound,
May the fruit of thy redemp-
tion
In our hearts and lives abound;
Ever faithful, ever faithful
To the ways of truth be found.

The King of Glory   49

W. F. Jabusch   Israeli Folksong

Refrain: **The King of Glory comes,
the people rejoices;
Open the gates before him,
lift up your voices.**

**1. Who is the King of Glory;
how shall we call him?
He is Emmanuel,
the promised of ages.**

**2. In all of Galilee,
In city or village,
He goes among his people
Curing their illness.**

Recorded on LP "Songs of Good News," © Copyright 1969 by ACTA Foundations, 4848 N. Clark St., Chicago, IL.

50 Psalm 23: Shepherd Me, O God

Music: Marty Haugen

Text: Psalm 23; Marty Haugen

Refrain

Shep-herd me, O God, be-yond my wants, be-yond my fears, from death in-to life.

Verses

1. God is my shepherd, so nothing shall I want,
I rest in the meadows of faithfulness and love,
I walk by the quiet waters of peace.

2. Gently you raise me and heal my weary soul,
you lead me by pathways of righteousness and truth,
my spirit shall sing the music of your name.

3. Though I should wander the valley of death,
I fear no evil, for you are at my side, your rod and your staff,
my comfort and my hope.

4. Surely your kindness and mercy follow me all the days of my life;
I will dwell in the house of my God for evermore.

Amazing Grace

1. A - maz - ing grace! how
2. 'Twas grace that taught my
3. The Lord has prom - ised
4. Through man - y dan - gers,
5. When we've been there ten

1. sweet the sound That saved a
2. heart to fear, And grace my
3. good to me, His word my
4. toils, and snares, I have al -
5. thou - sand years, Bright shin - ing

1. wretch like me! I once — was
2. fears re - leaved; How pre - cious
3. hope se - cures; He will — my
4. read - y come; 'Tis grace — has
5. as the sun, We've no less

1. lost, but now — am found, Was
2. did that grace — ap - pear The
3. shield and por - tion be, As
4. brought me safe — thus far, And
5. days to sing — God's praise Than

1. blind, but now I see.
2. hour I first be - lieved!
3. long as life en - dures.
4. grace will lead me home.
5. when we'd first be - gun.

643

Gather Us In

Tune: GATHER US IN, Irreg.,   Text: Marty Haugen, b. 1950
Marty Haugen, b. 1950

1. Here in this place   new light is stream-ing,
2. We are the young—our   lives are a mys-t'ry,
3. Here we will take   the   wine and the wa - ter,
4. Not in the dark   of   build-ings con - fin -ing,

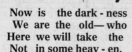

Now is the dark - ness   van-ished a - way,
We are the old— who   yearn for your face,
Here we will take the   bread of new birth,
Not in some heav - en,   light-years a - way, But

See in this space our   fears and our dream-ings,
We have been sung through-out all of his - t'ry,
Here you shall call   your   sons and your daugh-ters,
here in this place   the   new light is shin-ing,

Brought here to you in the   light of this   day.
Called to be light to the   whole hu-man race.
Call us a - new to be   salt for the earth.
Now is the King-dom,   now is the day.

Gath - er us in— the lost and for - sak - en,
Gath - er us in— the rich and the haugh-ty,
Give us to drink the wine of com - pas-sion,
Gath - er us in   and hold us for ev - er,

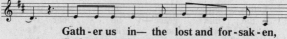

Gath-er us in— the blind and the lame;
Gath-er us in— the proud and the strong;
Give us to eat   the bread that is you;
Gath-er us in   and make us your own;

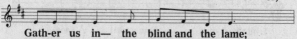

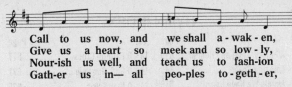

Call to us now, and we shall a-wak-en,
Give us a heart so meek and so low-ly,
Nour-ish us well, and teach us to fash-ion
Gath-er us in— all peo-ples to-geth-er,

We shall a-rise at the sound of our name.
Give us the cour-age to en-ter the song.
Lives that are ho-ly and hearts that are true.
Fire of love in our flesh and our bone.

Were You There

53

1. Were you there when they crucified my Lord?
   Were you there when they crucified my Lord?
   Oh! sometimes it causes me
   To tremble, tremble, tremble.
   Were you there when they crucified my Lord?

2. Were you there when they nailed him to the tree?
   Were you there when they nailed him to the tree?
   Oh! sometimes it causes me
   To tremble, tremble, tremble.
   Were you there when they nailed him to the tree?

3. Were you there when they laid him in the tomb?
   Were you there when they laid him in the tomb?
   Oh! sometimes it causes me
   To tremble, tremble, tremble.
   Were you there when they laid him in the tomb?

O Canada

54

R. S. Weir, 1908   A.B. Routhier

O Canada! Our home and na-
tive land!
True patriot love in all thy sons
command.
With glowing hearts we see
thee rise.
The True North strong and free;
From far and wide, O Canada,
We stand on guard for thee.
God keep our land glorious and
free!
O Canada! we stand on guard
for thee.

O Canada! Terre de nos aieux,
Ton front est ceint de fleurons
glorieux!
Car ton bras sait porter l'epee,
Il sait porter la croix!
Ton histoíre est une epopee
Des plus briliants exploits.
Et ta valeur, de foi trempee,
Protegera nos foyers et nos
droits.
Protegera nos foyers et nos
droits.

HYMN INDEX

TREASURY OF PRAYERS

These prayers reflect the traditions of the Catholic Church. Individuals and families may find them helpful as they pray.

PRAISE AND THANKS

Blessed are you, Lord God:
blessed are you for ever.
Holy is your name:
blessed are you for ever.
Great is your mercy for your people:
blessed are you for ever. Amen!

Father, Son, and Holy Spirit,
we praise you and give you glory:
we bless you for calling us to be your holy people.

Remain in our hearts,
and guide us in our love and service.
Help us to let our light shine before others
and lead them to the way of faith.

Holy Trinity of love,
we praise you now and for ever. Amen!

We praise you, Father of all:
we thank you for calling us to be your people,
and for choosing us to give you glory.
In a special way we thank you for . . .

Cleanse our hearts and our lives
with your holy word
and make our prayer pleasing to you.
Guide us by your Spirit
as we follow in the paths of Jesus our brother.

All glory and praise are yours, Father,
for ever and ever. Amen!

Let us give glory to the Father
through the Son
in the Holy Spirit,
for God has made us his people, his Church,
and calls us to sing his praises.

All honor and glory and thanks are his,
and praise and worship belong to him.
To God be glory in his Church
for ever and ever! Amen!

Thanks for a beautiful day: *On a beautiful day we may thank God and praise him for his many gifts:*

Father of Jesus,
we praise you and give you glory
for the wonderful things you do for us:
for life and health,
for friends and family,
for this splendid day.

For these reasons, we pray as Jesus taught us:
Our Father . . .

MORNING PRAYERS

With our risen Lord, we praise our Father and offer our day and our work.

**In the ✠ name of the Father, and of the Son,
and of the Holy Spirit. Amen!**

Father, help your people.
Be with us as we pray.

MORNING PSALM:

We may pray one of these psalms, or last Sunday's responsorial psalm, adding the Glory (be) to the Father *at the end.*

Ps. 23—from Mass for Second Scrutiny (4th Sun. of Lent)
Ps. 95—from Mass for First Scrutiny (3rd Sun. of Lent)

Ps. 97—from Mass of the Nativity (at Dawn)
Ps. 116—from Mass for Holy Thursday

*On Sunday, it is appropriate to use Ps. 118 from Easter
    Sunday Mass.*
*On Friday, it is appropriate to use Ps. 51 from Ash Wednes-
    day Mass.*

PSALM OF PRAISE:

One of these Psalms may be prayed, adding the Glory (be)
to the Father *at the end.*

Ps. 46(47)—from Mass for Palm Sunday of the Passion
Ps. 67—from Mass of January 1
Ps. 96—from Mass of the Nativity (During the Night)
Ps. 98—from Mass of the Nativity (During the Day)

READING:

*One of the first two readings from last Sunday, or another
appropriate text from God's word.*

A moment of silent prayer follows the reading.

Canticle of Zechariah
Lk. 1.68-79

Blessed ✠ be the Lord, the God of Israel,
for he has looked favorably on his people and re-
    deemed them.

He has raised up a mighty saviour for us
    in the house of his servant David,
as he spoke through the mouth of his holy prophets
        from of old,
        that we would be saved from our enemies and
        from the hand of all who hate us.
Thus he has shown the mercy promised to our an-
    cestors,
    and has remembered his holy covenant,
the oath that he swore to our ancestor Abraham,
    to grant us that we, being rescued from the hands
        of our enemies,

might serve him without fear, in holiness and righteousness
  before him all our days.
And you, child, will be called the prophet of the
   Most High;
  for you will go before the Lord to prepare his ways,
to give knowledge of salvation to his people
  by the forgiveness of their sins.
By the tender mercy of our God,
  the dawn from on high will break upon us,
to give light to those who sit in darkness and in the
   shadow of death,
  to guide our feet into the way of peace.

Glory to the Father . . . .

Or Glory to God in the highest *(see page 14) may be
prayed or sung.*

Prayers for All People

Lord Jesus, we come to you for help:
Lord, have mercy.

Help us to love you more this day. ℟.
Teach us to see you in other people. ℟.
Help us to be ready to serve others. ℟.
Give us strength to carry our cross with you. ℟.
In moments of sorrow, be with us today. ℟.
Help us to do everything for the glory of your Father.
  ℟.
Help us to build the kingdom by our life today. ℟.

Other petitions may be added.

Lord Jesus, our brother,
hear our prayers for your people.
Help us to work with you today
to honour your Father and save the world.

Lord Jesus,
we praise you for ever and ever. Amen!

THE LORD'S PRAYER: *With Jesus and all his people on earth and in heaven, we sing or say:* Our Father . . . *(page 72).*

BLESSING: *The parents, one of the family, or all may say:*

May our loving God bless us,
Father, Son, and Holy Spirit. Amen!

All may share in a sign of peace and love.

EVENING PRAYERS

At the end of the day, we join Jesus and his Church in offering thanks to our loving God. A candle may be lighted.

**In the ✠ name of the Father, and of the Son,
and of the Holy Spirit. Amen!**

Father, help your people.
Be with us as we pray.

PSALMS:

We may pray one or two of these psalms, or last Sunday's responsorial psalm, adding the Glory (be) to the Father *after each psalm:*

Ps. 30—from Easter Vigil Service after Fourth Reading
Ps. 51—from Mass for Ash Wednesday
Ps. 104—from Mass for Pentecost Sunday
Ps. 130—from Mass for Third Scrutiny (5th Sun. of Lent)

READING:

One of the first two readings from last Sunday, or another appropriate text from God's word.

A moment of silent prayer follows the reading.

Canticle of Mary Lk. 1.46-55

My soul ✠ proclaims the greatness of the Lord,
my spirit rejoices in God my Saviour
for he has looked with favour on his lowly servant.

From this day all generations will call me blessed:
the Almighty has done great things for me,
and holy is his Name.

He has mercy on those who fear him
in every generation.

He has shown the strength of his arm,
he has scattered the proud in their conceit.

He has cast down the mighty from their thrones,
and has lifted up the lowly.

He has filled the hungry with good things,
and the rich he has sent away empty.

He has come to the help of his servant Israel
for he has remembered his promise of mercy,
the promise he made to our fathers,
to Abraham and his children for ever.

Glory to the Father.

Or we may sing the Holy, Holy, Holy Lord, *from page 23.*

Prayers for all people:

Let us pray to God our Father:
Lord, hear our prayer.
For the people of God everywhere. ℟.
For peace in the world. ℟.
For the people who are suffering. ℟.
For the sick and the dying. ℟.
For our family, friends, and neighbours. ℟.
For . . .

Other petitions may be added.

Prayer:

Blessed are you, Father of light,
Lord of all the universe:
in the name of Jesus our Lord we pray for your
   world.
Grant peace to your people,
strength to the weak,
courage to the downhearted,
and guidance to all in despair.
Send your Spirit to conquer evil,
and make your kingdom come among us.

Father, we ask this grace
through Jesus Christ our Lord. Amen!

THE LORD'S PRAYER: *With Jesus and all his people
on earth and in heaven, we sing or say: Our Father . . .
(page 72).*

BLESSING: *The parents, one of the family, or all may say:*

May our loving God bless us,
Father, Son, ✠ and Holy Spirit. Amen!

All may share a sign of peace and love.

BEFORE AND AFTER SCRIPTURE

Before:

Lord, open our hearts:
let your Spirit speak to us
as we read your word.

After:

Father, we thank you
for speaking to us today
through your holy word.

Or another prayer of thanks may be said (pages 647-648).

MEAL PRAYERS

When we are eating or drinking, or doing anything else, we can do it for the glory of God (1 Cor. 10.31). We may use these prayers or other familiar ones, or make up our own.

Before our meal:

Lord Jesus, our brother,
we praise you for saving us.
Bless ✠ us in your love
as we gather in your name,
and bless ✠ this meal that we share.

Jesus, we praise you for ever. Amen!

or:

Father of us all,
this meal is a sign of your love for us:
bless ✠ us and bless ✠ our food,
and help us to give you glory each day
through Jesus Christ our Lord. Amen!

After our meal:

Loving Father, we praise you
for all the gifts you give us:
for life and health,
for faith and love,
and for this meal we have shared together.

Father, we thank you
through Christ our Lord. Amen!

or:

Thank you, Father, for your gifts:
help us to love you more. Amen!

or:

Father, we thank you for your love
and for giving us food and drink.
Help us to praise you today
in the name of Jesus our Lord. Amen!

A PRAYER FOR OUR FAMILY

Blessed are you, loving Father,
ruler of the universe:

You have given us your Son as your leader,
and have made us temples of your Holy Spirit.

Fill our family with your light and peace.
Have mercy on all who suffer,
and bring us to everlasting joy with you.

Father,
we bless your name for ever and ever. Amen!

PARENT'S PRAYER

All praise to you, Lord Jesus, lover of children:
bless our family,
and help us to lead our children to you.

Give us light and strength,
and courage when our task is difficult.
Let your Spirit fill us with love and peace,
so that we may help our children to love you.

All glory and praise are yours, Lord Jesus,
for ever and ever. Amen!

PRAYER OF SORROW

Psalm 51: *from the Mass for Ash Wednesday.*

A prayer for mercy:

Lord Jesus, you have called us
to be children of light:

Lord, have mercy.   **Lord, have mercy.**

Christ, you have suffered on the cross for us:
Christ, have mercy.   **Christ, have mercy.**

Lord Jesus, you are the saviour of the world:
Lord, have mercy.   **Lord, have mercy.**

Other prayers. We may sing or say Lamb of God *(see page 74), or* I confess to almighty God *(see page 12).*

JESUS PRAYER

We may use this simple prayer at any time.

Lord Jesus Christ, Son of God,
have mercy on me.

or:

Lord Jesus Christ, Son of God,
have mercy on us.

or:

Jesus, our Lord and our brother,
save us in your love.

MARIAN ANTHEM

Blessed are you, mother of my Lord,
for you have believed the word of God.

In faith and love,
you have pondered the words and actions of God
in your life and the life of God's people.

With Jesus we call you mother.
Pray for us,
and ask your Son to lead us to the Father. Amen!

PRAYER FOR PEACE

Lord Jesus Christ, we praise you:
bring peace into the world
by bringing your peace into the hearts of all.
Help us to turn away from sin
and to follow you in love and service.

Glory be yours, and honour,
for ever and ever. Amen!

A PRAYER FOR VOCATIONS

Heavenly Father, Lord of the harvest,
call many members of our community
to be generous workers for your people
and to gather in your harvest.
Send them to share the Good News of Jesus
with all the people of the earth.

Father,
we ask this prayer
through Christ our Lord. Amen!

THANKS FOR FAMILY AND FRIENDS

Blessed are you, loving Father,
for all your gifts to us.
Blessed are you for giving us family and friends
to be with us in times of joy and sorrow,
to help us in days of need,
and to rejoice with us in moments of celebration.

Father,
we praise you for your Son Jesus,
who knew the happiness of family and friends,
and in the love of your Holy Spirit.
Blessed are you for ever and ever. Amen!

FAMILY BLESSINGS

Family gathering: *When the family is gathered for a special occasion, a feast, a holiday, a reunion, or any other special time:*

Father in heaven,
we praise you for giving us your Son
to be our saviour and Lord.
Bless us all as we gather here today, [tonight,]
and let us live happily in your love.

Hear our prayer, loving Father,
for we ask this in Jesus' name. Amen!

Children: *Parents may bless their children each day, or on special occasions. These or similar words may be used:*

Simple form:

May God bless ✢ you, N.,
and keep you in love.

The child answers: Amen!

At bedtime:

Heavenly Father,
bless N., and keep him/her in your love.
Grant him/her a good rest tonight,
and send your angels to protect him/her.
In the name of the Father, and of the ✢ Son,
and of the Holy Spirit.

The child answers: Amen!

PRAYER FOR A BIRTHDAY
OF A FAMILY MEMBER

This prayer may be offered at a meal or birthday party:

Heavenly Father,
we praise you for all your gifts to us.
In a special way, we thank you for N.
Bless him/her on this birthday,
and keep him/her always in your love.

Bless us too, holy Father,
and this food with which we celebrate.
Help us all to praise you and give you glory
through Jesus Christ our Lord.

All answer: Amen!

PRAYER FOR
A WEDDING ANNIVERSARY

N. and N.,
may God bless you and grant you joy.
May he deepen your love for each other.
May he bless ✠ you in your family and friends,
and lead you to unending happiness in heaven.

May almighty God,
Father, Son, ✠ and Holy Spirit,
bless us all, and keep us in his love for ever.

All answer: Amen!

WHEN VISITING A SICK PERSON

Heavenly Father,
look with mercy on N.,
and help him/her in this time of sickness.
Restore him/her to health, we pray,
through Christ our Lord.

All answer: Amen!

or:

Lord Jesus,
lover of the sick,
be with *N.* in his/her sickness.
Help him/her to accept this illness
as a sharer in your cross,
and bring him/her back to full health.

Lord Jesus,
we praise you,
for you are Lord for ever and ever.

All answer: Amen!

PRAYER FOR THE POPE

All praise and glory are yours, Lord Jesus:
you have made us your body, your Church,
and help us to bear fruit for our heavenly Father.

You chose St. Peter as the rock,
and sent him to feed your flock
and to strengthen his brothers and sisters.
Continue to help your Church
through the guidance of our pope,
and keep us faithful in your service.

Jesus, our brother,
you are Lord for ever and ever. Amen!

PRAYERS BEFORE MASS

Act of Faith

Lord Jesus Christ, I firmly believe that you are present in this Blessed Sacrament as true God and true Man, with your Body and Blood, Soul and Divinity. My Redeemer and my Judge, I adore your Divine Majesty together with the angels and saints. I believe, O Lord; increase my faith.

Act of Contrition

O my Saviour, I am truly sorry for having offended you because you are infinitely good and sin displeases you. I detest all the sins of my life and I desire to atone for them. Through the merits of your Precious Blood, wash from my soul all stain of sin, so that, cleansed in body and soul, I may worthily approach the Most Holy Sacrament of the Altar.

PRAYER AFTER MASS

Anima Christi

Partial indulgence (No. 10)

Soul of Christ, sanctify me.
Body of Christ, save me.
Blood of Christ, inebriate me.
Water from the side of Christ, wash me.
Passion of Christ, strengthen me.
O good Jesus, hear me.
Within your wounds hide me.
Separated from you let me never be.
From the malignant enemy, defend me.
At the hour of death, call me.
And close to you bid me.
That with your saints I may be
Praising you, for all eternity. Amen.

Indulgenced Prayer before a Crucifix

Look down upon me, good and gentle Jesus, while before your face I humbly kneel, and with a burning soul pray and beseech you to fix deep in my heart lively sentiments of faith, hope and charity, true contrition for my sins, and a firm purpose of amendment, while I contemplate with great love and tender pity your five wounds, pondering over them within me, calling to mind the words which David, your prophet, said of you, my good Jesus: "They have pierced my hands and my feet; they have numbered all my bones" (Ps 21.17-18).

A *plenary indulgence* is granted on each Friday of Lent and Passiontide to the faithful, who after Communion piously recite the above prayer before an image of Christ crucified; on other days of the year the indulgence is *partial (No. 22)*.

Stations of the Cross

The Way of the Cross is a devotion in which we meditate on Christ's Passion and Death in order to put their meaning into our lives.

Heavenly Father, grant that I who meditate on the Passion and Death of Your Son, Jesus Christ, may imitate in my life His love and self-giving to You and to others. Grant this through Christ our Lord. Amen.

STATIONS
of the
CROSS

1. Jesus Is Condemned to Death

O Jesus, help me to appreciate Your sanctifying grace more and more.

2. Jesus Bears His Cross

O Jesus, You chose to die for me. Help me to love You always with all my heart.

3. Jesus Falls the First Time

O Jesus, make me strong to conquer my wicked passions, and to rise quickly from sin.

4. Jesus Meets His Mother

O Jesus, grant me a tender love for Your Mother, who offered You for love of me.

STATIONS
of the
CROSS

5. Jesus Is Helped by Simon

O Jesus, like Simon lead me ever closer to You through my daily crosses and trials.

6. Jesus and Veronica

O Jesus, imprint Your image on my heart that I may be faithful to You all my life.

7. Jesus Falls a Second Time

O Jesus, I repent for having offended You. Grant me forgiveness of all my sins.

8. Jesus Speaks to the Women

O Jesus, grant me tears of compassion for Your sufferings and of sorrow for my sins.

STATIONS
of the
CROSS

9. Jesus Falls a Third Time

O Jesus, let me never yield to despair. Let me come to You in hardship and spiritual distress.

10. He Is Stripped of His Garments

O Jesus, let me sacrifice all my attachments rather than imperil the divine life of my soul.

11. Jesus Is Nailed to the Cross

O Jesus, strengthen my faith and increase my love for You. Help me to accept my crosses.

12. Jesus Dies on the Cross

O Jesus, I thank You for making me a child of God. Help me to forgive others.

STATIONS
of the
CROSS

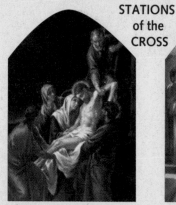

13. Jesus Is Taken down from the Cross

O Jesus, through the interces-sion of Your holy Mother, let me be pleasing to You.

14. Jesus Is Laid in the Tomb

O Jesus, strengthen my will to live for You on earth and bring me to eternal bliss in heaven.

Prayer after the Stations

JESUS, You became an example of humility, obedience and patience, and preceded me on the way of life bearing Your Cross. Grant that, in-flamed with Your love, I may cheerfully take upon myself the sweet yoke of Your Gospel together with the mortification of the Cross and follow You as a true disciple so that I may be united with You in heaven. Amen.

THE HOLY ROSARY

Prayer before the Rosary

QUEEN of the Holy Rosary, you have deigned to come to Fatima to reveal to the three shepherd children the treasures of grace hidden in the Rosary. Inspire my heart with a sincere love of this devotion, in order that by meditating on the Mysteries of our Redemption which are recalled in it, I may be enriched with its fruits and obtain peace for the world, the conversion of sinners, and the favor which I ask of you in this Rosary. *(Here mention your request.)* I ask it for the greater glory of God, for your own honor, and for the good of souls, especially for my own. Amen.

The Five
Joyful
Mysteries

Said on Mondays and Saturdays [except during Lent], and the Sundays from Advent to Lent.

3. The Nativity
For the spirit of poverty.

1. The Annunciation
For the love of humility.

4. The Presentation
For the virtue of obedience.

2. The Visitation
For charity toward my neighbor.

5. Finding in the Temple
For the virtue of piety.

The Five

Luminous

Mysteries *

1. The Baptism of Jesus
For living my Baptismal Promises.

Said on Thursdays [except during Lent].
* Added to the Mysteries of the Rosary by Pope John Paul II in his Apostolic Letter of October 16, 2002, entitled *The Rosary of the Virgin Mary.*

2. The Wedding at Cana
For doing whatever Jesus says.

4. The Transfiguration
Becoming a New Person in Christ.

3. Proclamation of the Kingdom
For seeking God's forgiveness.

5. Institution of the Eucharist
For active participation at Mass.

The Five
Sorrowful
Mysteries

Said on Tuesdays and Fridays throughout the year, and every day from Ash Wednesday until Easter.

3. Crowning with Thorns
For moral courage.

1. Agony in the Garden
For true contrition.

4. Carrying of the Cross
For the virtue of patience.

2. Scourging at the Pillar
For the virtue of purity.

5. The Crucifixion
For final perseverance.